Thank you for picking up volume 26! It's getting
warmer, so I'm taking more walks!

KOHEI HORIKOSHI

26

SHONEN JUMP Manga Edition

STORY & ART **KOHEI HORIKOSHI**

TRANSLATION & ENGLISH ADAPTATION **Caleb Cook**
TOUCH-UP ART & LETTERING **John Hunt**
DESIGNER **Julian [JR] Robinson**
SHONEN JUMP SERIES EDITOR **John Bae**
GRAPHIC NOVEL EDITOR **Mike Montesa**

BOKU NO HERO ACADEMIA © 2014 by Kohei Horikoshi
All rights reserved.
First published in Japan in 2014 by SHUEISHA Inc., Tokyo.
English translation rights arranged by SHUEISHA Inc.

Printed in the U.S.A.

Published by VIZ Media, LLC
P.O. Box 77010
San Francisco, CA 94107

10 9 8 7 6 5 4 3 2 1
First printing, January 2021

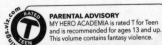

VIZ MEDIA
viz.com

MY HERO ACADEMIA vol.26

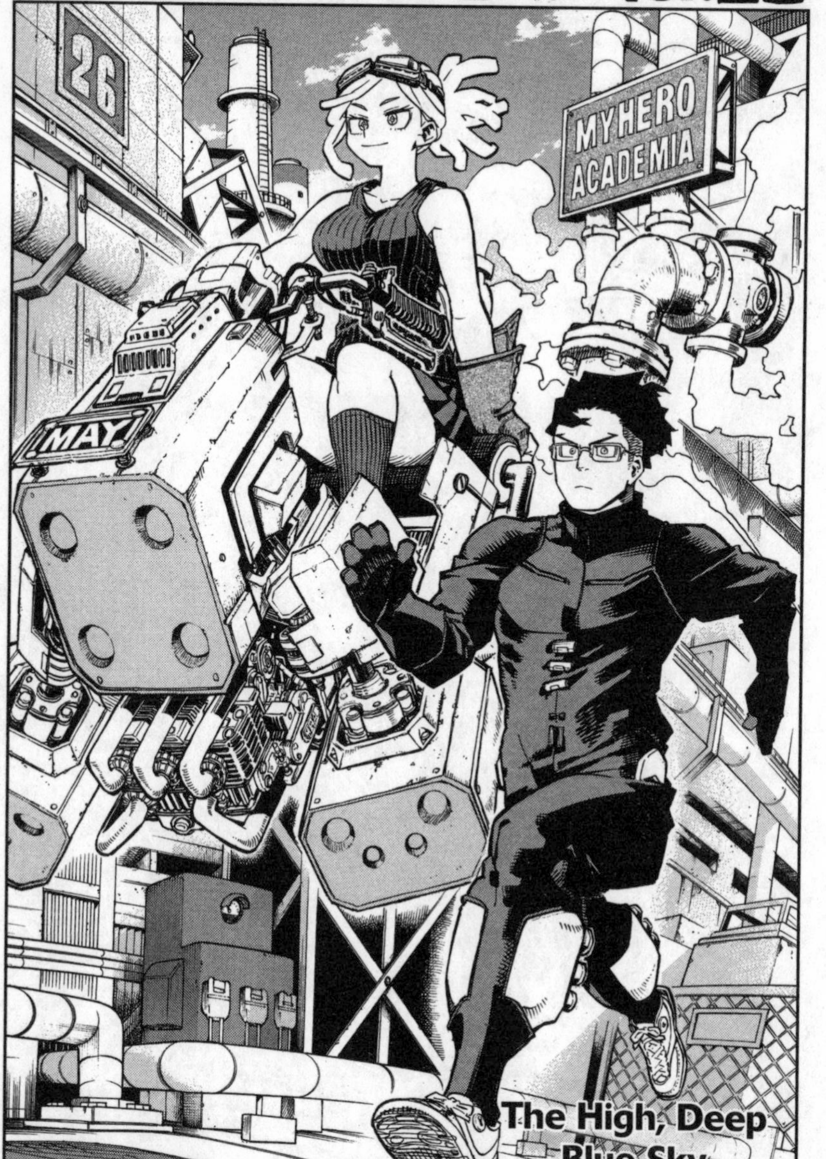
26
MY HERO ACADEMIA
MAY

The High, Deep Blue Sky

KOHEI HORIKOSHI

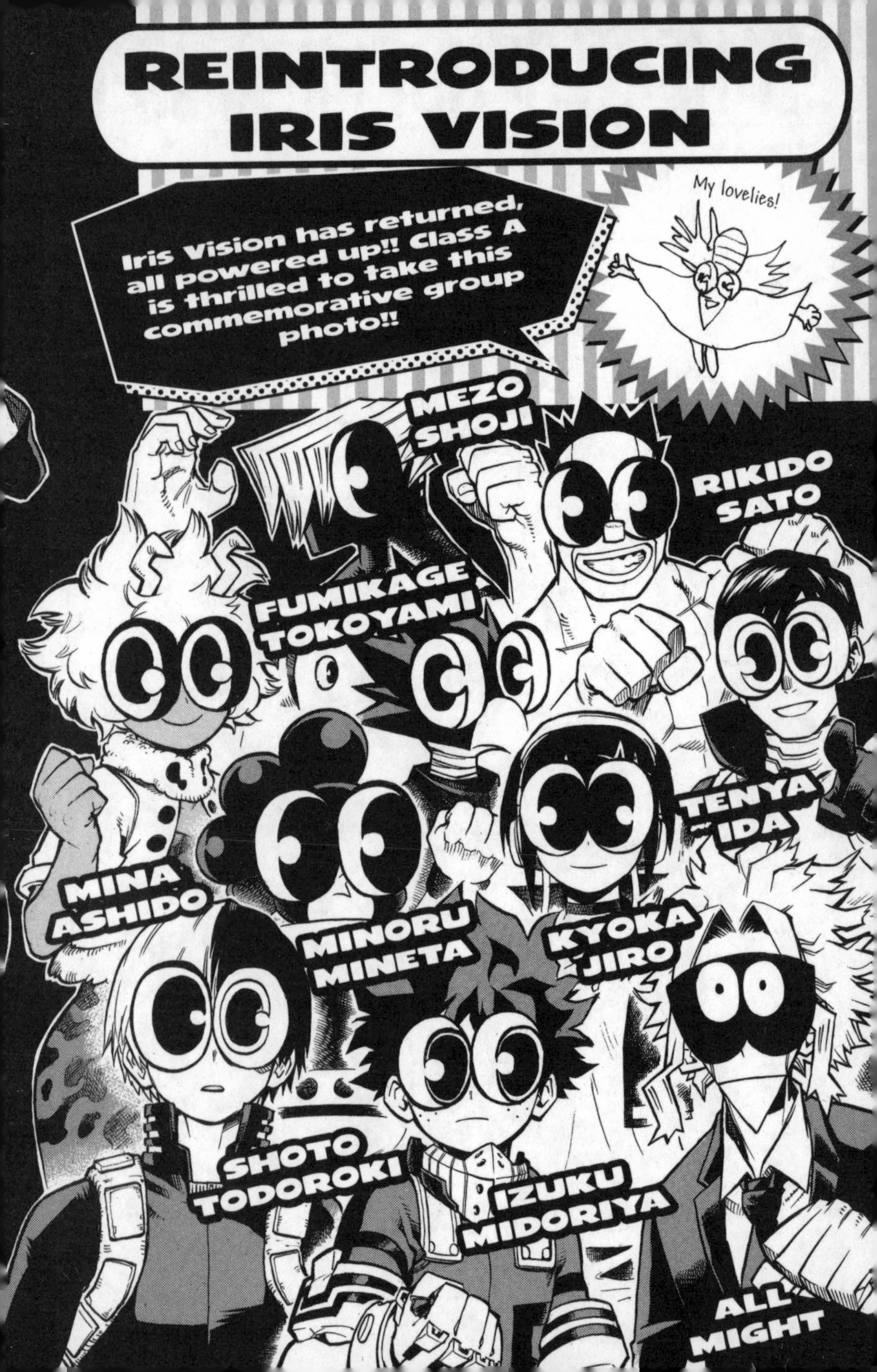
REINTRODUCING IRIS VISION
Iris Vision has returned, all powered up!! Class A is thrilled to take this commemorative group photo!!
My lovelies!
MEZO SHOJI
RIKIDO SATO
FUMIKAGE TOKOYAMI
TENYA IDA
MINA ASHIDO
MINORU MINETA
KYOKA JIRO
SHOTO TODOROKI
IZUKU MIDORIYA
ALL MIGHT

STORY

One day, people began manifesting special abilities that came to be known as "Quirks," and before long, the world was full of superpowered humans. But with the advent of these exceptional individuals came an increase in crime, and governments alone were unable to deal with the situation. At the same time, others emerged to oppose the spread of evil! As if straight from the comic books, these heroes keep the peace and are even officially authorized to fight crime. Our story begins when a certain Quirkless boy and lifelong hero fan meets the world's number one hero, starting him on his path to becoming the greatest hero ever!

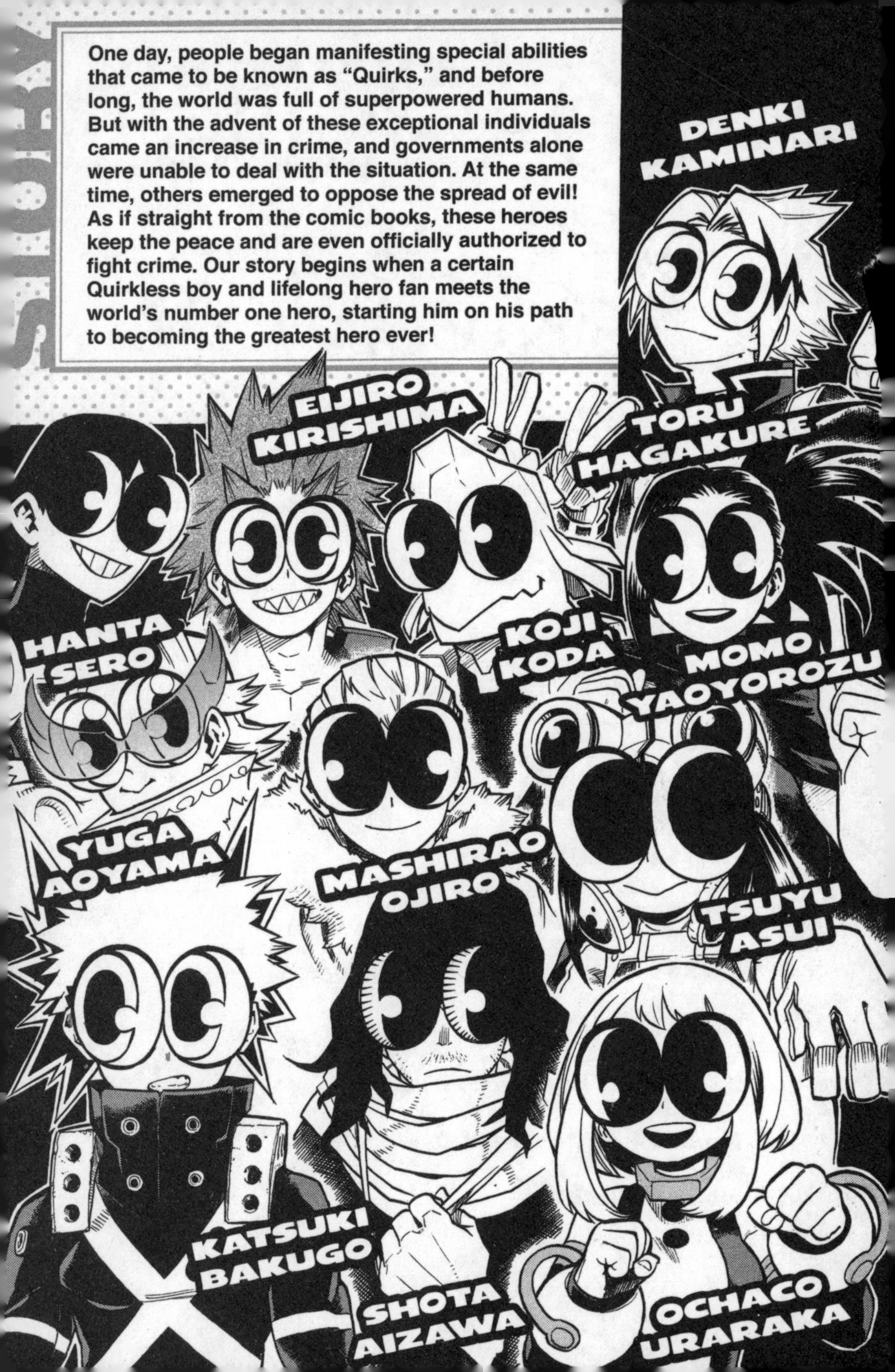
DENKI KAMINARI
TORU HAGAKURE
EIJIRO KIRISHIMA
MOMO YAOYOROZU
KOJI KODA
HANTA SERO
TSUYU ASUI
MASHIRAO OJIRO
YUGA AOYAMA
OCHACO URARAKA
SHOTA AIZAWA
KATSUKI BAKUGO

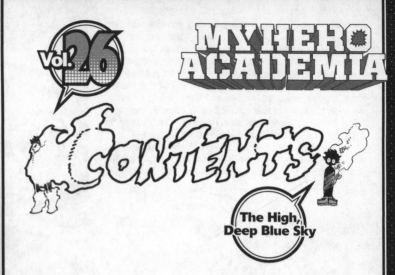

Vol. 26

MY HERO ACADEMIA

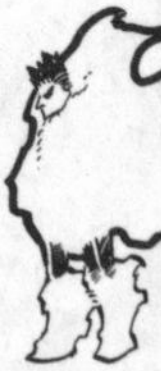

CONTENTS

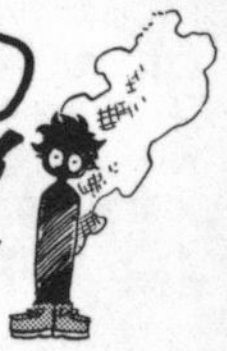

The High, Deep Blue Sky

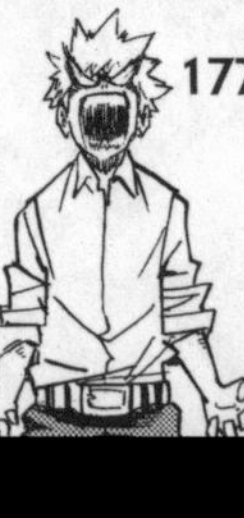

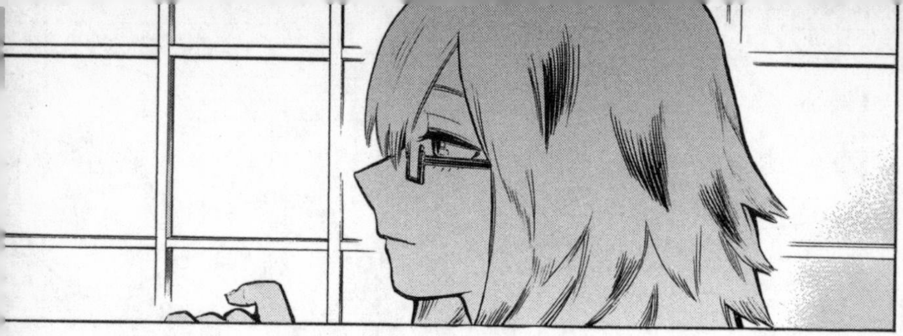

No. 247 - Status Report!

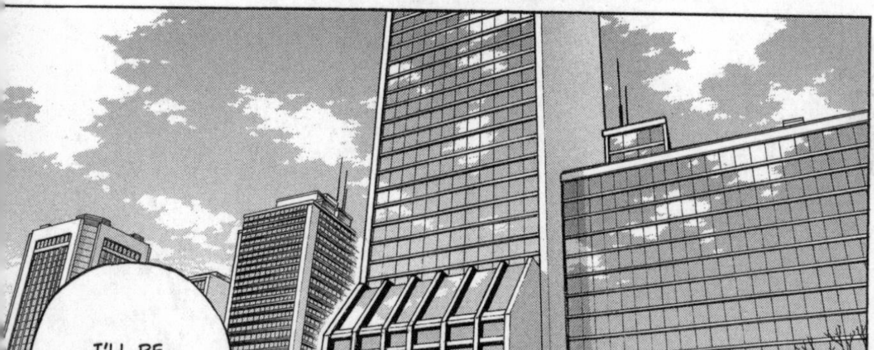
I'LL BE SUPERVISING YOU BOYS MYSELF.

*SIGN: FORGE

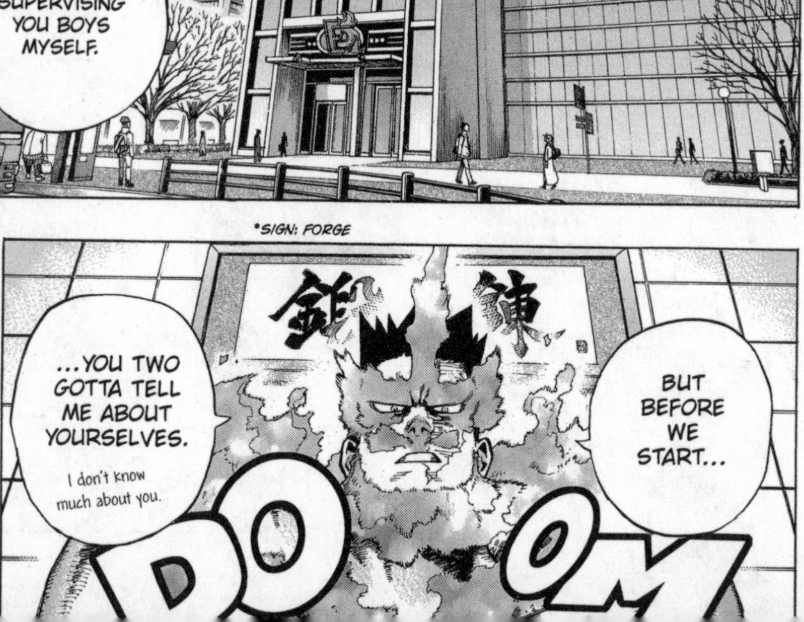
BUT BEFORE WE START...
...YOU TWO GOTTA TELL ME ABOUT YOURSELVES.
I don't know much about you.
DOOM

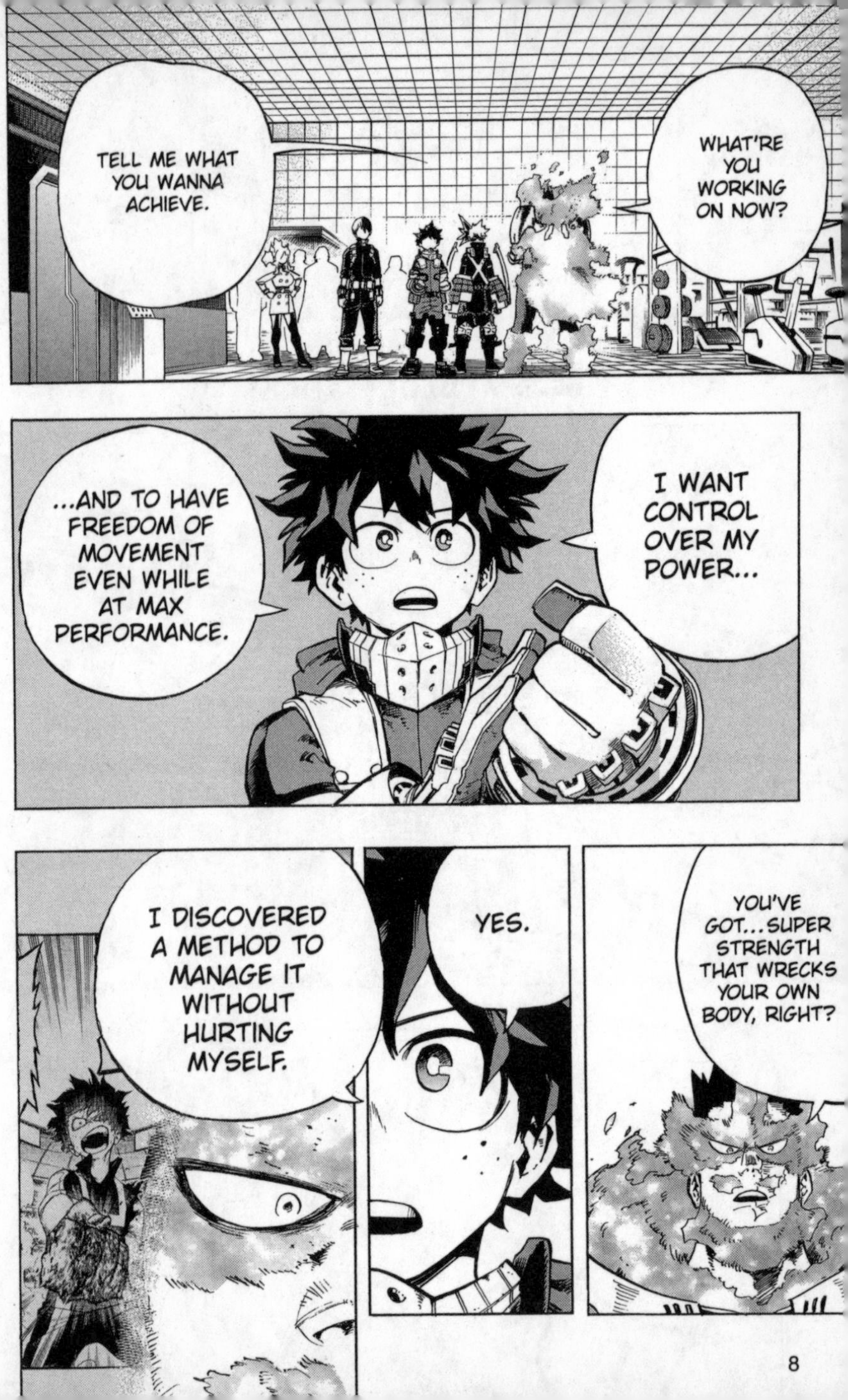
WHAT'RE YOU WORKING ON NOW?
TELL ME WHAT YOU WANNA ACHIEVE.
I WANT CONTROL OVER MY POWER...
...AND TO HAVE FREEDOM OF MOVEMENT EVEN WHILE AT MAX PERFORMANCE.
YOU'VE GOT...SUPER STRENGTH THAT WRECKS YOUR OWN BODY, RIGHT?
YES.
I DISCOVERED A METHOD TO MANAGE IT WITHOUT HURTING MYSELF.

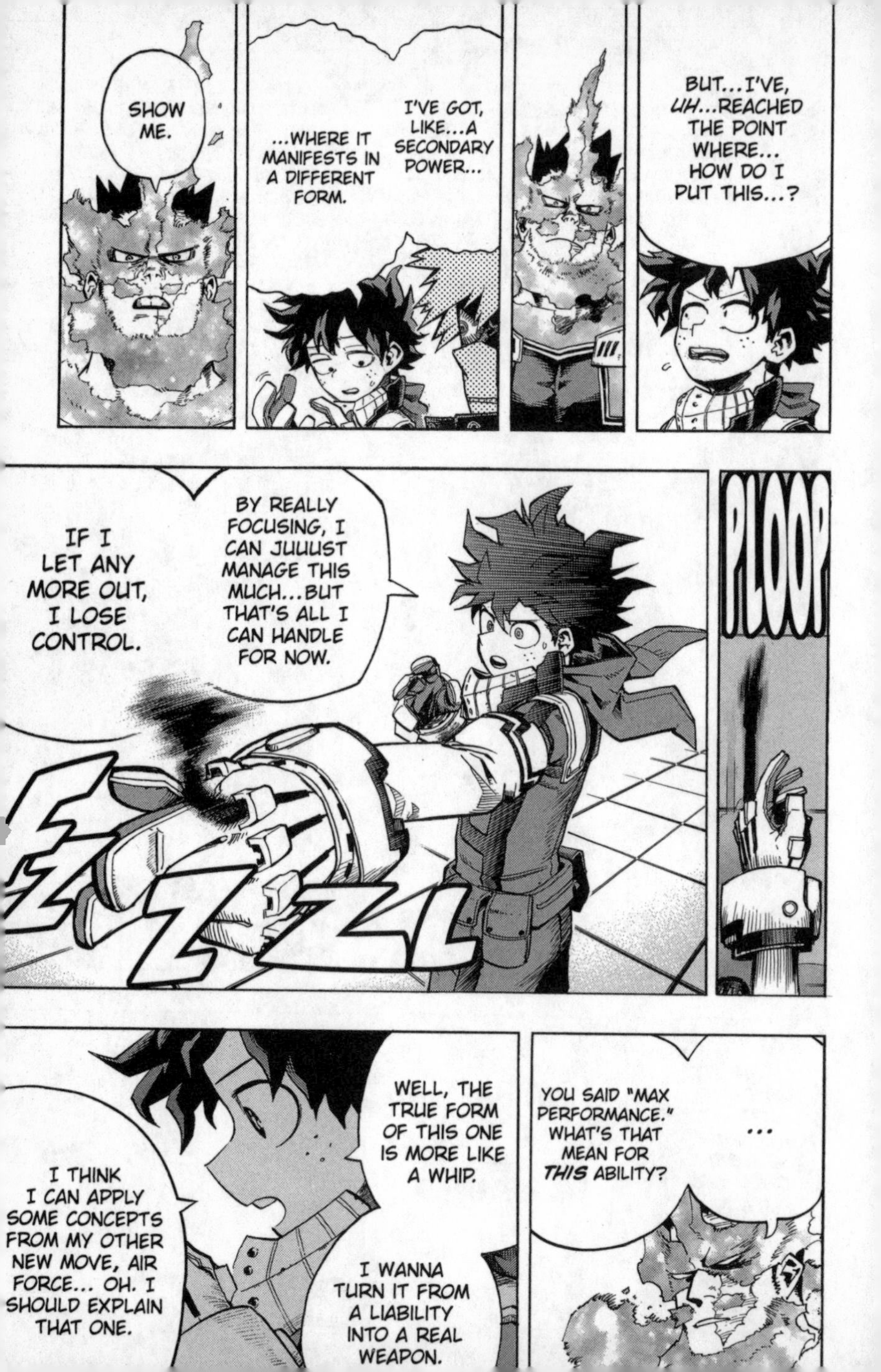
BUT...I'VE, *UH*...REACHED THE POINT WHERE... HOW DO I PUT THIS...?
I'VE GOT, LIKE...A SECONDARY POWER...
...WHERE IT MANIFESTS IN A DIFFERENT FORM.
SHOW ME.
PLOOP
BY REALLY FOCUSING, I CAN JUUUST MANAGE THIS MUCH...BUT THAT'S ALL I CAN HANDLE FOR NOW.
IF I LET ANY MORE OUT, I LOSE CONTROL.
ZZZZL
...
YOU SAID "MAX PERFORMANCE." WHAT'S THAT MEAN FOR *THIS* ABILITY?
WELL, THE TRUE FORM OF THIS ONE IS MORE LIKE A WHIP.
I WANNA TURN IT FROM A LIABILITY INTO A REAL WEAPON.
I THINK I CAN APPLY SOME CONCEPTS FROM MY OTHER NEW MOVE, AIR FORCE... OH. I SHOULD EXPLAIN THAT ONE.

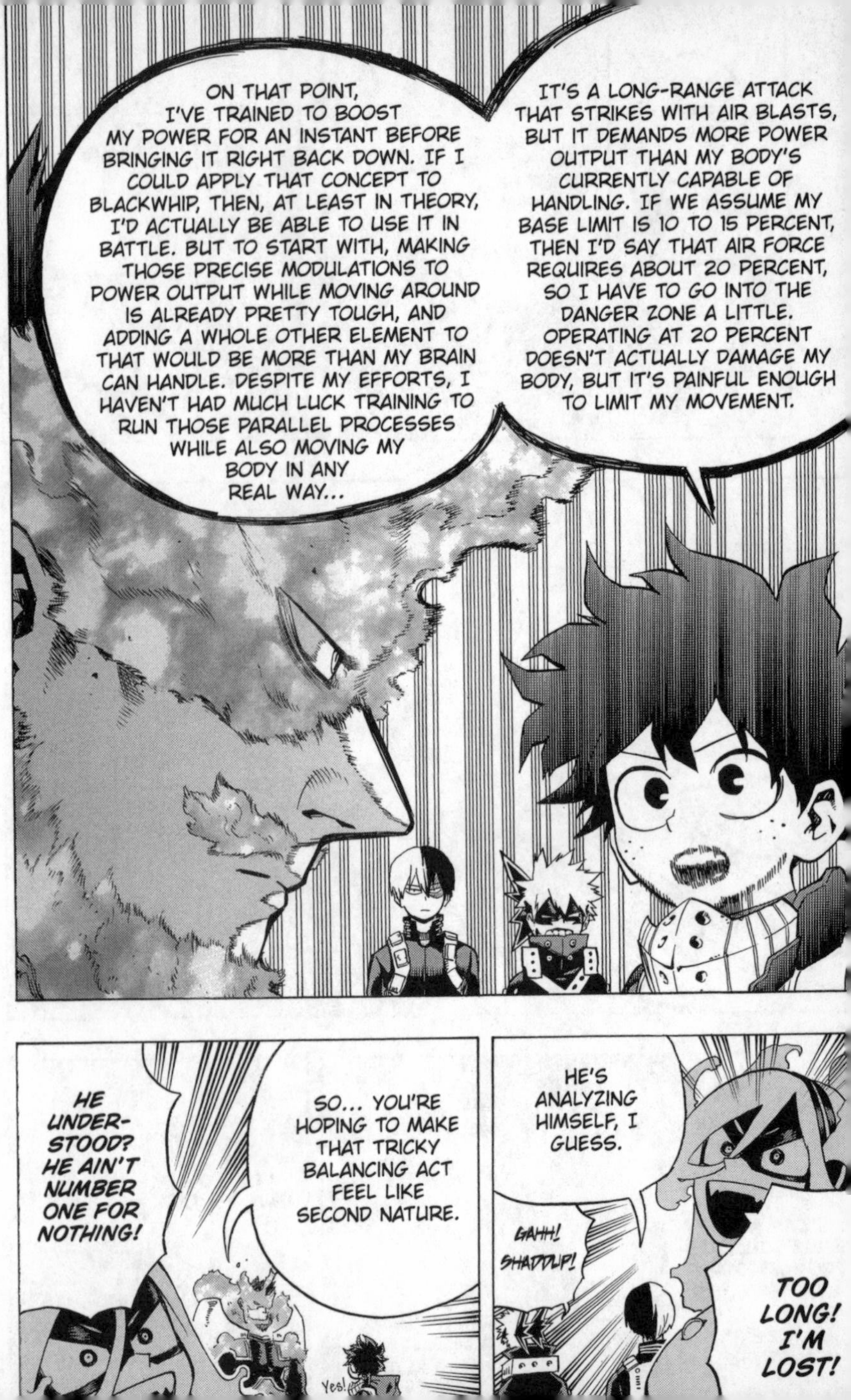
IT'S A LONG-RANGE ATTACK THAT STRIKES WITH AIR BLASTS, BUT IT DEMANDS MORE POWER OUTPUT THAN MY BODY'S CURRENTLY CAPABLE OF HANDLING. IF WE ASSUME MY BASE LIMIT IS 10 TO 15 PERCENT, THEN I'D SAY THAT AIR FORCE REQUIRES ABOUT 20 PERCENT, SO I HAVE TO GO INTO THE DANGER ZONE A LITTLE. OPERATING AT 20 PERCENT DOESN'T ACTUALLY DAMAGE MY BODY, BUT IT'S PAINFUL ENOUGH TO LIMIT MY MOVEMENT.
ON THAT POINT, I'VE TRAINED TO BOOST MY POWER FOR AN INSTANT BEFORE BRINGING IT RIGHT BACK DOWN. IF I COULD APPLY THAT CONCEPT TO BLACKWHIP, THEN, AT LEAST IN THEORY, I'D ACTUALLY BE ABLE TO USE IT IN BATTLE. BUT TO START WITH, MAKING THOSE PRECISE MODULATIONS TO POWER OUTPUT WHILE MOVING AROUND IS ALREADY PRETTY TOUGH, AND ADDING A WHOLE OTHER ELEMENT TO THAT WOULD BE MORE THAN MY BRAIN CAN HANDLE. DESPITE MY EFFORTS, I HAVEN'T HAD MUCH LUCK TRAINING TO RUN THOSE PARALLEL PROCESSES WHILE ALSO MOVING MY BODY IN ANY REAL WAY...
HE'S ANALYZING HIMSELF, I GUESS.
GAHH! SHADDUP!
TOO LONG! I'M LOST!
SO... YOU'RE HOPING TO MAKE THAT TRICKY BALANCING ACT FEEL LIKE SECOND NATURE.
HE UNDER-STOOD? HE AIN'T NUMBER ONE FOR NOTHING!
Yes!

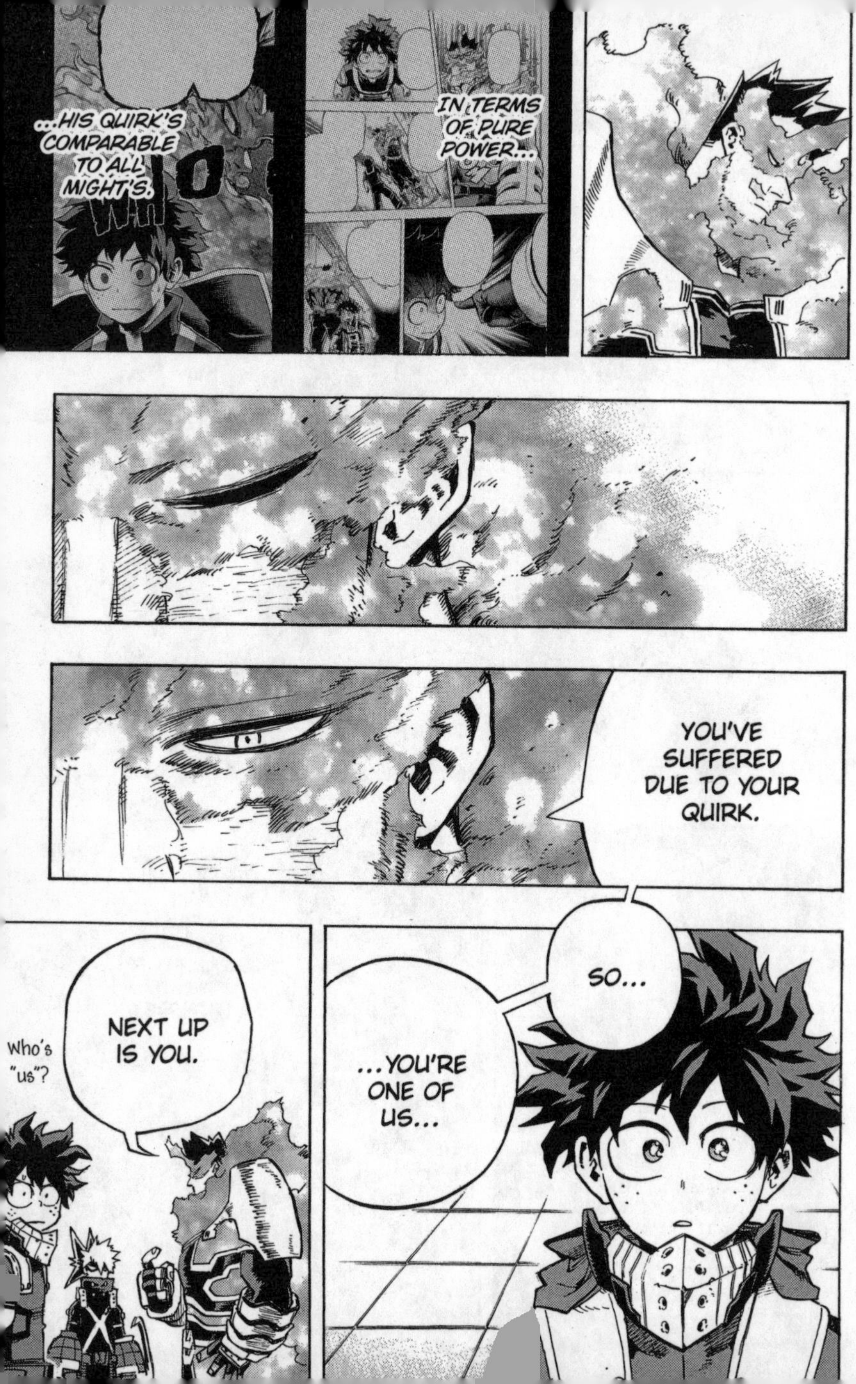
IN TERMS OF PURE POWER...
...HIS QUIRK'S COMPARABLE TO ALL MIGHT'S.
YOU'VE SUFFERED DUE TO YOUR QUIRK.
SO...
...YOU'RE ONE OF US...
NEXT UP IS YOU.
Who's "us"?

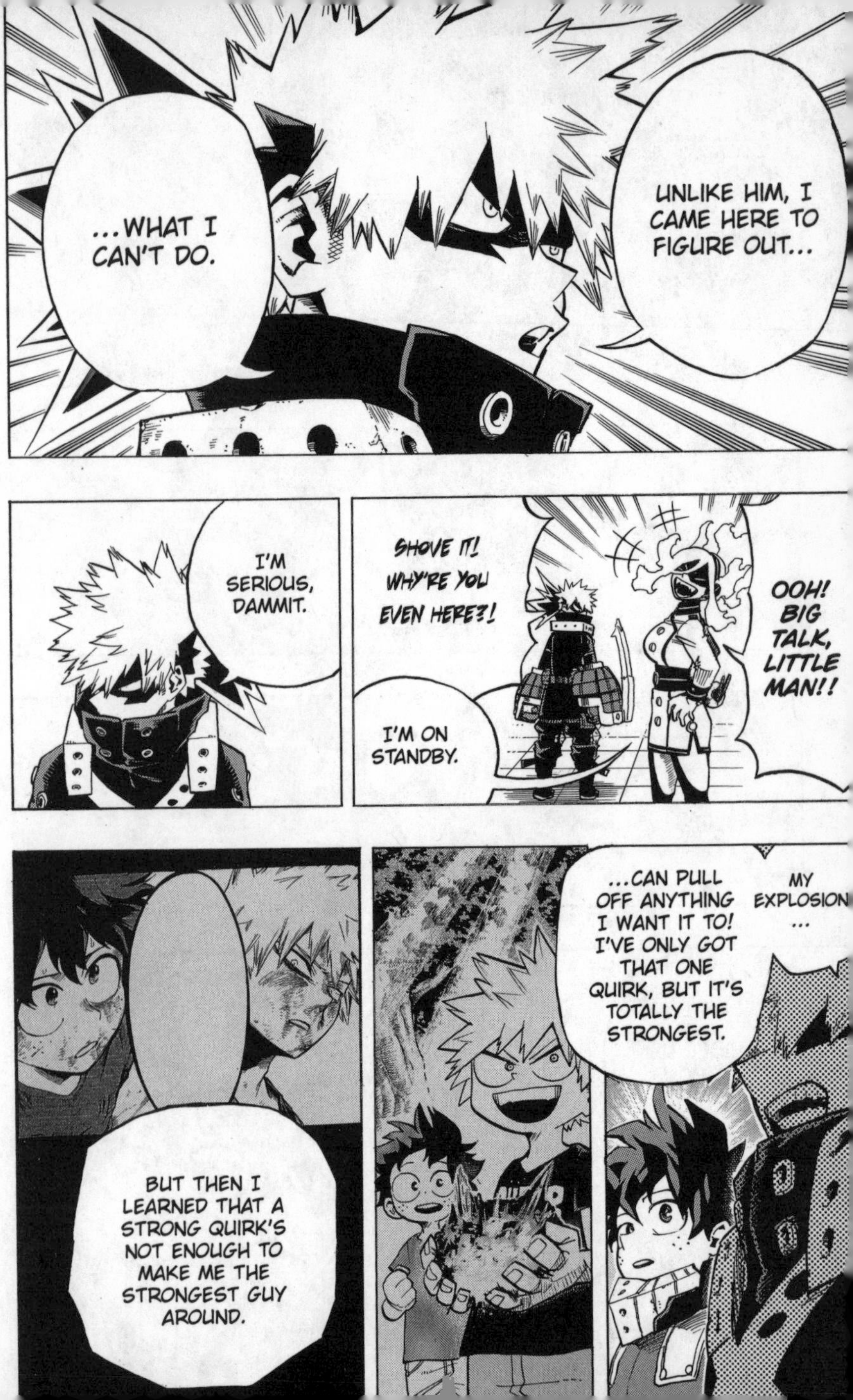
UNLIKE HIM, I CAME HERE TO FIGURE OUT...
...WHAT I CAN'T DO.
OOH! BIG TALK, LITTLE MAN!!
SHOVE IT! WHY'RE YOU EVEN HERE?!
I'M ON STANDBY.
I'M SERIOUS, DAMMIT.
MY EXPLOSION...
...CAN PULL OFF ANYTHING I WANT IT TO! I'VE ONLY GOT THAT ONE QUIRK, BUT IT'S TOTALLY THE STRONGEST.
BUT THEN I LEARNED THAT A STRONG QUIRK'S NOT ENOUGH TO MAKE ME THE STRONGEST GUY AROUND.

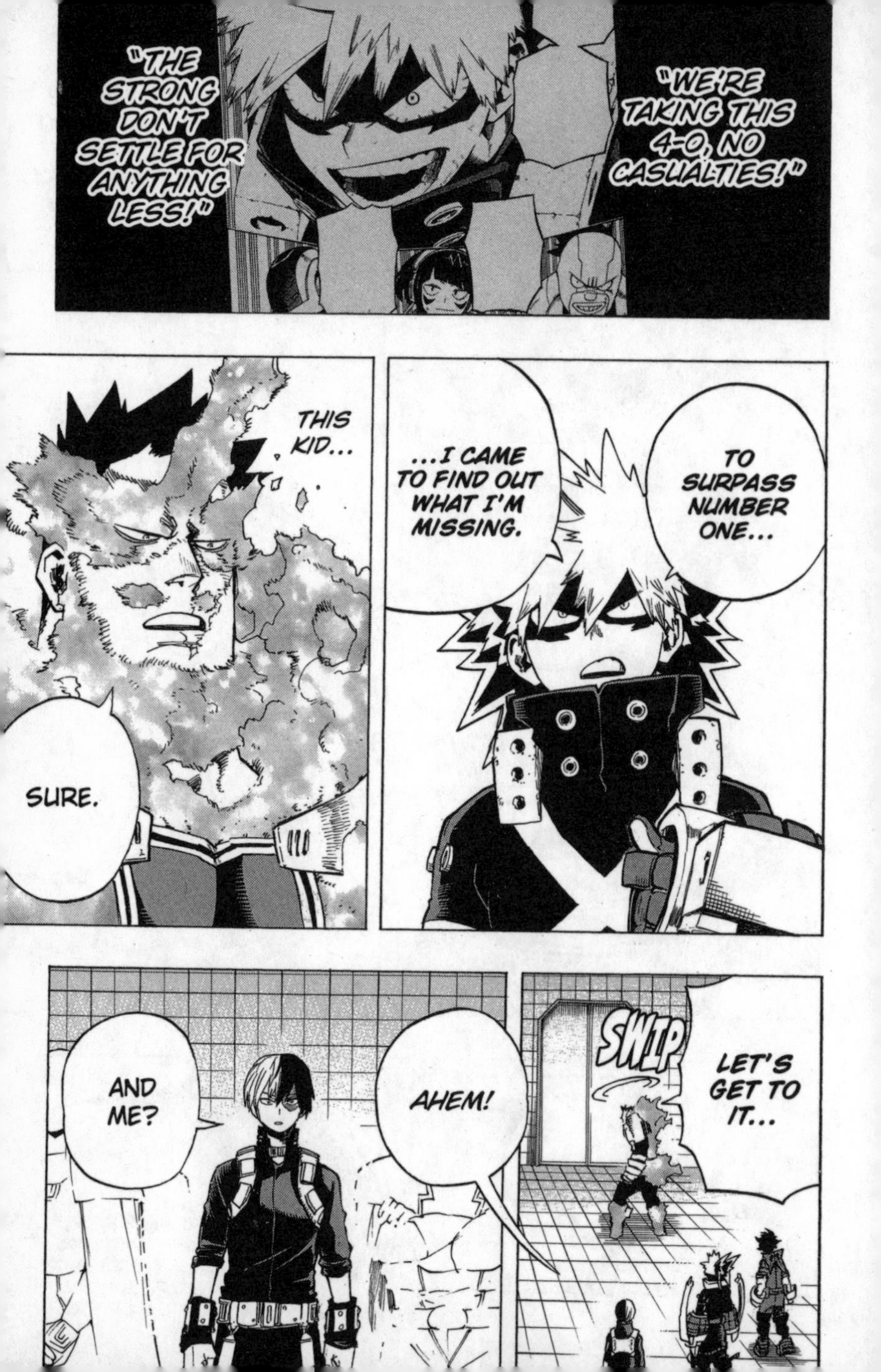
"WE'RE TAKING THIS 4-0, NO CASUALTIES!"
"THE STRONG DON'T SETTLE FOR ANYTHING LESS!"
TO SURPASS NUMBER ONE...
...I CAME TO FIND OUT WHAT I'M MISSING.
THIS KID...
SURE.
SWIP
LET'S GET TO IT...
AHEM!
AND ME?

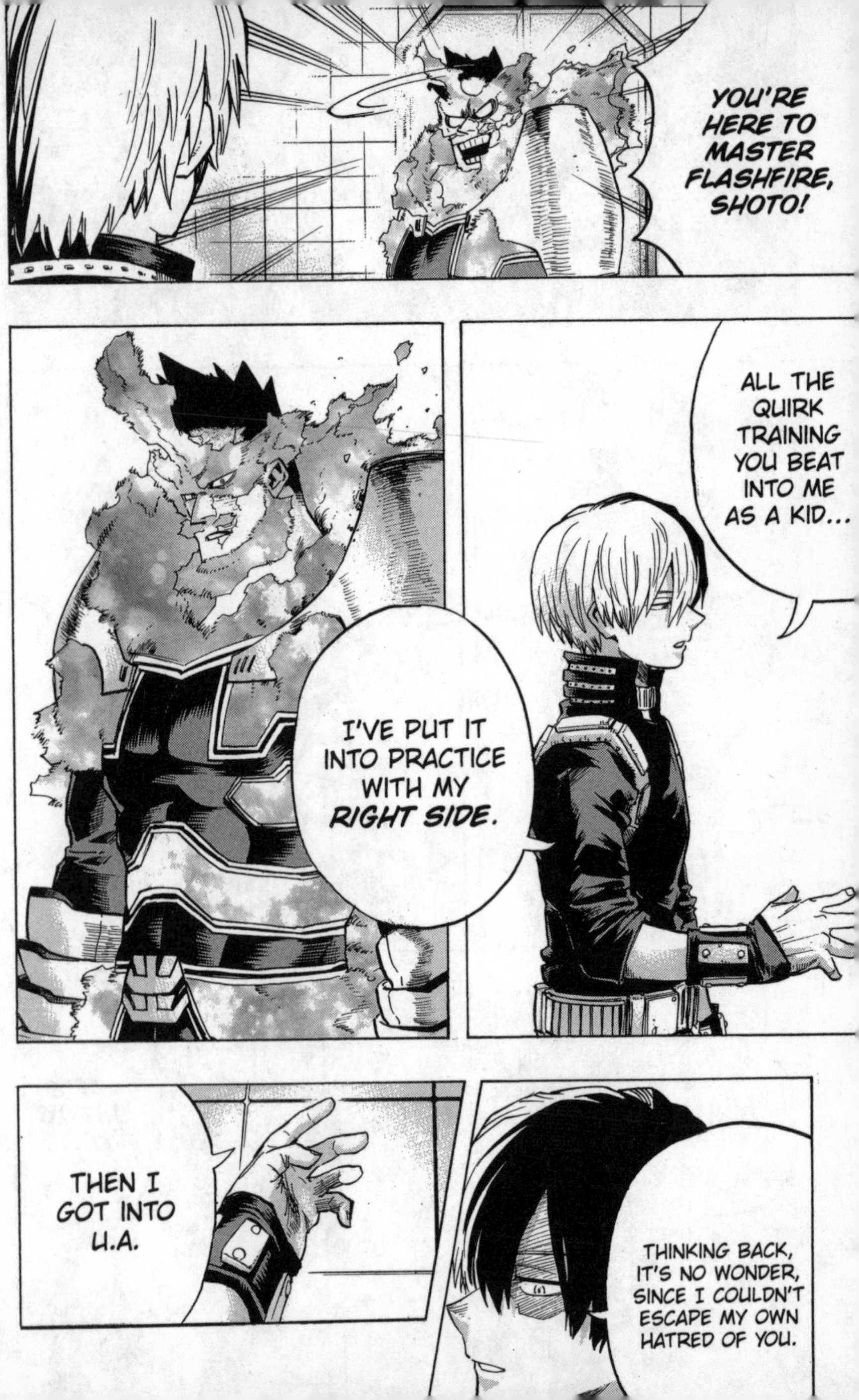
YOU'RE HERE TO MASTER FLASHFIRE, SHOTO!
ALL THE QUIRK TRAINING YOU BEAT INTO ME AS A KID...
I'VE PUT IT INTO PRACTICE WITH MY *RIGHT SIDE.*
THINKING BACK, IT'S NO WONDER, SINCE I COULDN'T ESCAPE MY OWN HATRED OF YOU.
THEN I GOT INTO U.A.

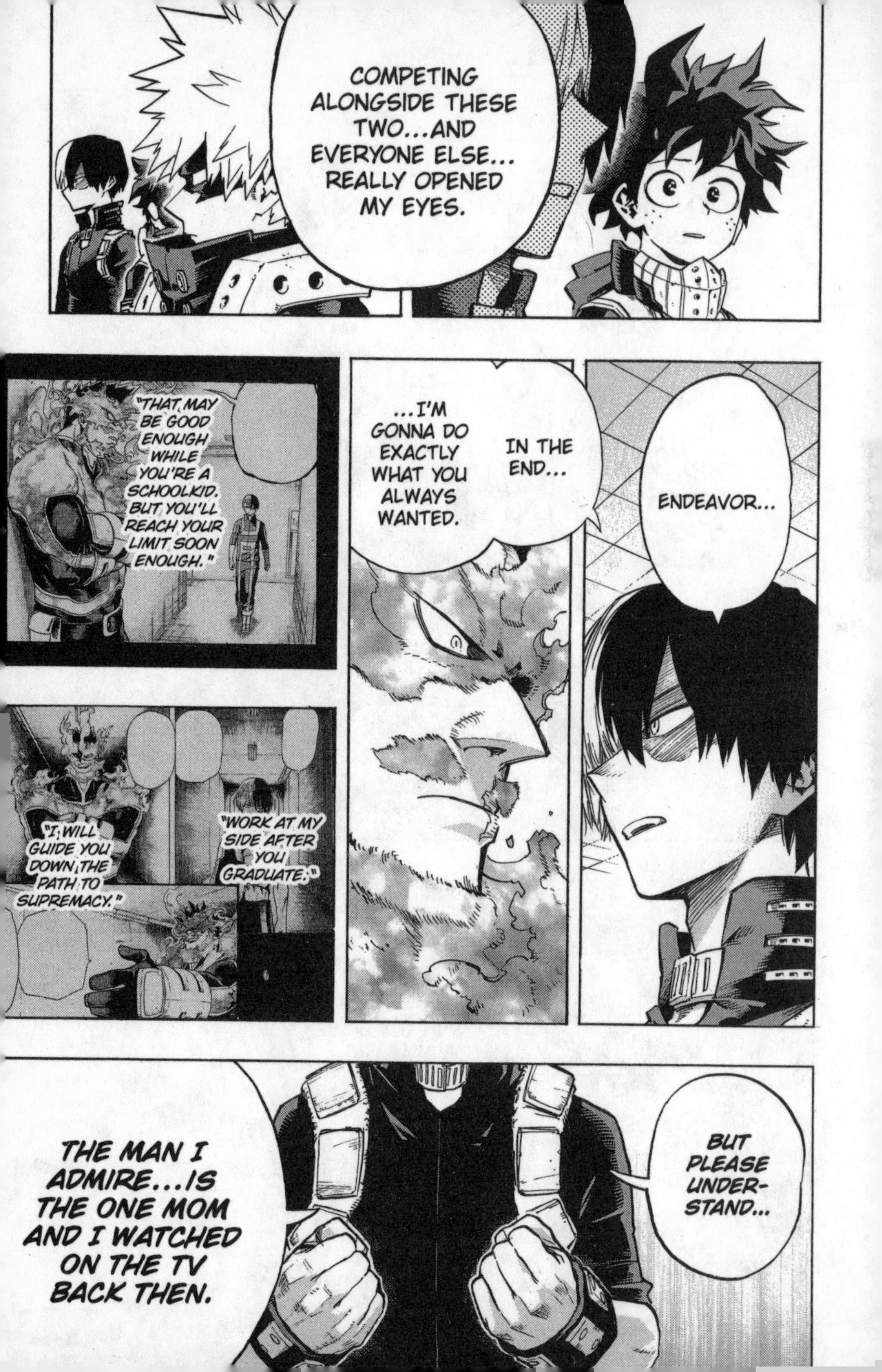
COMPETING ALONGSIDE THESE TWO...AND EVERYONE ELSE... REALLY OPENED MY EYES.
ENDEAVOR...
IN THE END...
...I'M GONNA DO EXACTLY WHAT YOU ALWAYS WANTED.
"THAT MAY BE GOOD ENOUGH WHILE YOU'RE A SCHOOLKID. BUT YOU'LL REACH YOUR LIMIT SOON ENOUGH."
"WORK AT MY SIDE AFTER YOU GRADUATE."
"I WILL GUIDE YOU DOWN THE PATH TO SUPREMACY."
BUT PLEASE UNDER-STAND...
THE MAN I ADMIRE...IS THE ONE MOM AND I WATCHED ON THE TV BACK THEN.

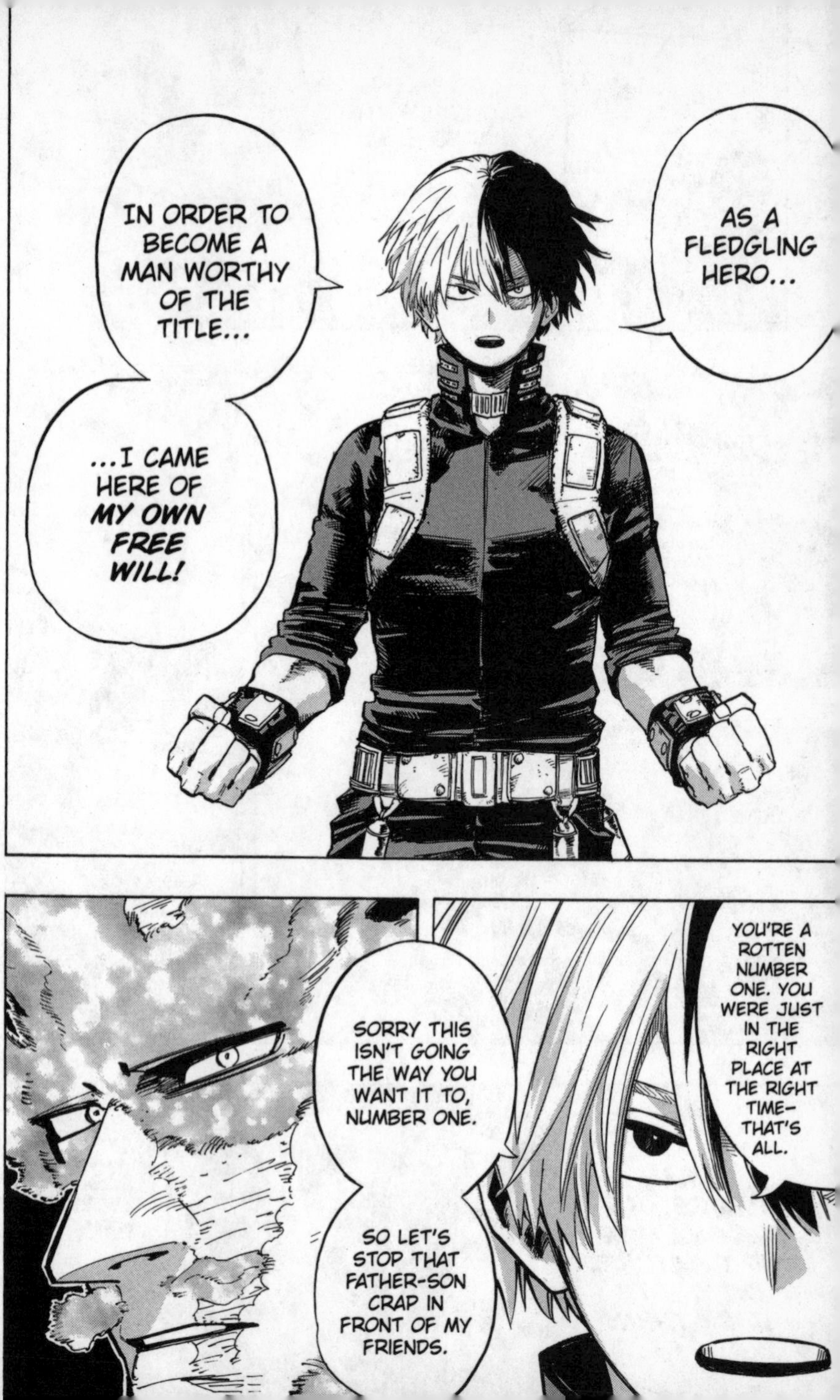
AS A FLEDGLING HERO...
IN ORDER TO BECOME A MAN WORTHY OF THE TITLE...
...I CAME HERE OF *MY OWN FREE WILL!*
YOU'RE A ROTTEN NUMBER ONE. YOU WERE JUST IN THE RIGHT PLACE AT THE RIGHT TIME— THAT'S ALL.
SORRY THIS ISN'T GOING THE WAY YOU WANT IT TO, NUMBER ONE.
SO LET'S STOP THAT FATHER-SON CRAP IN FRONT OF MY FRIENDS.

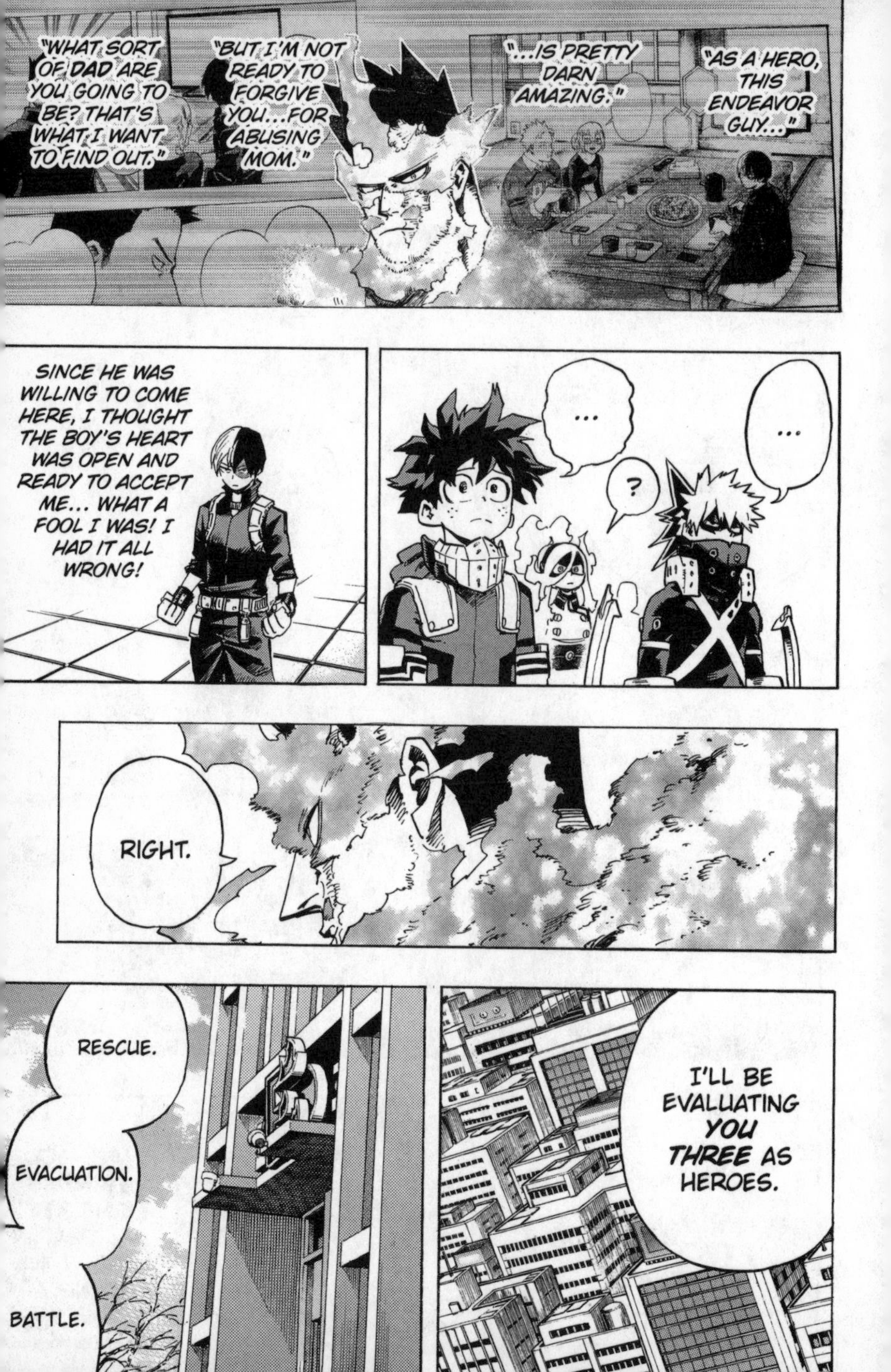
"AS A HERO, THIS ENDEAVOR GUY..."
"...IS PRETTY DARN AMAZING."
"BUT I'M NOT READY TO FORGIVE YOU...FOR ABUSING MOM."
"WHAT SORT OF DAD ARE YOU GOING TO BE? THAT'S WHAT I WANT TO FIND OUT."
...
...
?
SINCE HE WAS WILLING TO COME HERE, I THOUGHT THE BOY'S HEART WAS OPEN AND READY TO ACCEPT ME... WHAT A FOOL I WAS! I HAD IT ALL WRONG!
RIGHT.
I'LL BE EVALUATING YOU THREE AS HEROES.
RESCUE.
EVACUATION.
BATTLE.

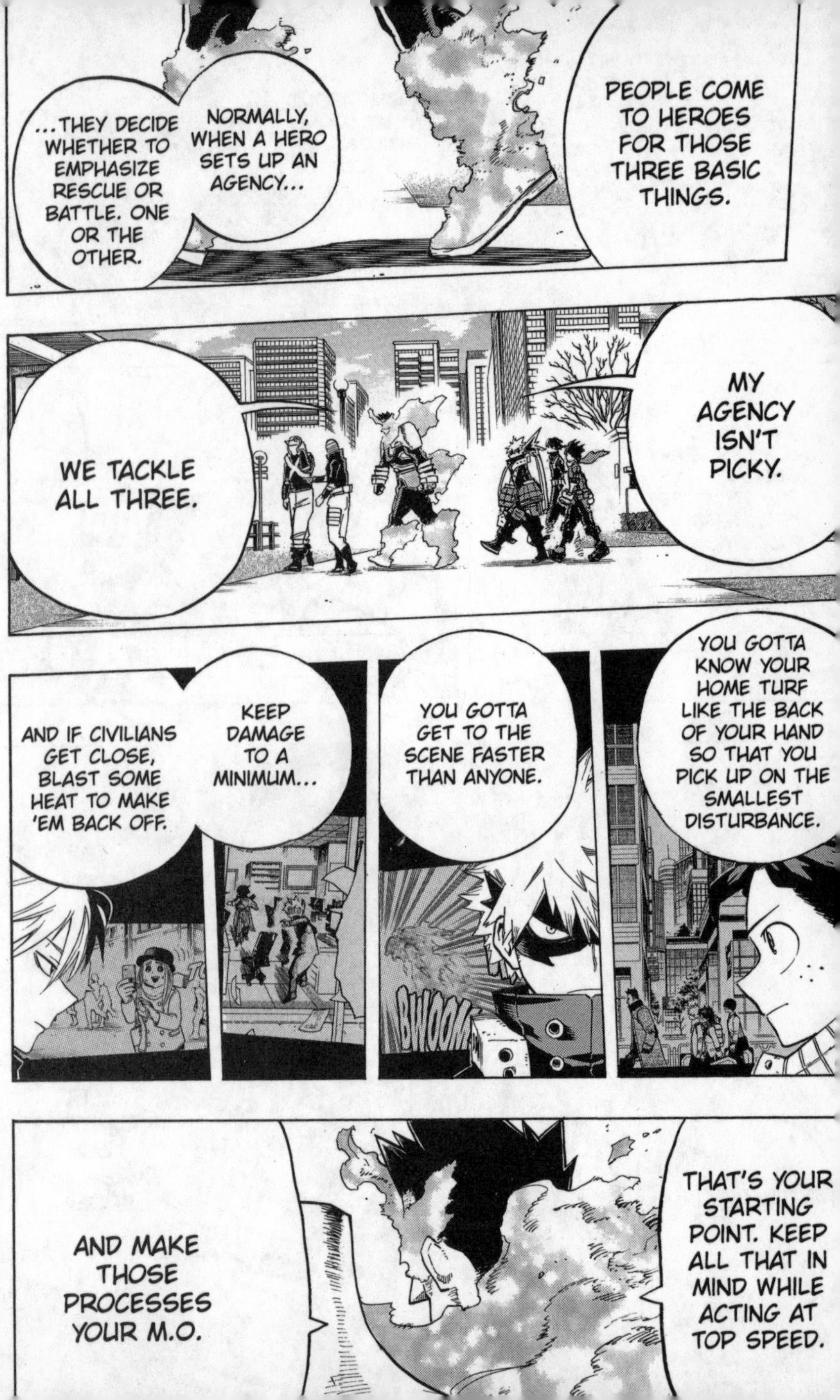
PEOPLE COME TO HEROES FOR THOSE THREE BASIC THINGS.
NORMALLY, WHEN A HERO SETS UP AN AGENCY...
...THEY DECIDE WHETHER TO EMPHASIZE RESCUE OR BATTLE. ONE OR THE OTHER.
MY AGENCY ISN'T PICKY.
WE TACKLE ALL THREE.
YOU GOTTA KNOW YOUR HOME TURF LIKE THE BACK OF YOUR HAND SO THAT YOU PICK UP ON THE SMALLEST DISTURBANCE.
YOU GOTTA GET TO THE SCENE FASTER THAN ANYONE.
BWOOM
KEEP DAMAGE TO A MINIMUM...
AND IF CIVILIANS GET CLOSE, BLAST SOME HEAT TO MAKE 'EM BACK OFF.
THAT'S YOUR STARTING POINT. KEEP ALL THAT IN MIND WHILE ACTING AT TOP SPEED.
AND MAKE THOSE PROCESSES YOUR M.O.

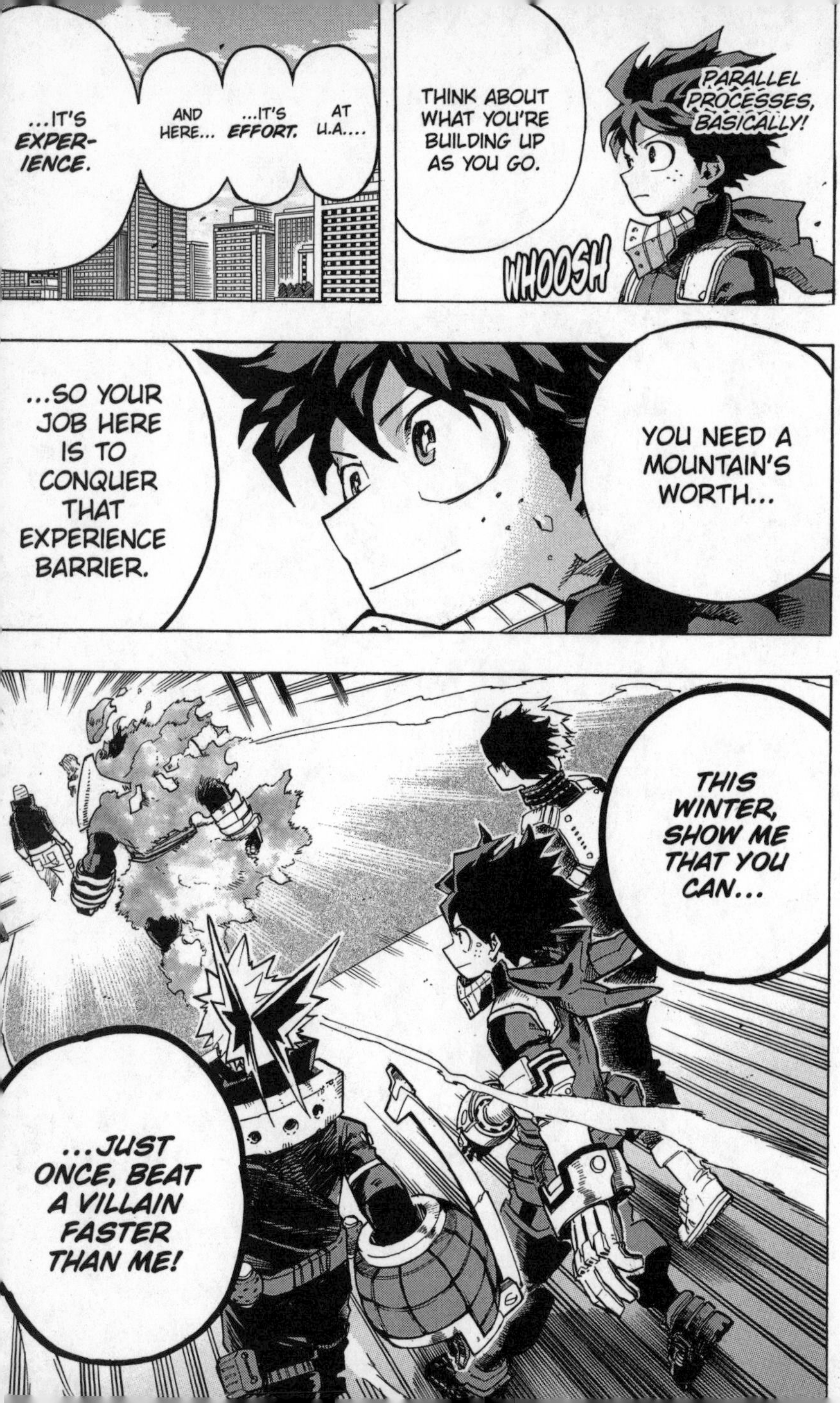
PARALLEL PROCESSES, BASICALLY!
THINK ABOUT WHAT YOU'RE BUILDING UP AS YOU GO.
WHOOSH
AT U.A.... ...IT'S EFFORT. AND HERE... ...IT'S EXPERIENCE.
YOU NEED A MOUNTAIN'S WORTH...
...SO YOUR JOB HERE IS TO CONQUER THAT EXPERIENCE BARRIER.
THIS WINTER, SHOW ME THAT YOU CAN...
...JUST ONCE, BEAT A VILLAIN FASTER THAN ME!

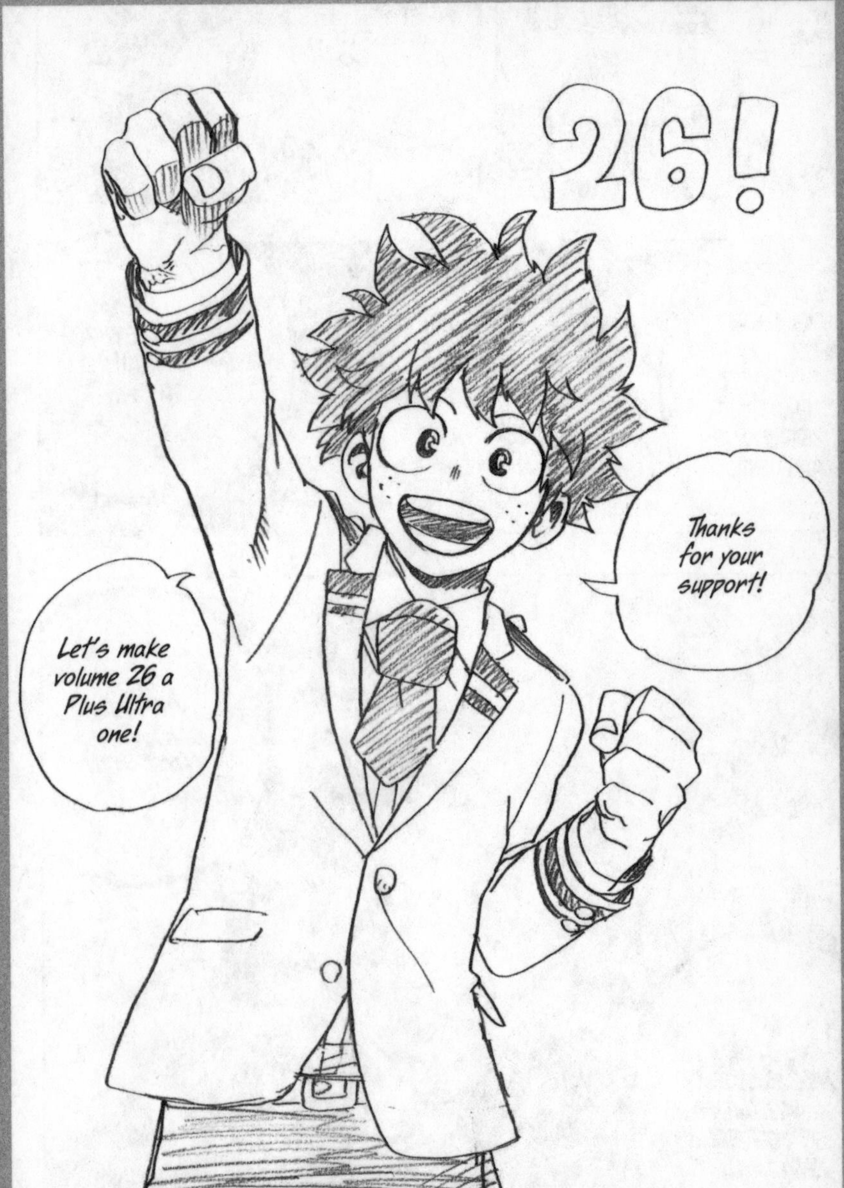
26!
Thanks for your support!
Let's make volume 26 a Plus Ultra one!

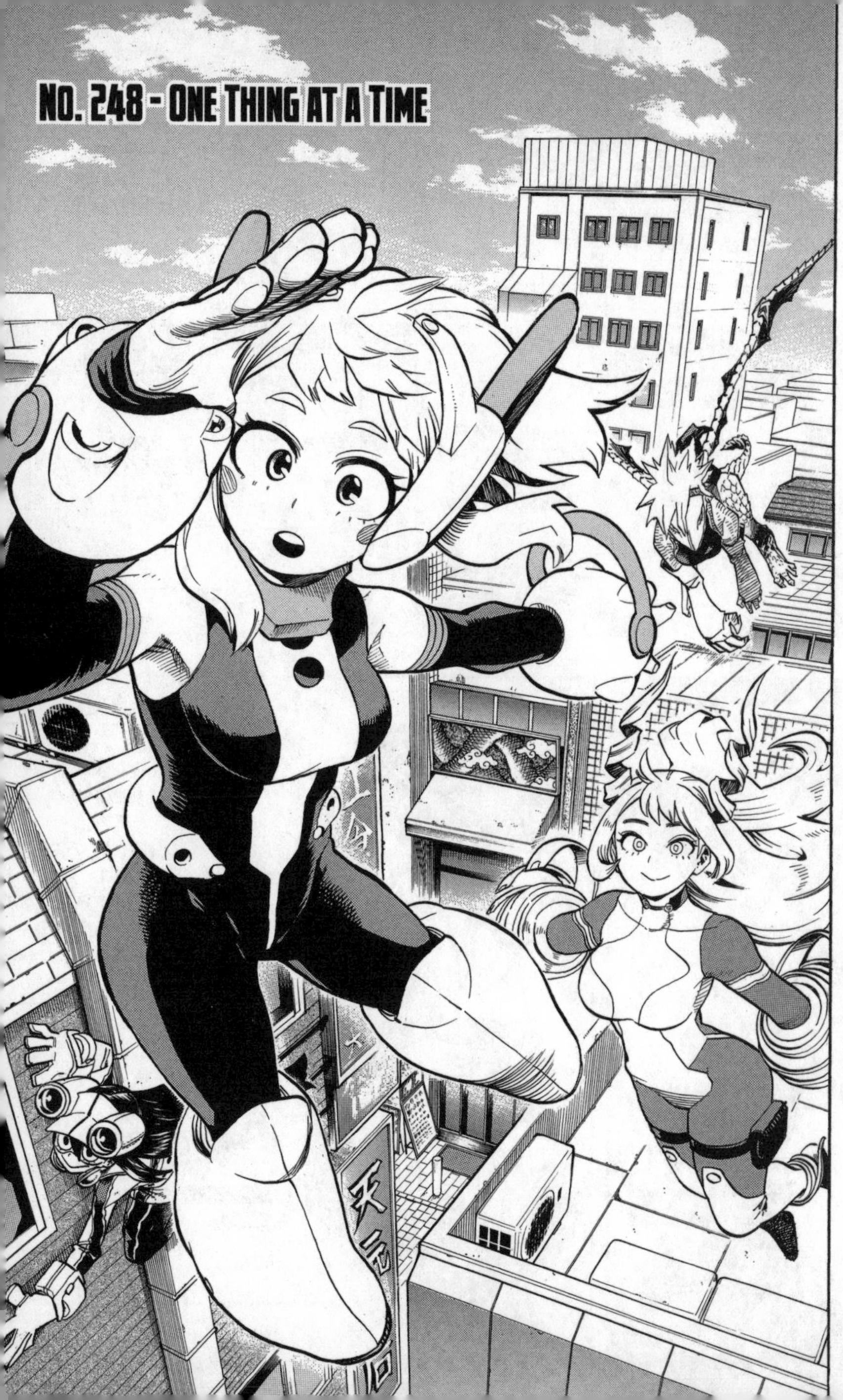
No. 248 - One Thing at a Time

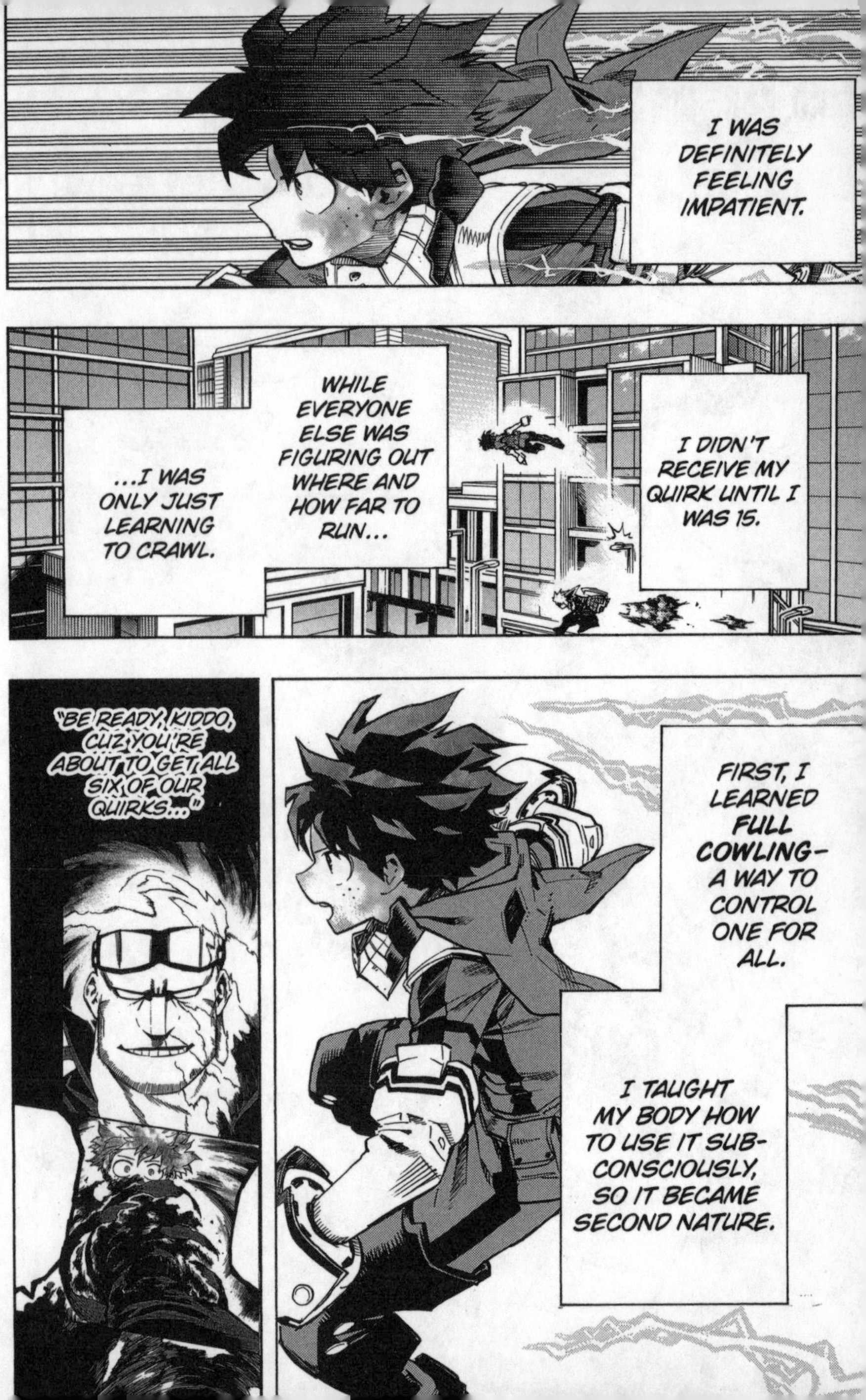
I WAS DEFINITELY FEELING IMPATIENT.
I DIDN'T RECEIVE MY QUIRK UNTIL I WAS 15.
WHILE EVERYONE ELSE WAS FIGURING OUT WHERE AND HOW FAR TO RUN...
...I WAS ONLY JUST LEARNING TO CRAWL.
FIRST, I LEARNED FULL COWLING- A WAY TO CONTROL ONE FOR ALL.
I TAUGHT MY BODY HOW TO USE IT SUB-CONSCIOUSLY, SO IT BECAME SECOND NATURE.
"BE READY, KIDDO, CUZ YOU'RE ABOUT TO GET ALL SIX OF OUR QUIRKS..."

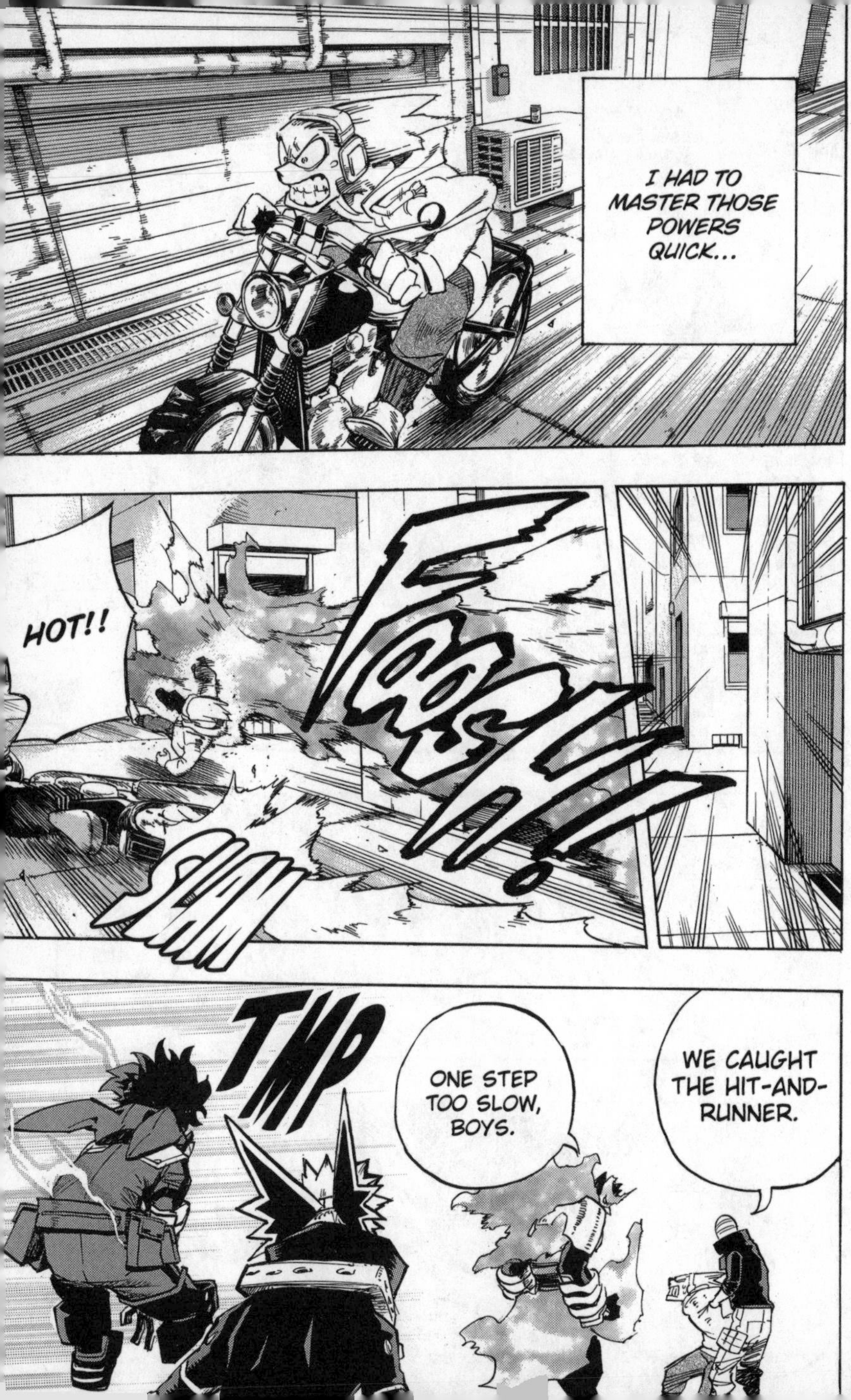
I HAD TO MASTER THOSE POWERS QUICK...
FOOSH!!
HOT!!
SHH
WE CAUGHT THE HIT-AND-RUNNER.
ONE STEP TOO SLOW, BOYS.
TMP

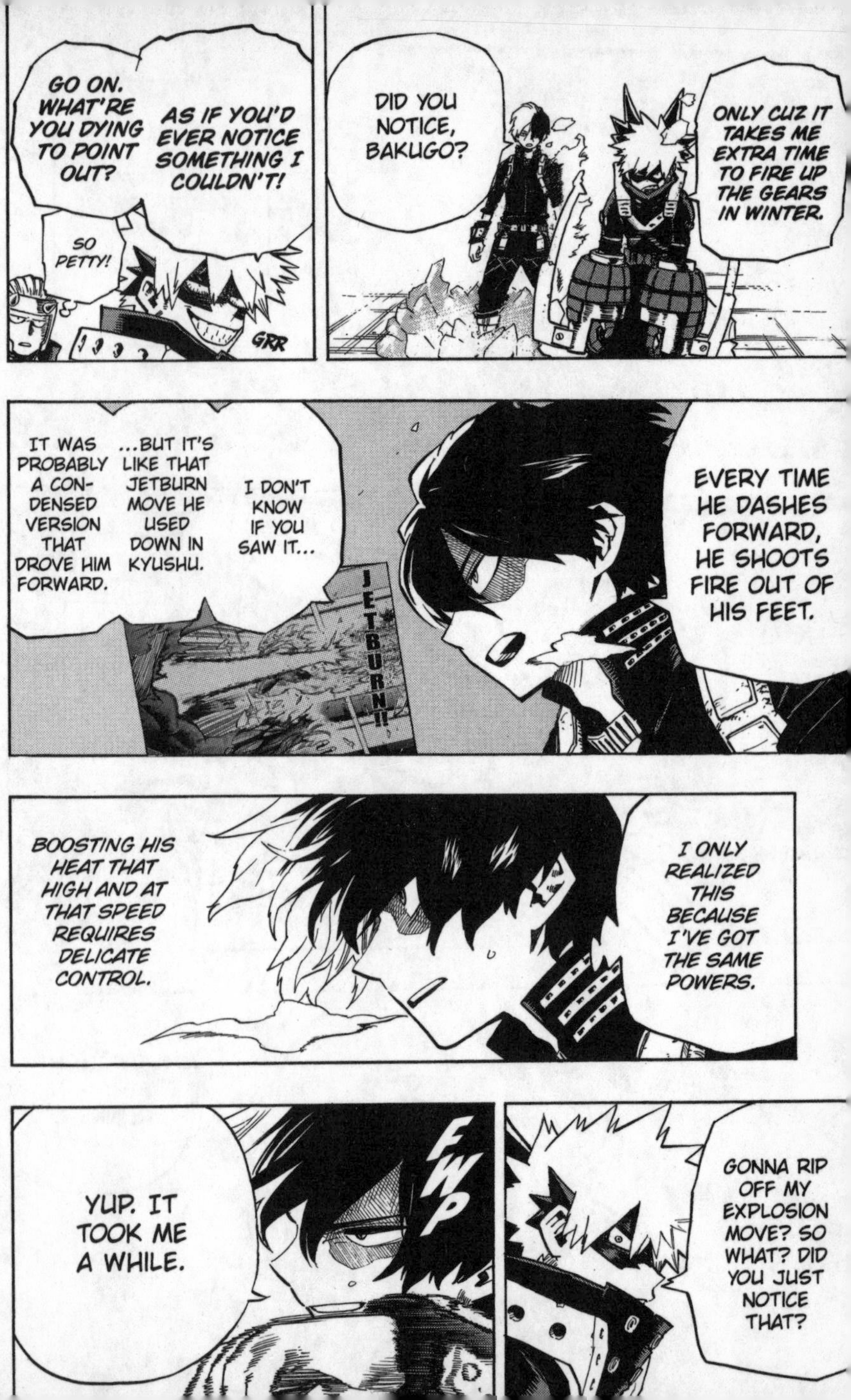
ONLY CUZ IT TAKES ME EXTRA TIME TO FIRE UP THE GEARS IN WINTER.
DID YOU NOTICE, BAKUGO?
AS IF YOU'D EVER NOTICE SOMETHING I COULDN'T!
GO ON. WHAT'RE YOU DYING TO POINT OUT?
SO PETTY!
GRR
EVERY TIME HE DASHES FORWARD, HE SHOOTS FIRE OUT OF HIS FEET.
I DON'T KNOW IF YOU SAW IT...
...BUT IT'S LIKE THAT JETBURN MOVE HE USED DOWN IN KYUSHU.
IT WAS PROBABLY A CON-DENSED VERSION THAT DROVE HIM FORWARD.
JETBURN!!
I ONLY REALIZED THIS BECAUSE I'VE GOT THE SAME POWERS.
BOOSTING HIS HEAT THAT HIGH AND AT THAT SPEED REQUIRES DELICATE CONTROL.
GONNA RIP OFF MY EXPLOSION MOVE? SO WHAT? DID YOU JUST NOTICE THAT?
FWP
YUP. IT TOOK ME A WHILE.

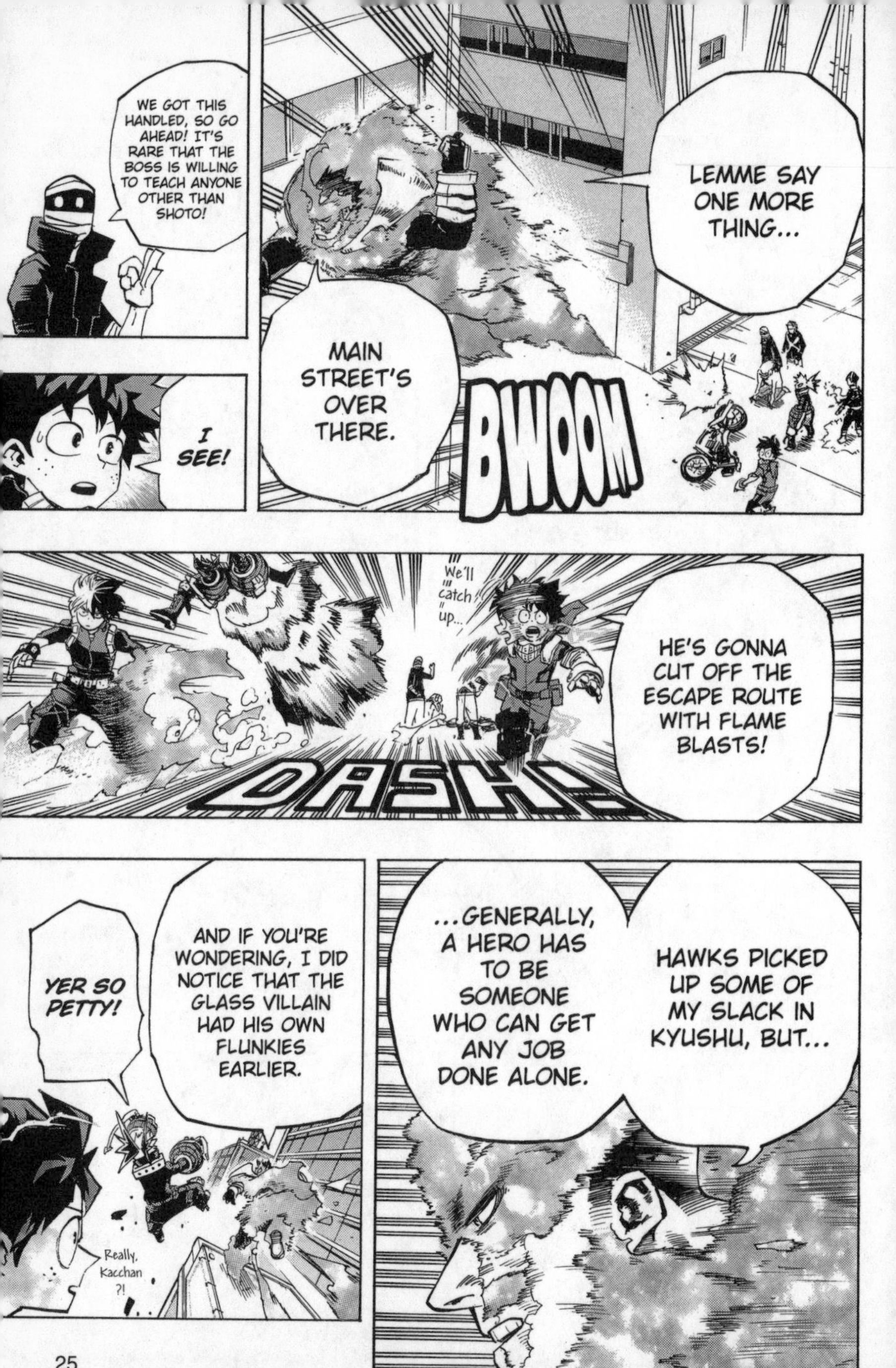
LEMME SAY ONE MORE THING...
MAIN STREET'S OVER THERE.
BWOOM
WE GOT THIS HANDLED, SO GO AHEAD! IT'S RARE THAT THE BOSS IS WILLING TO TEACH ANYONE OTHER THAN SHOTO!
I SEE!
HE'S GONNA CUT OFF THE ESCAPE ROUTE WITH FLAME BLASTS!
We'll catch up...
DASH!!
HAWKS PICKED UP SOME OF MY SLACK IN KYUSHU, BUT...
...GENERALLY, A HERO HAS TO BE SOMEONE WHO CAN GET ANY JOB DONE ALONE.
AND IF YOU'RE WONDERING, I DID NOTICE THAT THE GLASS VILLAIN HAD HIS OWN FLUNKIES EARLIER.
YER SO PETTY!
Really, Kacchan ?!

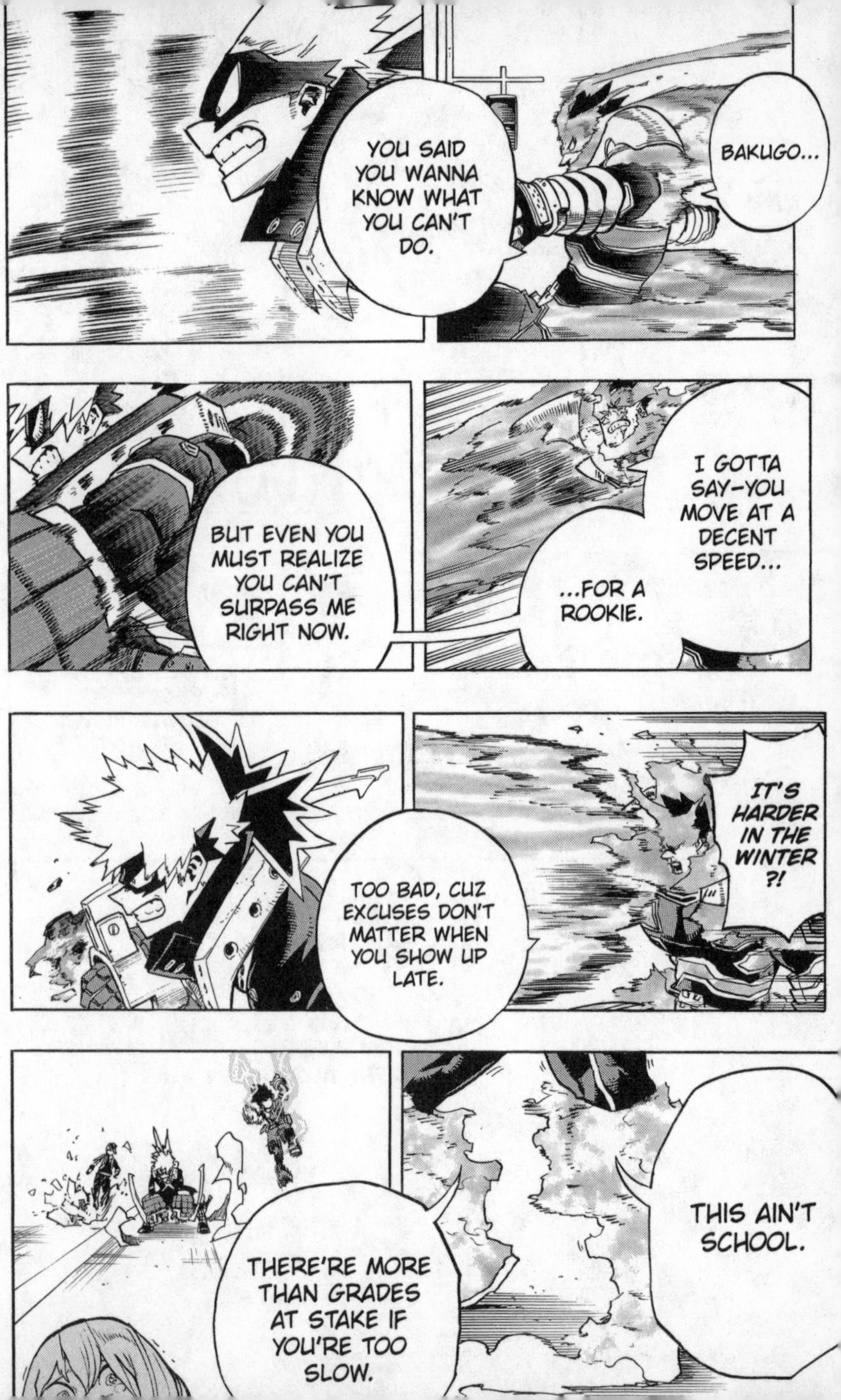
BAKUGO...
YOU SAID YOU WANNA KNOW WHAT YOU CAN'T DO.
I GOTTA SAY—YOU MOVE AT A DECENT SPEED...
...FOR A ROOKIE.
BUT EVEN YOU MUST REALIZE YOU CAN'T SURPASS ME RIGHT NOW.
IT'S HARDER IN THE WINTER?!
TOO BAD, CUZ EXCUSES DON'T MATTER WHEN YOU SHOW UP LATE.
THIS AIN'T SCHOOL.
THERE'RE MORE THAN GRADES AT STAKE IF YOU'RE TOO SLOW.

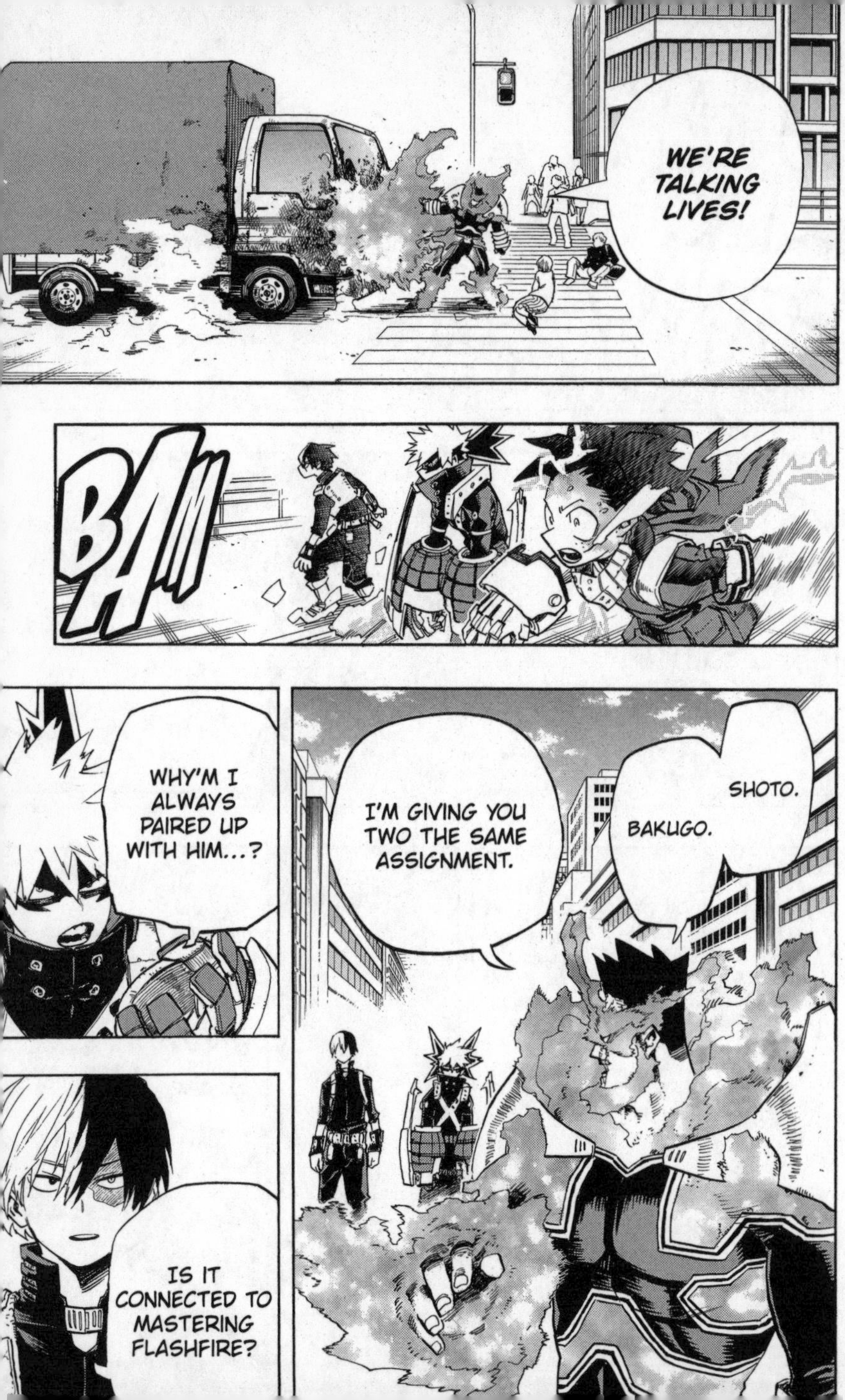

WE'RE TALKING LIVES!
BA
SHOTO.
BAKUGO.
I'M GIVING YOU TWO THE SAME ASSIGNMENT.
WHY'M I ALWAYS PAIRED UP WITH HIM...?
IS IT CONNECTED TO MASTERING FLASHFIRE?

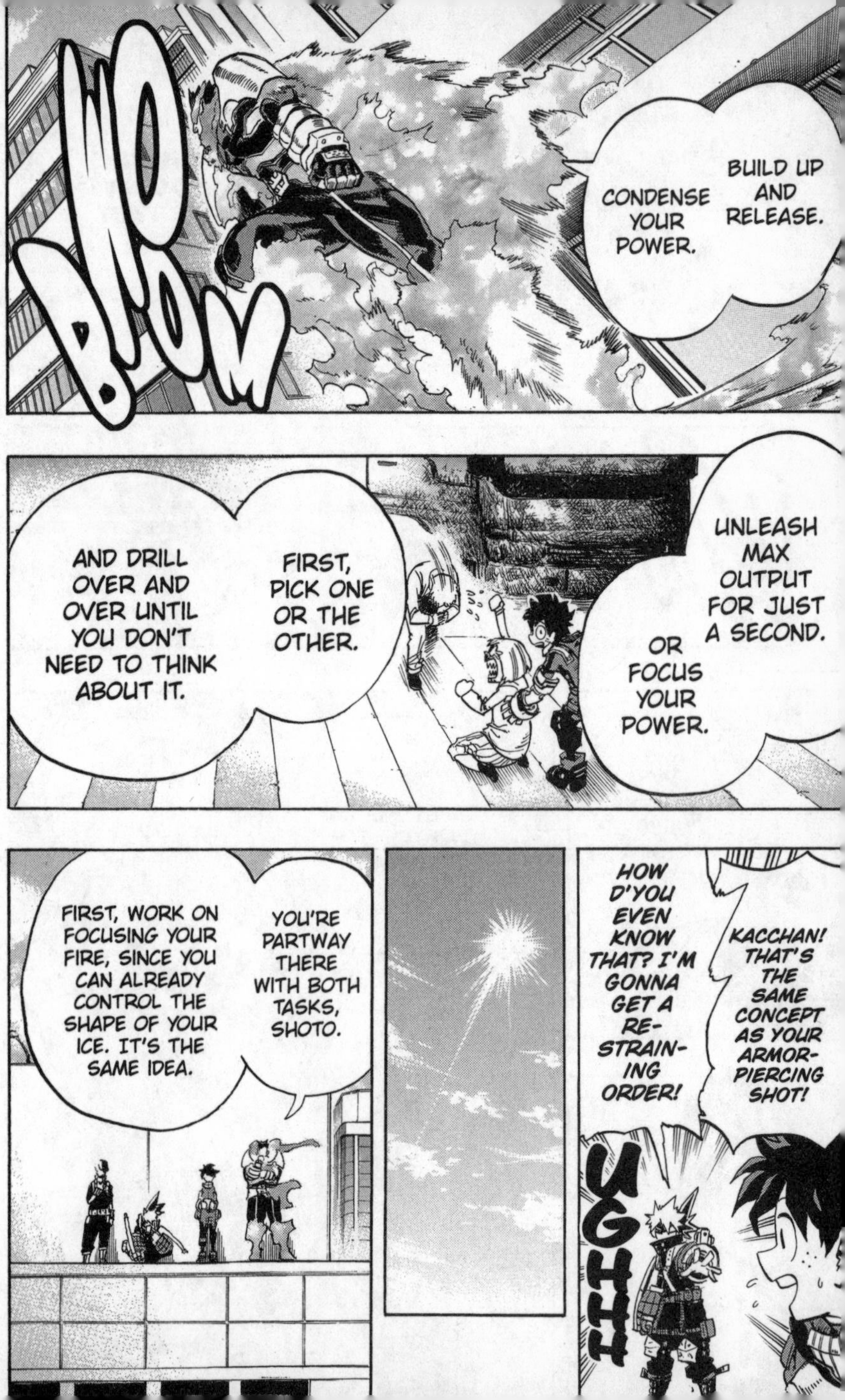
BUILD UP AND RELEASE.
CONDENSE YOUR POWER.
BOOM
UNLEASH MAX OUTPUT FOR JUST A SECOND.
OR FOCUS YOUR POWER.
FIRST, PICK ONE OR THE OTHER.
AND DRILL OVER AND OVER UNTIL YOU DON'T NEED TO THINK ABOUT IT.
KACCHAN! THAT'S THE SAME CONCEPT AS YOUR ARMOR-PIERCING SHOT!
HOW D'YOU EVEN KNOW THAT? I'M GONNA GET A RE-STRAIN-ING ORDER!
UGHHH
YOU'RE PARTWAY THERE WITH BOTH TASKS, SHOTO.
FIRST, WORK ON FOCUSING YOUR FIRE, SINCE YOU CAN ALREADY CONTROL THE SHAPE OF YOUR ICE. IT'S THE SAME IDEA.

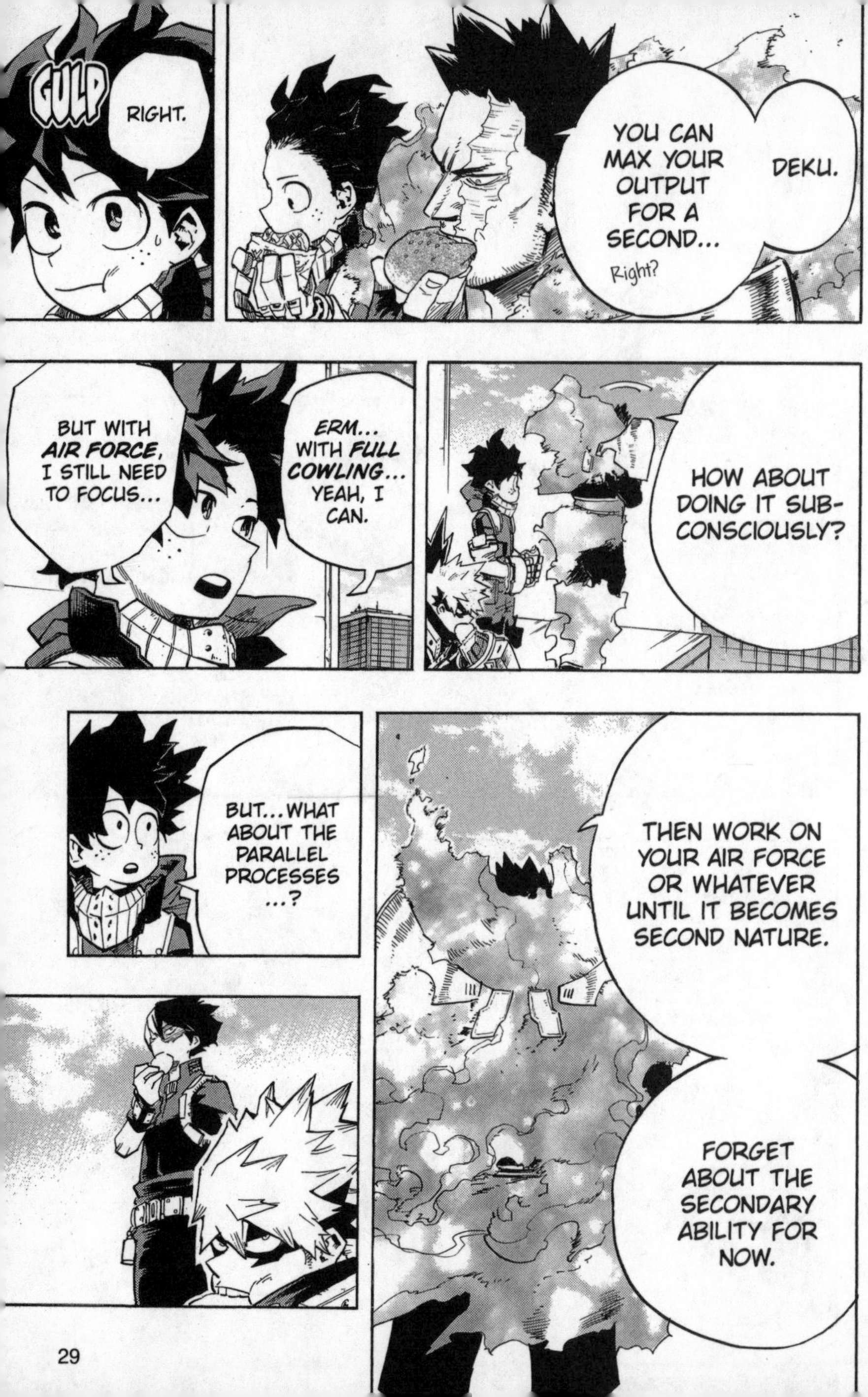
DEKU.
YOU CAN MAX YOUR OUTPUT FOR A SECOND... Right?
GULP
RIGHT.
HOW ABOUT DOING IT SUB-CONSCIOUSLY?
ERM... WITH FULL COWLING... YEAH, I CAN.
BUT WITH AIR FORCE, I STILL NEED TO FOCUS...
THEN WORK ON YOUR AIR FORCE OR WHATEVER UNTIL IT BECOMES SECOND NATURE.
FORGET ABOUT THE SECONDARY ABILITY FOR NOW.
BUT...WHAT ABOUT THE PARALLEL PROCESSES ...?

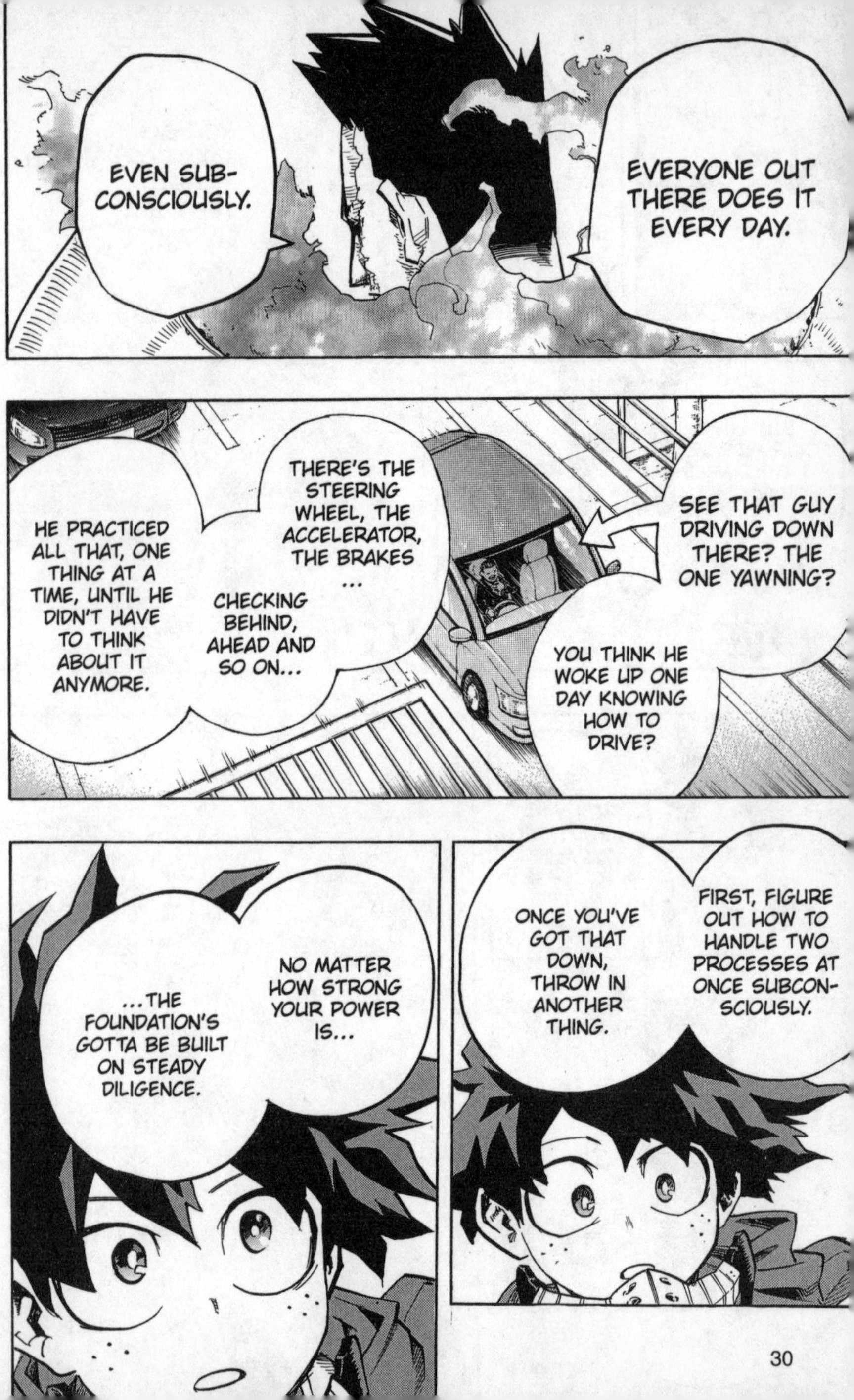
EVERYONE OUT THERE DOES IT EVERY DAY.
EVEN SUB-CONSCIOUSLY.
SEE THAT GUY DRIVING DOWN THERE? THE ONE YAWNING?
YOU THINK HE WOKE UP ONE DAY KNOWING HOW TO DRIVE?
THERE'S THE STEERING WHEEL, THE ACCELERATOR, THE BRAKES ...
CHECKING BEHIND, AHEAD AND SO ON...
HE PRACTICED ALL THAT, ONE THING AT A TIME, UNTIL HE DIDN'T HAVE TO THINK ABOUT IT ANYMORE.
FIRST, FIGURE OUT HOW TO HANDLE TWO PROCESSES AT ONCE SUBCON-SCIOUSLY.
ONCE YOU'VE GOT THAT DOWN, THROW IN ANOTHER THING.
NO MATTER HOW STRONG YOUR POWER IS...
...THE FOUNDATION'S GOTTA BE BUILT ON STEADY DILIGENCE.

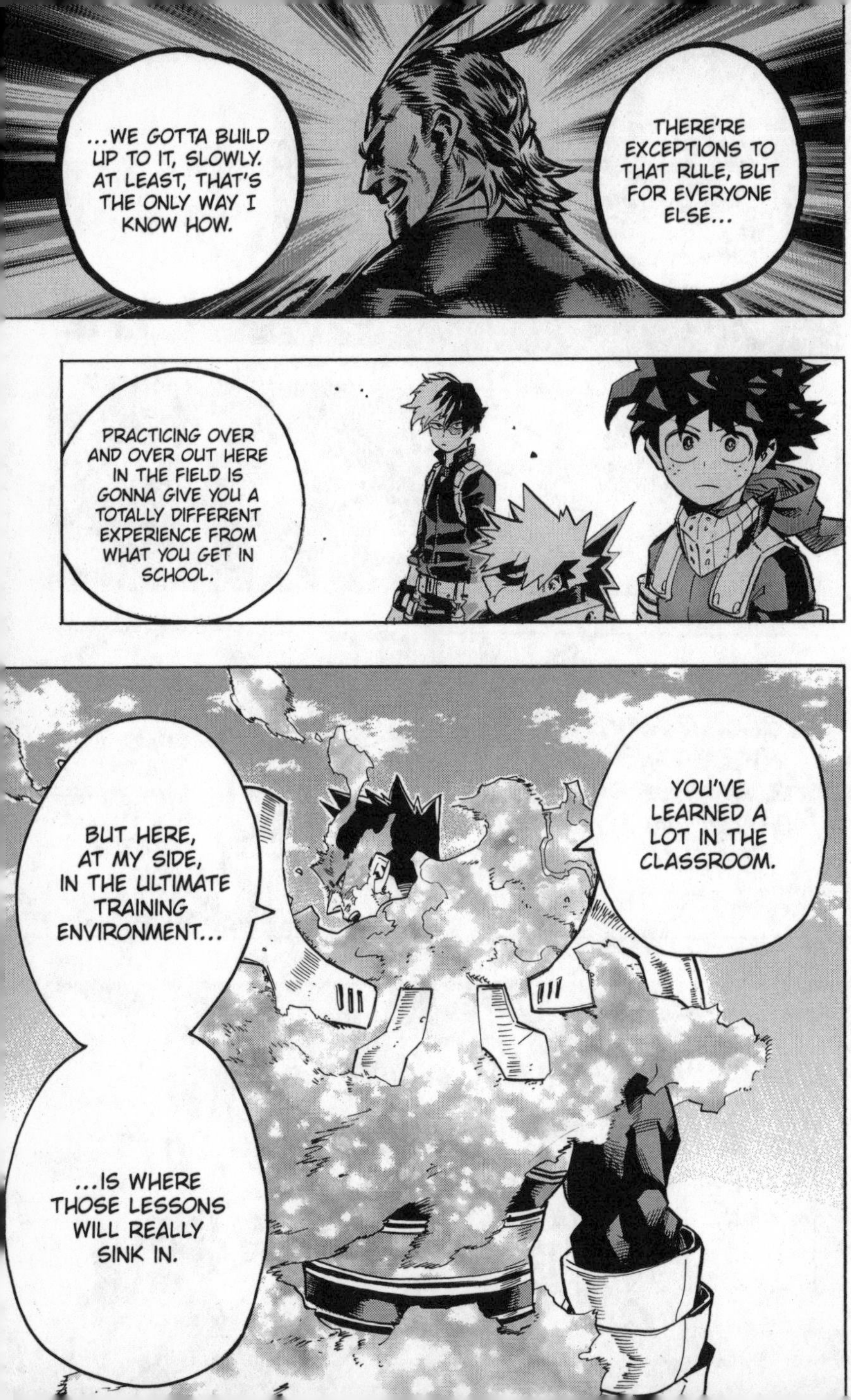
THERE'RE EXCEPTIONS TO THAT RULE, BUT FOR EVERYONE ELSE...
...WE GOTTA BUILD UP TO IT, SLOWLY. AT LEAST, THAT'S THE ONLY WAY I KNOW HOW.
PRACTICING OVER AND OVER OUT HERE IN THE FIELD IS GONNA GIVE YOU A TOTALLY DIFFERENT EXPERIENCE FROM WHAT YOU GET IN SCHOOL.
YOU'VE LEARNED A LOT IN THE CLASSROOM.
BUT HERE, AT MY SIDE, IN THE ULTIMATE TRAINING ENVIRONMENT...
...IS WHERE THOSE LESSONS WILL REALLY SINK IN.

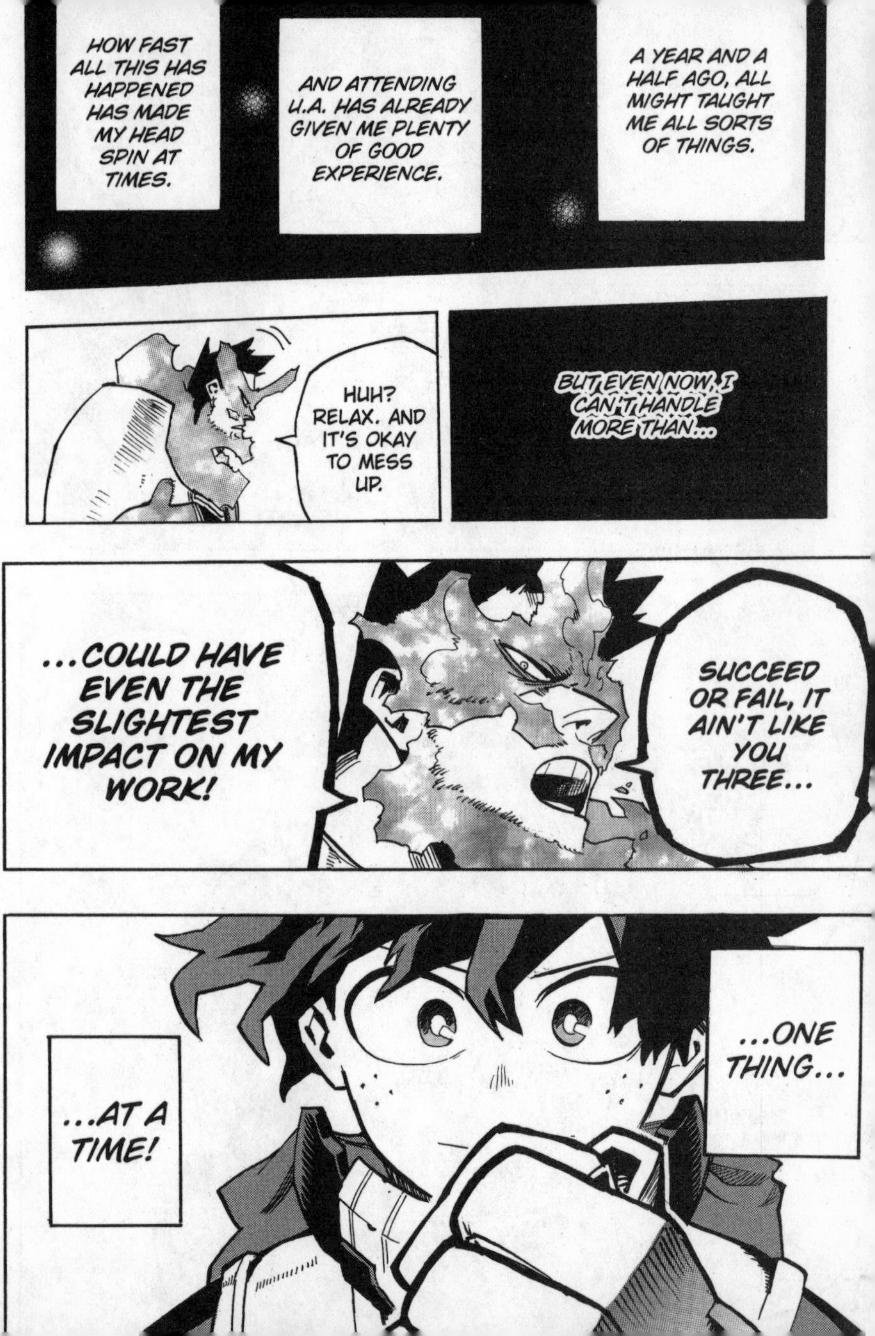
A YEAR AND A HALF AGO, ALL MIGHT TAUGHT ME ALL SORTS OF THINGS.
AND ATTENDING U.A. HAS ALREADY GIVEN ME PLENTY OF GOOD EXPERIENCE.
HOW FAST ALL THIS HAS HAPPENED HAS MADE MY HEAD SPIN AT TIMES.
BUT EVEN NOW, I CAN'T HANDLE MORE THAN...
HUH? RELAX. AND IT'S OKAY TO MESS UP.
SUCCEED OR FAIL, IT AIN'T LIKE YOU THREE...
...COULD HAVE EVEN THE SLIGHTEST IMPACT ON MY WORK!
...ONE THING...
...AT A TIME!

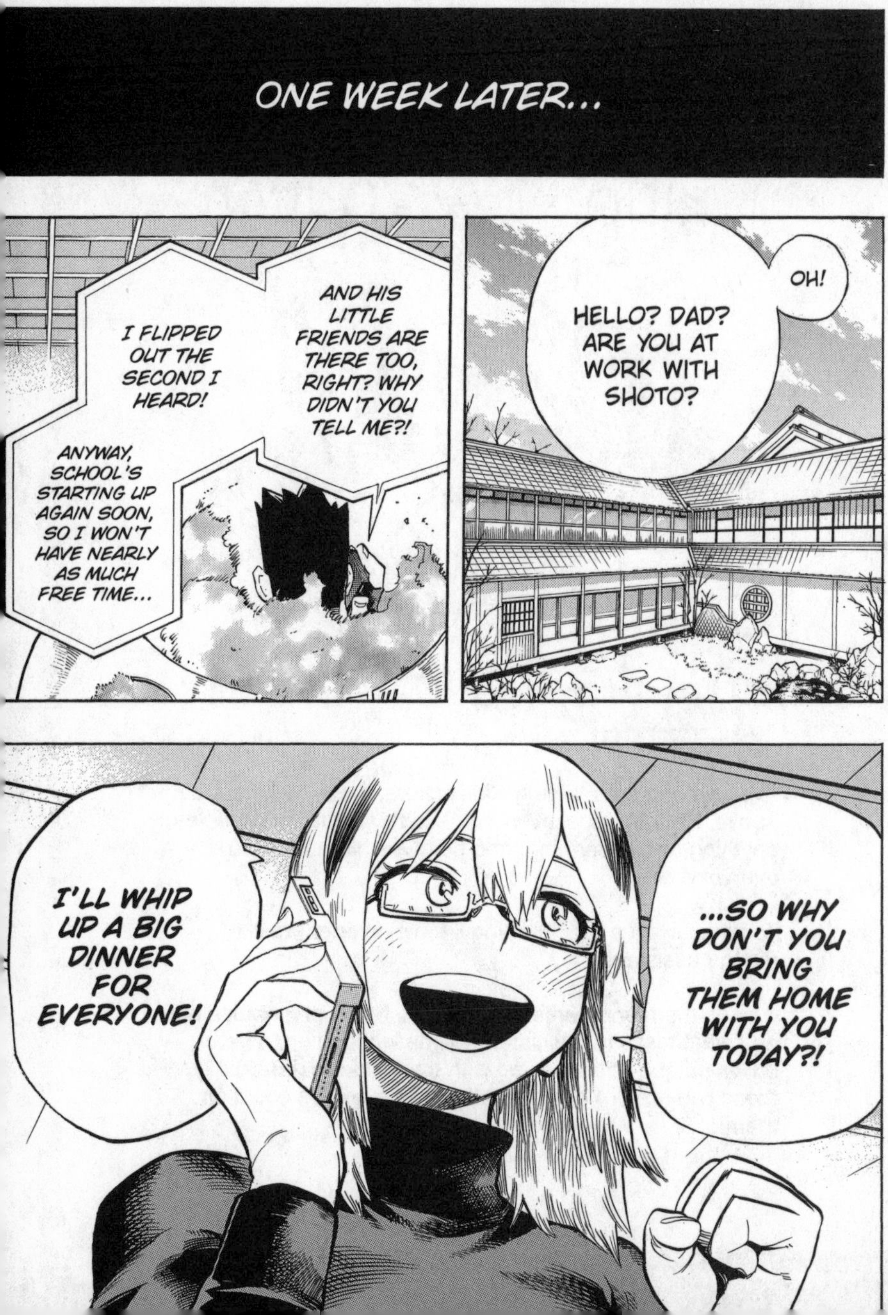
ONE WEEK LATER...
OH!
HELLO? DAD? ARE YOU AT WORK WITH SHOTO?
AND HIS LITTLE FRIENDS ARE THERE TOO, RIGHT? WHY DIDN'T YOU TELL ME?!
I FLIPPED OUT THE SECOND I HEARD!
ANYWAY, SCHOOL'S STARTING UP AGAIN SOON, SO I WON'T HAVE NEARLY AS MUCH FREE TIME...
...SO WHY DON'T YOU BRING THEM HOME WITH YOU TODAY?!
I'LL WHIP UP A BIG DINNER FOR EVERYONE!

KIDO   ONIMA

Even among the Flaming Sidekickers, these two are a cut above. Endeavor believes that a hero should be capable of anything and everything, and he gives his support to everyone else.

To use a manga-artist analogy, the sidekicks are like manga assistants.

Just as the manga artist decides the terms of employment and what tasks the assistant will be working on, a hero builds unique relationships with each sidekick! Basically, these two are pro assistants!! You can always count on them!!

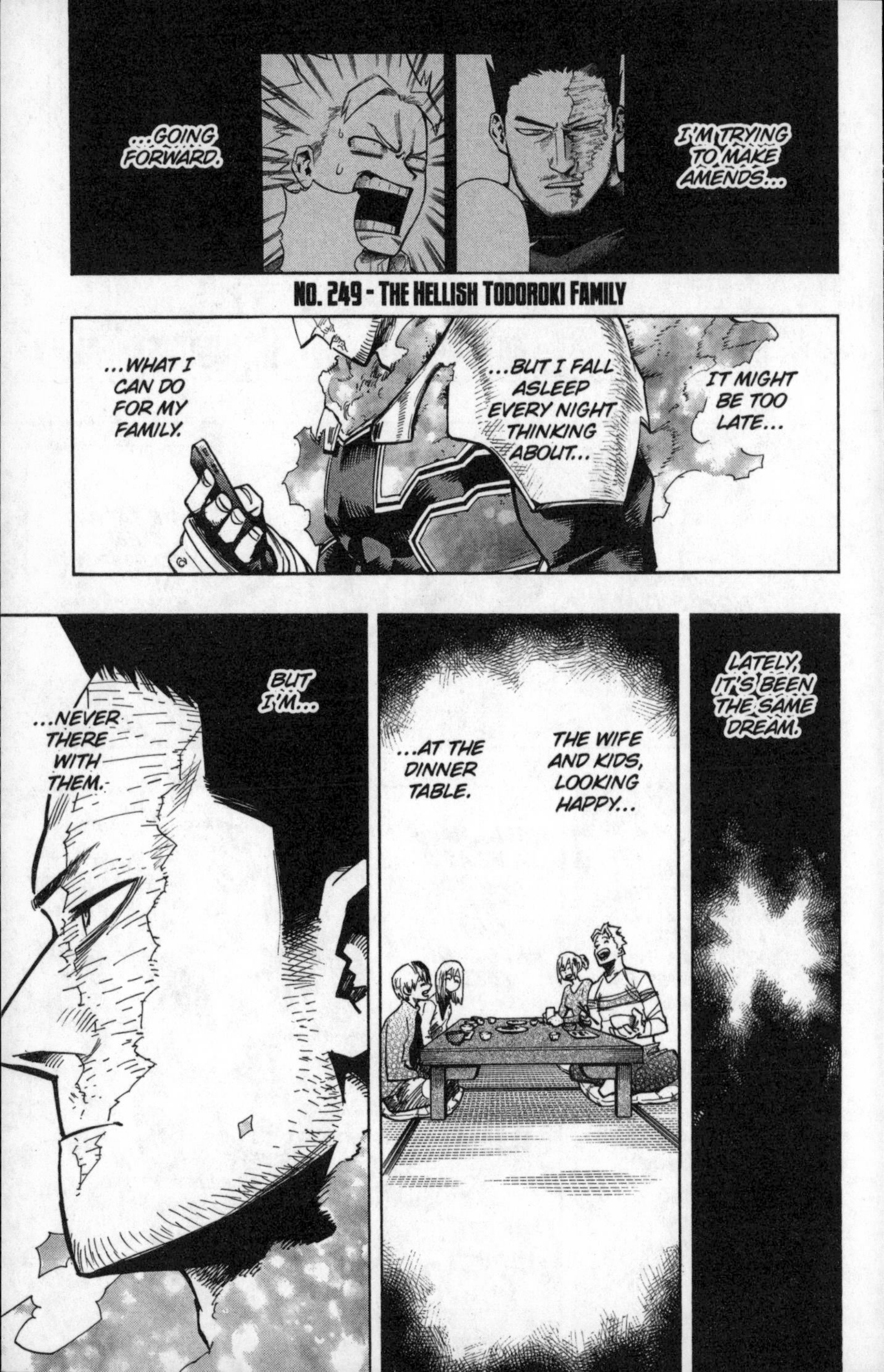
I'M TRYING TO MAKE AMENDS...
...GOING FORWARD.
No. 249 - The Hellish Todoroki Family
IT MIGHT BE TOO LATE...
...BUT I FALL ASLEEP EVERY NIGHT THINKING ABOUT...
...WHAT I CAN DO FOR MY FAMILY.
LATELY, IT'S BEEN THE SAME DREAM.
THE WIFE AND KIDS, LOOKING HAPPY...
...AT THE DINNER TABLE.
BUT I'M...
...NEVER THERE WITH THEM.

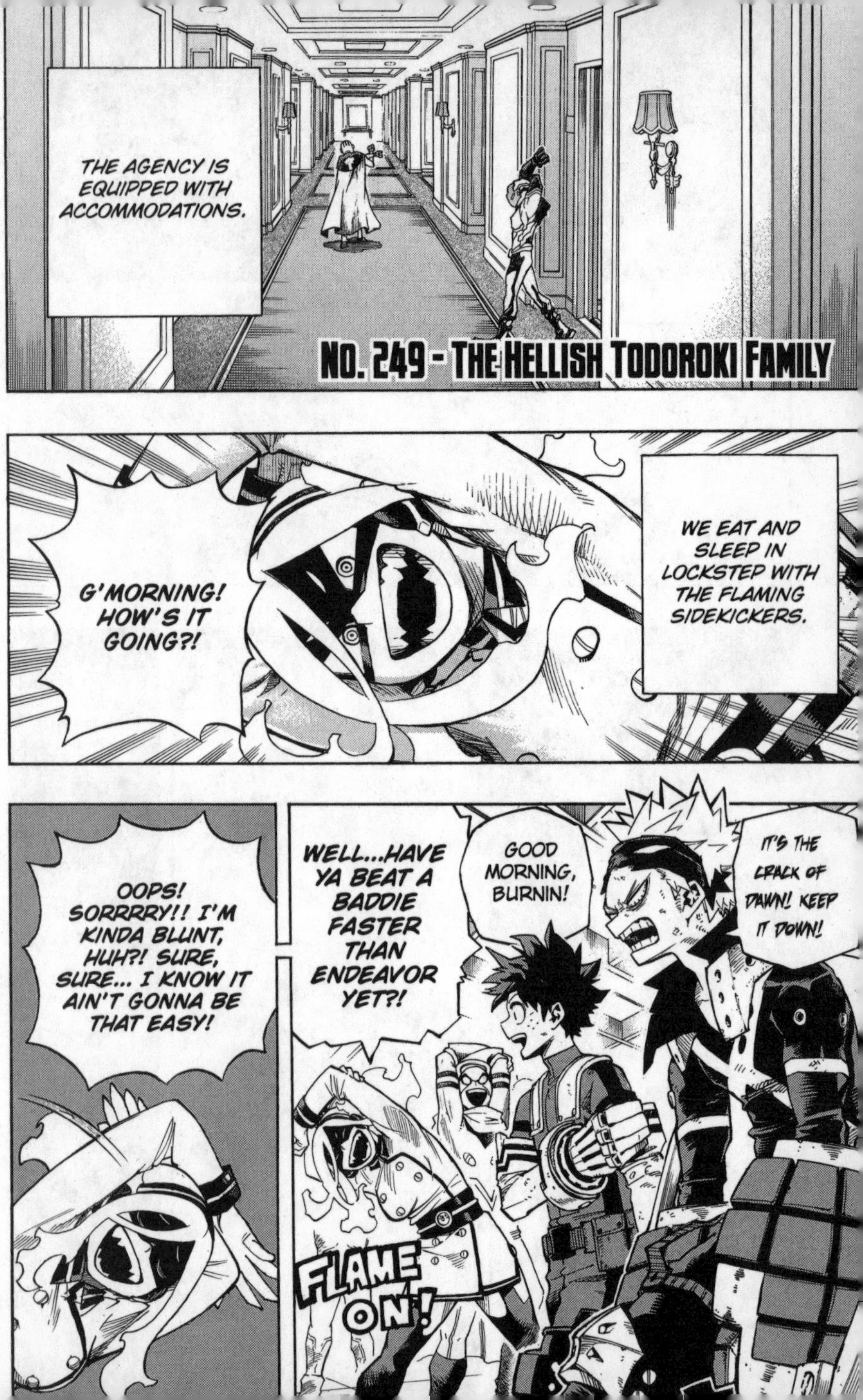
THE AGENCY IS EQUIPPED WITH ACCOMMODATIONS.
NO. 249 - THE HELLISH TODOROKI FAMILY
WE EAT AND SLEEP IN LOCKSTEP WITH THE FLAMING SIDEKICKERS.
G'MORNING! HOW'S IT GOING?!
IT'S THE CRACK OF DAWN! KEEP IT DOWN!
GOOD MORNING, BURNIN!
WELL...HAVE YA BEAT A BADDIE FASTER THAN ENDEAVOR YET?!
FLAME ON!
OOPS! SORRRRY!! I'M KINDA BLUNT, HUH?! SURE, SURE... I KNOW IT AIN'T GONNA BE THAT EASY!

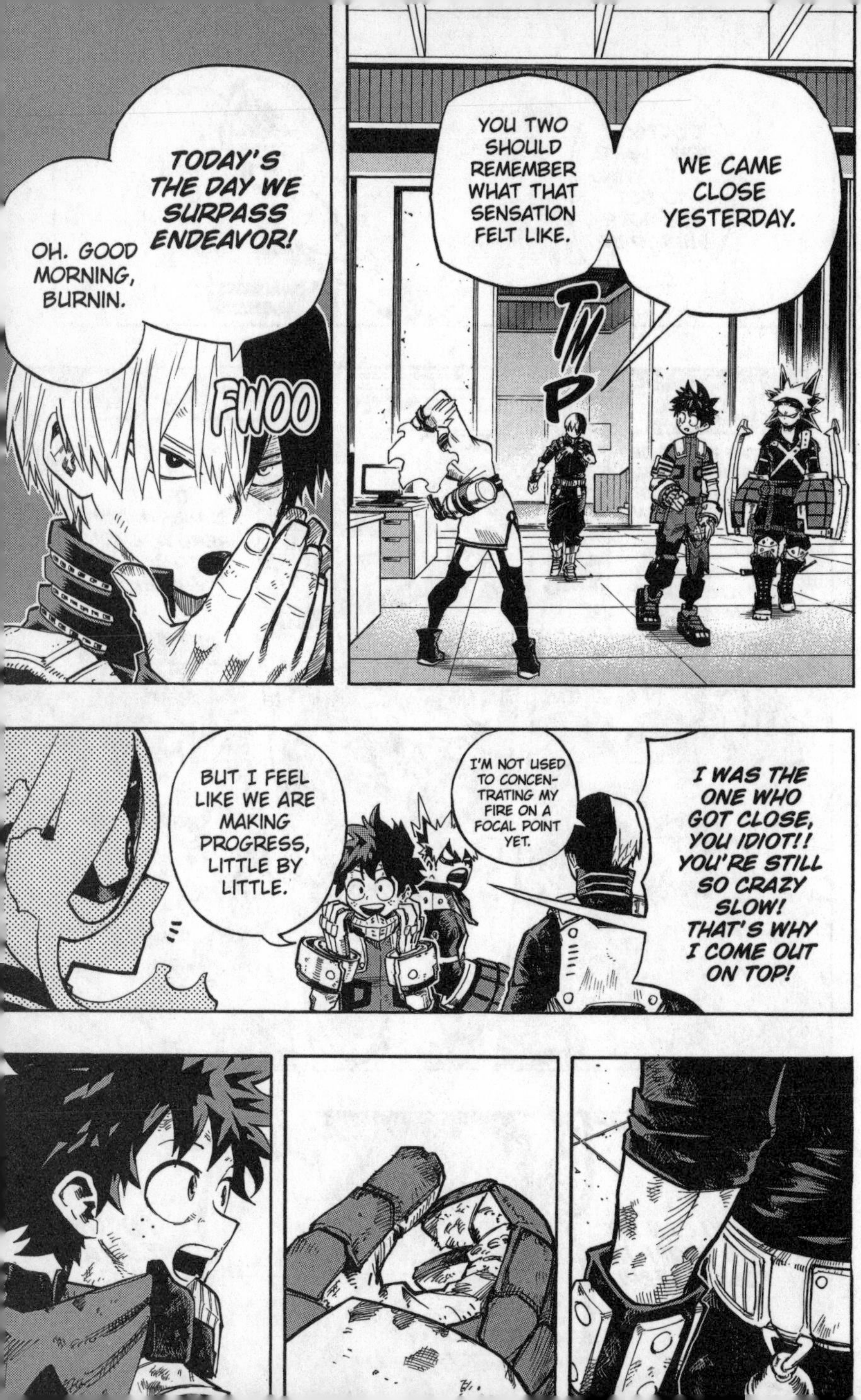
WE CAME CLOSE YESTERDAY.
YOU TWO SHOULD REMEMBER WHAT THAT SENSATION FELT LIKE.
TMP
TODAY'S THE DAY WE SURPASS ENDEAVOR!
OH. GOOD MORNING, BURNIN.
FWOO
I WAS THE ONE WHO GOT CLOSE, YOU IDIOT!! YOU'RE STILL SO CRAZY SLOW! THAT'S WHY I COME OUT ON TOP!
I'M NOT USED TO CONCEN-TRATING MY FIRE ON A FOCAL POINT YET.
BUT I FEEL LIKE WE ARE MAKING PROGRESS, LITTLE BY LITTLE.

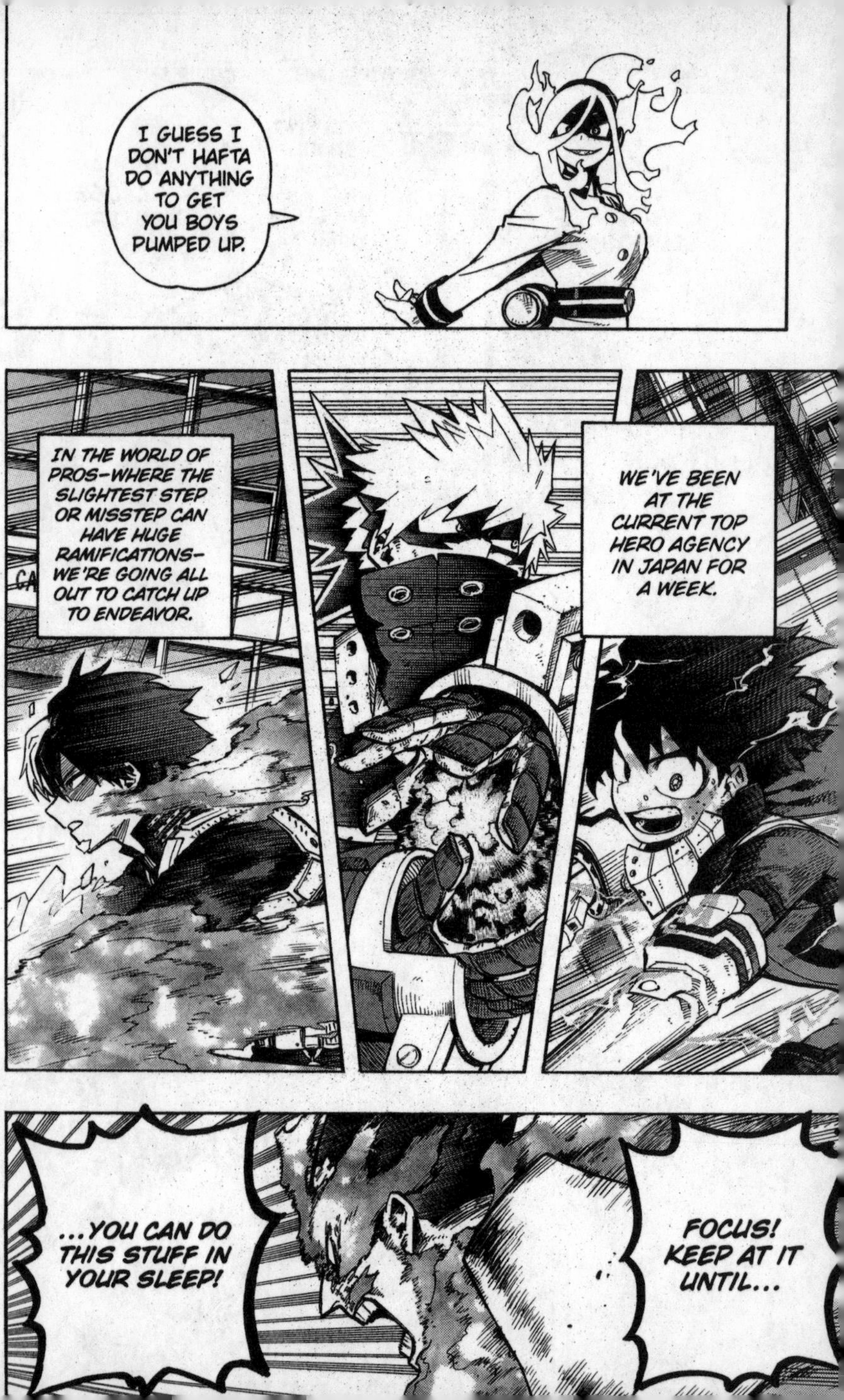
I GUESS I DON'T HAFTA DO ANYTHING TO GET YOU BOYS PUMPED UP.
WE'VE BEEN AT THE CURRENT TOP HERO AGENCY IN JAPAN FOR A WEEK.
IN THE WORLD OF PROS—WHERE THE SLIGHTEST STEP OR MISSTEP CAN HAVE HUGE RAMIFICATIONS—WE'RE GOING ALL OUT TO CATCH UP TO ENDEAVOR.
FOCUS! KEEP AT IT UNTIL...
...YOU CAN DO THIS STUFF IN YOUR SLEEP!

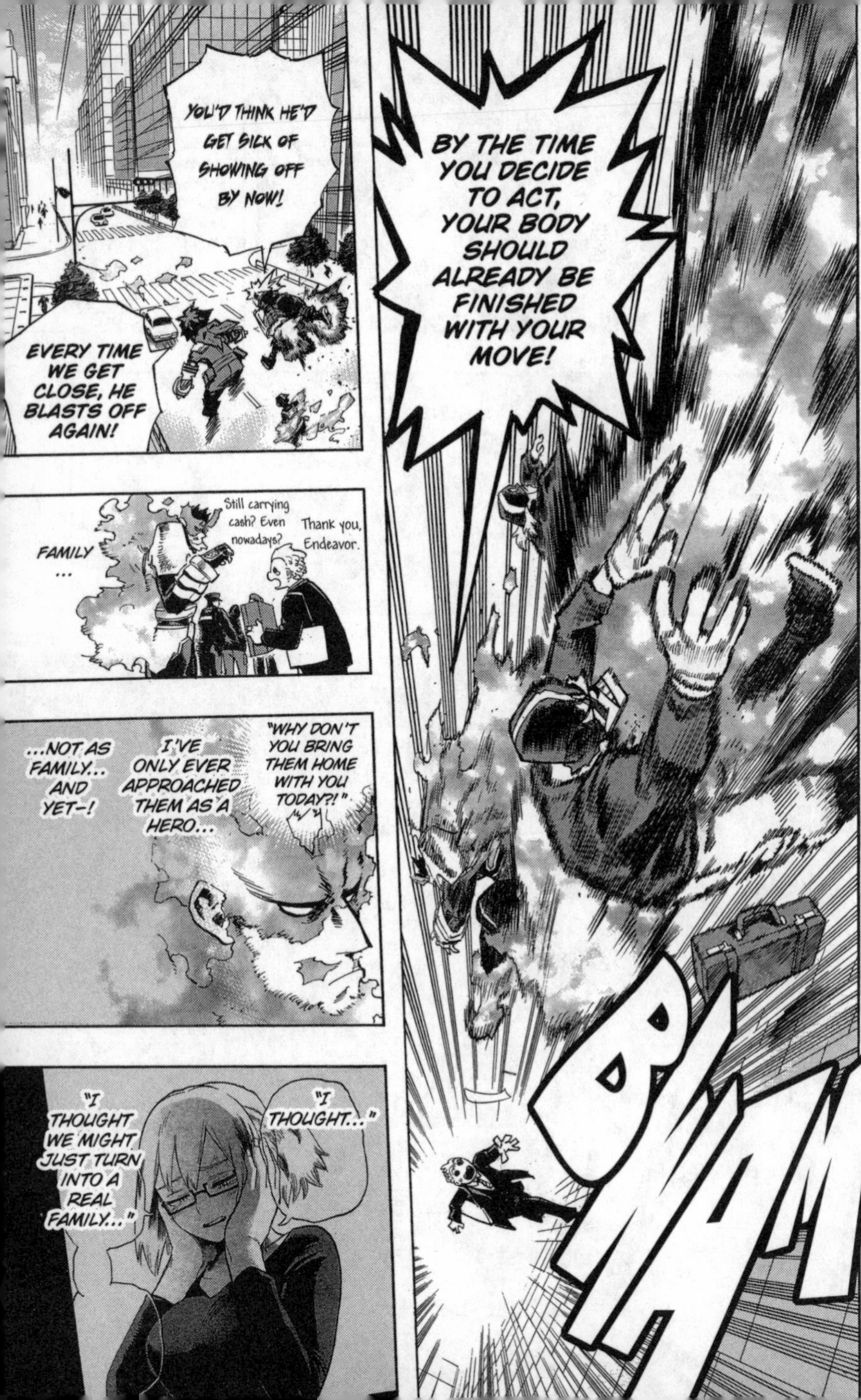
BY THE TIME YOU DECIDE TO ACT, YOUR BODY SHOULD ALREADY BE FINISHED WITH YOUR MOVE!
YOU'D THINK HE'D GET SICK OF SHOWING OFF BY NOW!
EVERY TIME WE GET CLOSE, HE BLASTS OFF AGAIN!
Thank you, Endeavor.
Still carrying cash? Even nowadays?
FAMILY ...
"WHY DON'T YOU BRING THEM HOME WITH YOU TODAY?!"
I'VE ONLY EVER APPROACHED THEM AS A HERO...
...NOT AS FAMILY... AND YET—!
"I THOUGHT..."
"I THOUGHT WE MIGHT JUST TURN INTO A REAL FAMILY..."

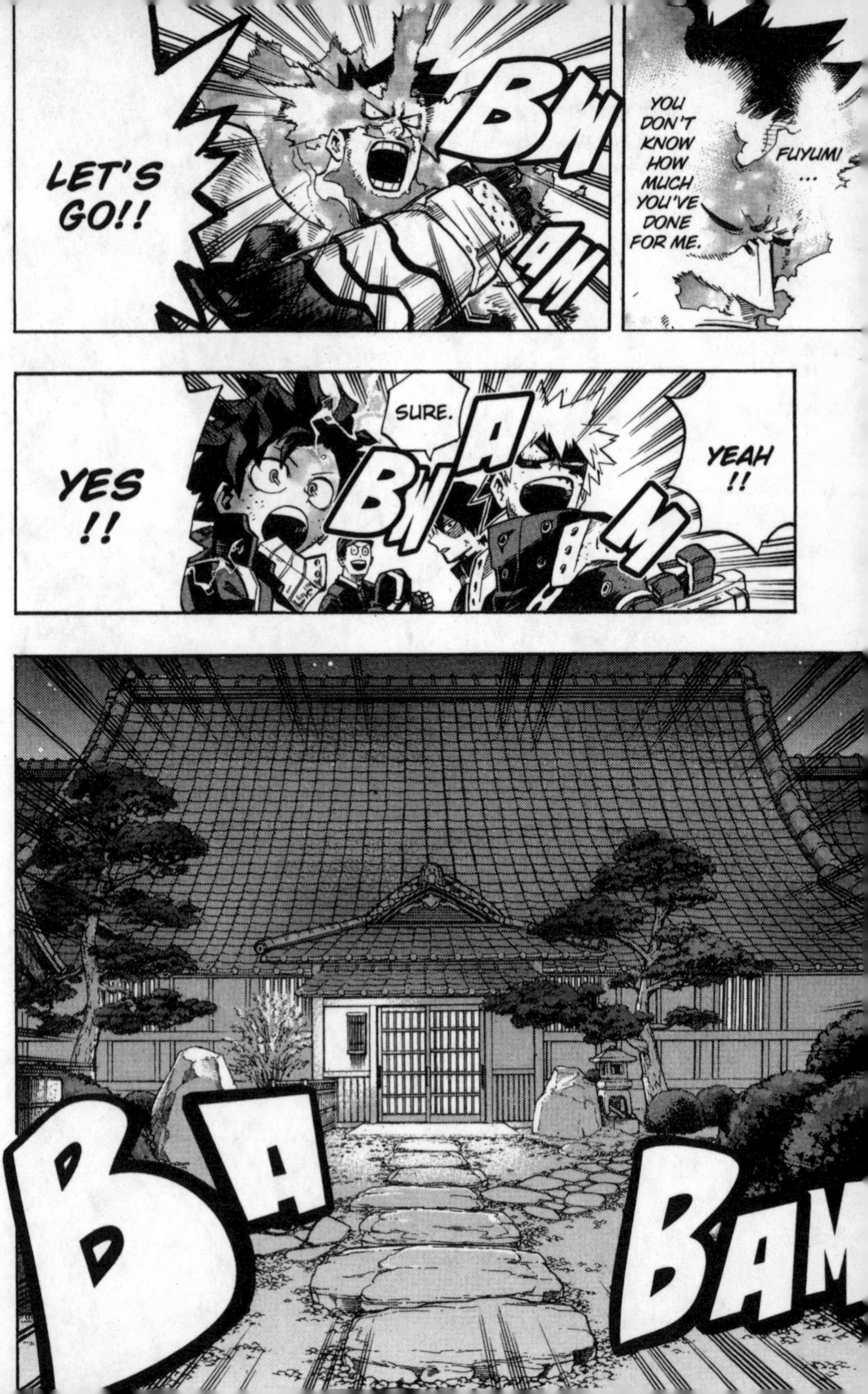

FUYUMI ...
YOU DON'T KNOW HOW MUCH YOU'VE DONE FOR ME.
BWAM
LET'S GO!!
YEAH !!
BWAM
SURE.
YES !!
BA
BAM

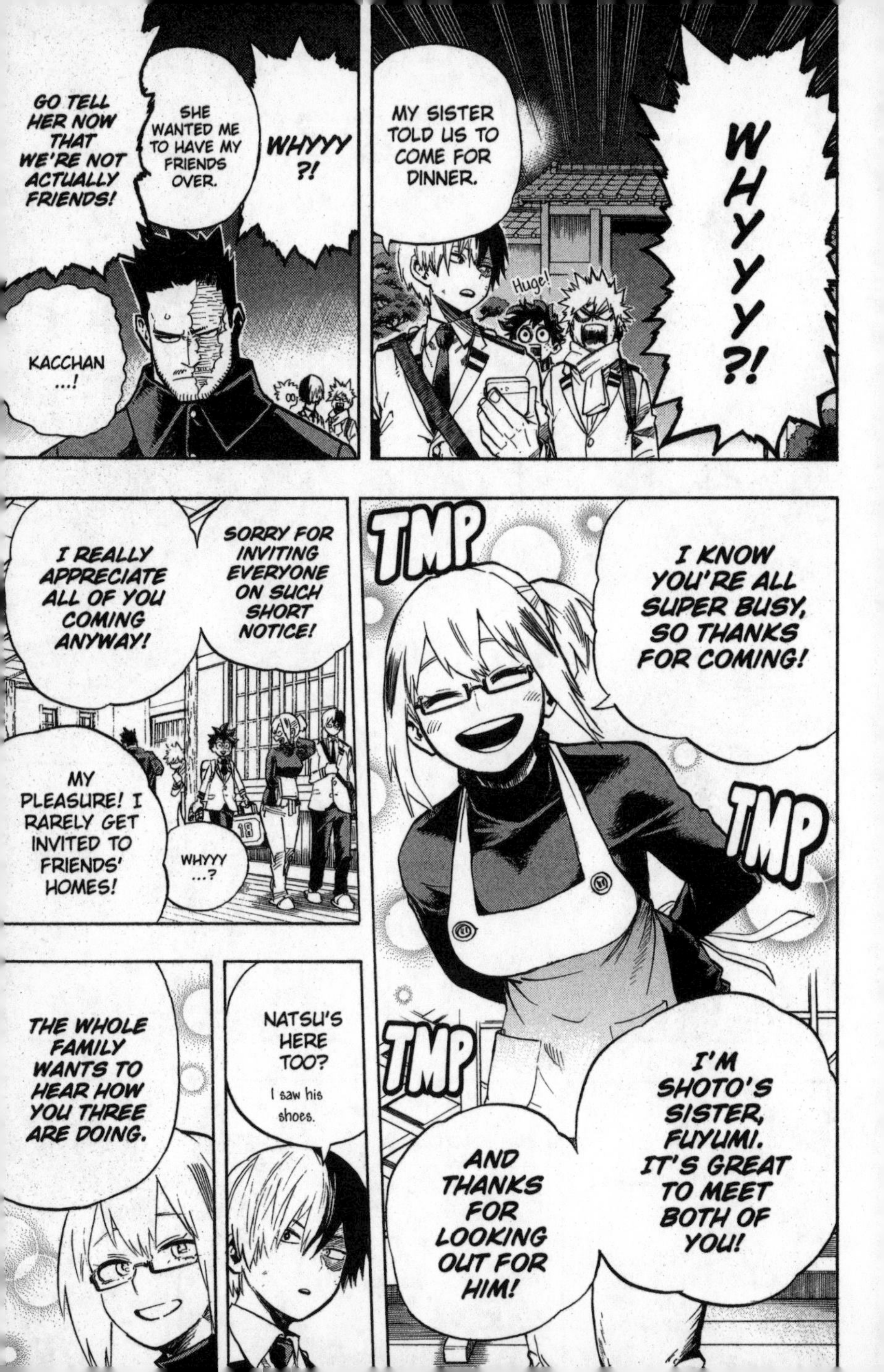
WHYYYY?!
MY SISTER TOLD US TO COME FOR DINNER.
Huge!
WHYYY?!
SHE WANTED ME TO HAVE MY FRIENDS OVER.
GO TELL HER NOW THAT WE'RE NOT ACTUALLY FRIENDS!
KACCHAN...!
TMP
I KNOW YOU'RE ALL SUPER BUSY, SO THANKS FOR COMING!
TMP
TMP
I'M SHOTO'S SISTER, FUYUMI. IT'S GREAT TO MEET BOTH OF YOU!
AND THANKS FOR LOOKING OUT FOR HIM!
SORRY FOR INVITING EVERYONE ON SUCH SHORT NOTICE!
I REALLY APPRECIATE ALL OF YOU COMING ANYWAY!
MY PLEASURE! I RARELY GET INVITED TO FRIENDS' HOMES!
WHYYY...?
NATSU'S HERE TOO?
I saw his shoes.
THE WHOLE FAMILY WANTS TO HEAR HOW YOU THREE ARE DOING.

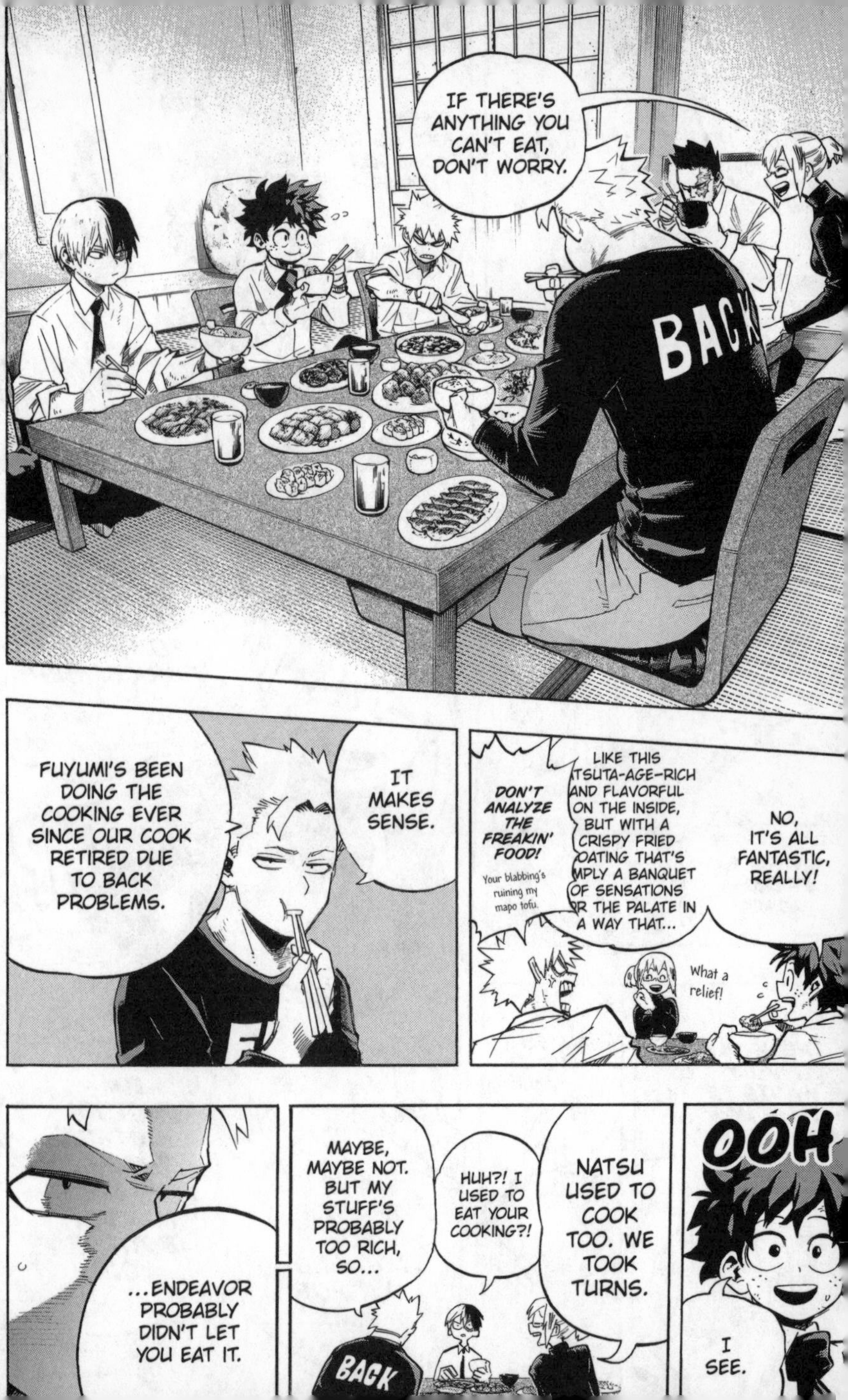
IF THERE'S ANYTHING YOU CAN'T EAT, DON'T WORRY.
BACK
NO, IT'S ALL FANTASTIC, REALLY!
LIKE THIS TSUTA-AGE-RICH AND FLAVORFUL ON THE INSIDE, BUT WITH A CRISPY FRIED OATING THAT'S MPLY A BANQUET OF SENSATIONS R THE PALATE IN A WAY THAT...
DON'T ANALYZE THE FREAKIN' FOOD!
Your blabbing's ruining my mapo tofu.
What a relief!
IT MAKES SENSE.
FUYUMI'S BEEN DOING THE COOKING EVER SINCE OUR COOK RETIRED DUE TO BACK PROBLEMS.
OOH
I SEE.
NATSU USED TO COOK TOO. WE TOOK TURNS.
HUH?! I USED TO EAT YOUR COOKING?!
MAYBE, MAYBE NOT. BUT MY STUFF'S PROBABLY TOO RICH, SO...
BACK
...ENDEAVOR PROBABLY DIDN'T LET YOU EAT IT.

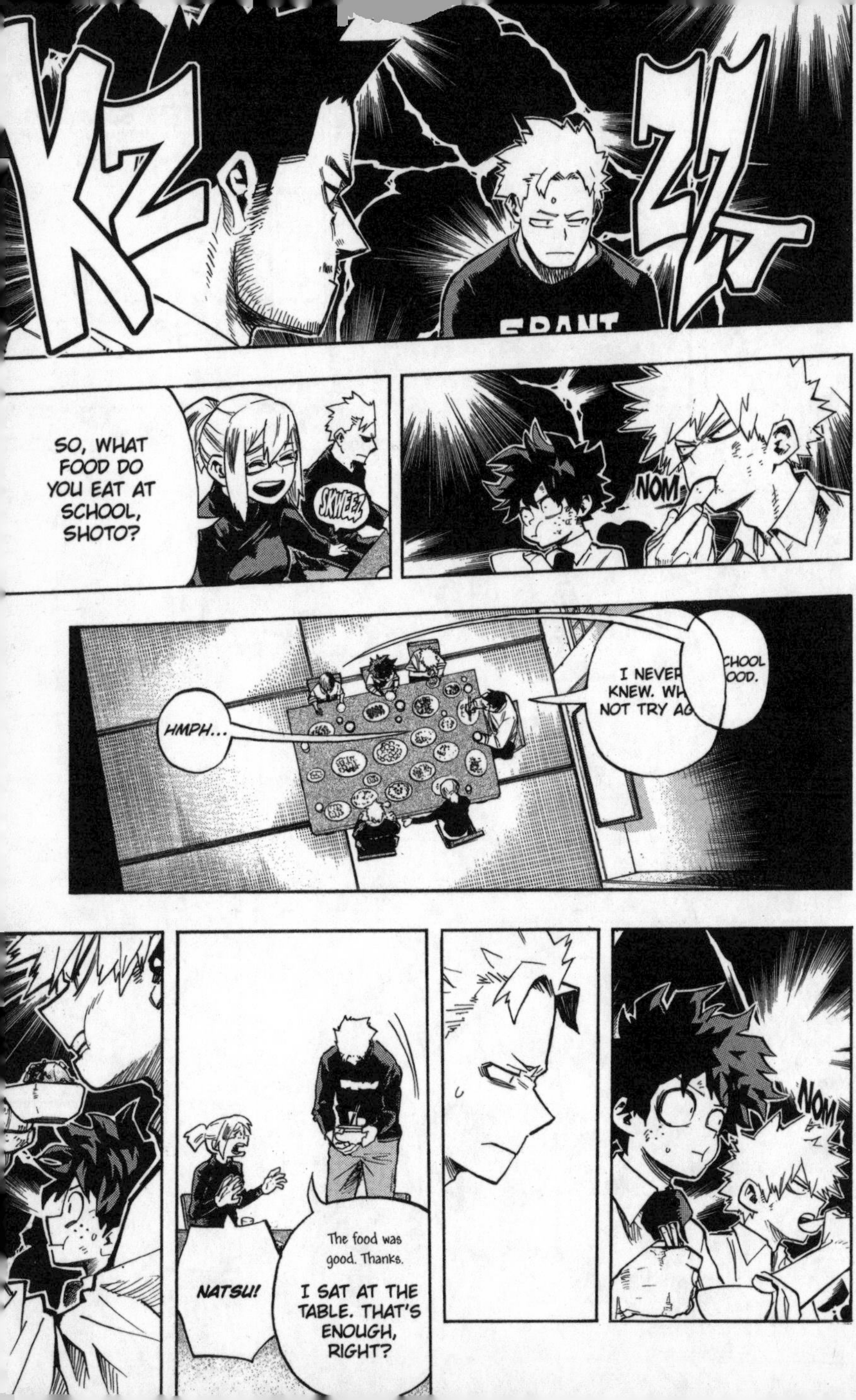
KZ
ZZT
NOM
SO, WHAT FOOD DO YOU EAT AT SCHOOL, SHOTO?
SKWEEZ
I NEVER KNEW. WH NOT TRY AG
CHOOL OOD.
HMPH...
NOM
The food was good. Thanks.
I SAT AT THE TABLE. THAT'S ENOUGH, RIGHT?
NATSU!

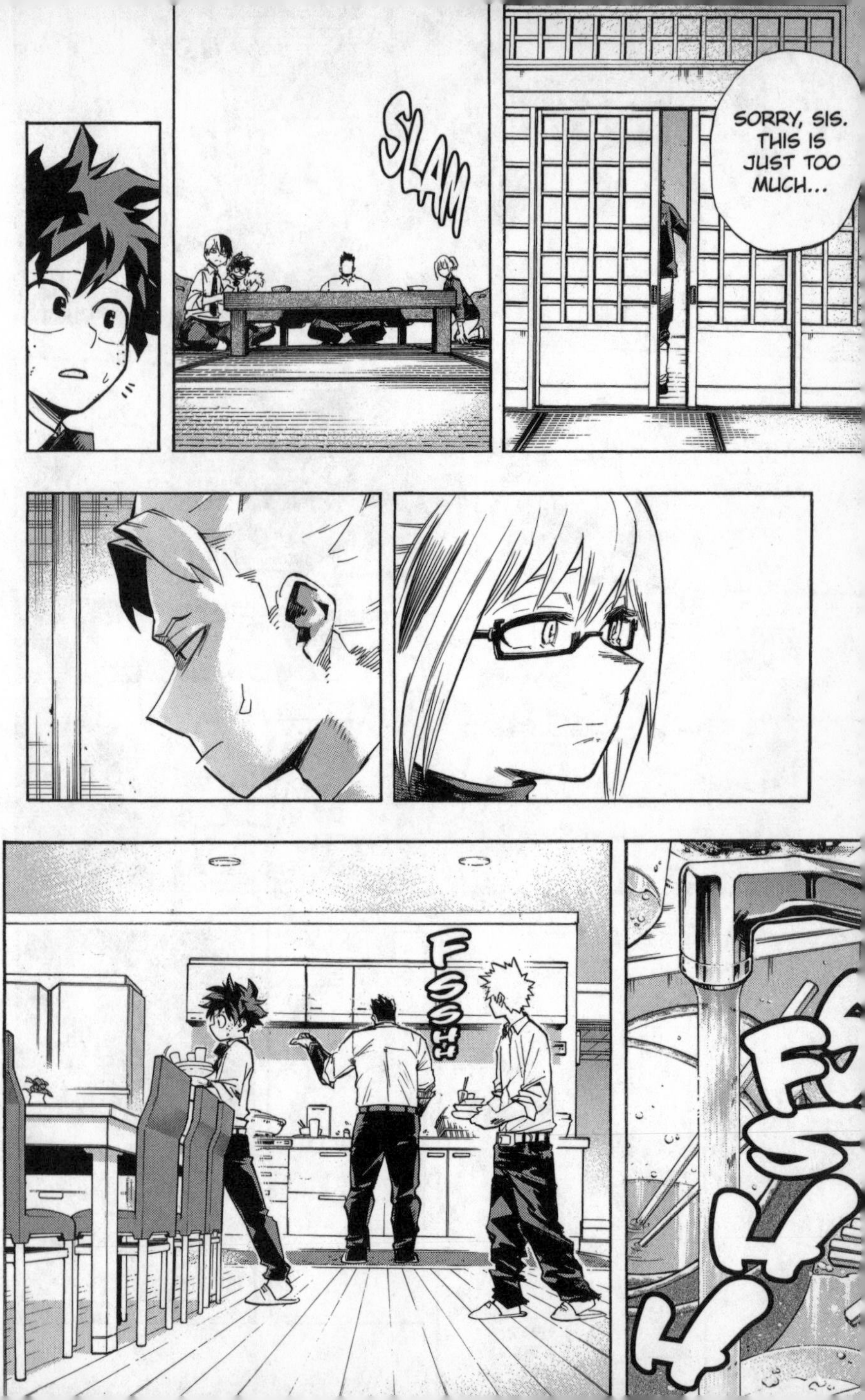
SORRY, SIS. THIS IS JUST TOO MUCH...
SLAM
FSSHH
FSSHH

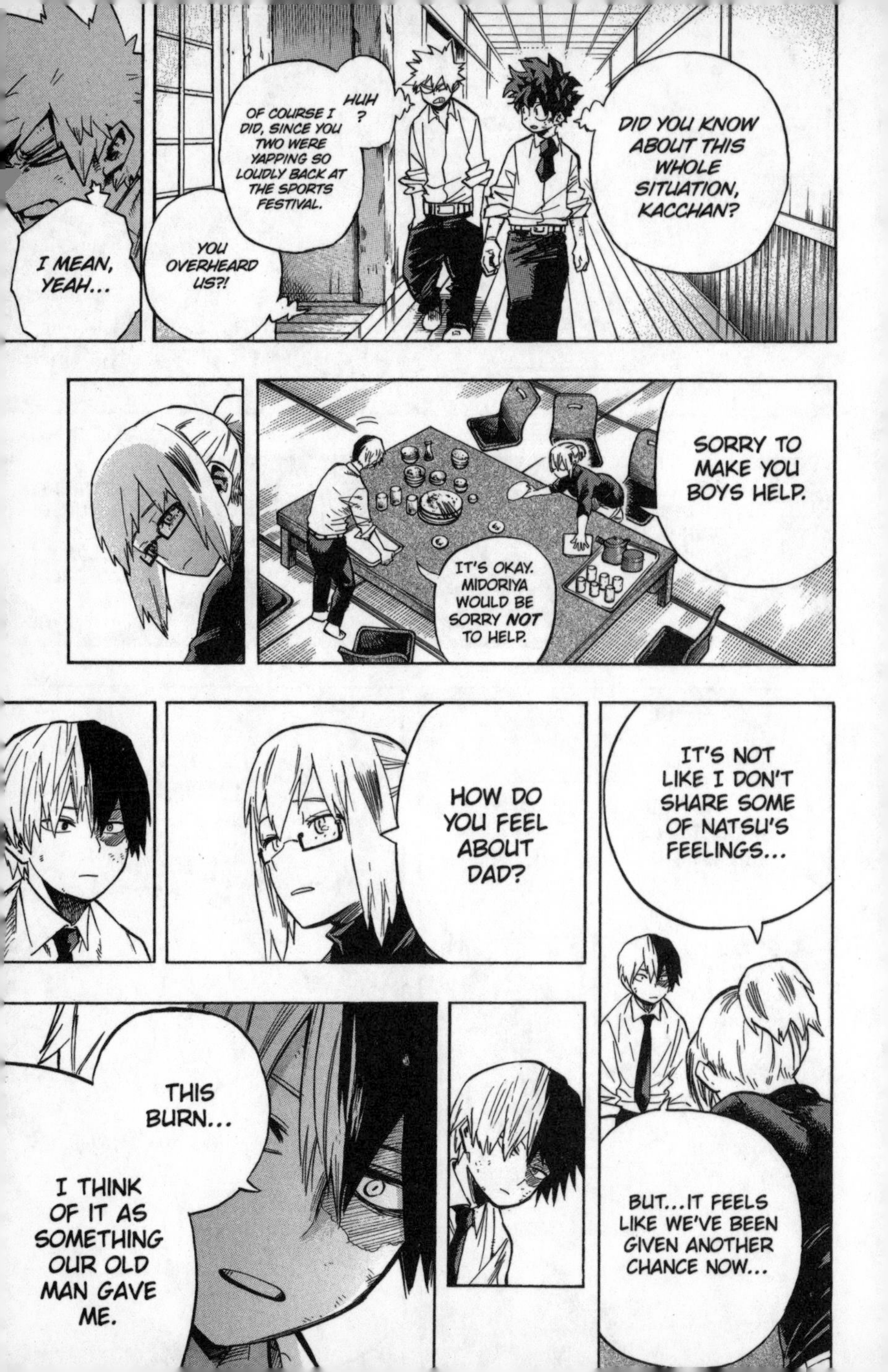
DID YOU KNOW ABOUT THIS WHOLE SITUATION, KACCHAN?
HUH?
OF COURSE I DID, SINCE YOU TWO WERE YAPPING SO LOUDLY BACK AT THE SPORTS FESTIVAL.
YOU OVERHEARD US?!
I MEAN, YEAH...
SORRY TO MAKE YOU BOYS HELP.
IT'S OKAY. MIDORIYA WOULD BE SORRY NOT TO HELP.
IT'S NOT LIKE I DON'T SHARE SOME OF NATSU'S FEELINGS...
BUT...IT FEELS LIKE WE'VE BEEN GIVEN ANOTHER CHANCE NOW...
HOW DO YOU FEEL ABOUT DAD?
THIS BURN...
I THINK OF IT AS SOMETHING OUR OLD MAN GAVE ME.

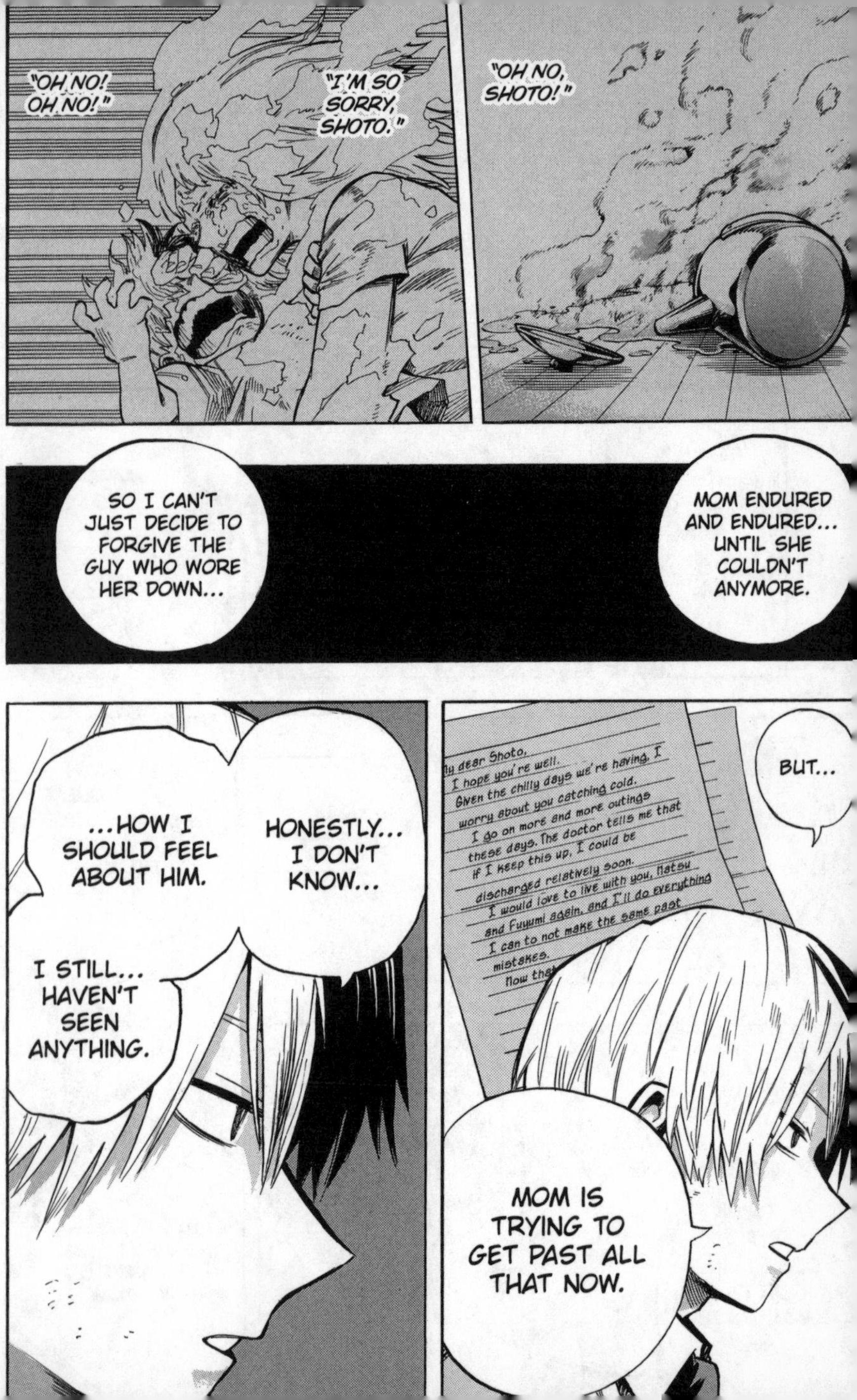
"OH NO, SHOTO!"
"I'M SO SORRY, SHOTO."
"OH NO! OH NO!"
MOM ENDURED AND ENDURED... UNTIL SHE COULDN'T ANYMORE.
SO I CAN'T JUST DECIDE TO FORGIVE THE GUY WHO WORE HER DOWN...
BUT...
dear Shoto,
I hope you're well.
Given the chilly days we're having, I
worry about you catching cold.
I go on more and more outings
these days. The doctor tells me that
if I keep this up, I could be
discharged relatively soon.
I would love to live with you, Natsu
and Fuyumi again, and I'll do everything
I can to not make the same past
mistakes.
MOM IS TRYING TO GET PAST ALL THAT NOW.
HONESTLY... I DON'T KNOW...
...HOW I SHOULD FEEL ABOUT HIM.
I STILL... HAVEN'T SEEN ANYTHING.

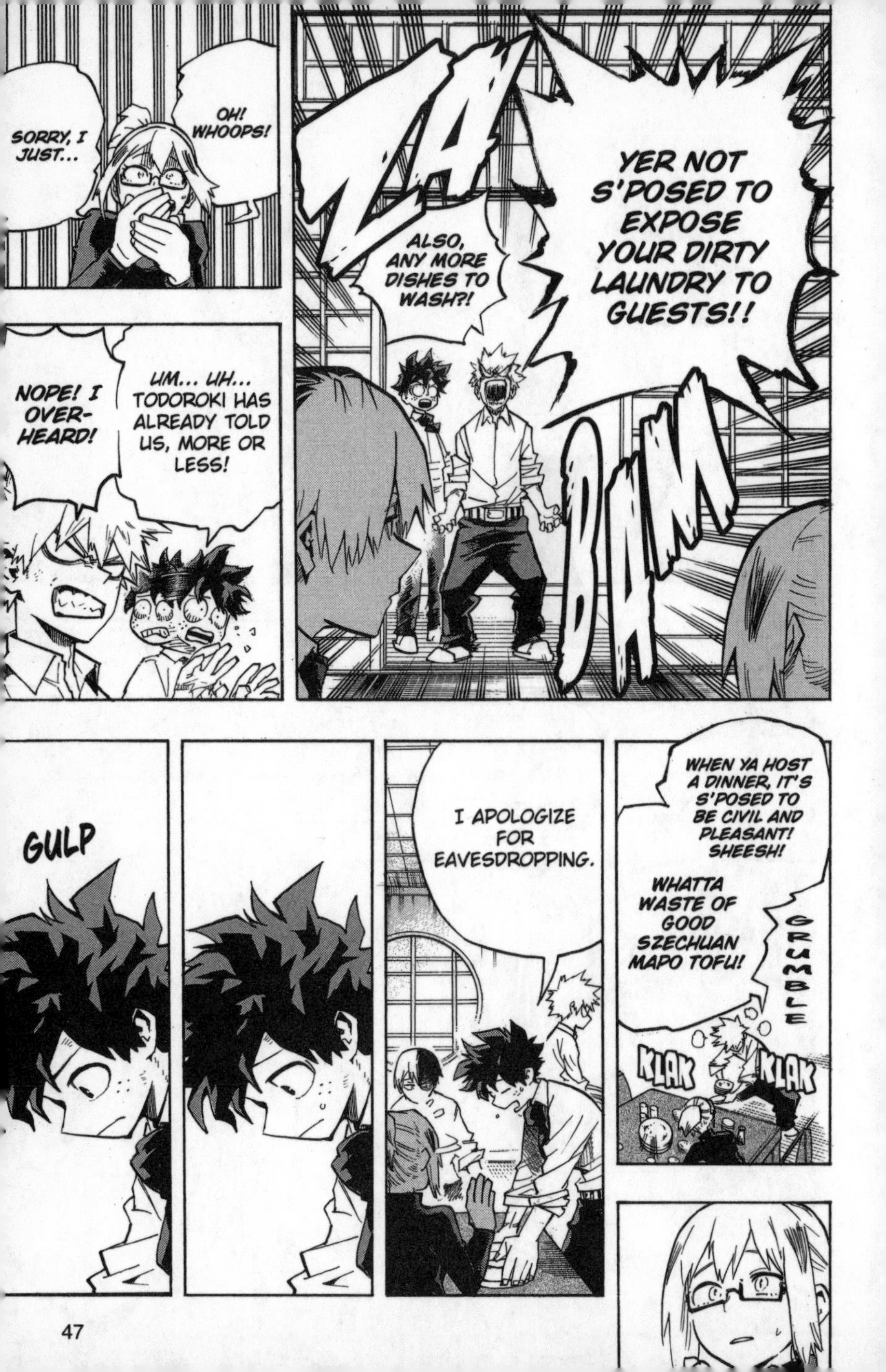
YER NOT S'POSED TO EXPOSE YOUR DIRTY LAUNDRY TO GUESTS!!
ZA
ALSO, ANY MORE DISHES TO WASH?!
BAM
OH! WHOOPS!
SORRY, I JUST...
UM... UH... TODOROKI HAS ALREADY TOLD US, MORE OR LESS!
NOPE! I OVER-HEARD!
WHEN YA HOST A DINNER, IT'S S'POSED TO BE CIVIL AND PLEASANT! SHEESH!
WHATTA WASTE OF GOOD SZECHUAN MAPO TOFU!
GRUMBLE
KLAK
KLAK
I APOLOGIZE FOR EAVESDROPPING.
GULP

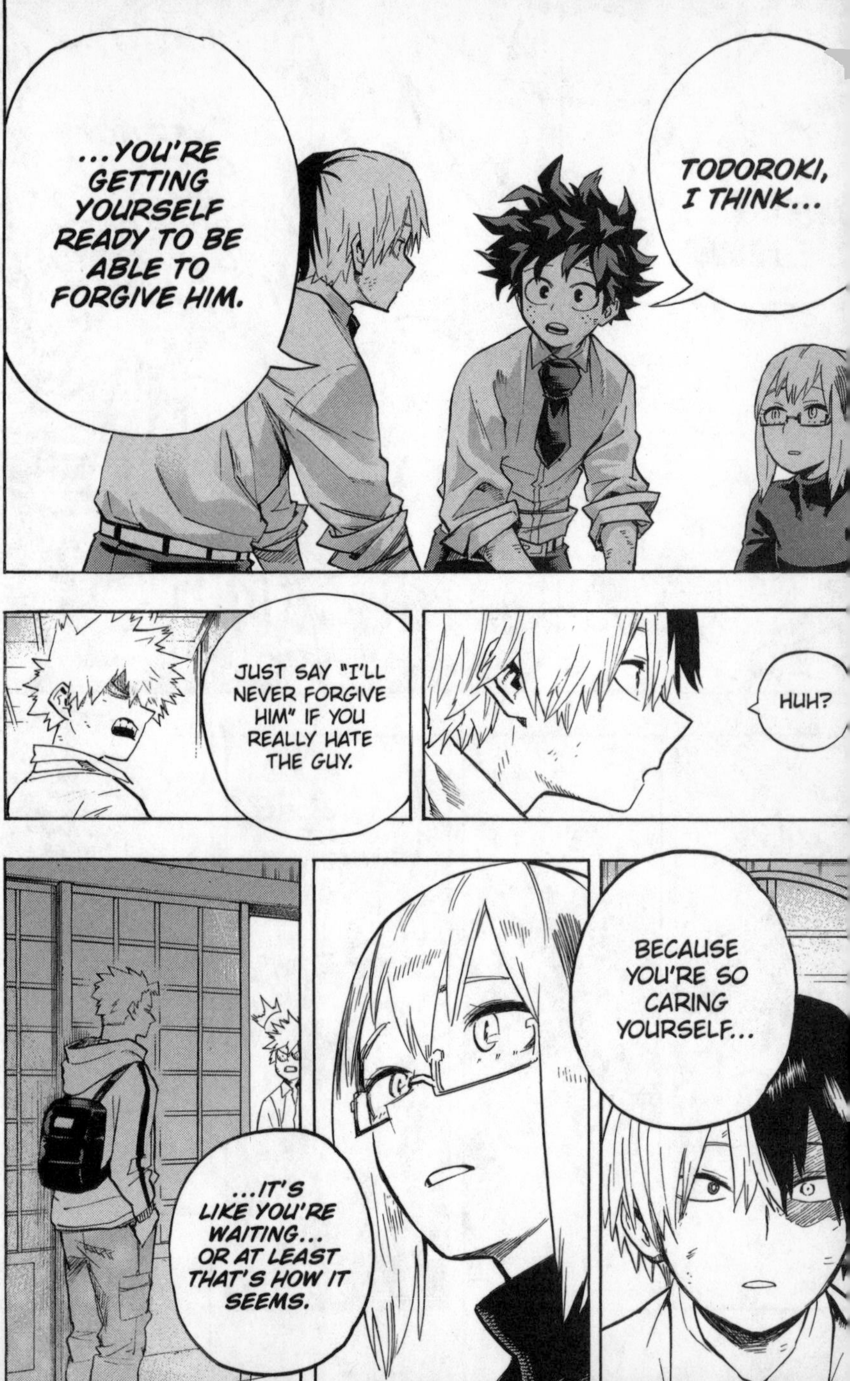
TODOROKI, I THINK...
...YOU'RE GETTING YOURSELF READY TO BE ABLE TO FORGIVE HIM.
HUH?
JUST SAY "I'LL NEVER FORGIVE HIM" IF YOU REALLY HATE THE GUY.
BECAUSE YOU'RE SO CARING YOURSELF...
...IT'S LIKE YOU'RE WAITING... OR AT LEAST THAT'S HOW IT SEEMS.

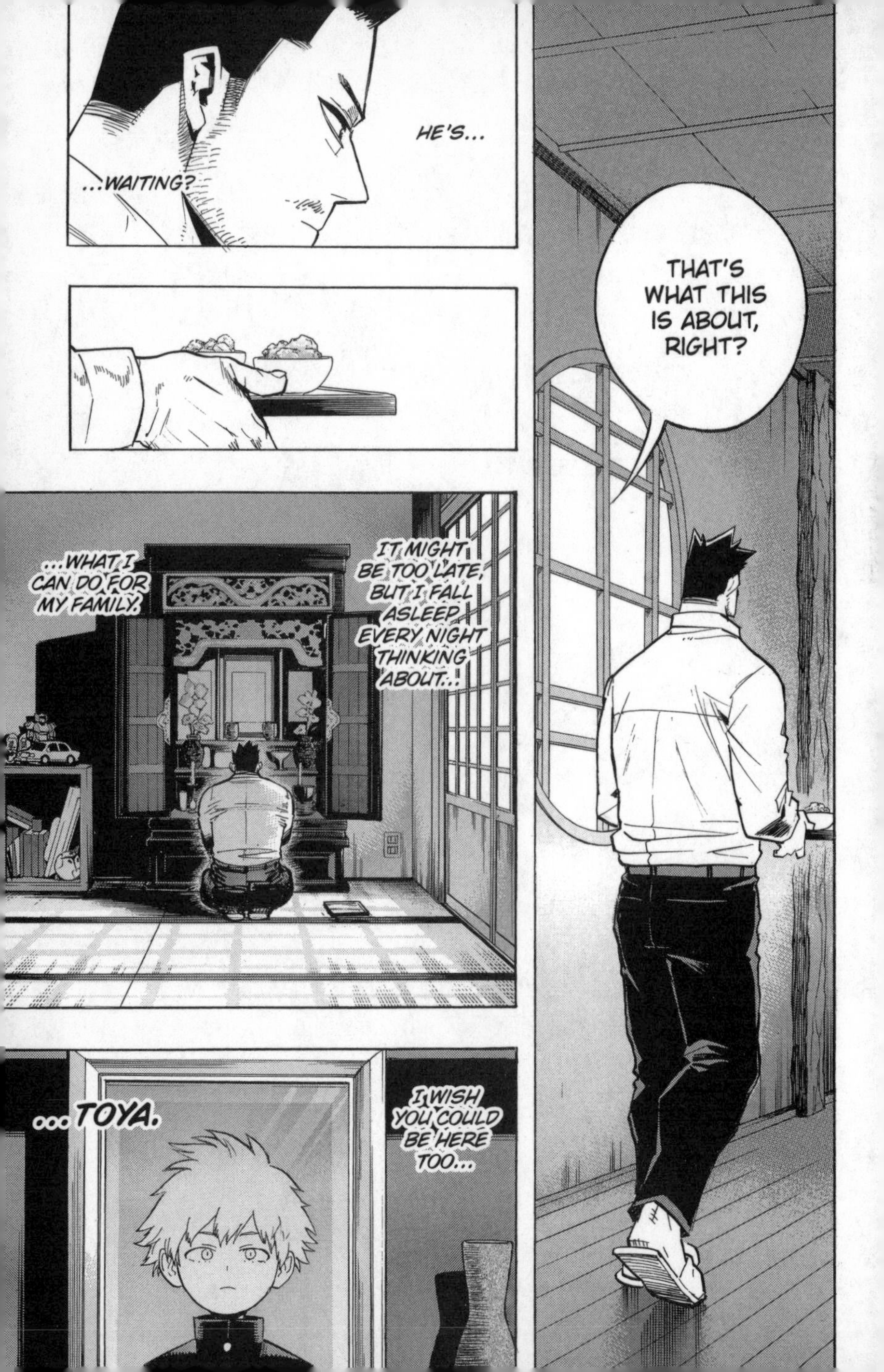
THAT'S WHAT THIS IS ABOUT, RIGHT?
HE'S...
...WAITING?
IT MIGHT BE TOO LATE, BUT I FALL ASLEEP EVERY NIGHT THINKING ABOUT...
...WHAT I CAN DO FOR MY FAMILY.
I WISH YOU COULD BE HERE TOO...
...TOYA.

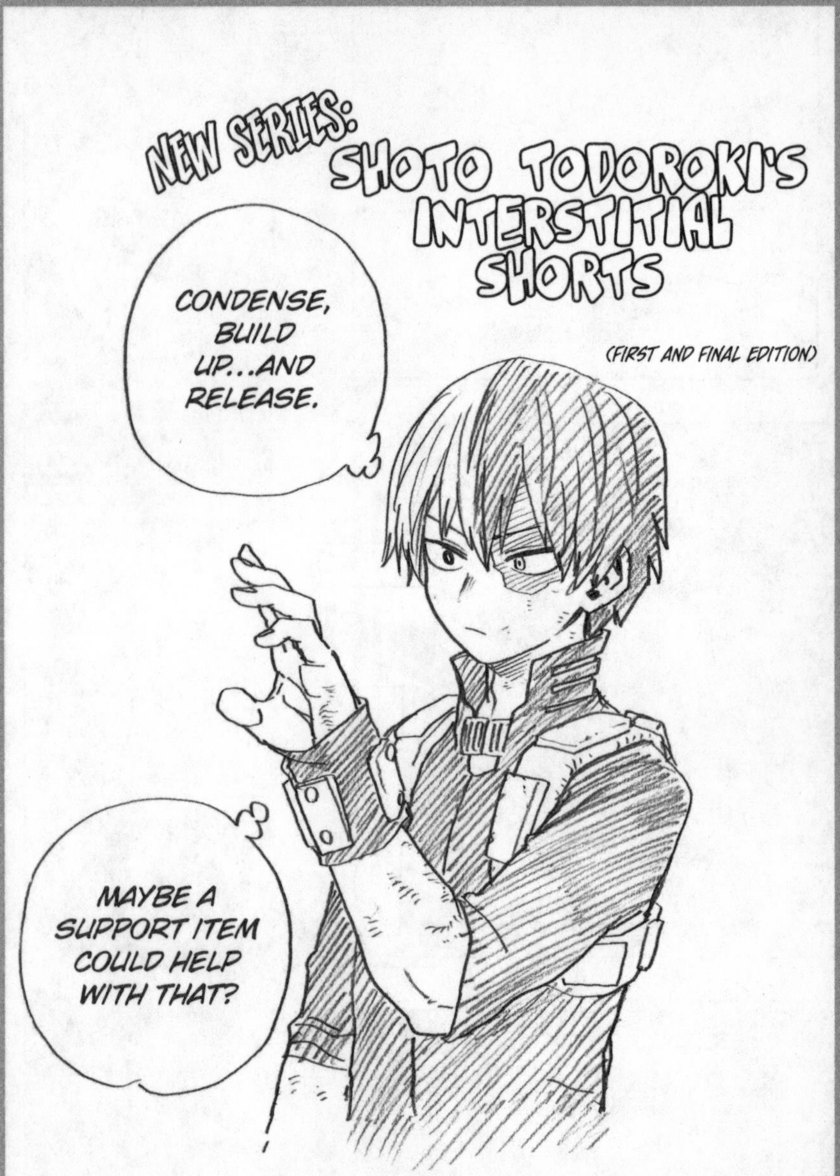
NEW SERIES:
SHOTO TODOROKI'S INTERSTITIAL SHORTS
(FIRST AND FINAL EDITION)
CONDENSE, BUILD UP...AND RELEASE.
MAYBE A SUPPORT ITEM COULD HELP WITH THAT?

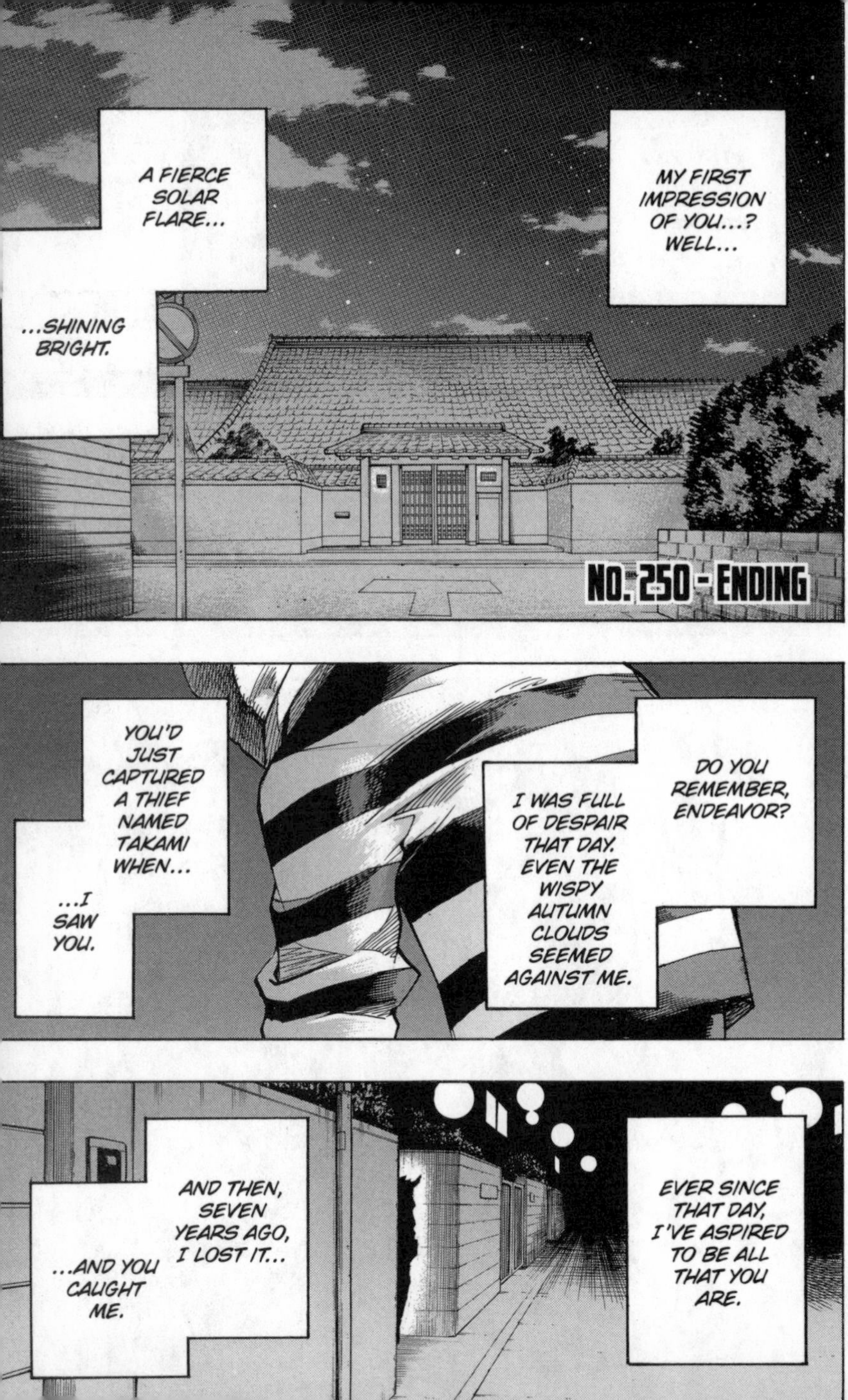
MY FIRST IMPRESSION OF YOU...? WELL...
A FIERCE SOLAR FLARE...
...SHINING BRIGHT.
No. 250 - ENDING
DO YOU REMEMBER, ENDEAVOR?
I WAS FULL OF DESPAIR THAT DAY. EVEN THE WISPY AUTUMN CLOUDS SEEMED AGAINST ME.
YOU'D JUST CAPTURED A THIEF NAMED TAKAMI WHEN...
...I SAW YOU.
EVER SINCE THAT DAY, I'VE ASPIRED TO BE ALL THAT YOU ARE.
AND THEN, SEVEN YEARS AGO, I LOST IT...
...AND YOU CAUGHT ME.

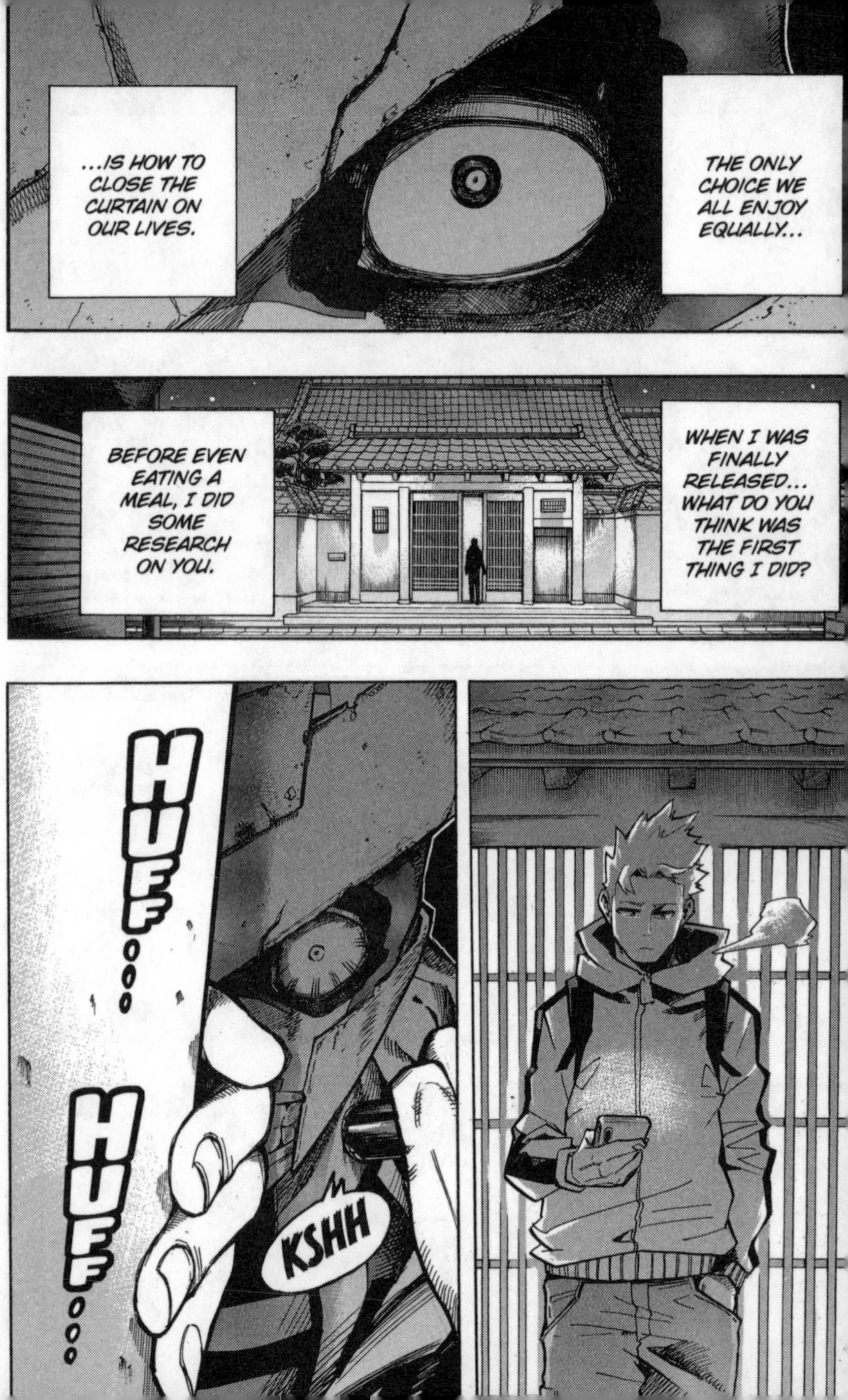
THE ONLY CHOICE WE ALL ENJOY EQUALLY...
...IS HOW TO CLOSE THE CURTAIN ON OUR LIVES.
WHEN I WAS FINALLY RELEASED... WHAT DO YOU THINK WAS THE FIRST THING I DID?
BEFORE EVEN EATING A MEAL, I DID SOME RESEARCH ON YOU.
HUFF...
HUFF...
KSHH

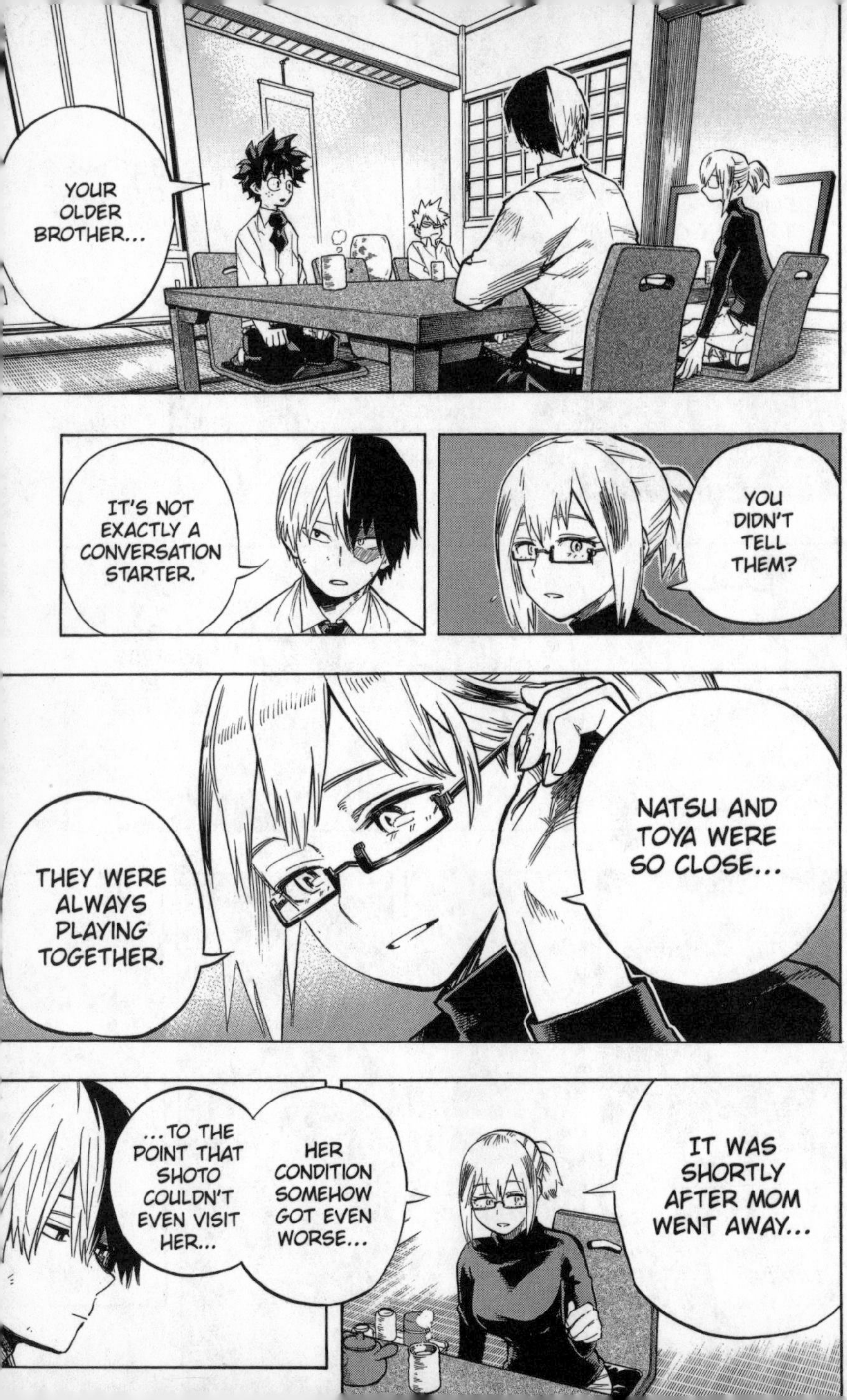
YOUR OLDER BROTHER...
YOU DIDN'T TELL THEM?
IT'S NOT EXACTLY A CONVERSATION STARTER.
NATSU AND TOYA WERE SO CLOSE...
THEY WERE ALWAYS PLAYING TOGETHER.
IT WAS SHORTLY AFTER MOM WENT AWAY...
HER CONDITION SOMEHOW GOT EVEN WORSE...
...TO THE POINT THAT SHOTO COULDN'T EVEN VISIT HER...

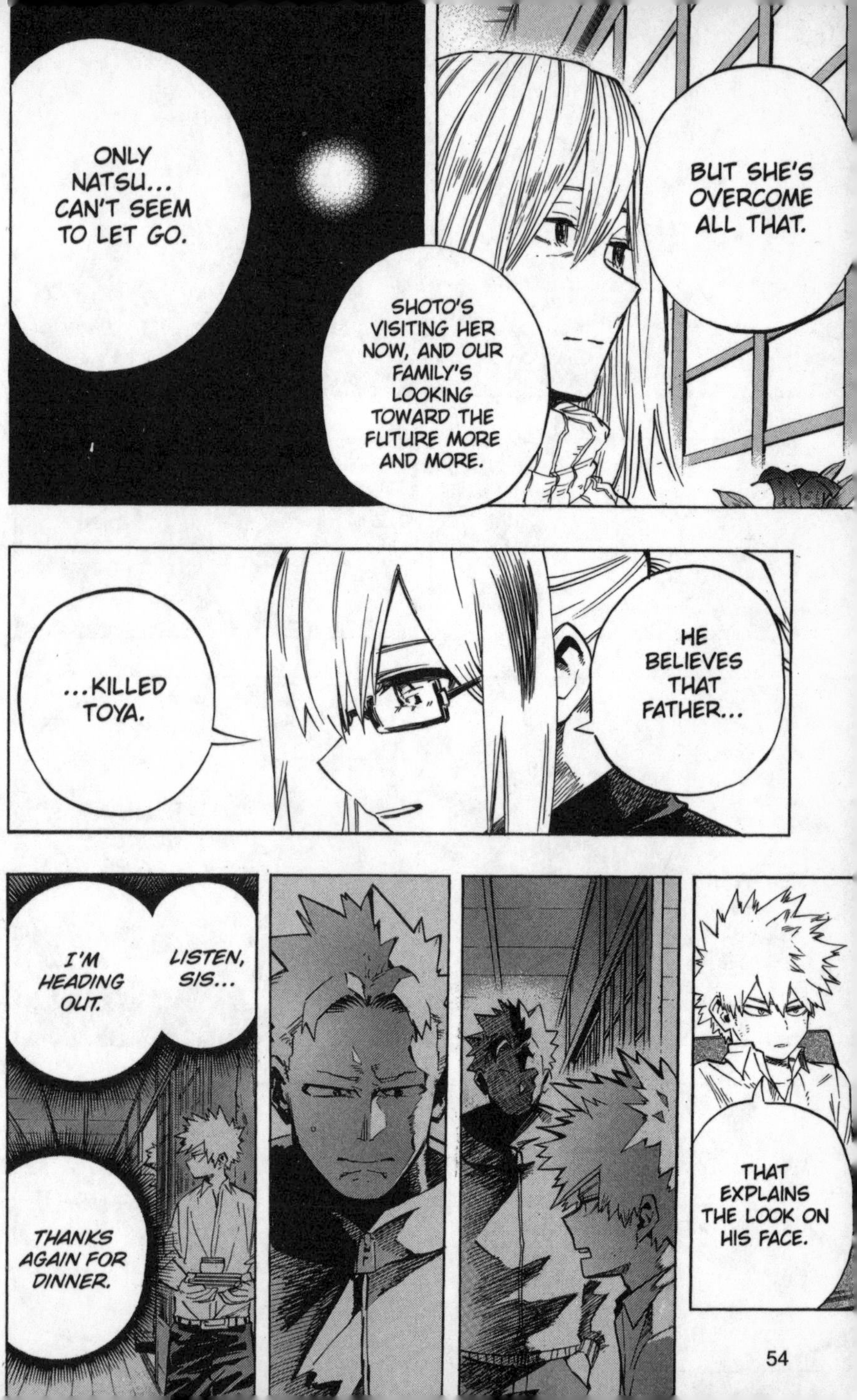

BUT SHE'S OVERCOME ALL THAT.
SHOTO'S VISITING HER NOW, AND OUR FAMILY'S LOOKING TOWARD THE FUTURE MORE AND MORE.
ONLY NATSU... CAN'T SEEM TO LET GO.
HE BELIEVES THAT FATHER...
...KILLED TOYA.
THAT EXPLAINS THE LOOK ON HIS FACE.
LISTEN, SIS...
I'M HEADING OUT.
THANKS AGAIN FOR DINNER.

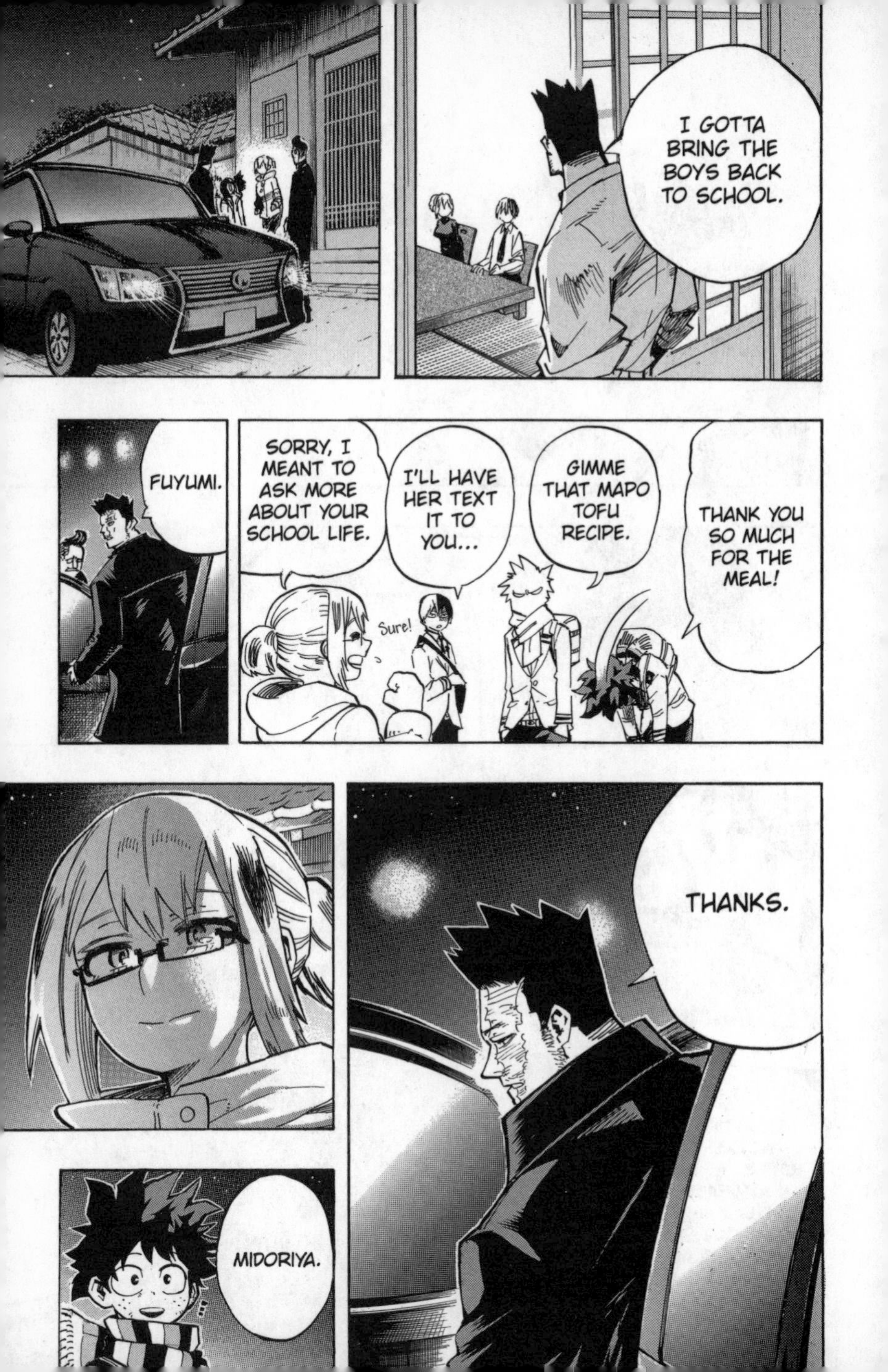
I GOTTA BRING THE BOYS BACK TO SCHOOL.
THANK YOU SO MUCH FOR THE MEAL!
GIMME THAT MAPO TOFU RECIPE.
I'LL HAVE HER TEXT IT TO YOU...
SORRY, I MEANT TO ASK MORE ABOUT YOUR SCHOOL LIFE.
Sure!
FUYUMI.
THANKS.
MIDORIYA.

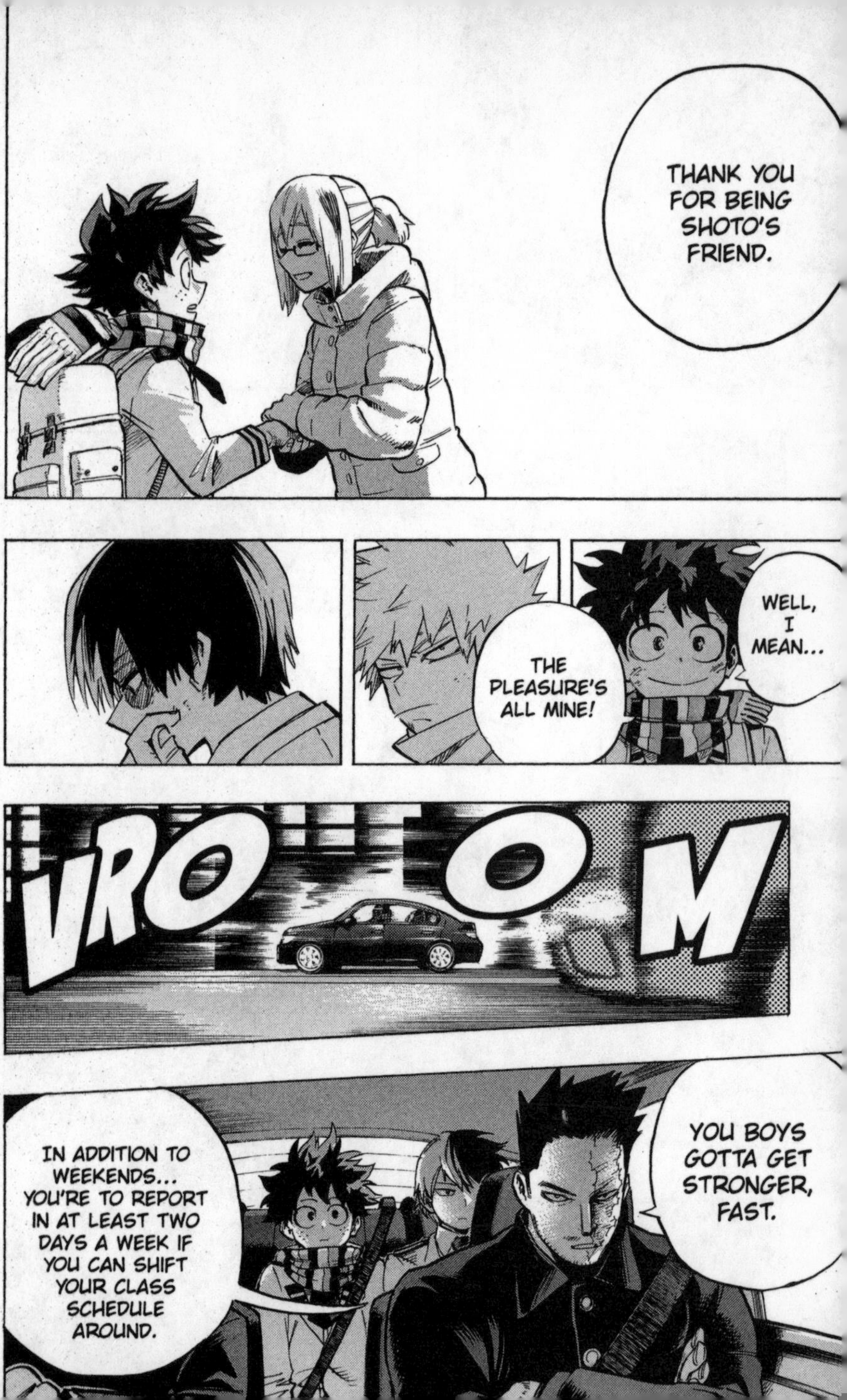
THANK YOU FOR BEING SHOTO'S FRIEND.
WELL, I MEAN...
THE PLEASURE'S ALL MINE!
VROOOM
YOU BOYS GOTTA GET STRONGER, FAST.
IN ADDITION TO WEEKENDS... YOU'RE TO REPORT IN AT LEAST TWO DAYS A WEEK IF YOU CAN SHIFT YOUR CLASS SCHEDULE AROUND.

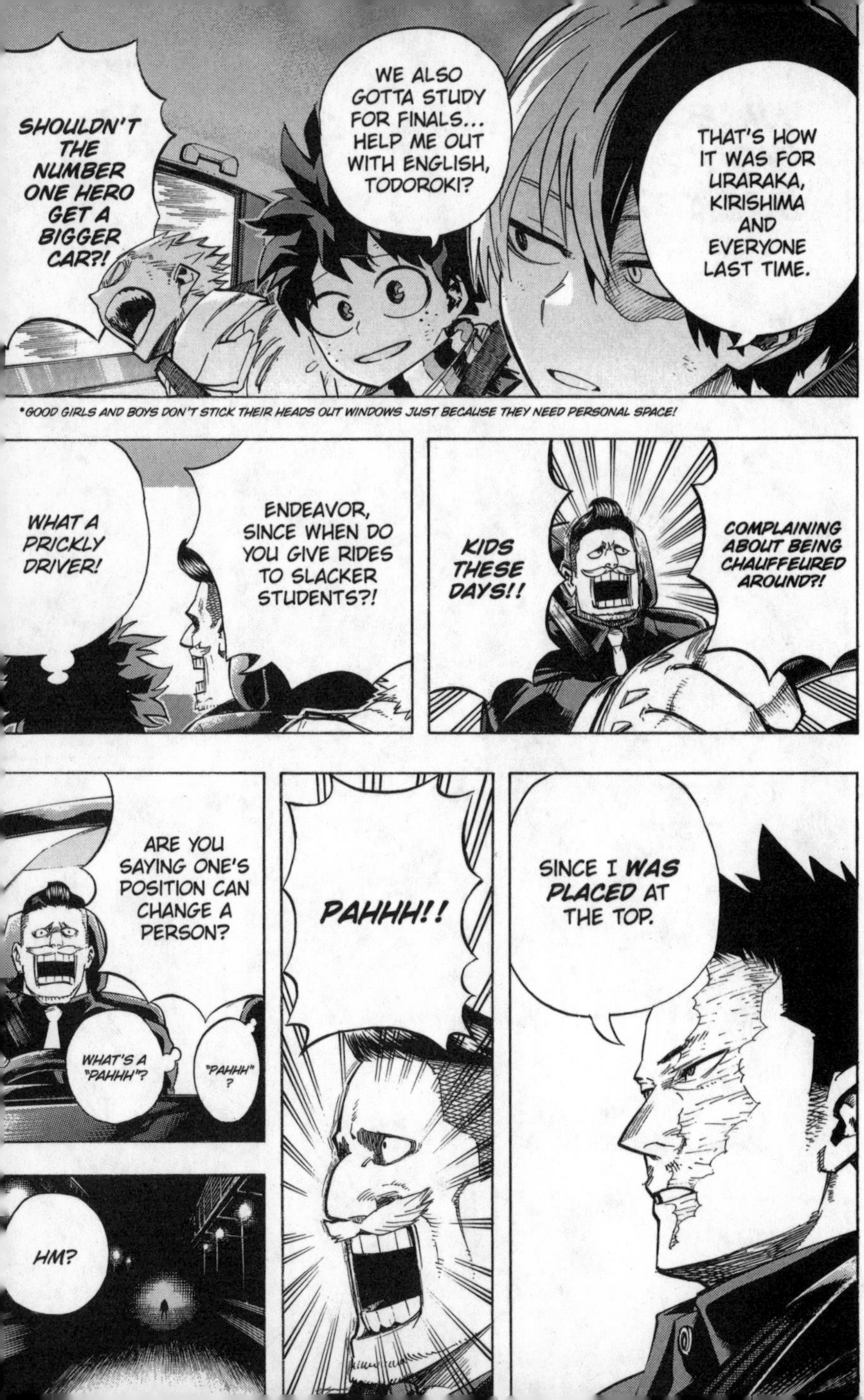
THAT'S HOW IT WAS FOR URARAKA, KIRISHIMA AND EVERYONE LAST TIME.
WE ALSO GOTTA STUDY FOR FINALS... HELP ME OUT WITH ENGLISH, TODOROKI?
SHOULDN'T THE NUMBER ONE HERO GET A BIGGER CAR?!
*GOOD GIRLS AND BOYS DON'T STICK THEIR HEADS OUT WINDOWS JUST BECAUSE THEY NEED PERSONAL SPACE!
COMPLAINING ABOUT BEING CHAUFFEURED AROUND?!
KIDS THESE DAYS!!
ENDEAVOR, SINCE WHEN DO YOU GIVE RIDES TO SLACKER STUDENTS?!
WHAT A PRICKLY DRIVER!
SINCE I ***WAS PLACED*** AT THE TOP.
PAHHH!!
ARE YOU SAYING ONE'S POSITION CAN CHANGE A PERSON?
"PAHHH"?
WHAT'S A "PAHHH"?
HM?

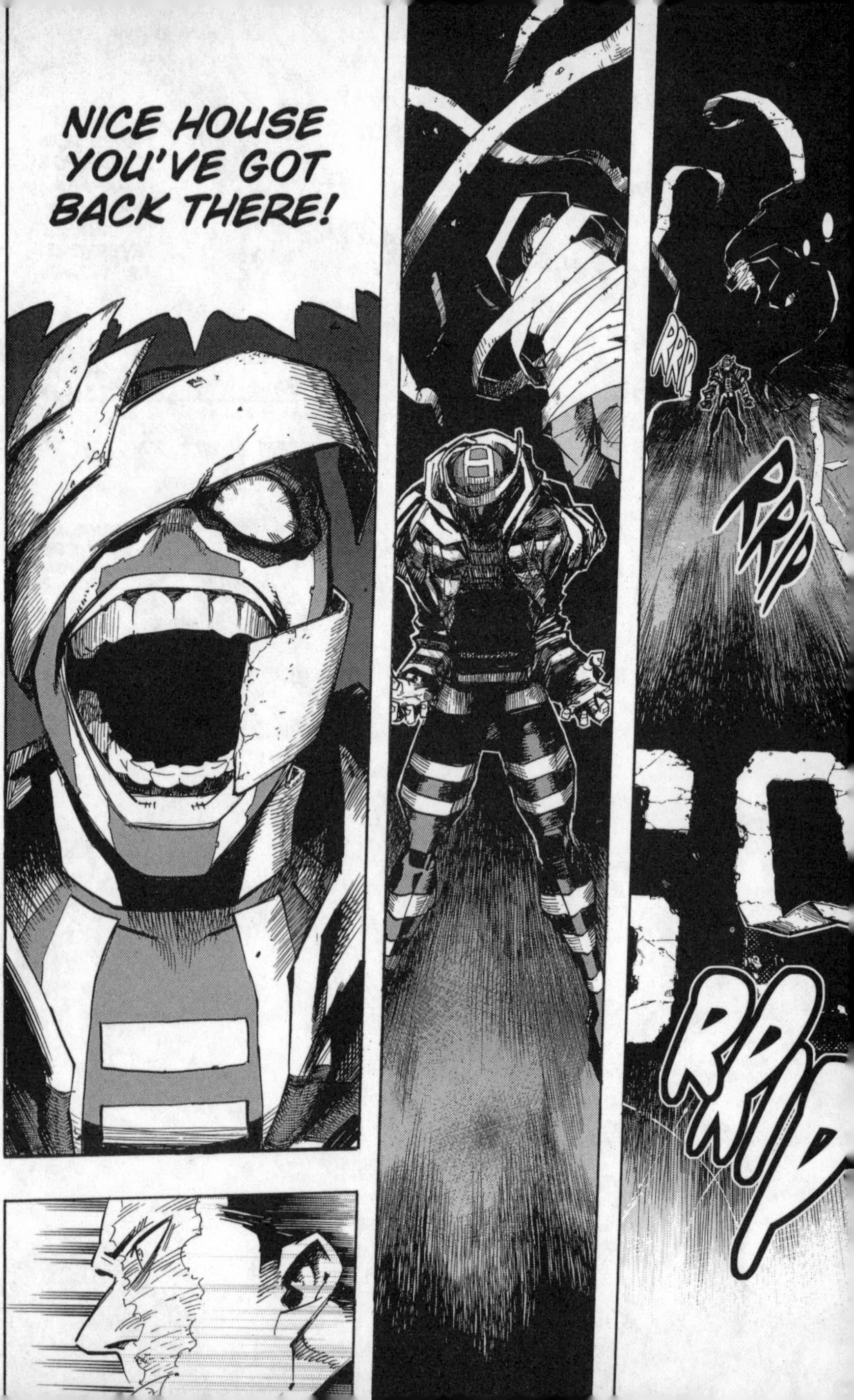
RRIP
RRIP
RRIP
NICE HOUSE YOU'VE GOT BACK THERE!

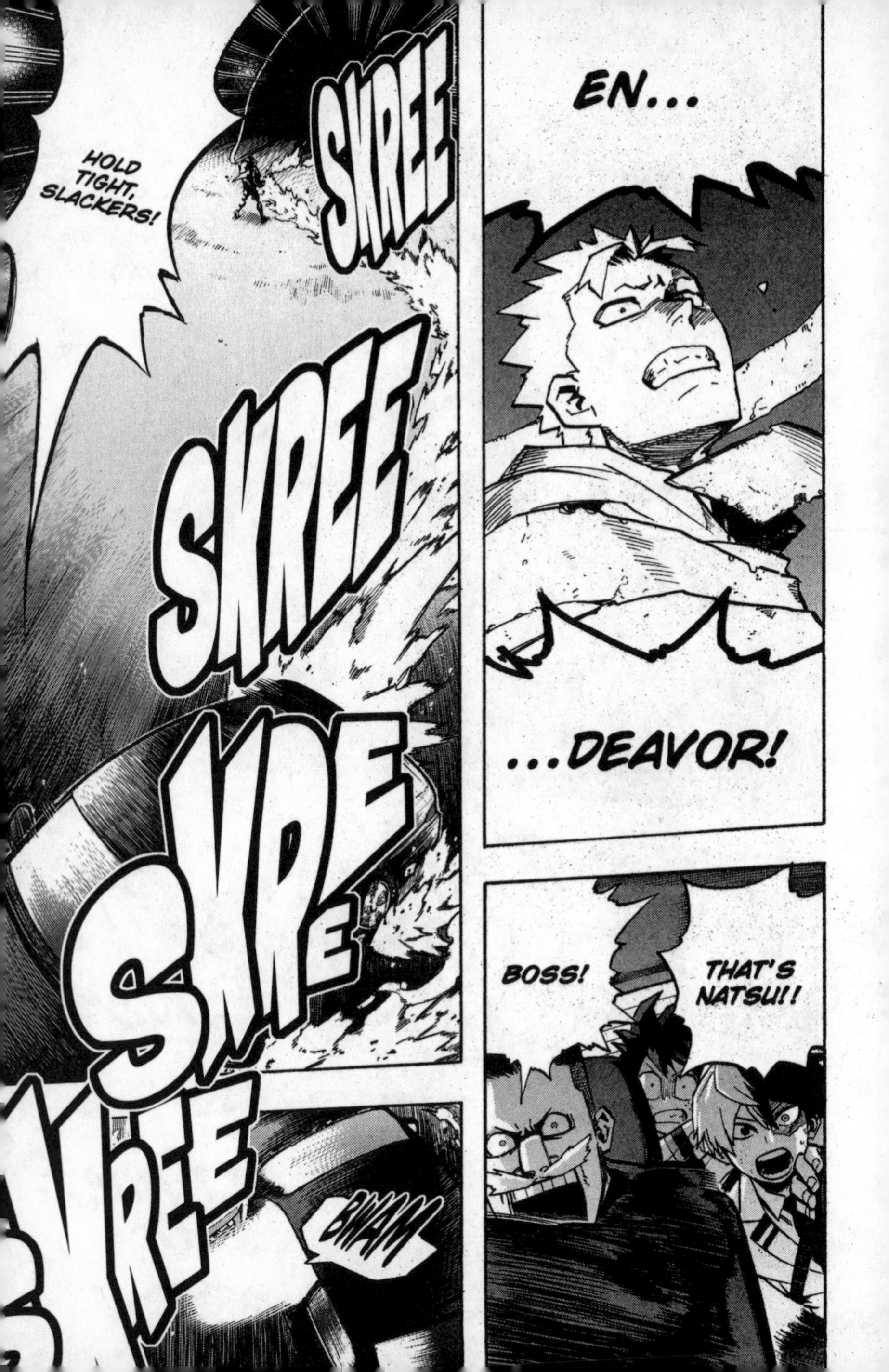

EN...
...DEAVOR!
THAT'S NATSU!!
BOSS!
SKREE
HOLD TIGHT, SLACKERS!
SKREE
SKREE
SKREE
BWAM

?! SHWNRL

LET HIM GO!

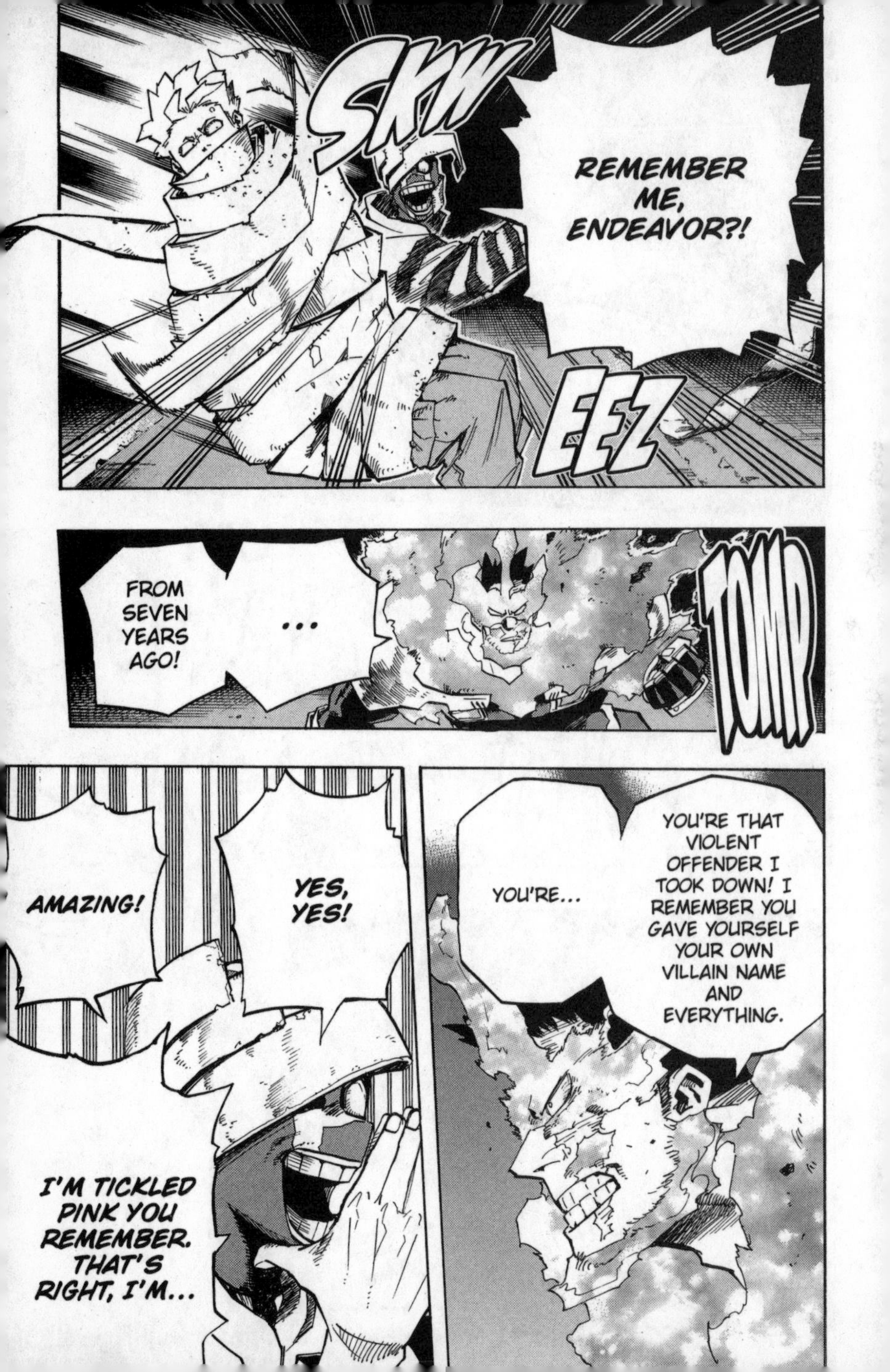
SKW
EEZ
REMEMBER ME, ENDEAVOR?!
TOMP
...
FROM SEVEN YEARS AGO!
YOU'RE THAT VIOLENT OFFENDER I TOOK DOWN! I REMEMBER YOU GAVE YOURSELF YOUR OWN VILLAIN NAME AND EVERYTHING.
YOU'RE...
YES, YES!
AMAZING!
I'M TICKLED PINK YOU REMEMBER. THAT'S RIGHT, I'M...

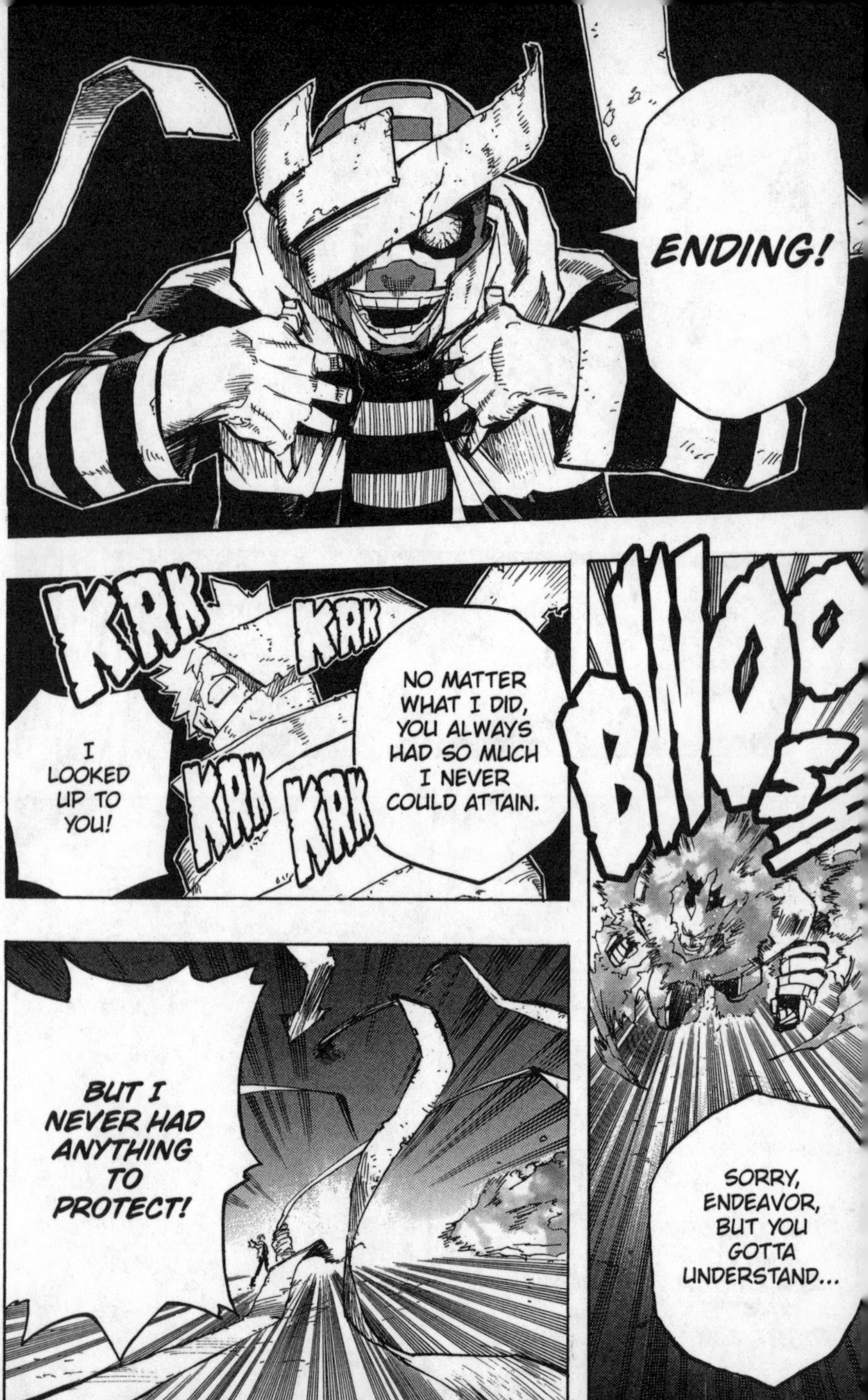
ENDING!
BWOOSH
SORRY, ENDEAVOR, BUT YOU GOTTA UNDERSTAND...
KRK
KRK
KRK
KRK
NO MATTER WHAT I DID, YOU ALWAYS HAD SO MUCH I NEVER COULD ATTAIN.
I LOOKED UP TO YOU!
BUT I NEVER HAD ANYTHING TO PROTECT!

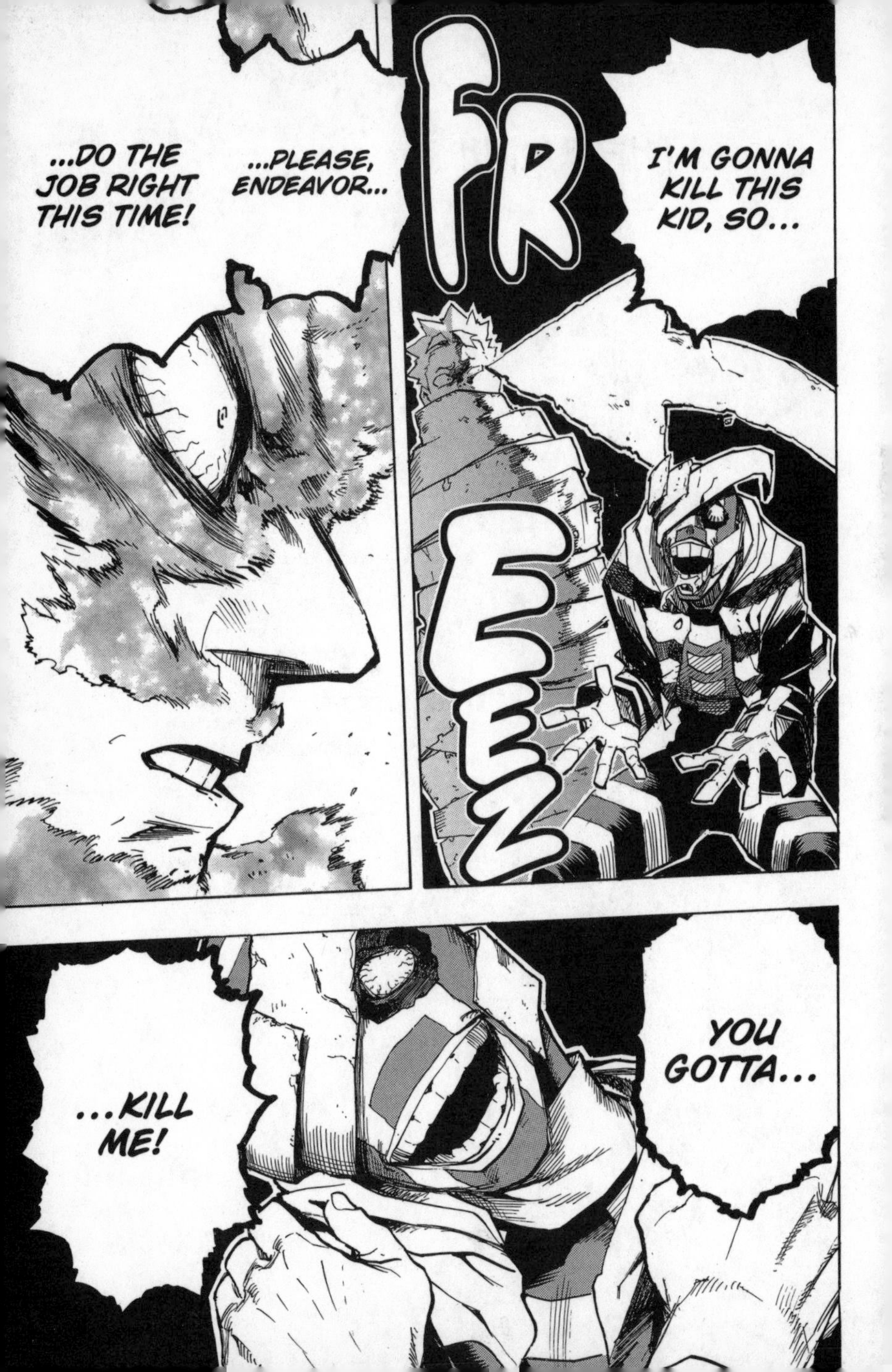
I'M GONNA KILL THIS KID, SO...
FREEZ
...PLEASE, ENDEAVOR...
...DO THE JOB RIGHT THIS TIME!
YOU GOTTA...
...KILL ME!

Aggressive Driver

UNTENMARU KURUMADA [47]

THE PAHHH

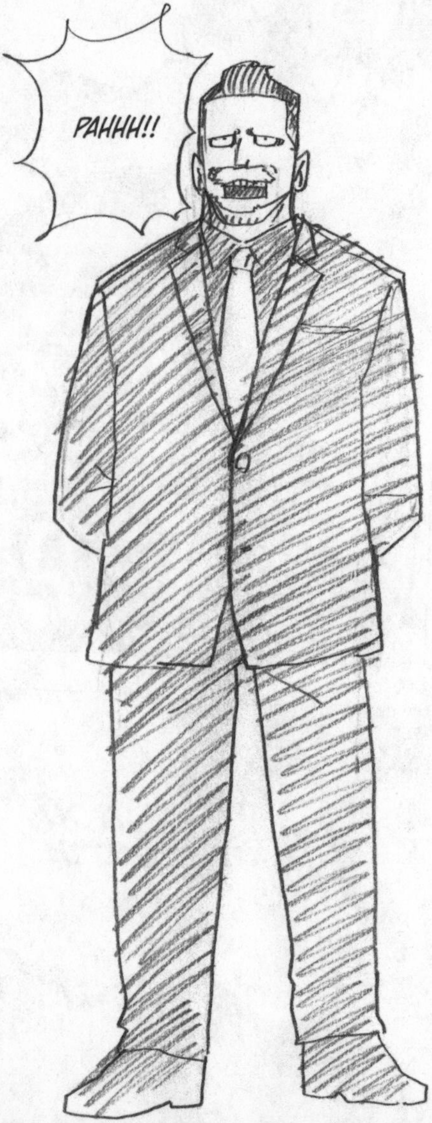
PAHHH!!

Birthday: 3/4
Height: 180 cm
Favorite Thing: Flowers

THE DRIVER

Unlike most hired drivers, this guy only caters to heroes. Kurumada actually has an exclusive contract with Endeavor. They've known each other for a long time.

While writing the draft for this chapter, that "Pahhh!!" thing was all the rage, and I couldn't help but burst out laughing while drawing. I think it was throwing my nervous system out of whack.

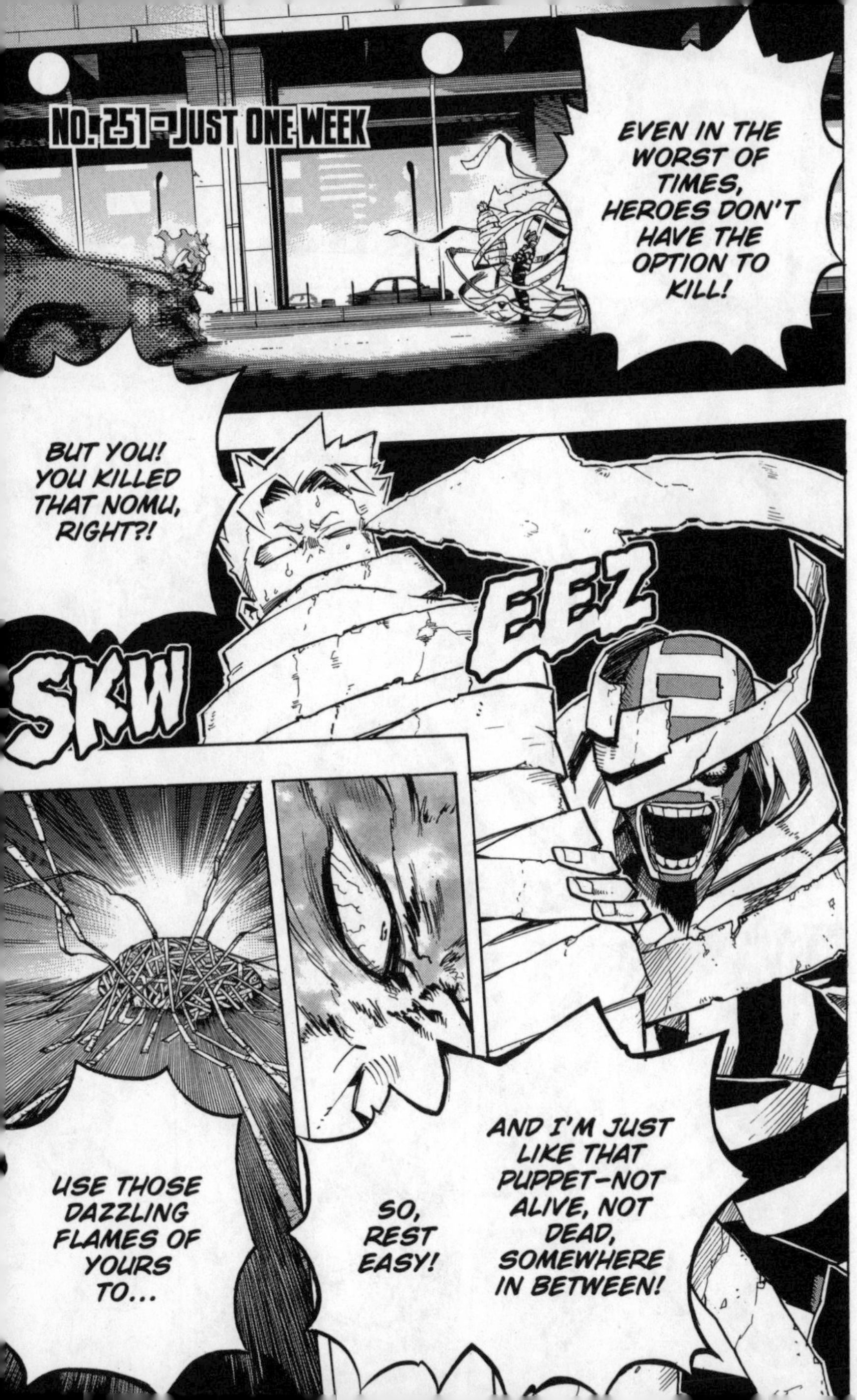
No. 251 - Just One Week
EVEN IN THE WORST OF TIMES, HEROES DON'T HAVE THE OPTION TO KILL!
BUT YOU! YOU KILLED THAT NOMU, RIGHT?!
SKW
EEZ
AND I'M JUST LIKE THAT PUPPET—NOT ALIVE, NOT DEAD, SOMEWHERE IN BETWEEN!
SO, REST EASY!
USE THOSE DAZZLING FLAMES OF YOURS TO...

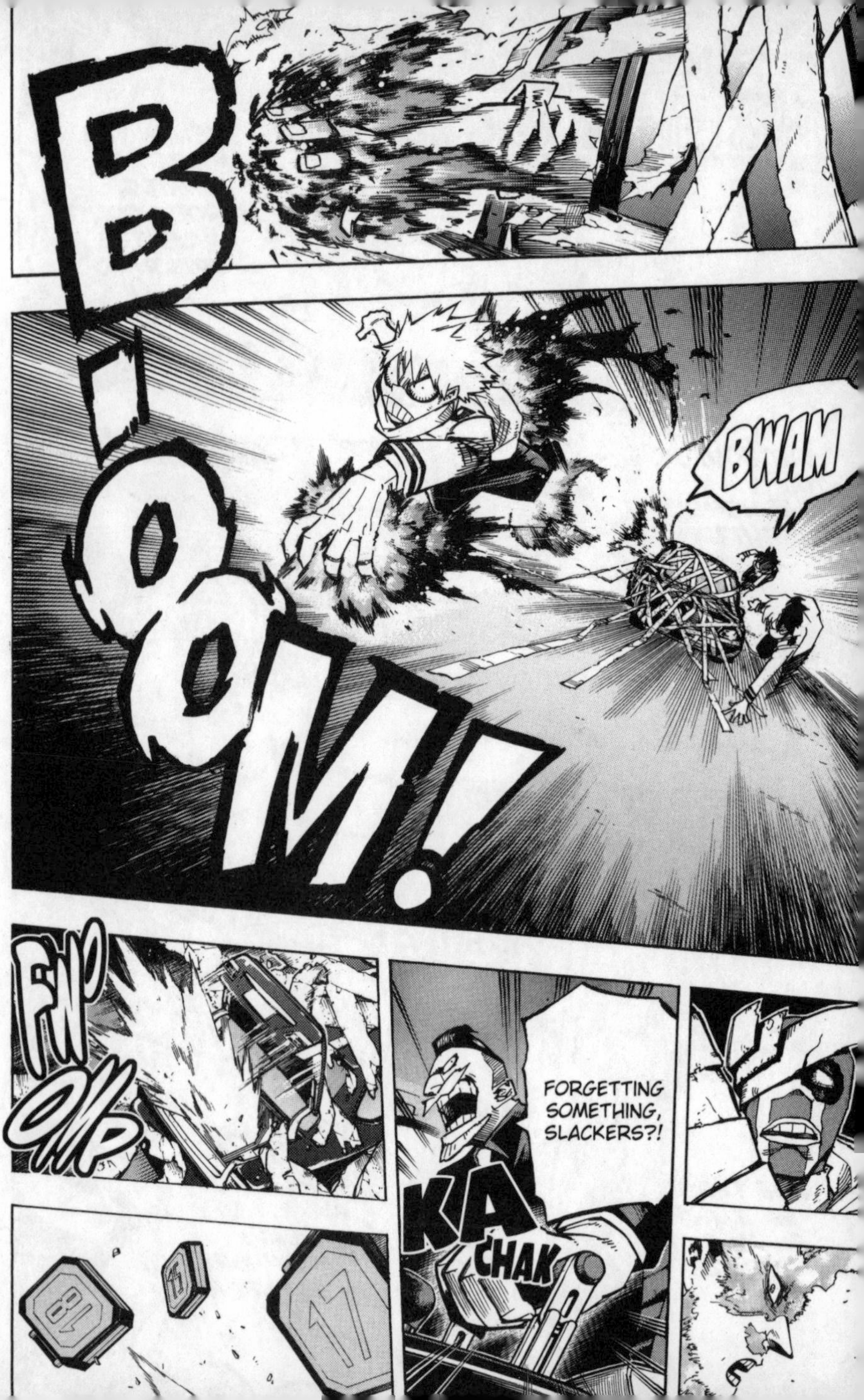
BOOM!
BWAM
FORGETTING SOMETHING, SLACKERS?!
FWOOMP
KA CHAK
18
17

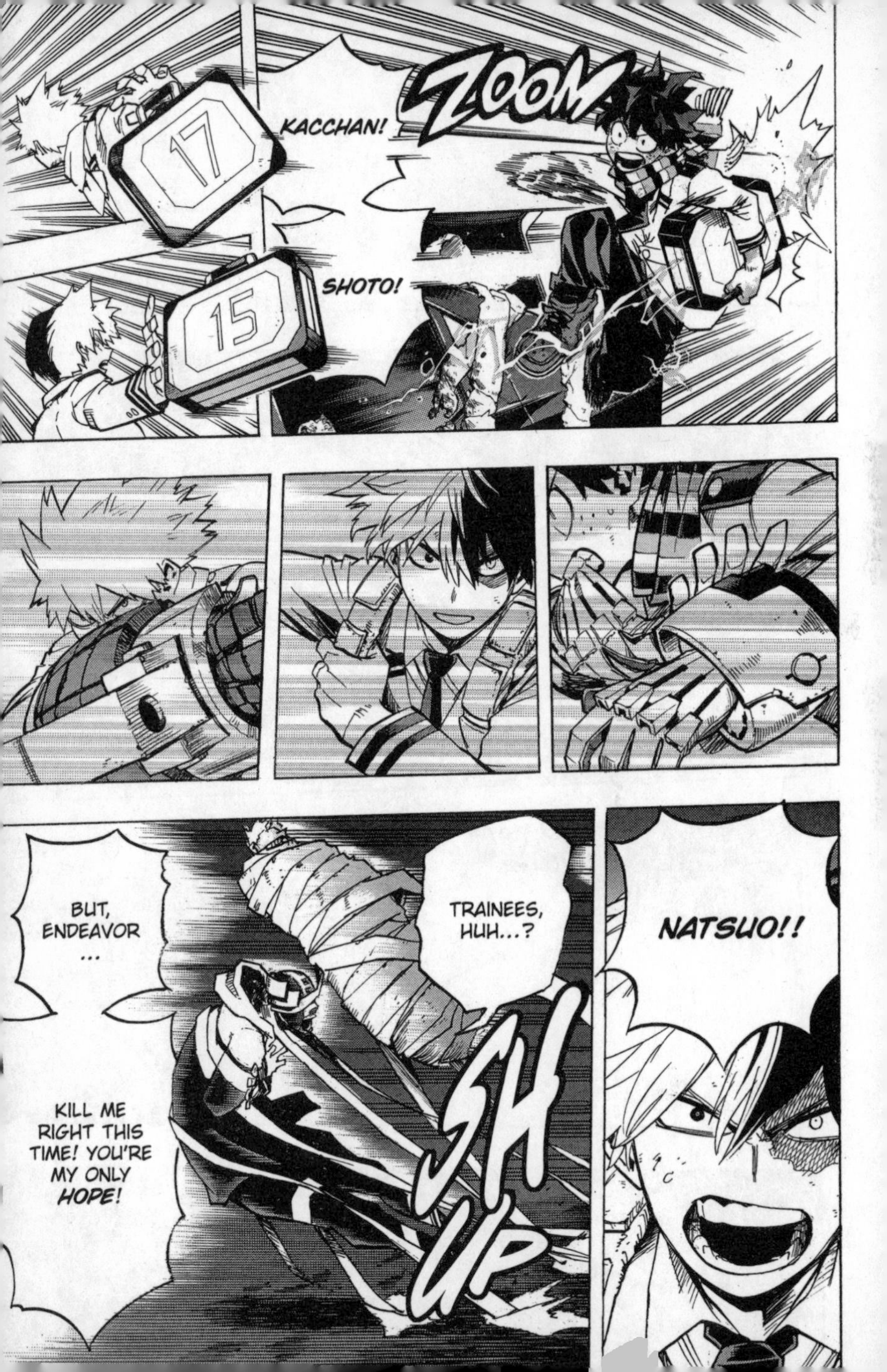
ZOOM
KACCHAN!
SHOTO!
NATSUO!!
TRAINEES, HUH...?
BUT, ENDEAVOR ...
SHUP
KILL ME RIGHT THIS TIME! YOU'RE MY ONLY HOPE!

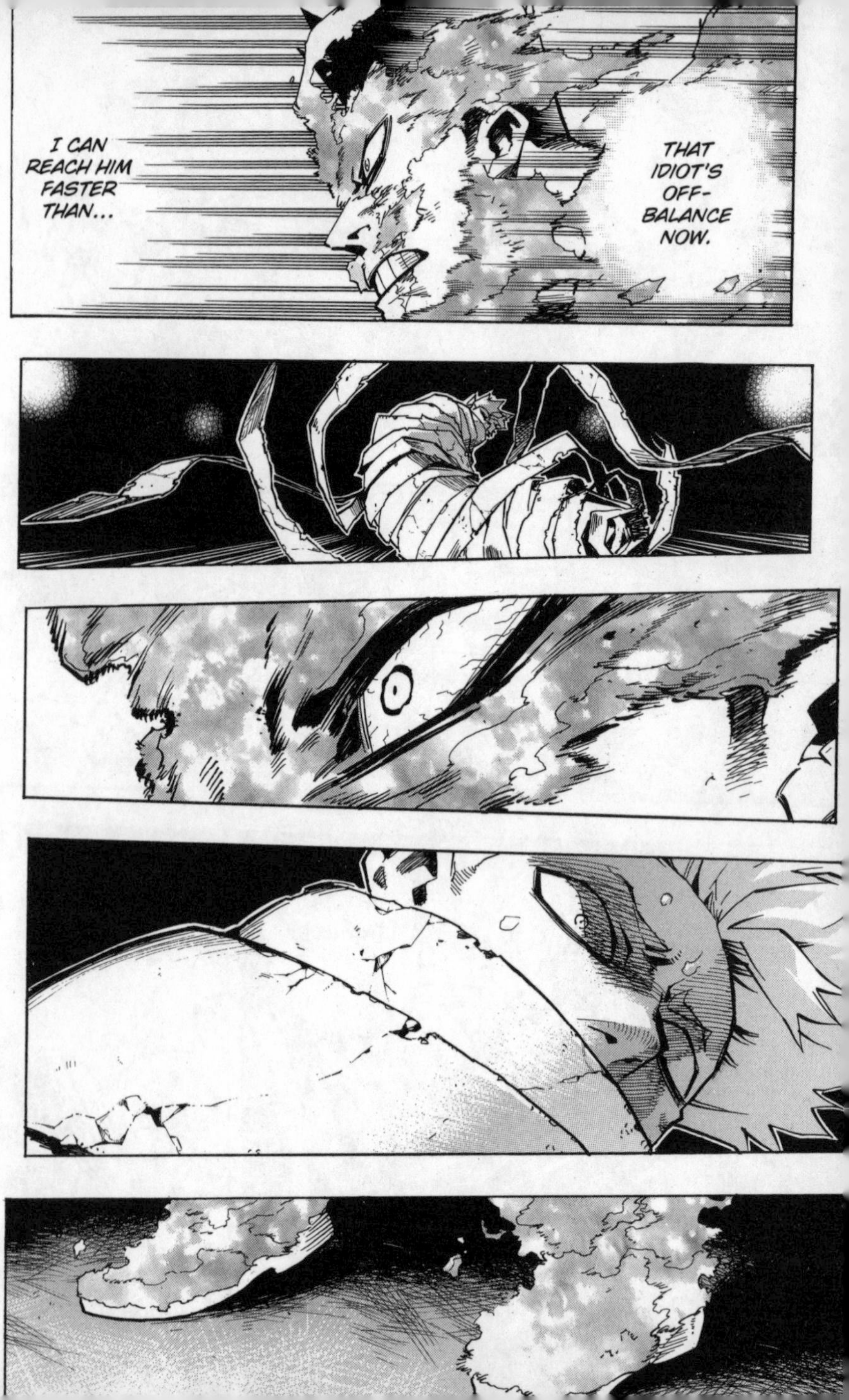
THAT IDIOT'S OFF-BALANCE NOW.
I CAN REACH HIM FASTER THAN...

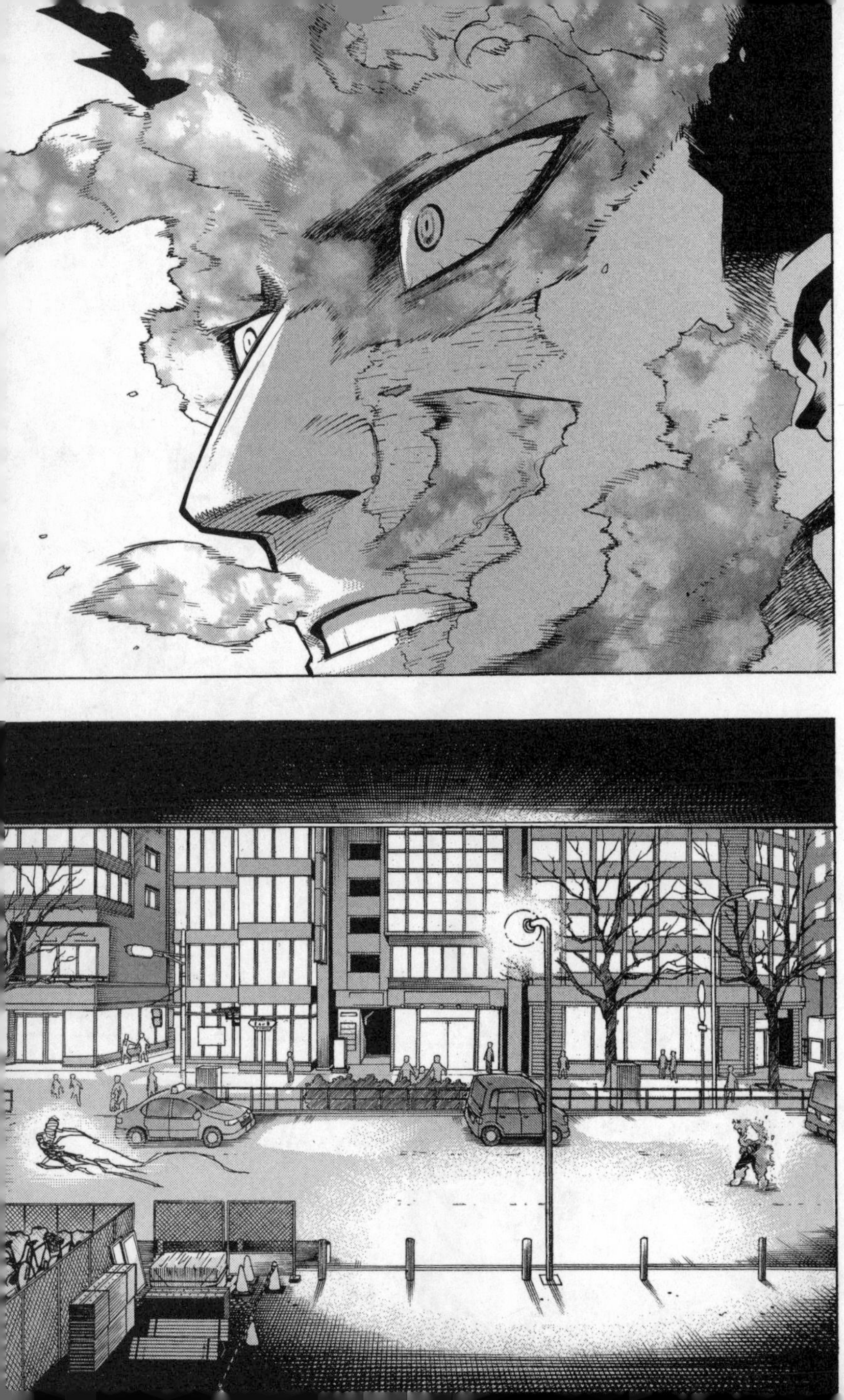

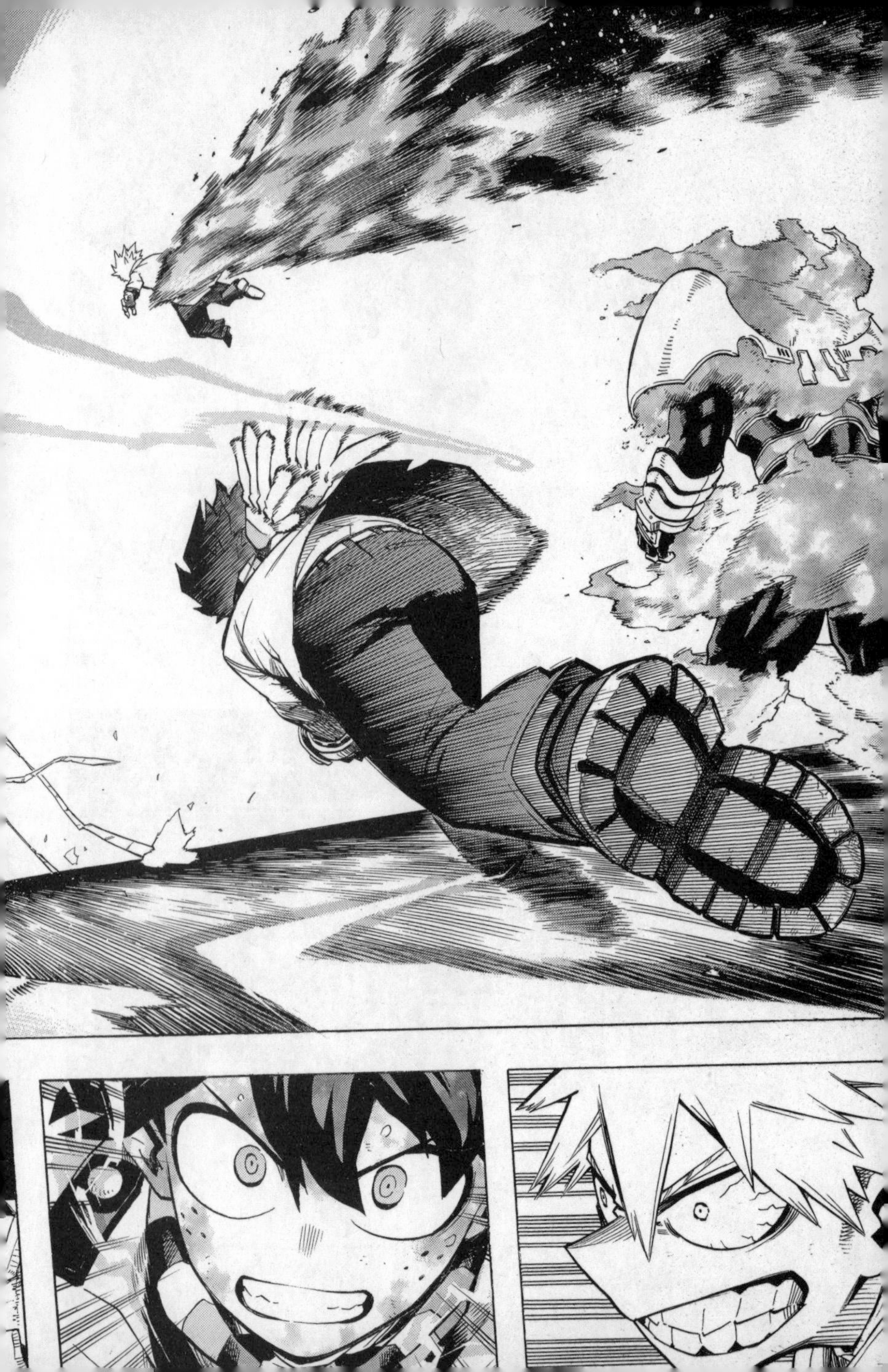

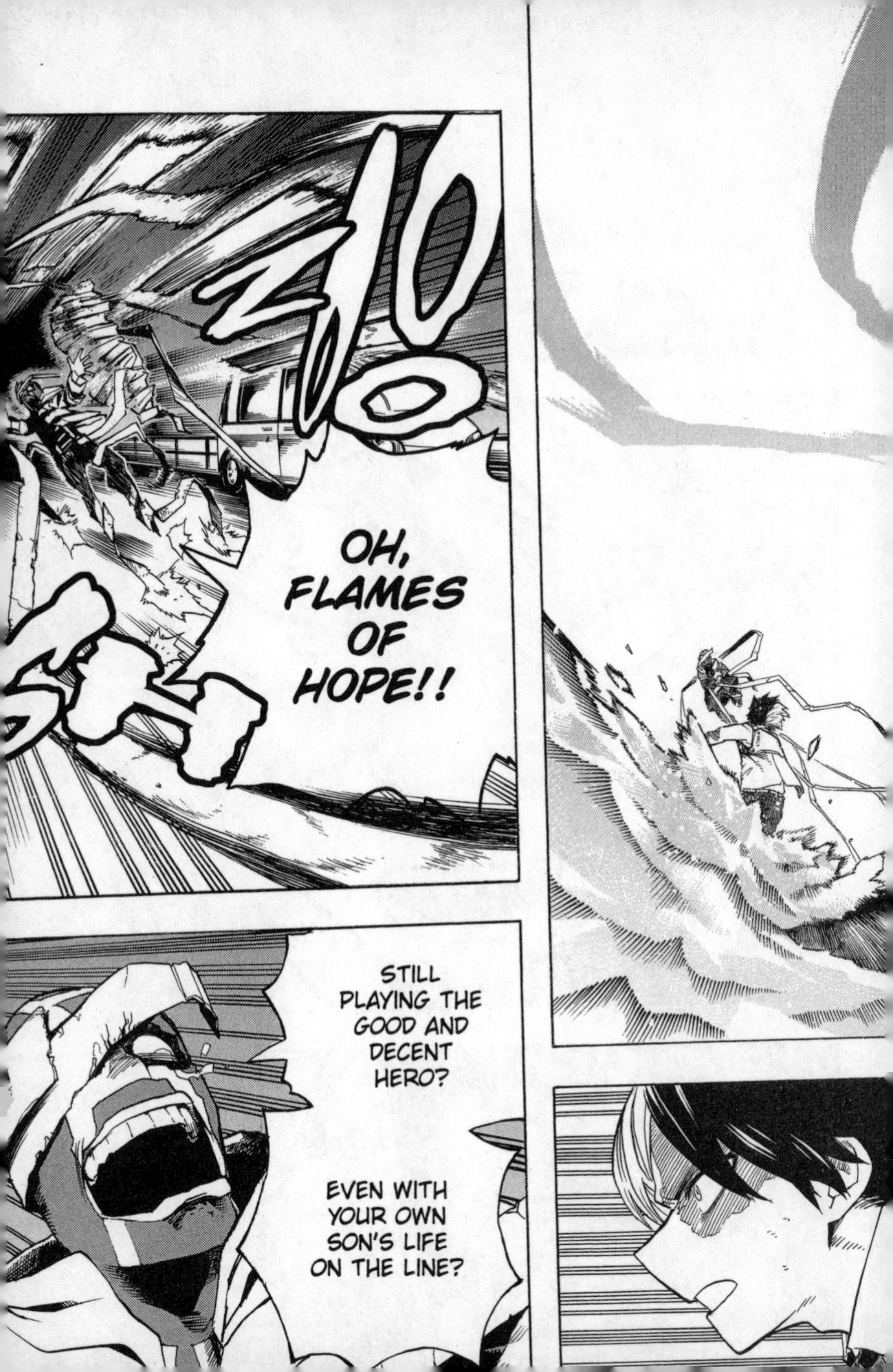
OH, FLAMES OF HOPE!!
STILL PLAYING THE GOOD AND DECENT HERO?
EVEN WITH YOUR OWN SON'S LIFE ON THE LINE?

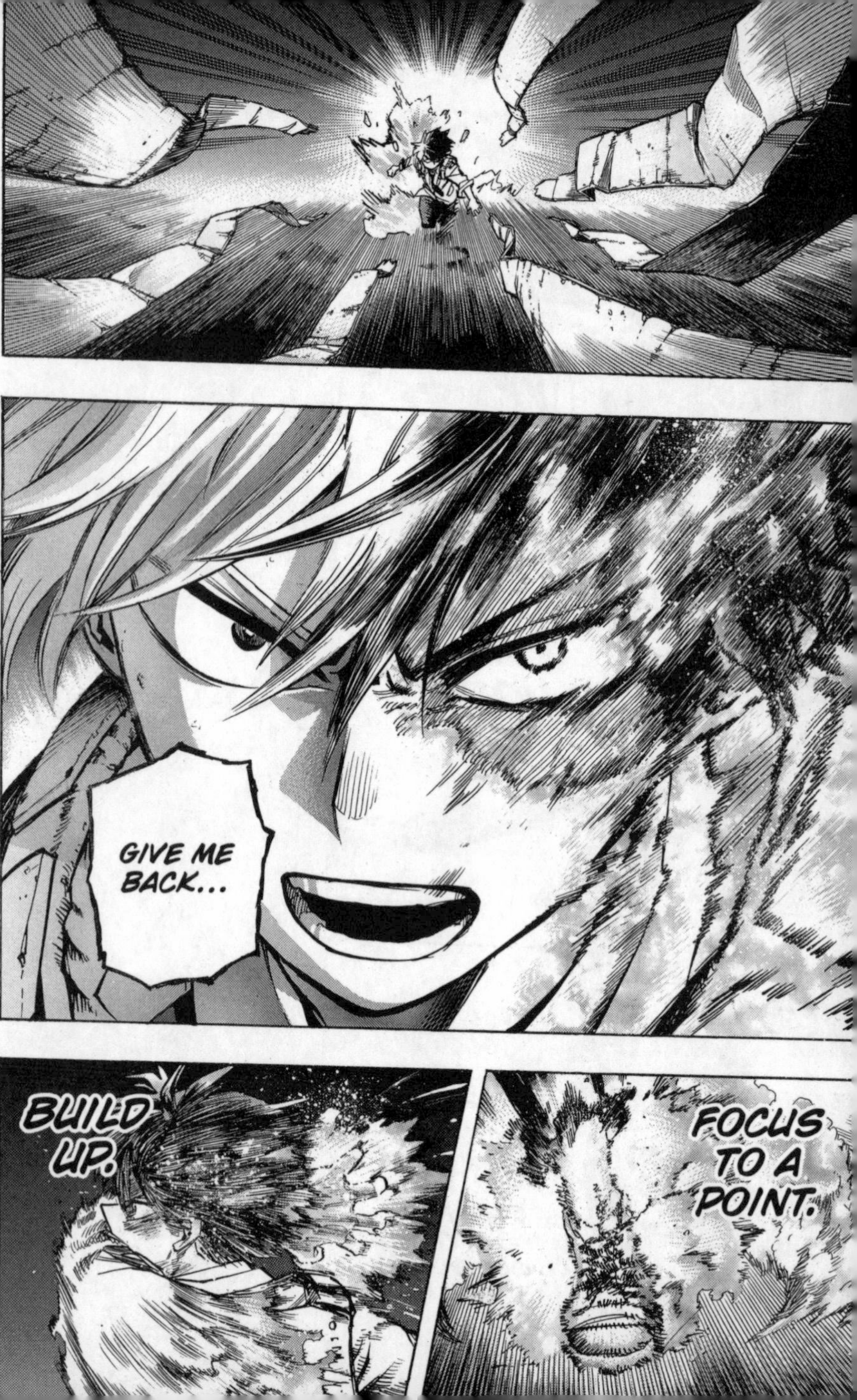
GIVE ME BACK...
FOCUS TO A POINT.
BUILD UP.

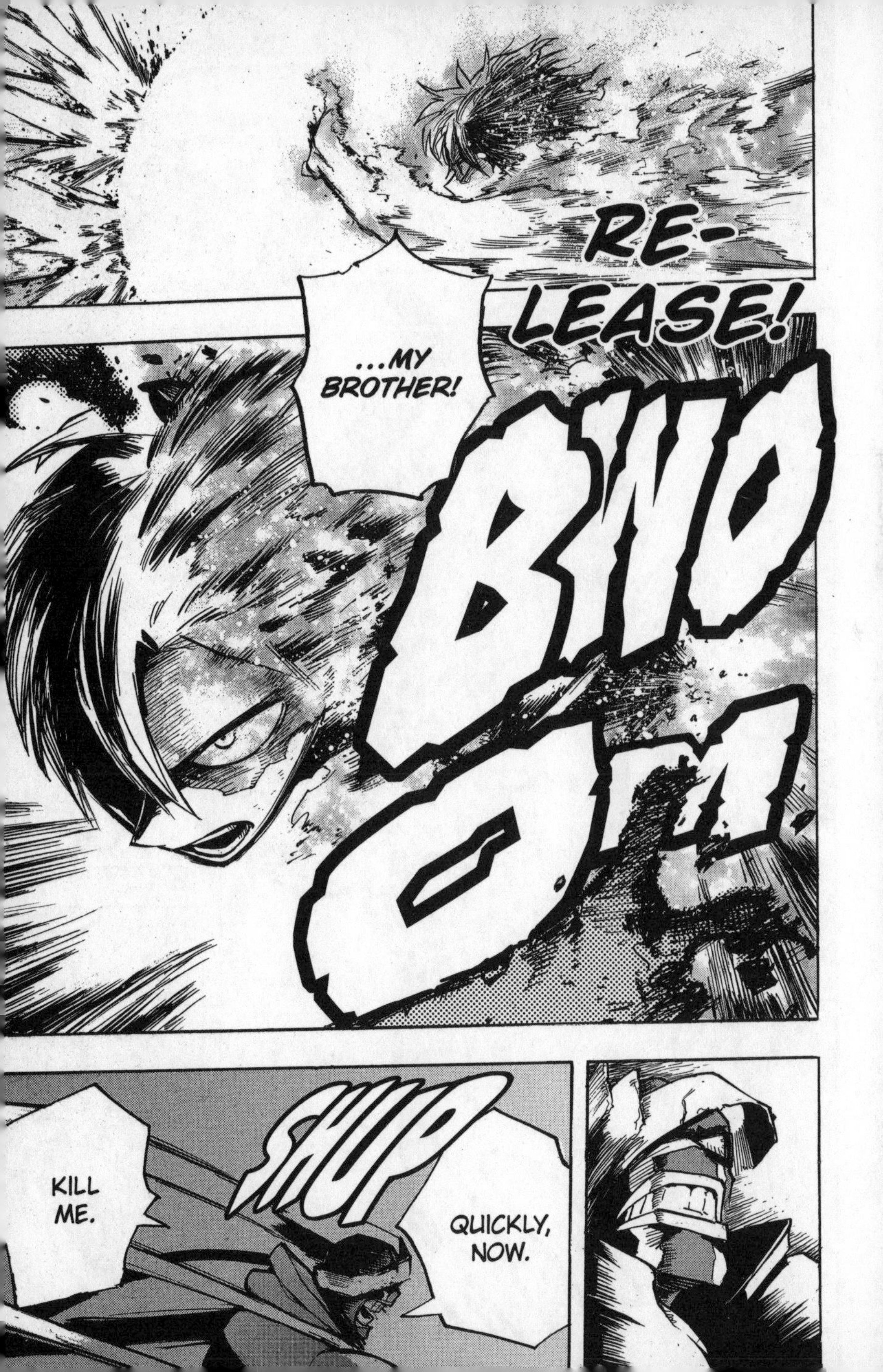
RE-
LEASE!
...MY BROTHER!
SHUP
KILL ME.
QUICKLY, NOW.

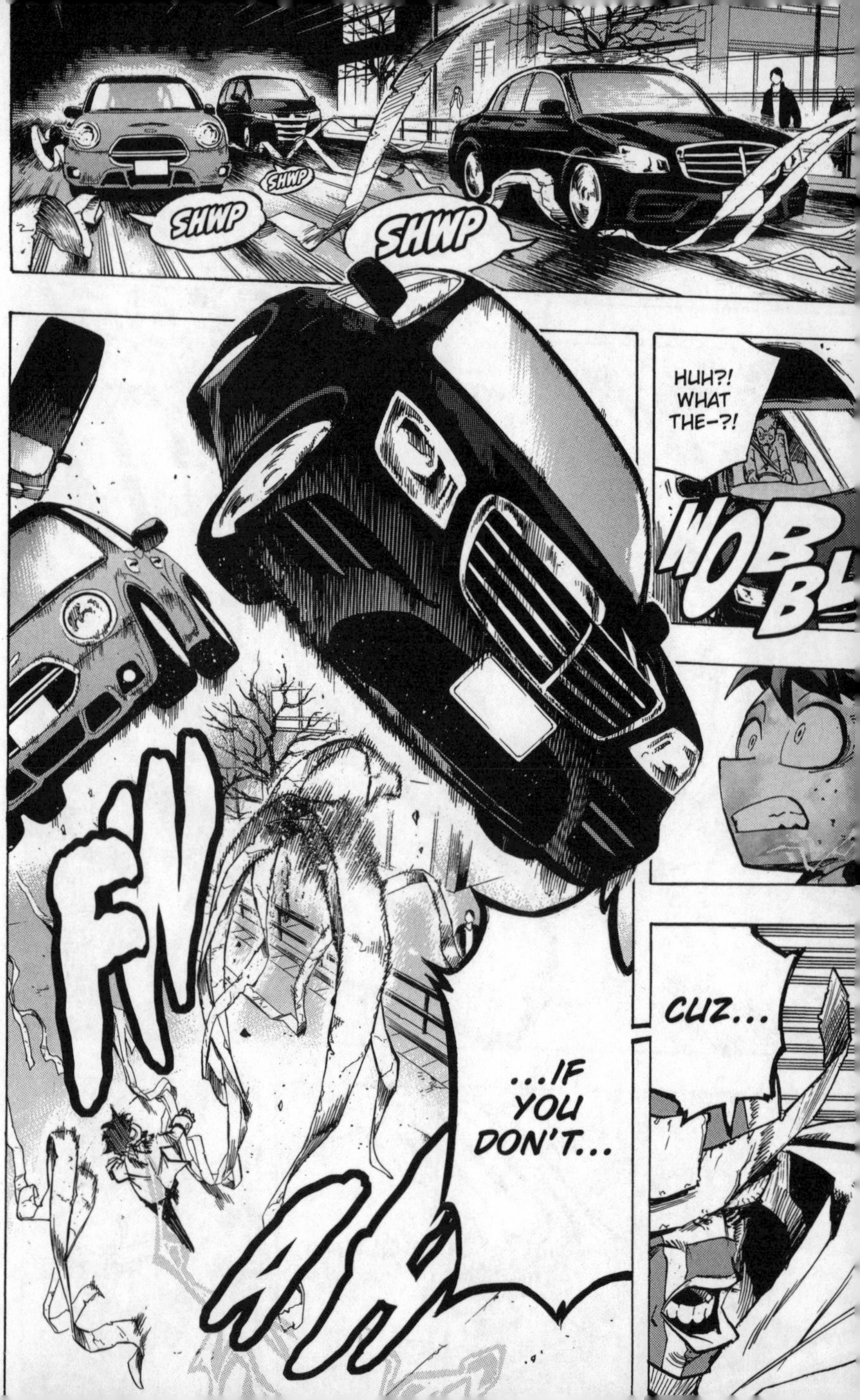

SHWP
SHWP
SHWP
HUH?! WHAT THE-?!
WOBB
CUZ...
...IF YOU DON'T...

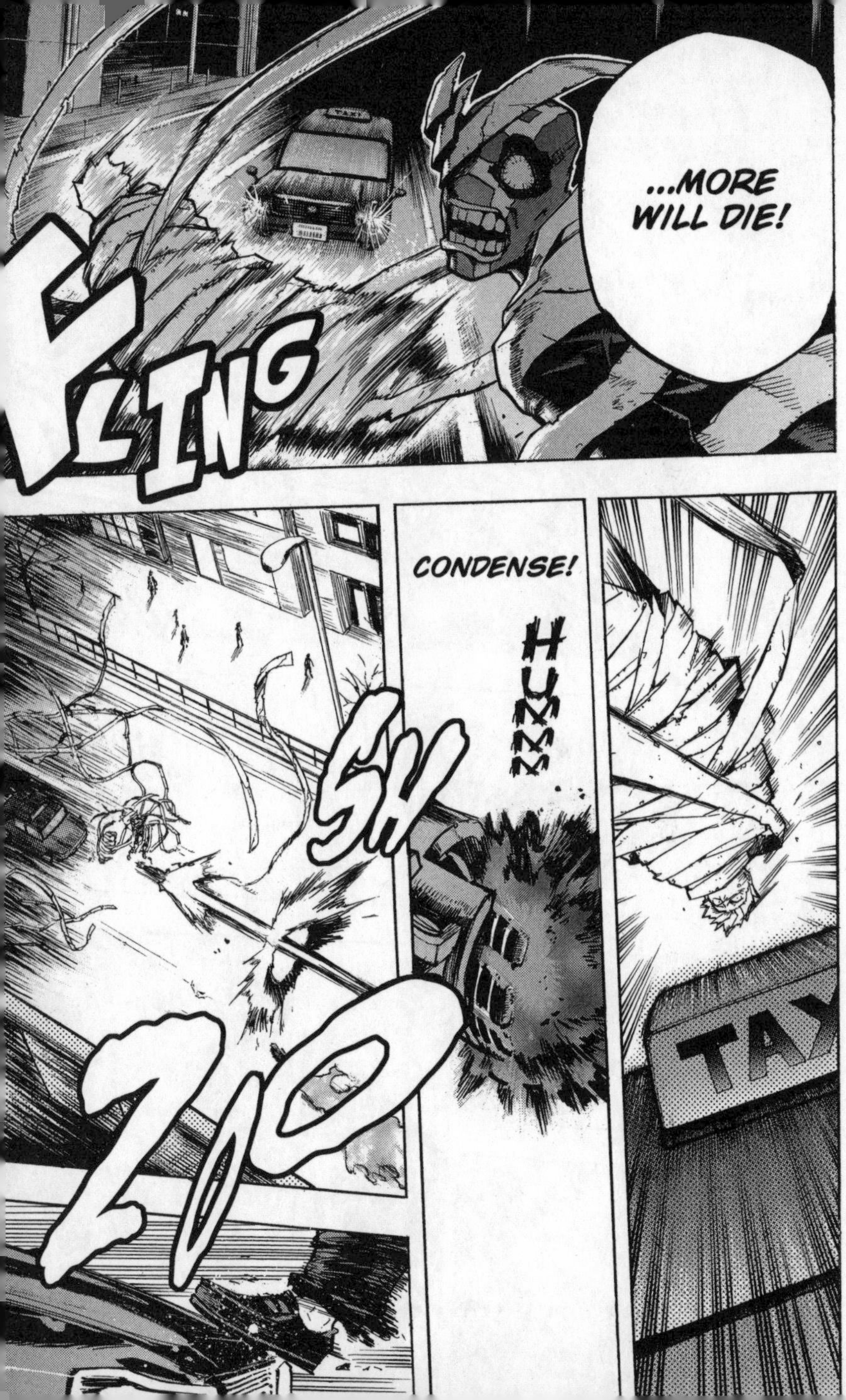
...MORE WILL DIE!
LING
TAX
CONDENSE!
HUMMM
SH
ZOO

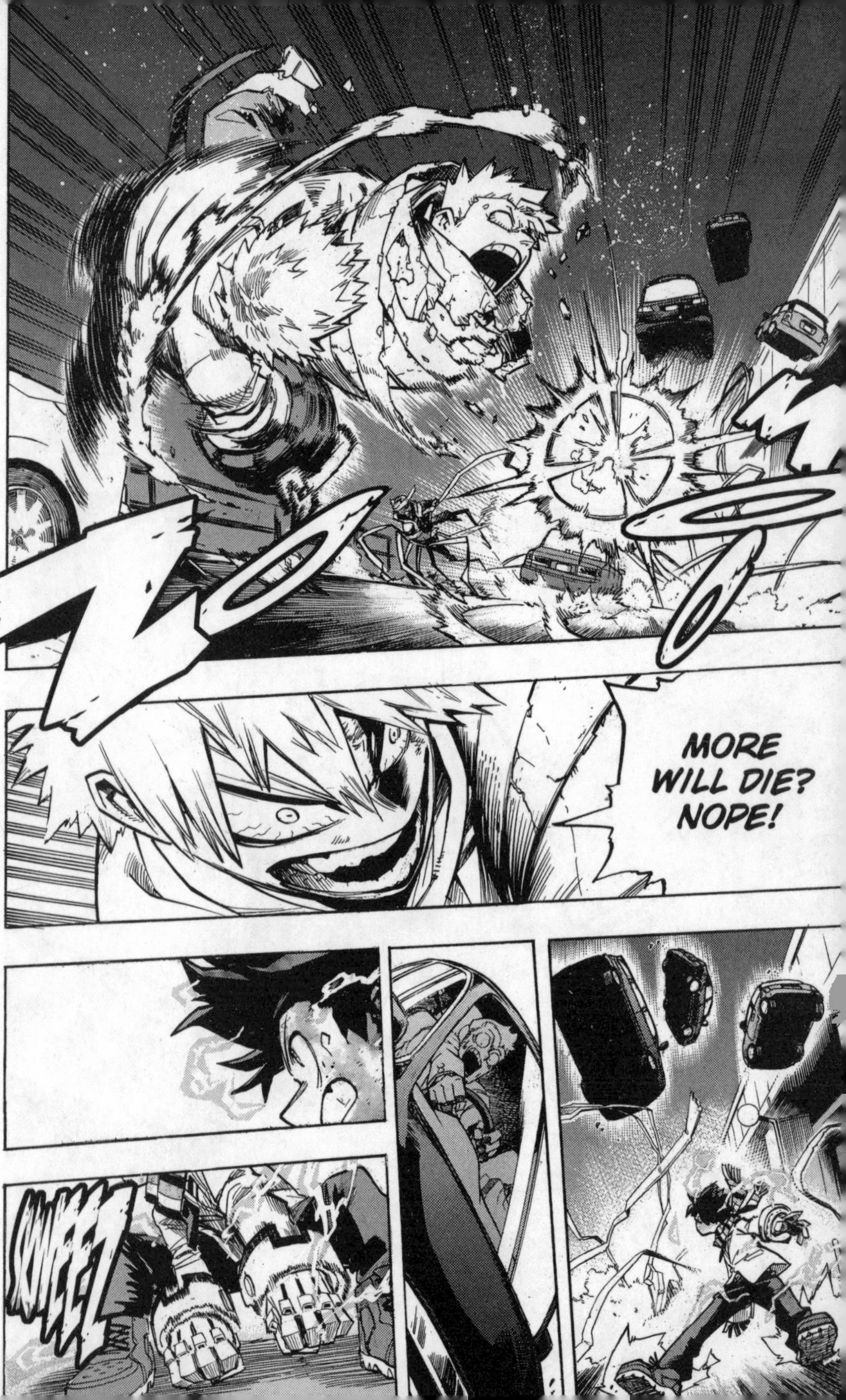
MORE WILL DIE? NOPE!

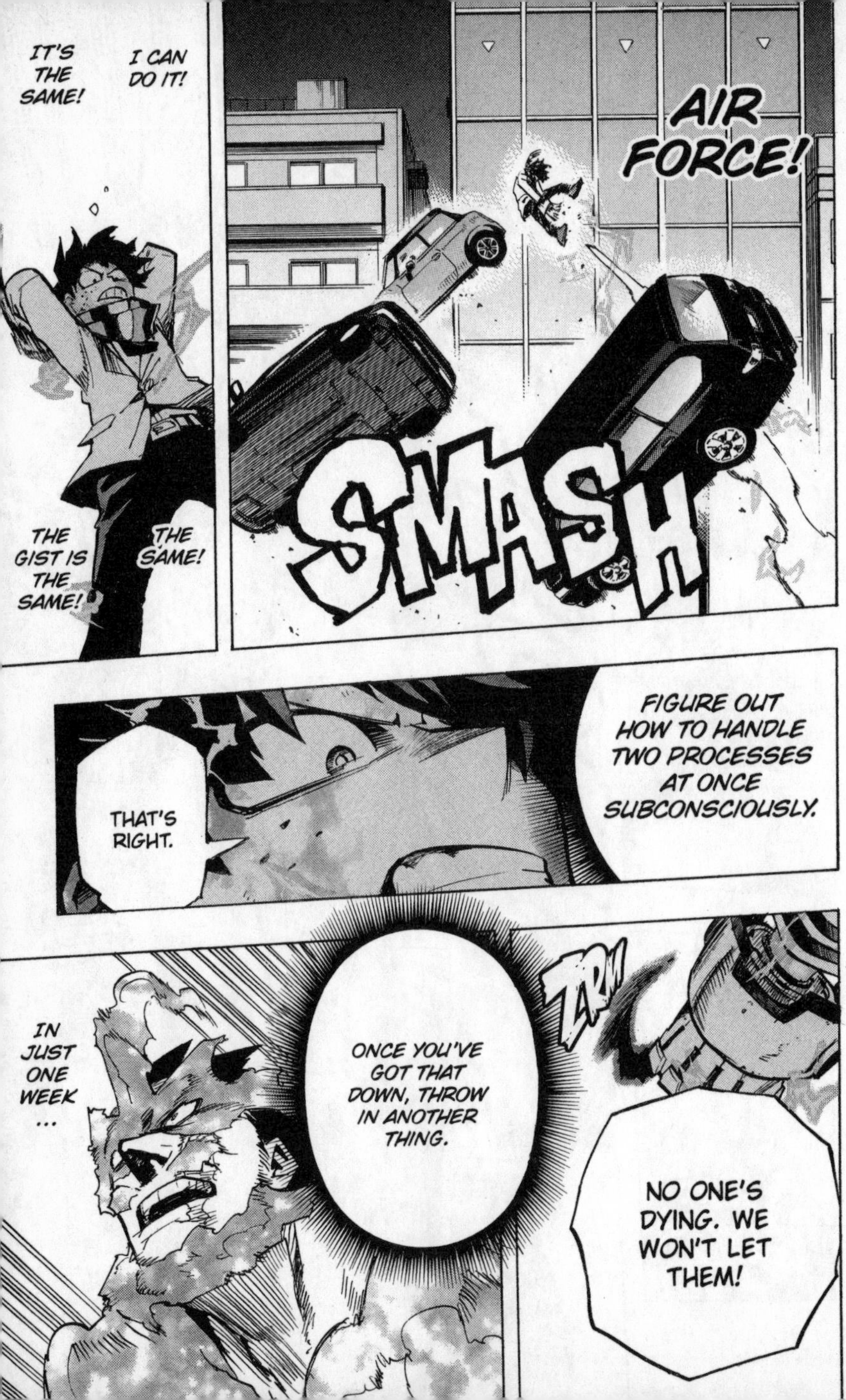
AIR FORCE!
SMASH
I CAN DO IT!
IT'S THE SAME!
THE SAME!
THE GIST IS THE SAME!
FIGURE OUT HOW TO HANDLE TWO PROCESSES AT ONCE SUBCONSCIOUSLY.
THAT'S RIGHT.
ZRM
ONCE YOU'VE GOT THAT DOWN, THROW IN ANOTHER THING.
NO ONE'S DYING. WE WON'T LET THEM!
IN JUST ONE WEEK...

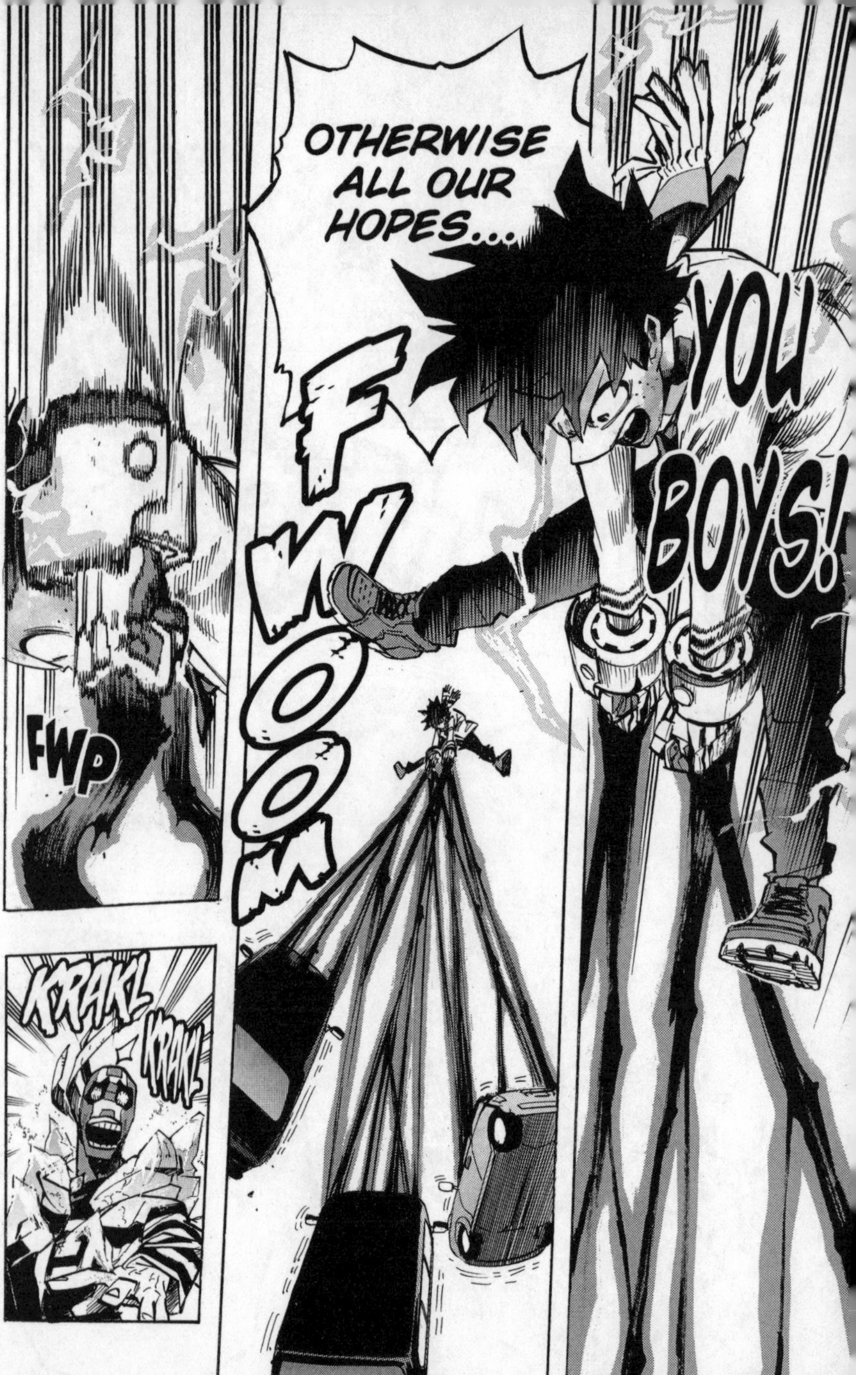
OTHERWISE ALL OUR HOPES...
YOU BOYS!
FWOOOOM
FWP
KRAKL
KRAKL

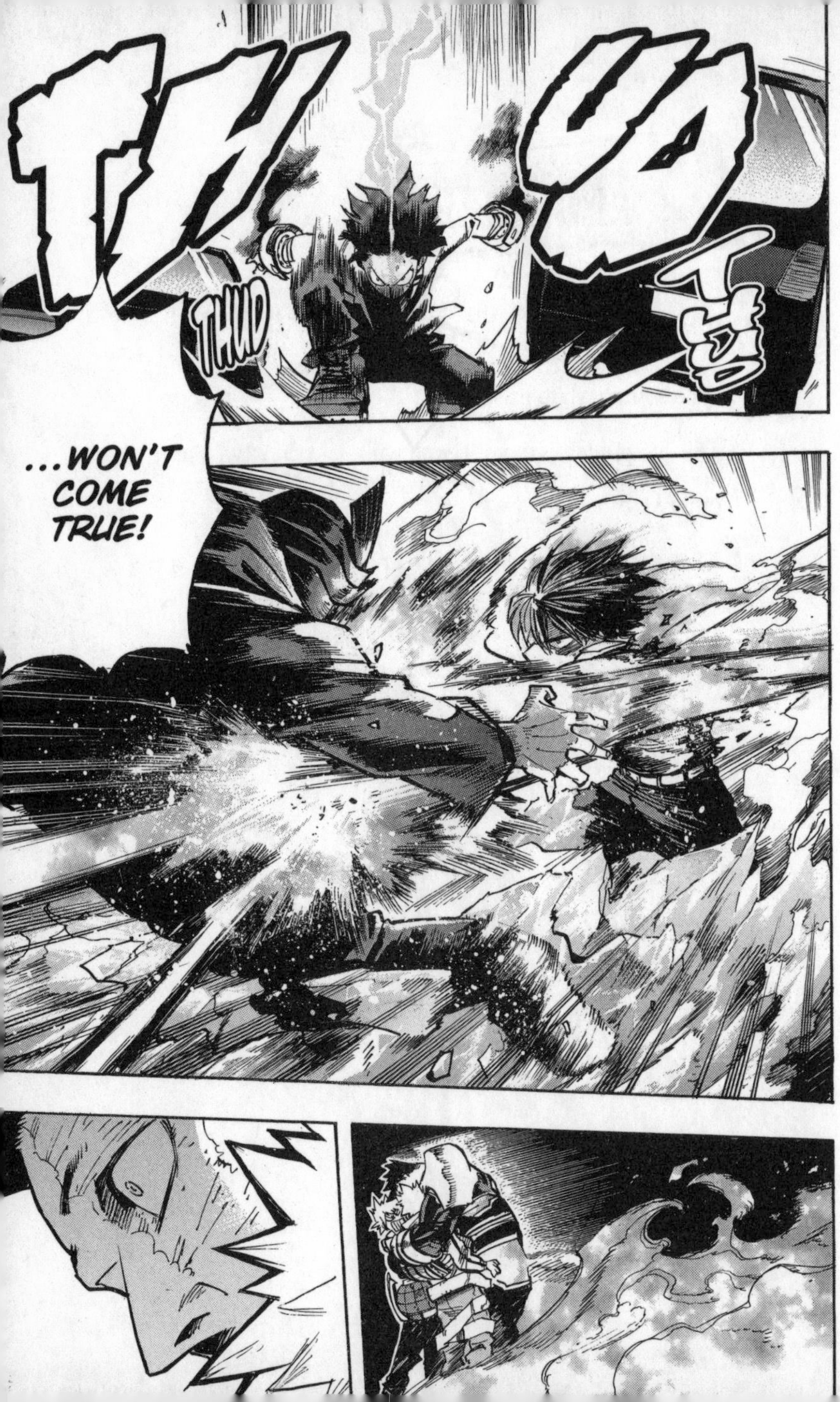
THUD
...WON'T COME TRUE!

QUIRK: WHITELINE

He controls white lines.

This is a Quirk I came up with while out on a walk and one that I definitely never would've thought of otherwise.

Taking the booster drug makes his Quirk much more powerful. Scary. I love it.

I want Endeavor to kill me.

No. 252 - The Unforgiven

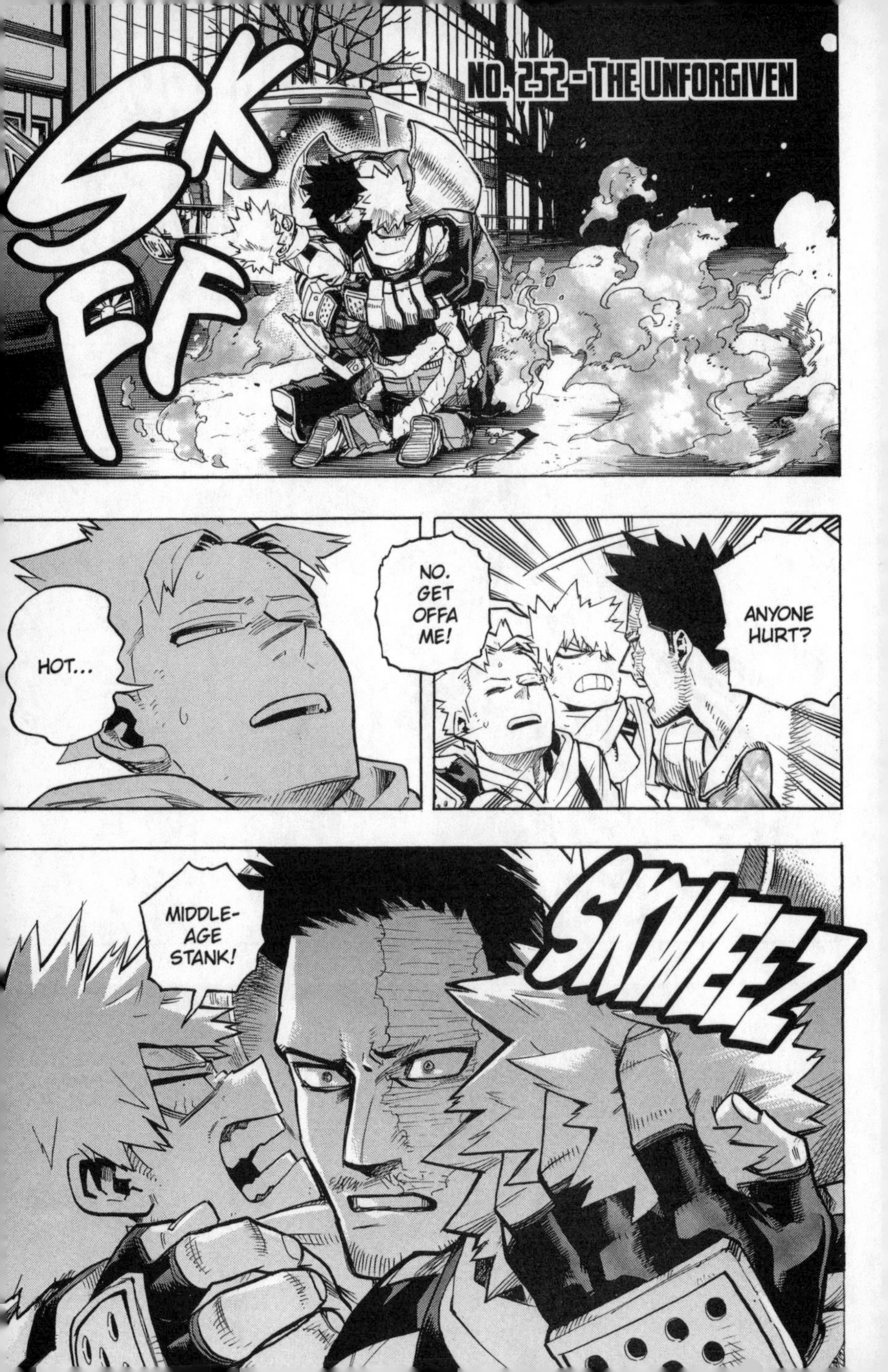
SK
FF
ANYONE HURT?
NO. GET OFFA ME!
HOT...
SKWEEZ
MIDDLE-AGE STANK!

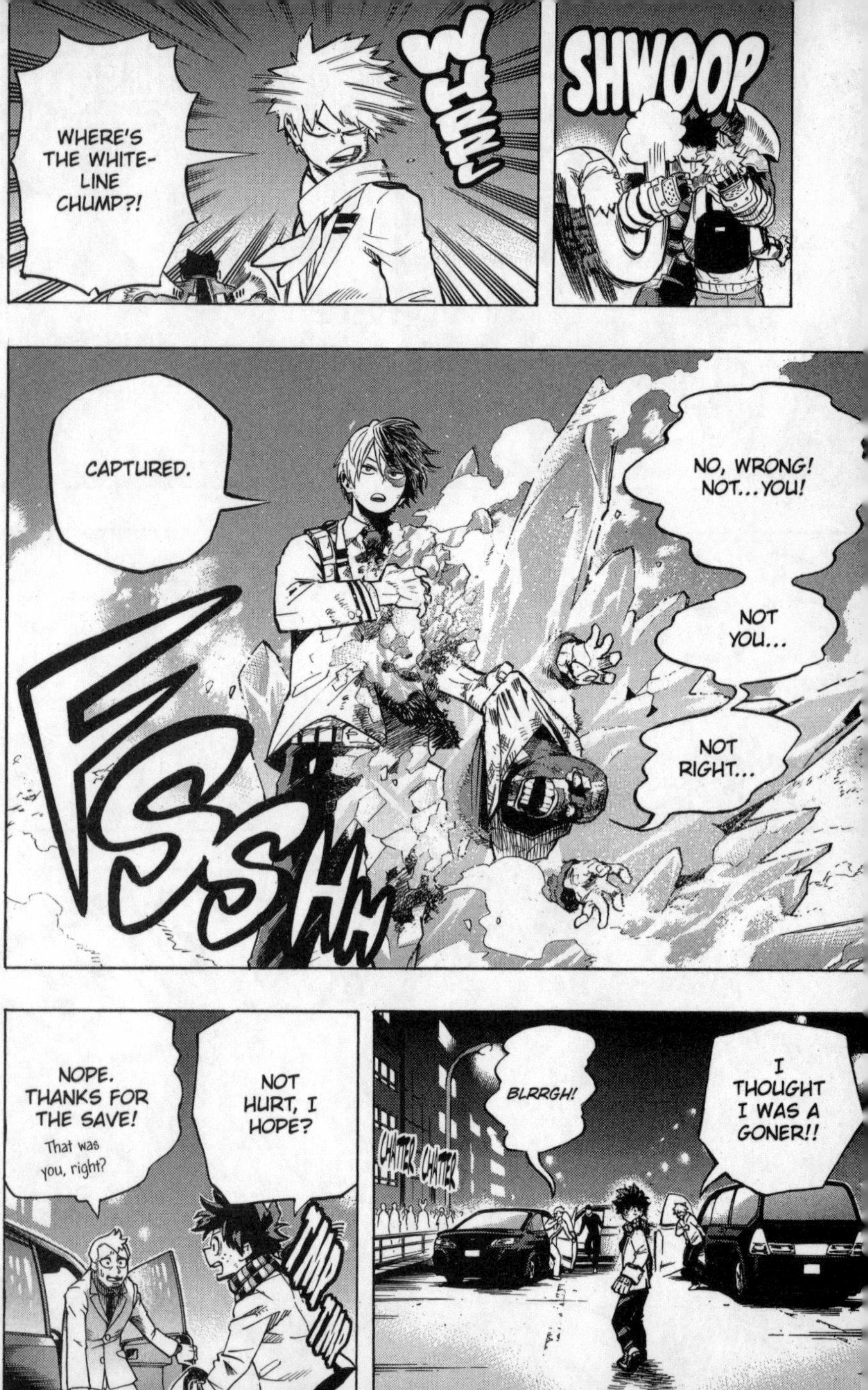
SHWOOP
WHERE'S THE WHITE-LINE CHUMP?!
NO, WRONG! NOT...YOU!
NOT YOU...
NOT RIGHT...
CAPTURED.
I THOUGHT I WAS A GONER!!
BLRRGH!
CHATTER CHATTER
NOT HURT, I HOPE?
NOPE. THANKS FOR THE SAVE!
That was you, right?
TMP TMP

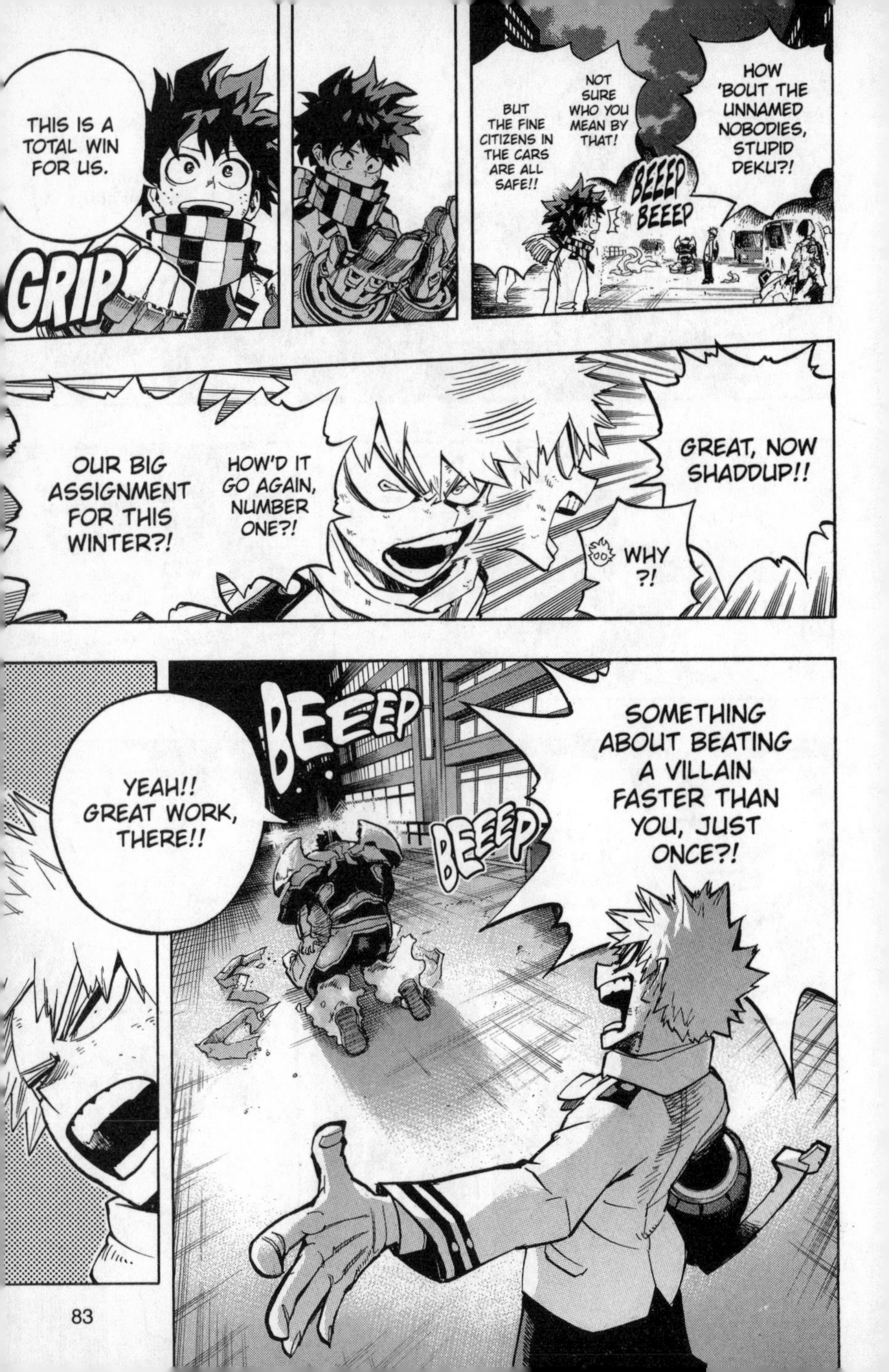
HOW 'BOUT THE UNNAMED NOBODIES, STUPID DEKU?!
BEEEP BEEEP
NOT SURE WHO YOU MEAN BY THAT!
BUT THE FINE CITIZENS IN THE CARS ARE ALL SAFE!!
THIS IS A TOTAL WIN FOR US.
GRIP
GREAT, NOW SHADDUP!!
WHY ?!
HOW'D IT GO AGAIN, NUMBER ONE?!
OUR BIG ASSIGNMENT FOR THIS WINTER?!
SOMETHING ABOUT BEATING A VILLAIN FASTER THAN YOU, JUST ONCE?!
BEEEP
BEEEP
YEAH!! GREAT WORK, THERE!!

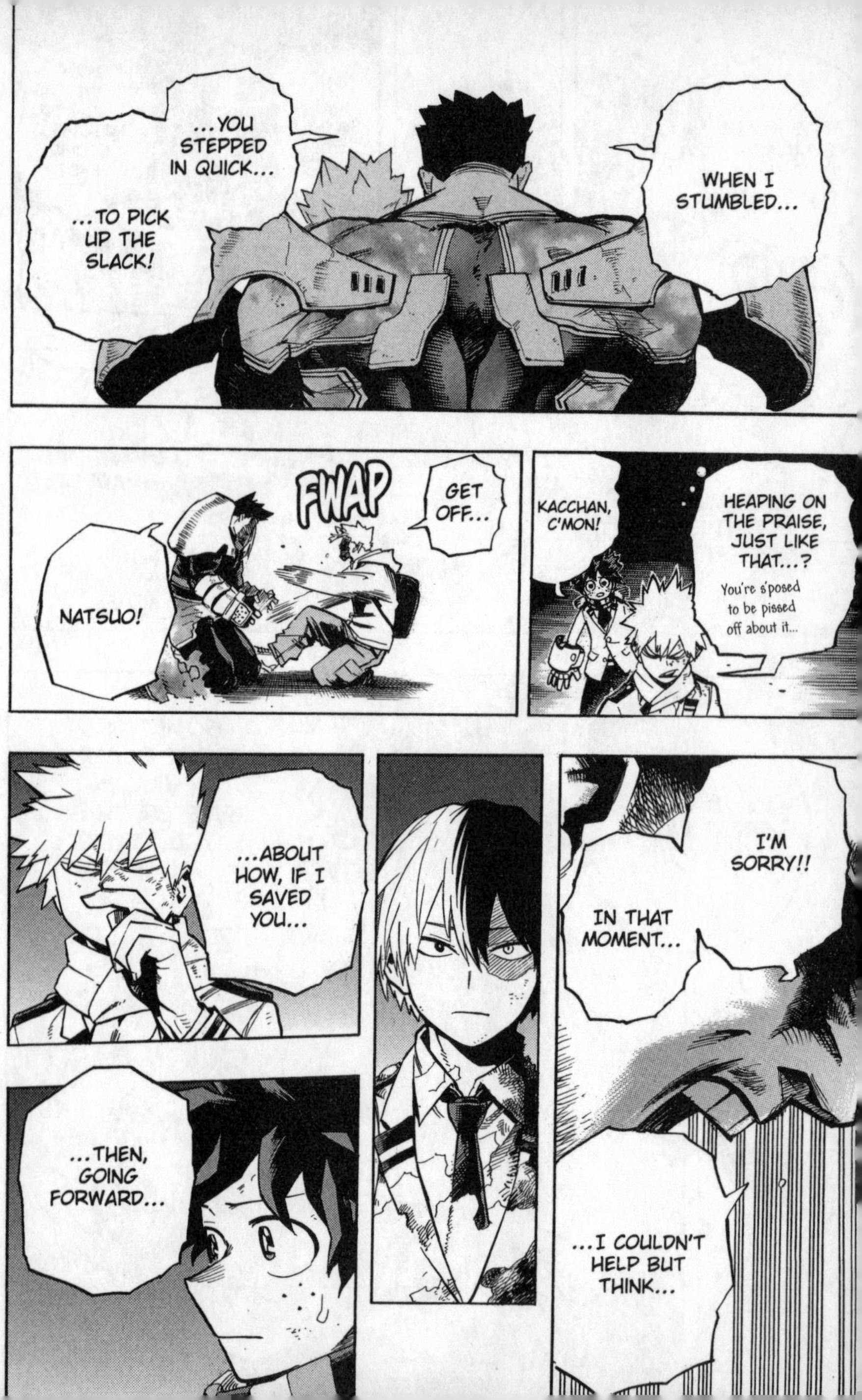
WHEN I STUMBLED...
...YOU STEPPED IN QUICK...
...TO PICK UP THE SLACK!
HEAPING ON THE PRAISE, JUST LIKE THAT...?
You're s'posed to be pissed off about it...
KACCHAN, C'MON!
GET OFF...
FWAP
NATSUO!
I'M SORRY!!
IN THAT MOMENT...
...I COULDN'T HELP BUT THINK...
...ABOUT HOW, IF I SAVED YOU...
...THEN, GOING FORWARD...

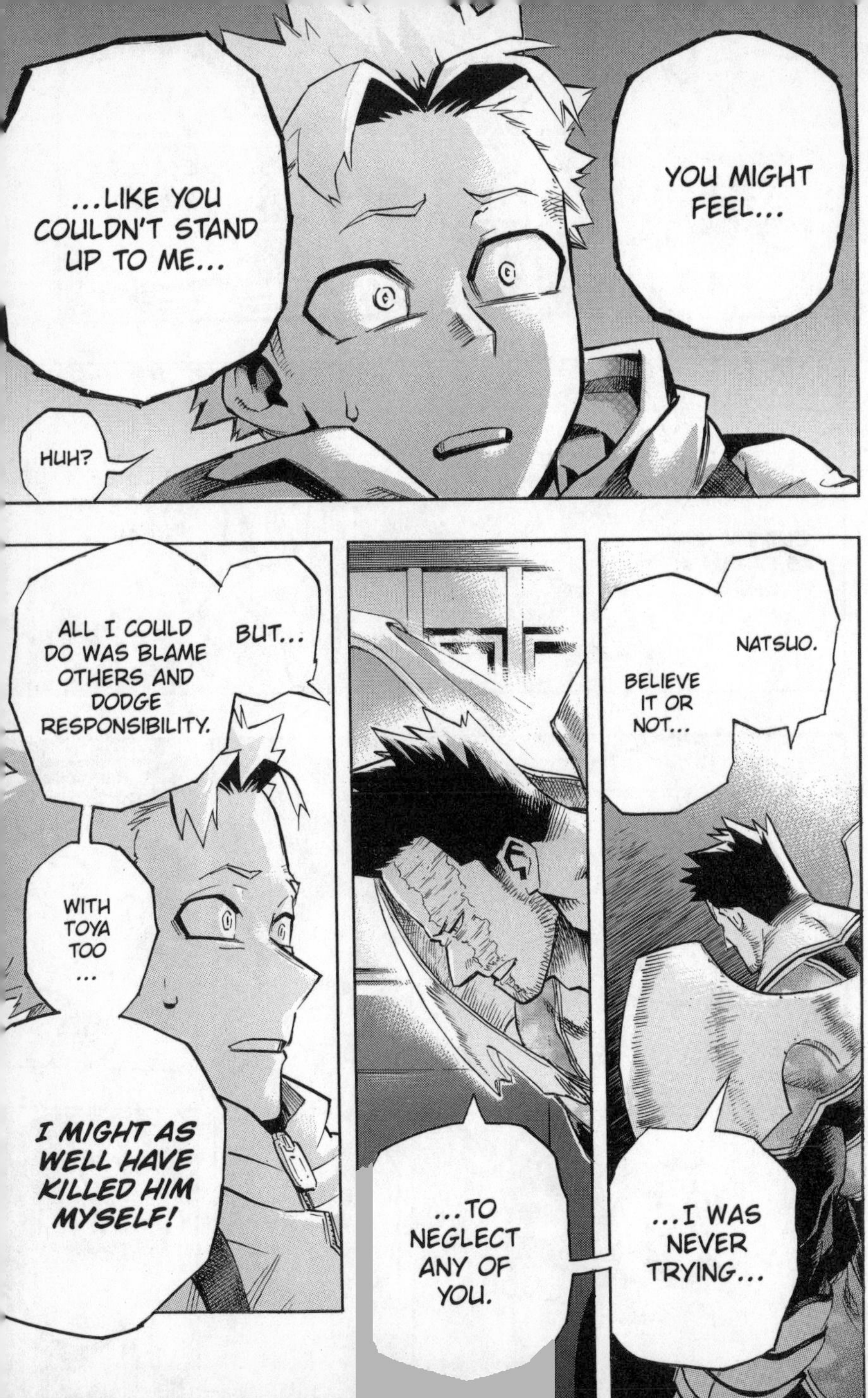
YOU MIGHT FEEL...
...LIKE YOU COULDN'T STAND UP TO ME...
HUH?
NATSUO.
BELIEVE IT OR NOT...
...I WAS NEVER TRYING...
...TO NEGLECT ANY OF YOU.
BUT...
ALL I COULD DO WAS BLAME OTHERS AND DODGE RESPONSIBILITY.
WITH TOYA TOO...
I MIGHT AS WELL HAVE KILLED HIM MYSELF!

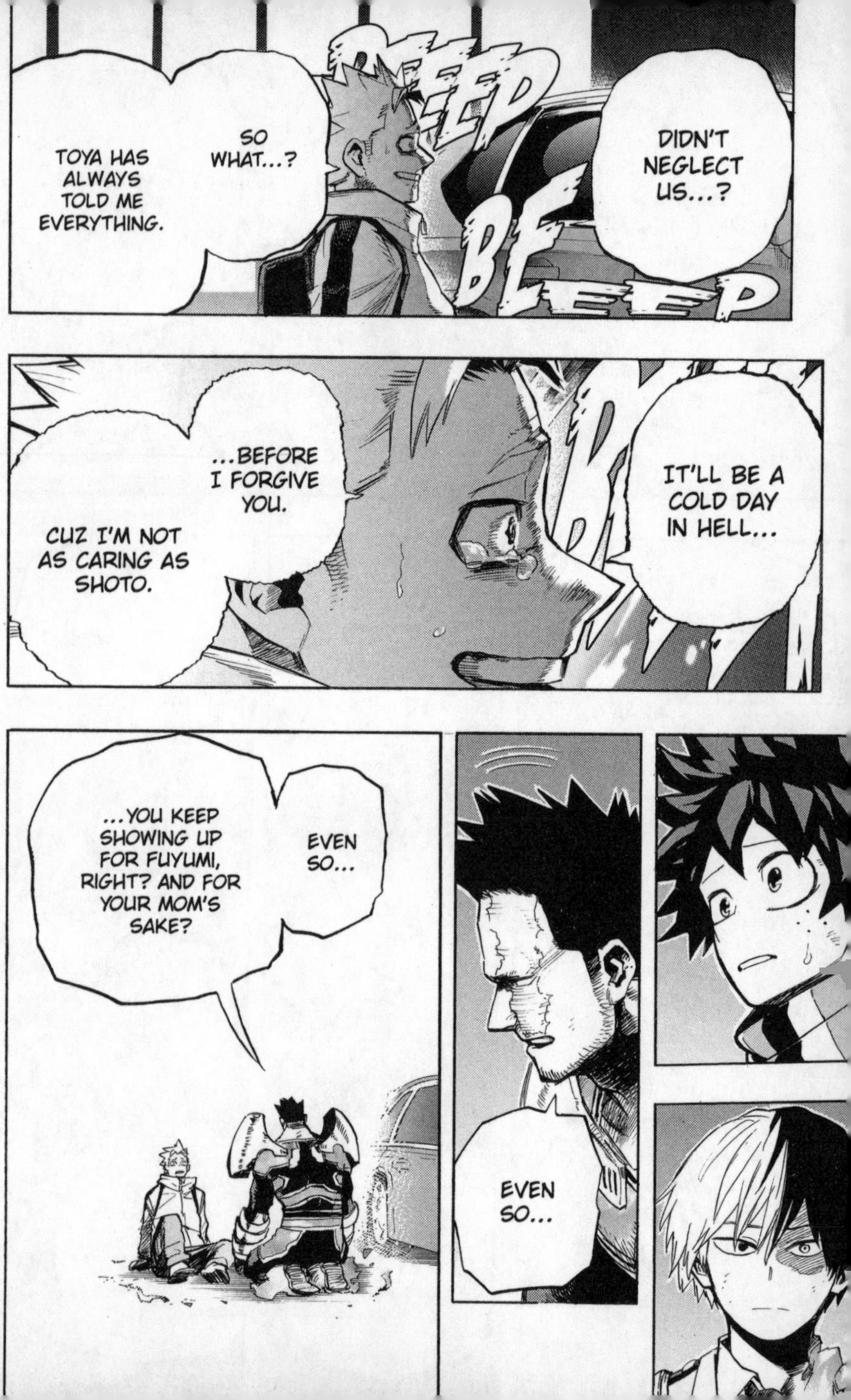
DIDN'T NEGLECT US...?
SO WHAT...?
TOYA HAS ALWAYS TOLD ME EVERYTHING.
IT'LL BE A COLD DAY IN HELL...
...BEFORE I FORGIVE YOU.
CUZ I'M NOT AS CARING AS SHOTO.
EVEN SO...
EVEN SO...
...YOU KEEP SHOWING UP FOR FUYUMI, RIGHT? AND FOR YOUR MOM'S SAKE?

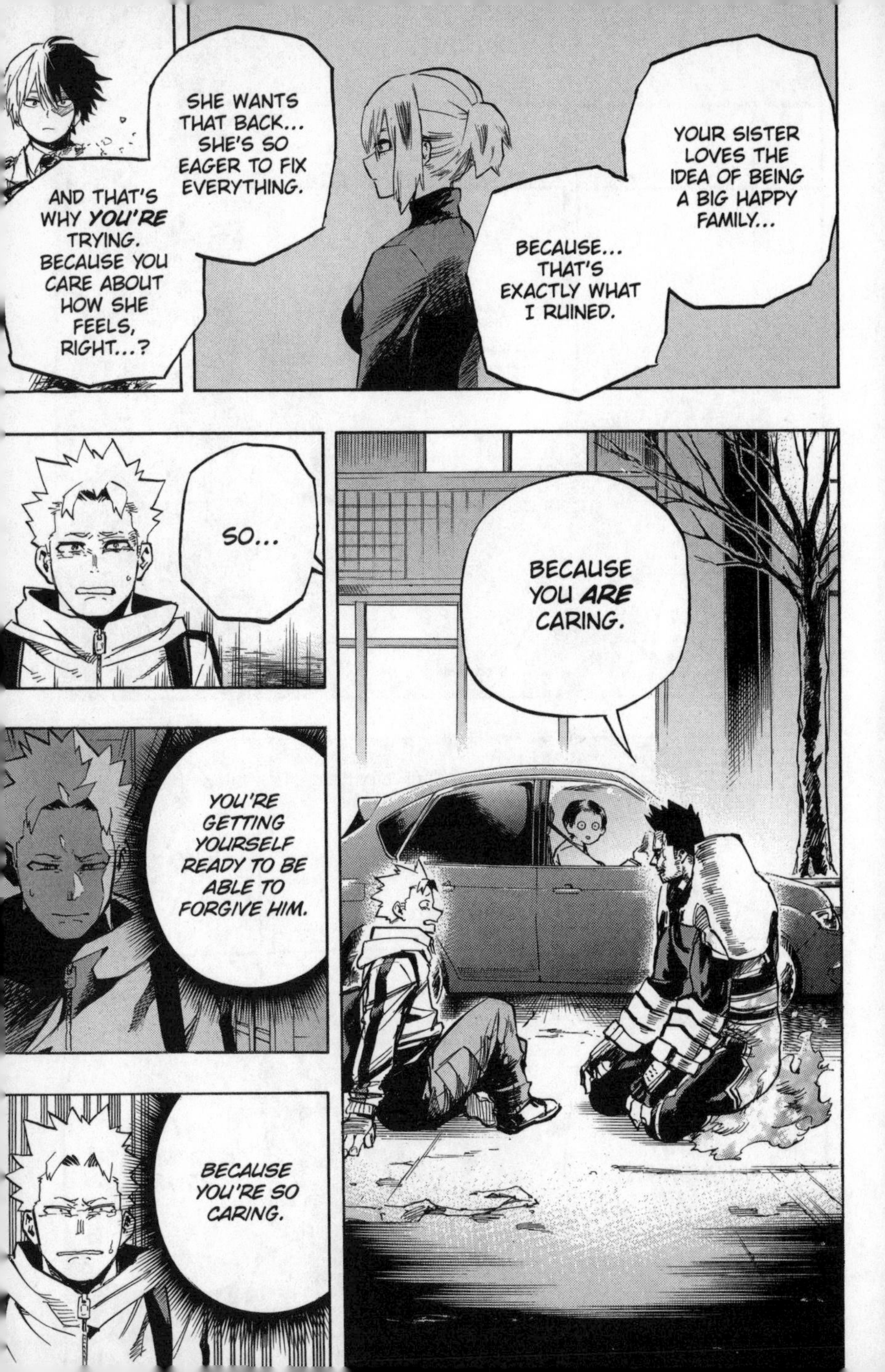
YOUR SISTER LOVES THE IDEA OF BEING A BIG HAPPY FAMILY...
BECAUSE... THAT'S EXACTLY WHAT I RUINED.
SHE WANTS THAT BACK... SHE'S SO EAGER TO FIX EVERYTHING.
AND THAT'S WHY *YOU'RE* TRYING. BECAUSE YOU CARE ABOUT HOW SHE FEELS, RIGHT...?
BECAUSE YOU *ARE* CARING.
SO...
YOU'RE GETTING YOURSELF READY TO BE ABLE TO FORGIVE HIM.
BECAUSE YOU'RE SO CARING.

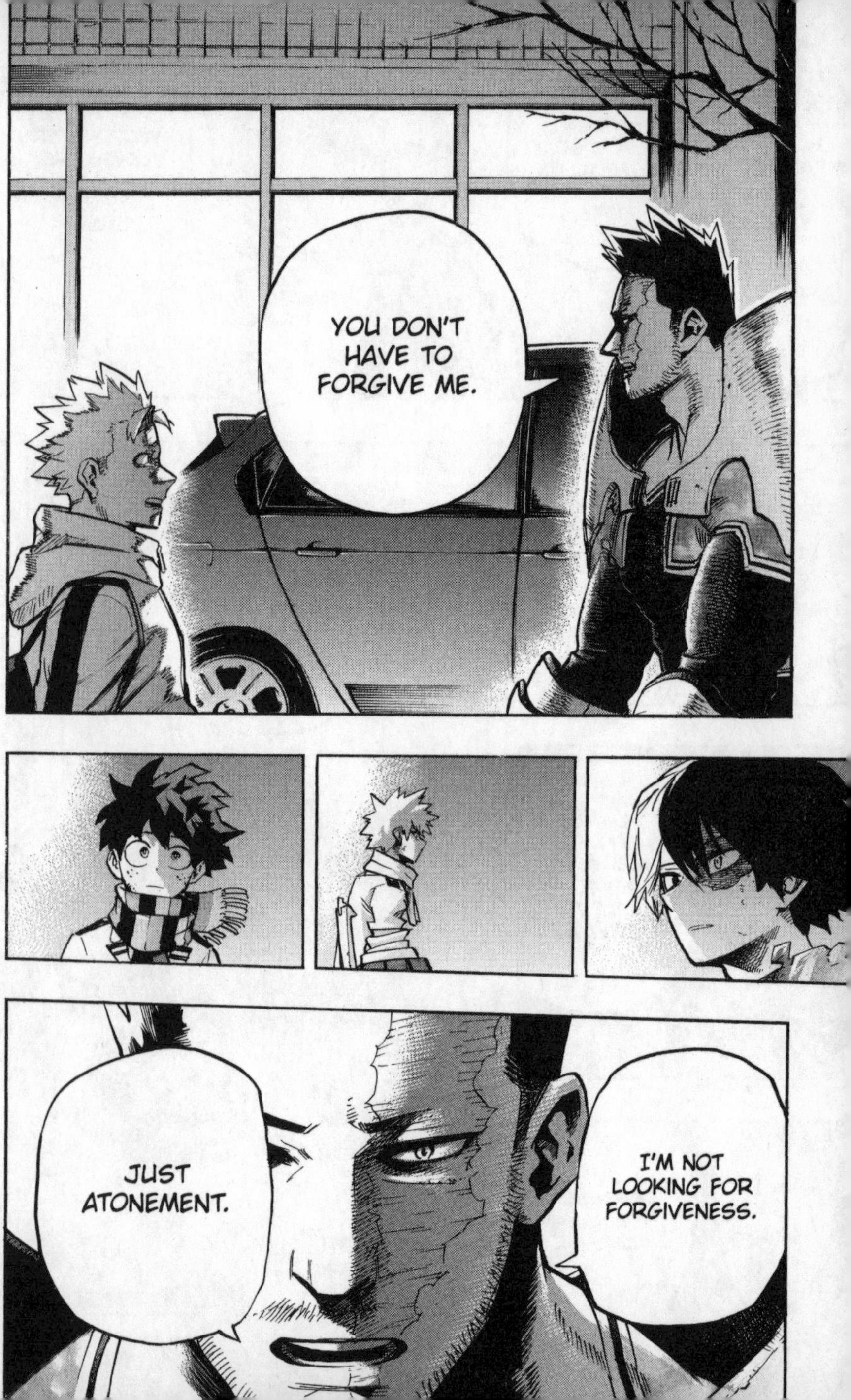
YOU DON'T HAVE TO FORGIVE ME.
I'M NOT LOOKING FOR FORGIVENESS.
JUST ATONEMENT.

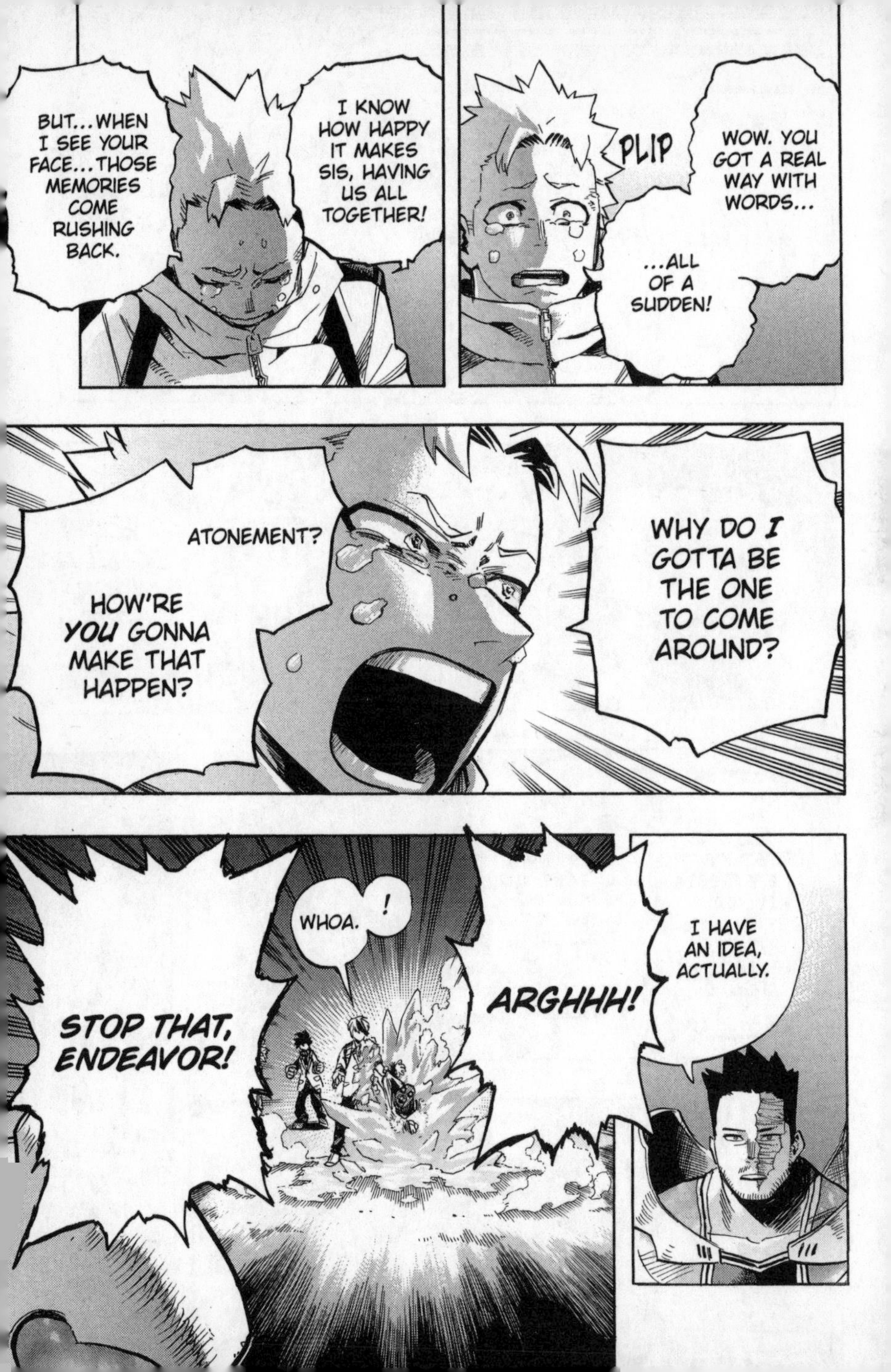
WOW. YOU GOT A REAL WAY WITH WORDS...
PLIP
...ALL OF A SUDDEN!
I KNOW HOW HAPPY IT MAKES SIS, HAVING US ALL TOGETHER!
BUT...WHEN I SEE YOUR FACE...THOSE MEMORIES COME RUSHING BACK.
WHY DO I GOTTA BE THE ONE TO COME AROUND?
ATONEMENT?
HOW'RE YOU GONNA MAKE THAT HAPPEN?
I HAVE AN IDEA, ACTUALLY.
ARGHHH!
!
WHOA.
STOP THAT, ENDEAVOR!

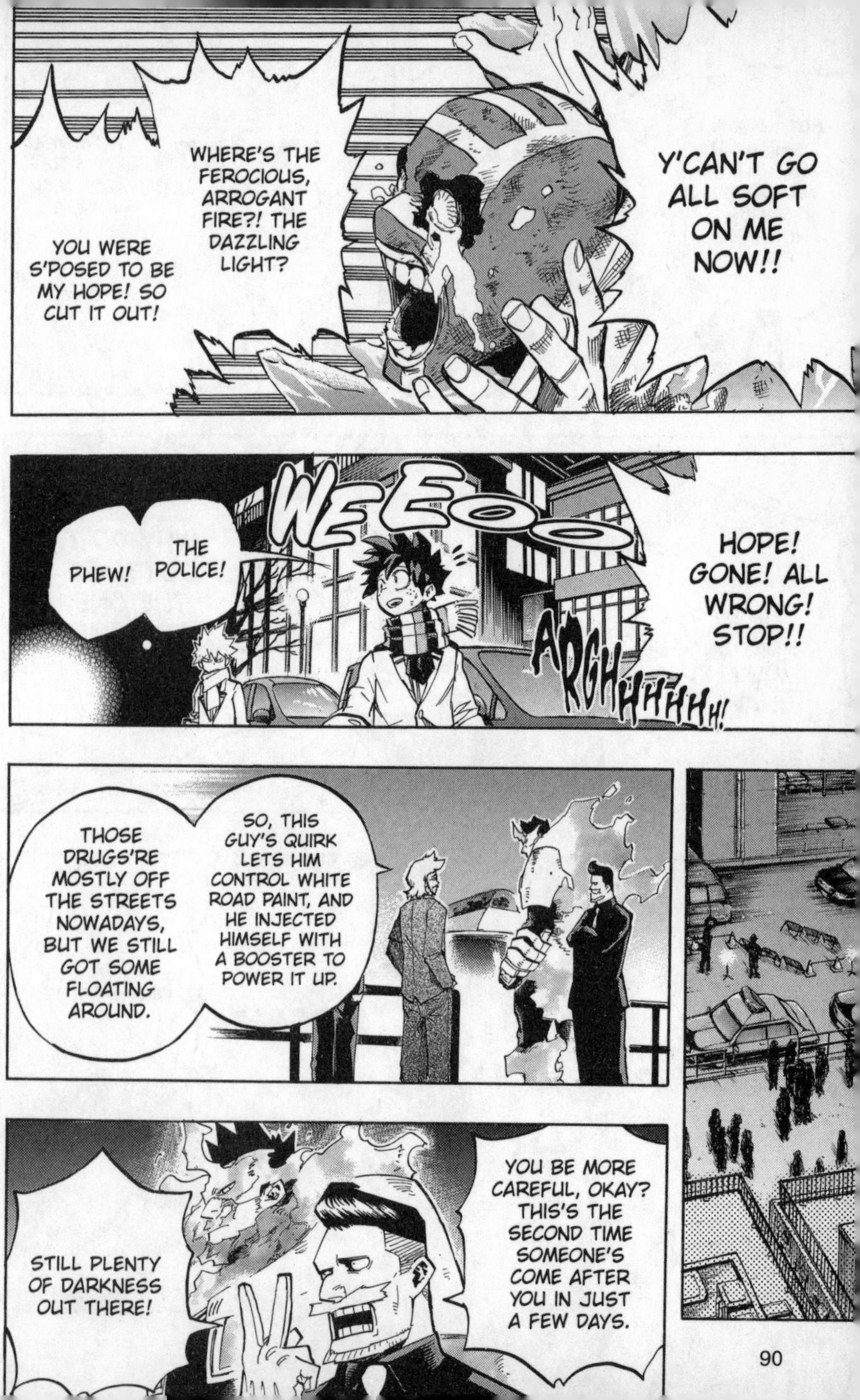
Y'CAN'T GO ALL SOFT ON ME NOW!!
WHERE'S THE FEROCIOUS, ARROGANT FIRE?! THE DAZZLING LIGHT?
YOU WERE S'POSED TO BE MY HOPE! SO CUT IT OUT!
HOPE! GONE! ALL WRONG! STOP!!
WEEOOO
ARGHHHHHH!
THE POLICE!
PHEW!
SO, THIS GUY'S QUIRK LETS HIM CONTROL WHITE ROAD PAINT, AND HE INJECTED HIMSELF WITH A BOOSTER TO POWER IT UP.
THOSE DRUGS'RE MOSTLY OFF THE STREETS NOWADAYS, BUT WE STILL GOT SOME FLOATING AROUND.
YOU BE MORE CAREFUL, OKAY? THIS'S THE SECOND TIME SOMEONE'S COME AFTER YOU IN JUST A FEW DAYS.
STILL PLENTY OF DARKNESS OUT THERE!

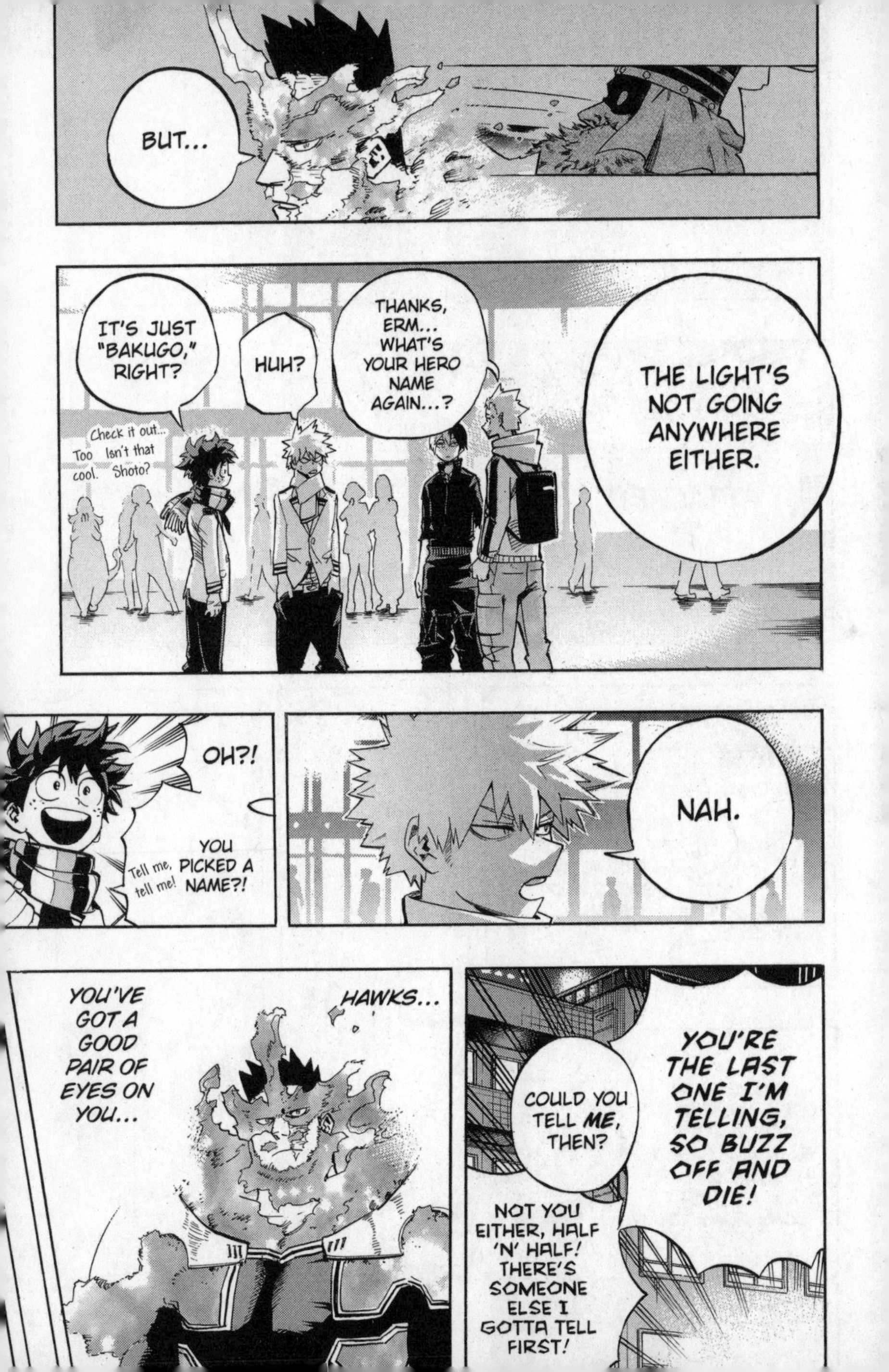
BUT...
THE LIGHT'S NOT GOING ANYWHERE EITHER.
THANKS, ERM... WHAT'S YOUR HERO NAME AGAIN...?
HUH?
IT'S JUST "BAKUGO," RIGHT?
Check it out... Isn't that Shoto?
Too cool.
NAH.
OH?!
YOU PICKED A NAME?!
Tell me, tell me!
YOU'RE THE LAST ONE I'M TELLING, SO BUZZ OFF AND DIE!
COULD YOU TELL ME, THEN?
NOT YOU EITHER, HALF 'N' HALF! THERE'S SOMEONE ELSE I GOTTA TELL FIRST!
HAWKS...
YOU'VE GOT A GOOD PAIR OF EYES ON YOU...

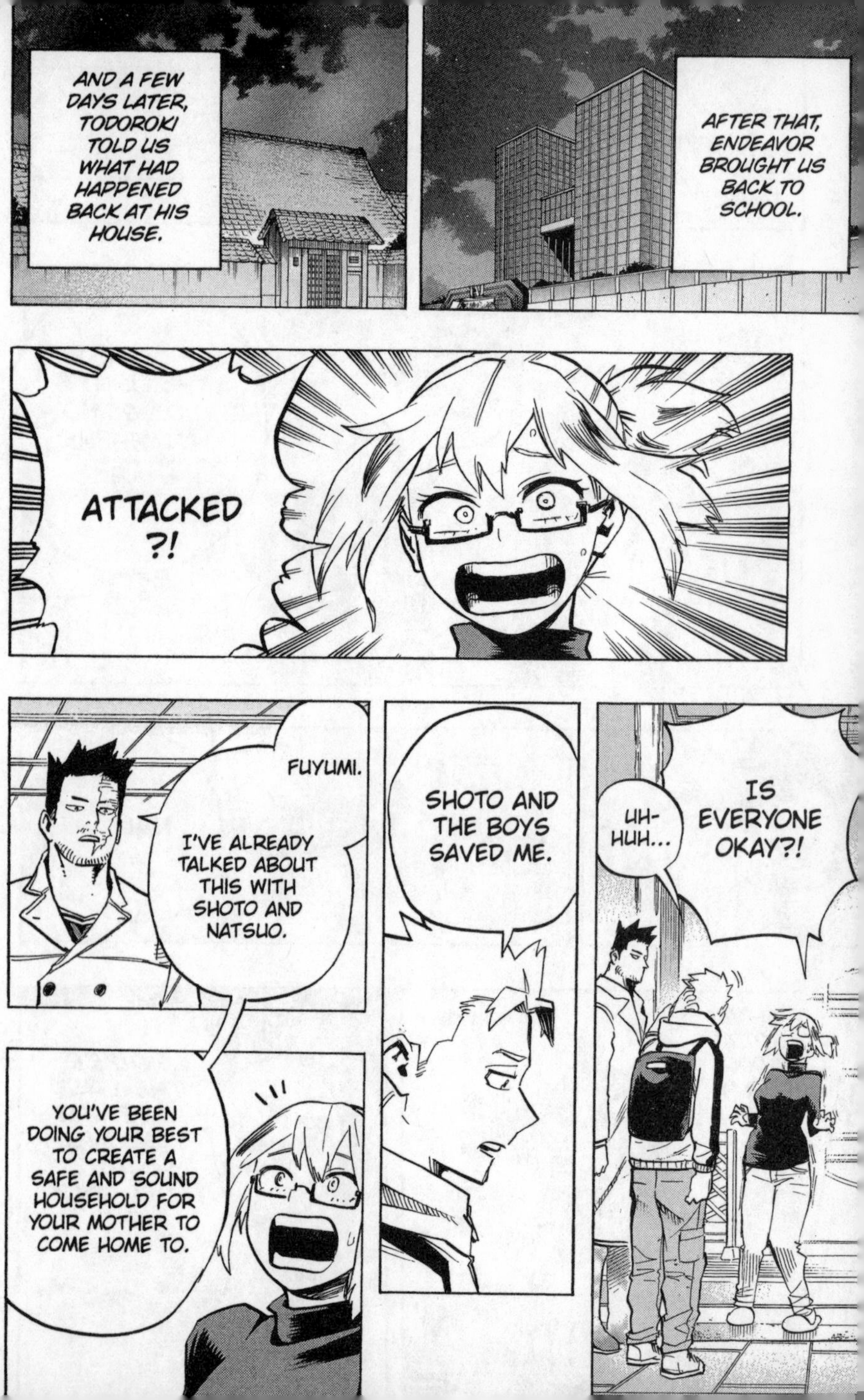
AFTER THAT, ENDEAVOR BROUGHT US BACK TO SCHOOL.
AND A FEW DAYS LATER, TODOROKI TOLD US WHAT HAD HAPPENED BACK AT HIS HOUSE.
ATTACKED ?!
IS EVERYONE OKAY?!
UH-HUH...
SHOTO AND THE BOYS SAVED ME.
FUYUMI.
I'VE ALREADY TALKED ABOUT THIS WITH SHOTO AND NATSUO.
YOU'VE BEEN DOING YOUR BEST TO CREATE A SAFE AND SOUND HOUSEHOLD FOR YOUR MOTHER TO COME HOME TO.

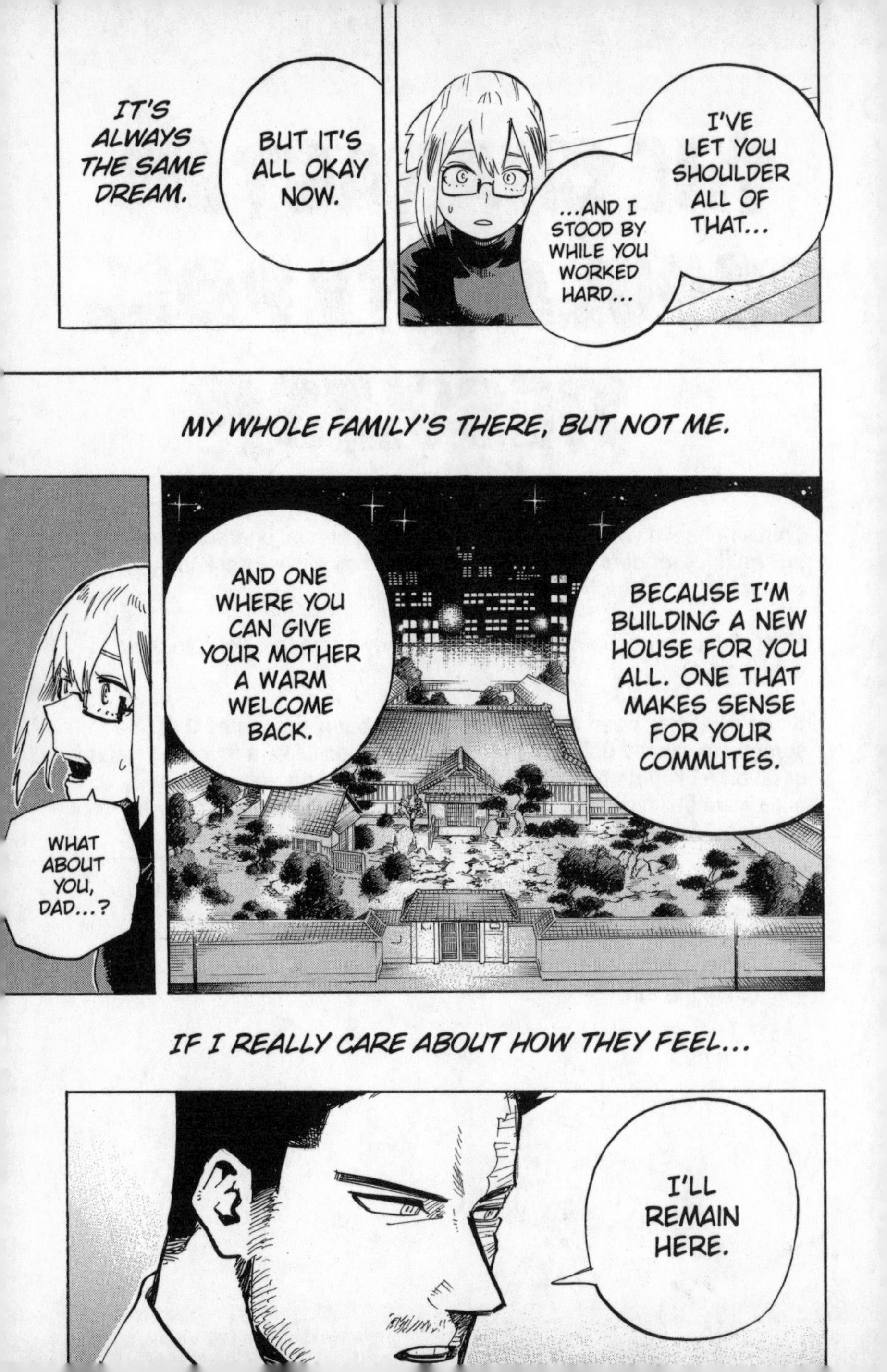
I'VE LET YOU SHOULDER ALL OF THAT...
...AND I STOOD BY WHILE YOU WORKED HARD...
BUT IT'S ALL OKAY NOW.
IT'S ALWAYS THE SAME DREAM.
MY WHOLE FAMILY'S THERE, BUT NOT ME.
BECAUSE I'M BUILDING A NEW HOUSE FOR YOU ALL. ONE THAT MAKES SENSE FOR YOUR COMMUTES.
AND ONE WHERE YOU CAN GIVE YOUR MOTHER A WARM WELCOME BACK.
WHAT ABOUT YOU, DAD...?
IF I REALLY CARE ABOUT HOW THEY FEEL...
I'LL REMAIN HERE.

THE CHARACTER POPULARITY POLL RESULTS!!

We just keep doing this thing!!

That's right, we've got the results of the fifth annual character popularity poll held for readers of *Jump* and the volumes alike. Thanks to everyone who voted!

Most *Jump* series have some sort of yearly event to celebrate their anniversaries.

Since *MHA* has been going five years, it's been suggested that I try something slightly different than a character poll, like a favorite location or favorite ultimate move poll, but as a kid, the character popularity polls were always my favorite, so that's what I've decided to go with. It's fun, right? Like some sort of festival.

The results are at the end of this book! Who's gonna dominate those rankings?!

I don't know if there will be a sixth poll next year, but if there is, I hope you join in the fun!

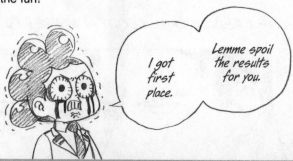

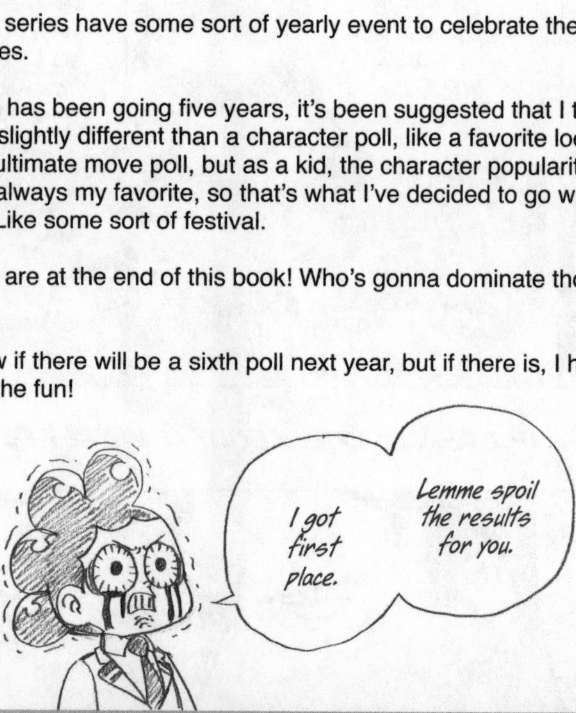

Lemme spoil the results for you.
I got first place.

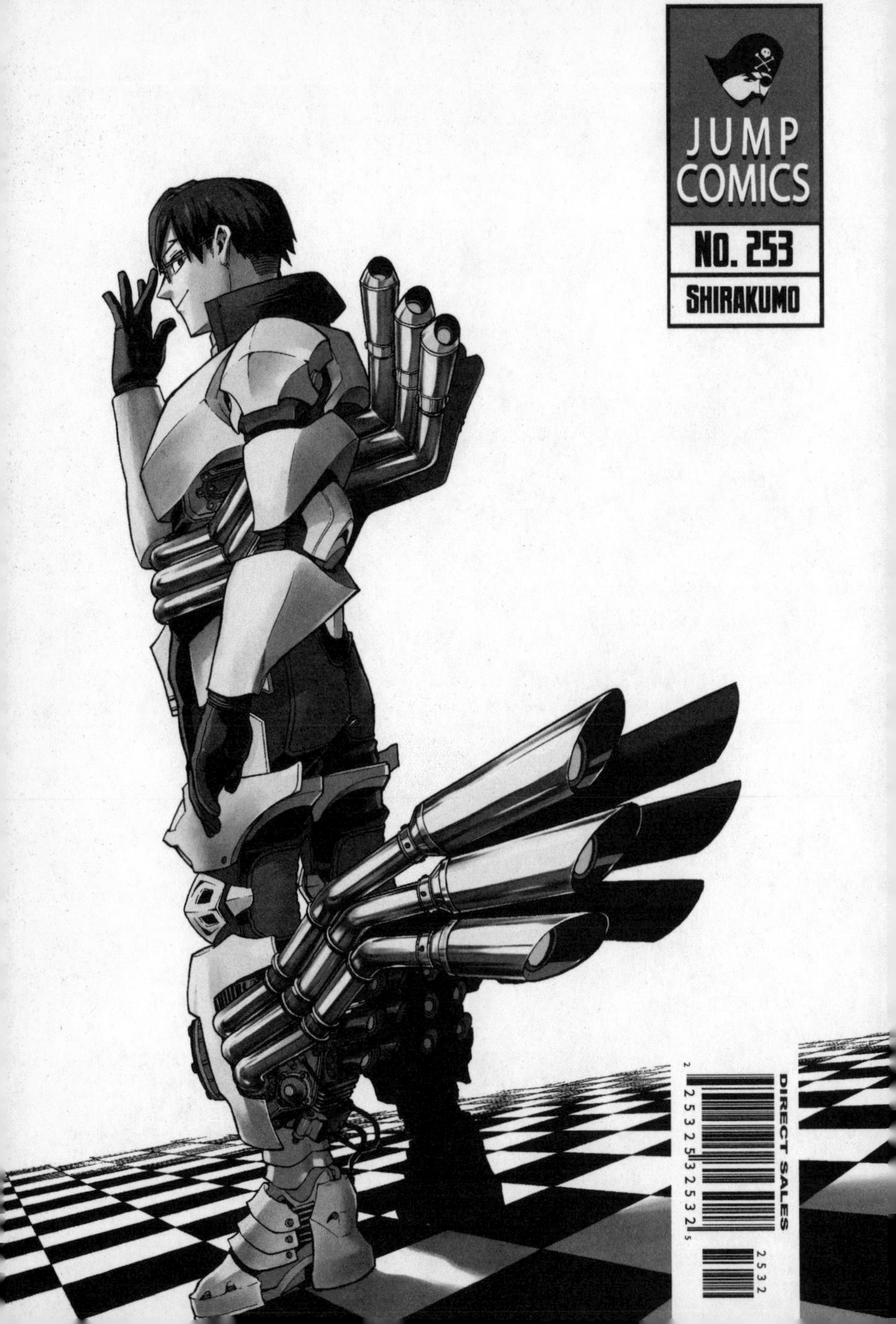
JUMP COMICS
NO. 253
SHIRAKUMO
DIRECT SALES

MY HERO
ACADEMIA

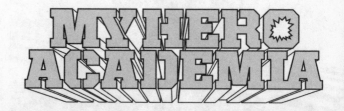

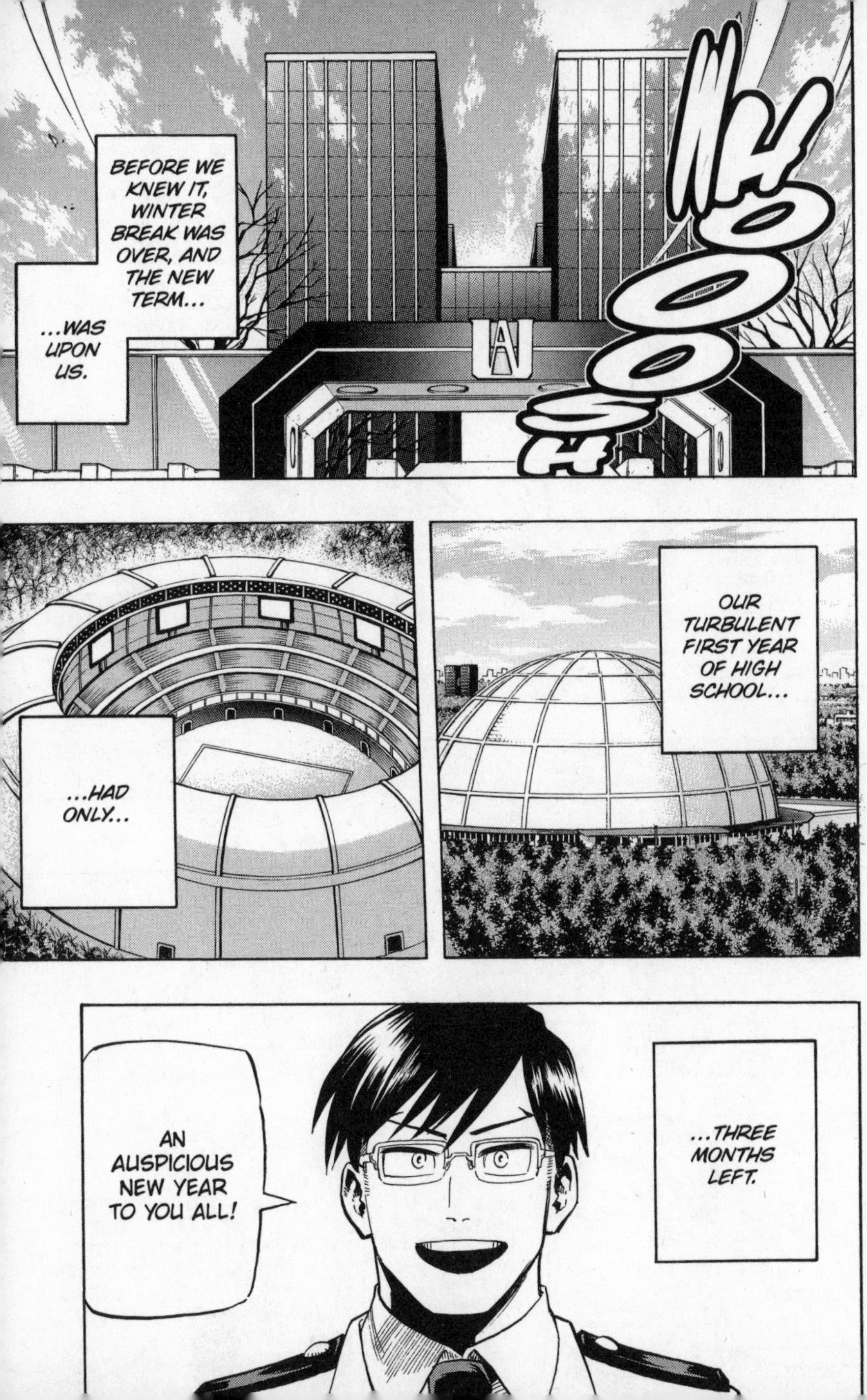
BEFORE WE KNEW IT, WINTER BREAK WAS OVER, AND THE NEW TERM...
...WAS UPON US.
WHOOSH
OUR TURBULENT FIRST YEAR OF HIGH SCHOOL...
...HAD ONLY...
...THREE MONTHS LEFT.
AN AUSPICIOUS NEW YEAR TO YOU ALL!

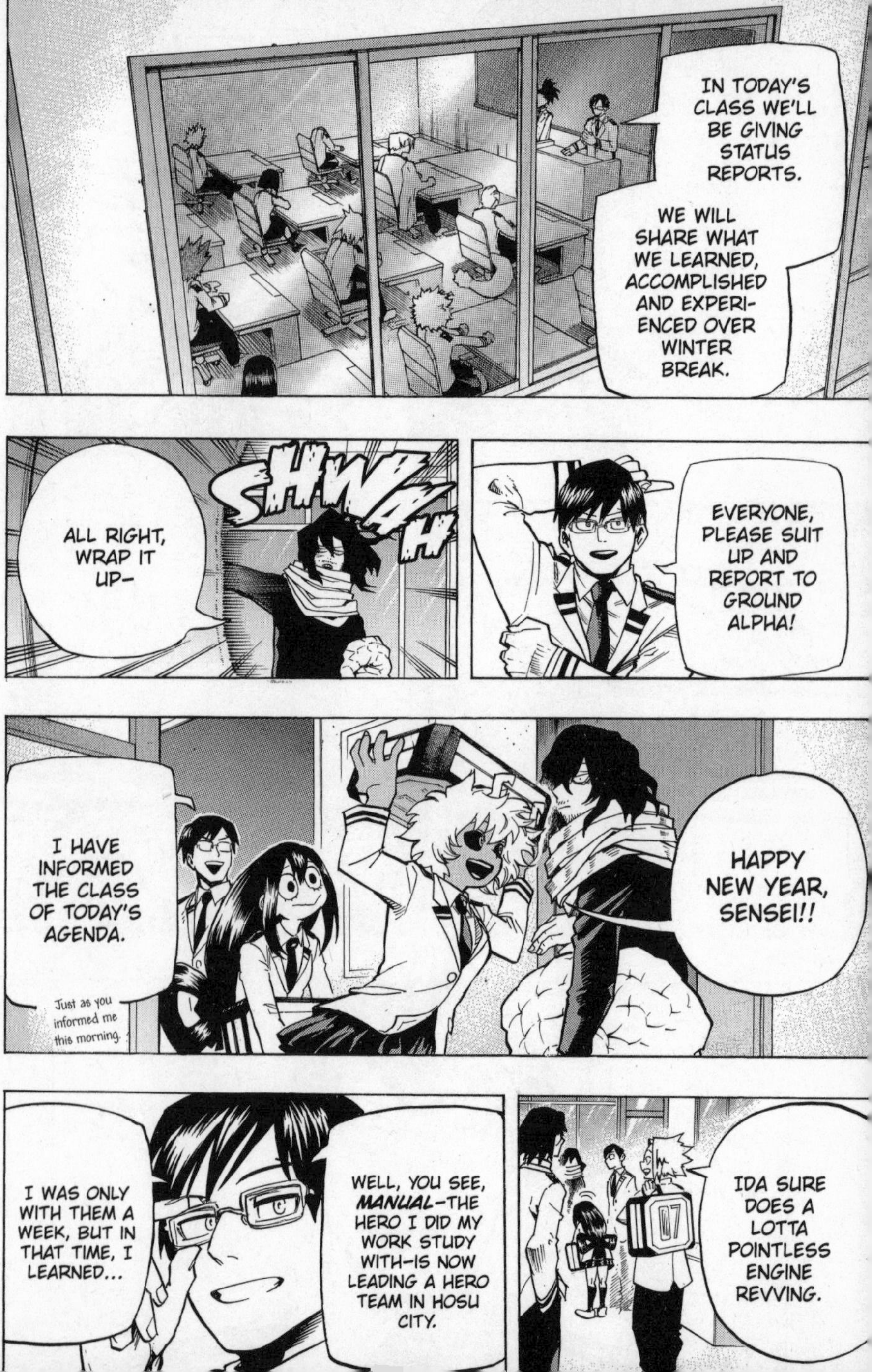
IN TODAY'S CLASS WE'LL BE GIVING STATUS REPORTS.
WE WILL SHARE WHAT WE LEARNED, ACCOMPLISHED AND EXPERIENCED OVER WINTER BREAK.
EVERYONE, PLEASE SUIT UP AND REPORT TO GROUND ALPHA!
SHWAAH
ALL RIGHT, WRAP IT UP–
HAPPY NEW YEAR, SENSEI!!
I HAVE INFORMED THE CLASS OF TODAY'S AGENDA.
Just as you informed me this morning.
IDA SURE DOES A LOTTA POINTLESS ENGINE REVVING.
07
WELL, YOU SEE, ***MANUAL***–THE HERO I DID MY WORK STUDY WITH–IS NOW LEADING A HERO TEAM IN HOSU CITY.
I WAS ONLY WITH THEM A WEEK, BUT IN THAT TIME, I LEARNED...

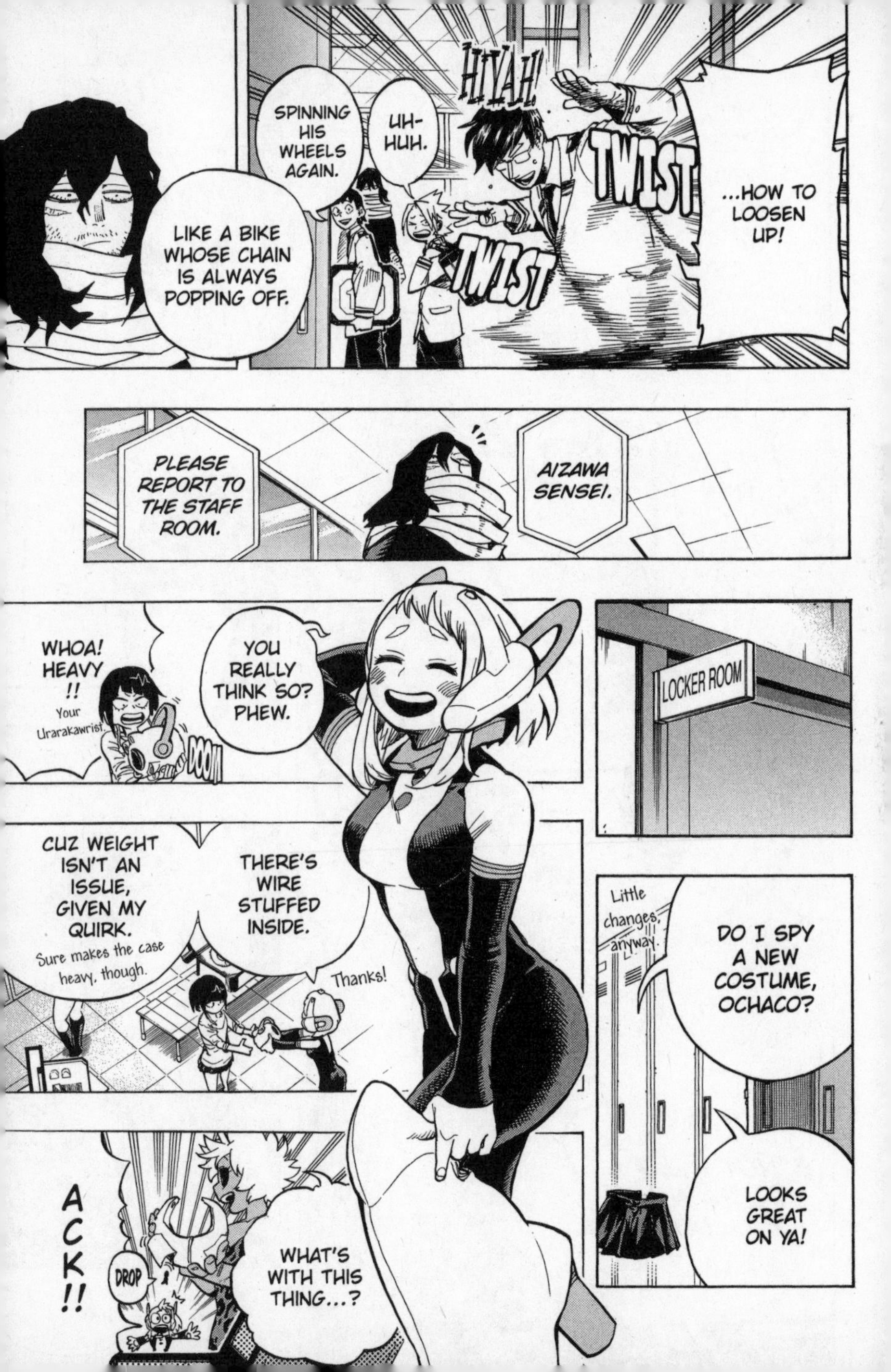
...HOW TO LOOSEN UP!
HIYAH!
TWIST
TWIST
UH-HUH.
SPINNING HIS WHEELS AGAIN.
LIKE A BIKE WHOSE CHAIN IS ALWAYS POPPING OFF.
AIZAWA SENSEI.
PLEASE REPORT TO THE STAFF ROOM.
LOCKER ROOM
DO I SPY A NEW COSTUME, OCHACO?
Little changes, anyway.
LOOKS GREAT ON YA!
YOU REALLY THINK SO? PHEW.
WHAT'S WITH THIS THING...?
WHOA! HEAVY!!
Your Urarakawrist.
DOOM
THERE'S WIRE STUFFED INSIDE.
CUZ WEIGHT ISN'T AN ISSUE, GIVEN MY QUIRK.
Sure makes the case heavy, though.
Thanks!
ACK!!
DROP

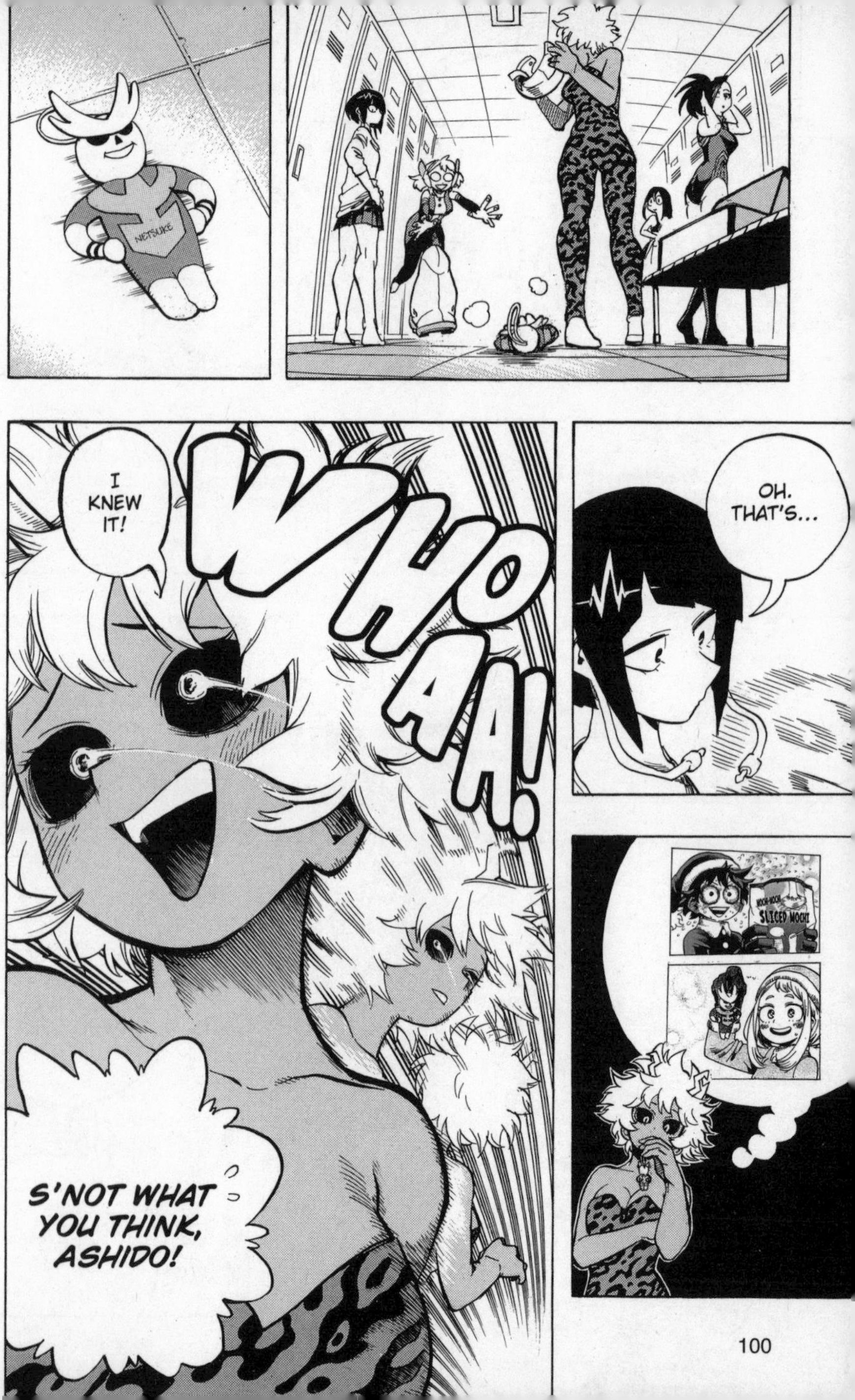
NETSUKE
OH. THAT'S...
SLICED MOCHI
I KNEW IT!
WHOAA!
S'NOT WHAT YOU THINK, ASHIDO!

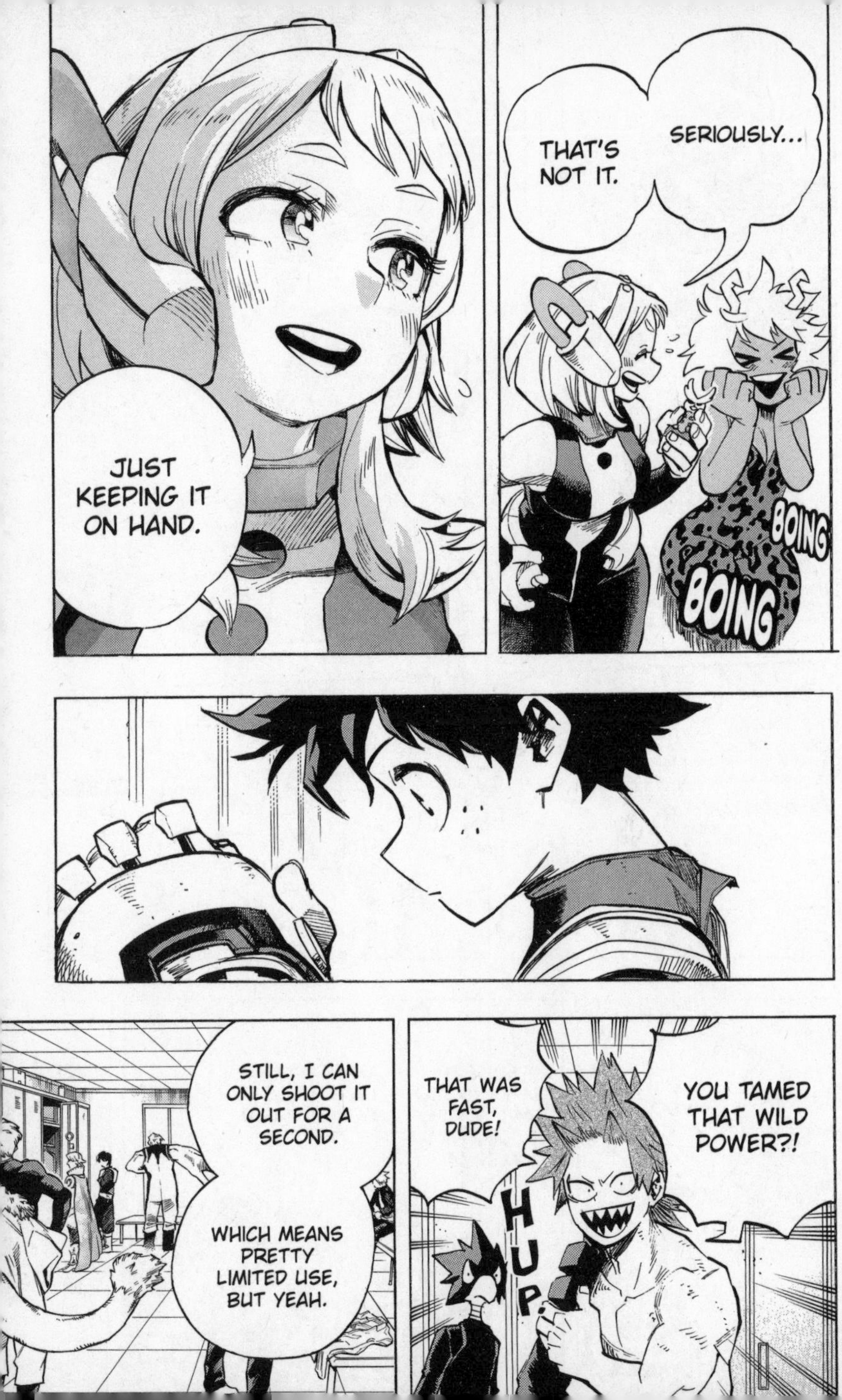
SERIOUSLY...
THAT'S NOT IT.
BOING
BOING
JUST KEEPING IT ON HAND.
YOU TAMED THAT WILD POWER?!
THAT WAS FAST, DUDE!
HUP.
STILL, I CAN ONLY SHOOT IT OUT FOR A SECOND.
WHICH MEANS PRETTY LIMITED USE, BUT YEAH.

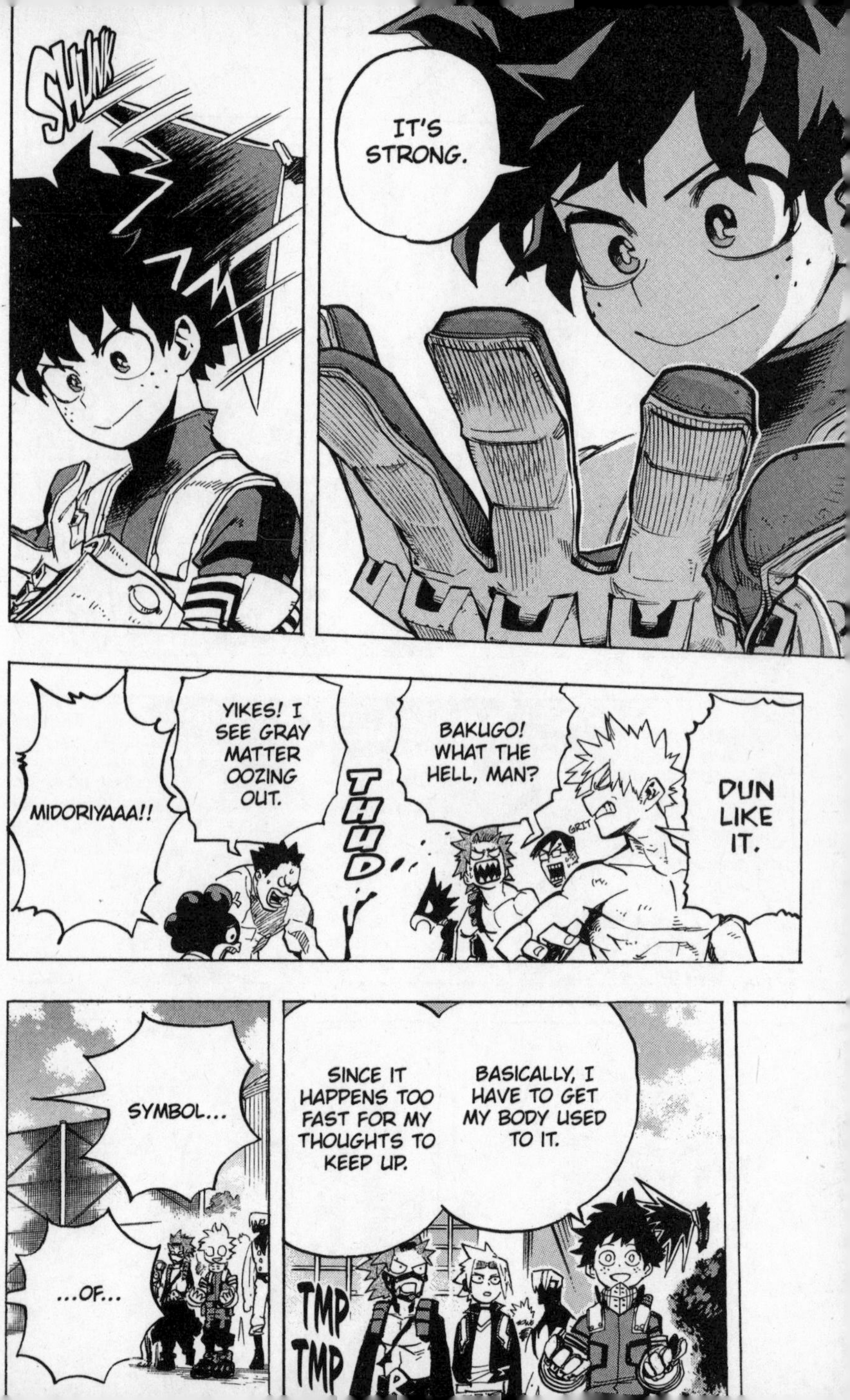

IT'S STRONG.
SHUNK
DUN LIKE IT.
BAKUGO! WHAT THE HELL, MAN?
GRIT
THUD
YIKES! I SEE GRAY MATTER OOZING OUT.
MIDORIYAAA!!
BASICALLY, I HAVE TO GET MY BODY USED TO IT.
SINCE IT HAPPENS TOO FAST FOR MY THOUGHTS TO KEEP UP.
TMP TMP
SYMBOL...
...OF...

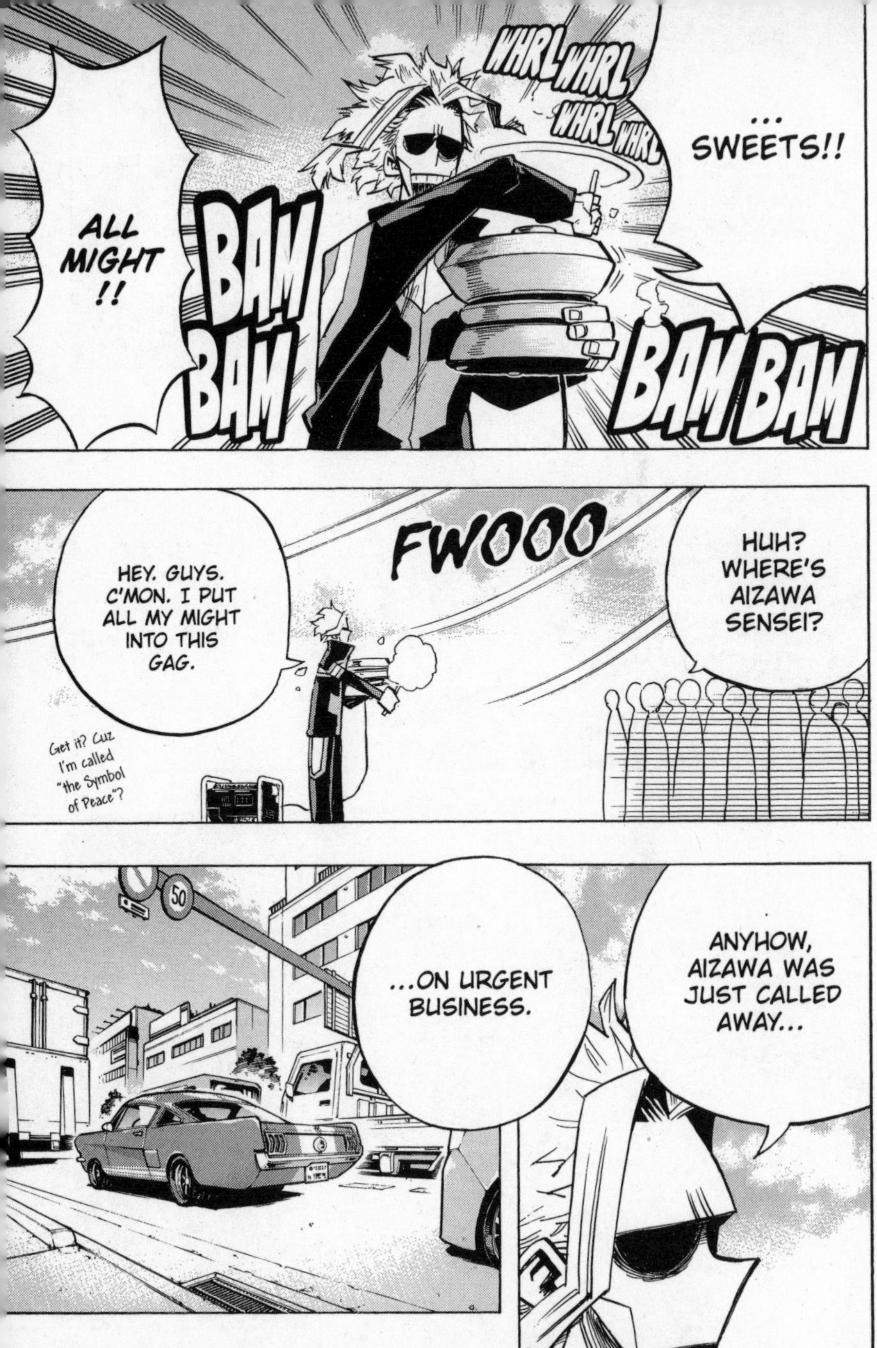
WHRL WHRL WHRL WHRL
...SWEETS!!
BAM BAM
ALL MIGHT !!
BAM BAM
HUH? WHERE'S AIZAWA SENSEI?
FWOOO
HEY. GUYS. C'MON. I PUT ALL MY MIGHT INTO THIS GAG.
Get it? Cuz I'm called "the Symbol of Peace"?
ANYHOW, AIZAWA WAS JUST CALLED AWAY...
...ON URGENT BUSINESS.
50

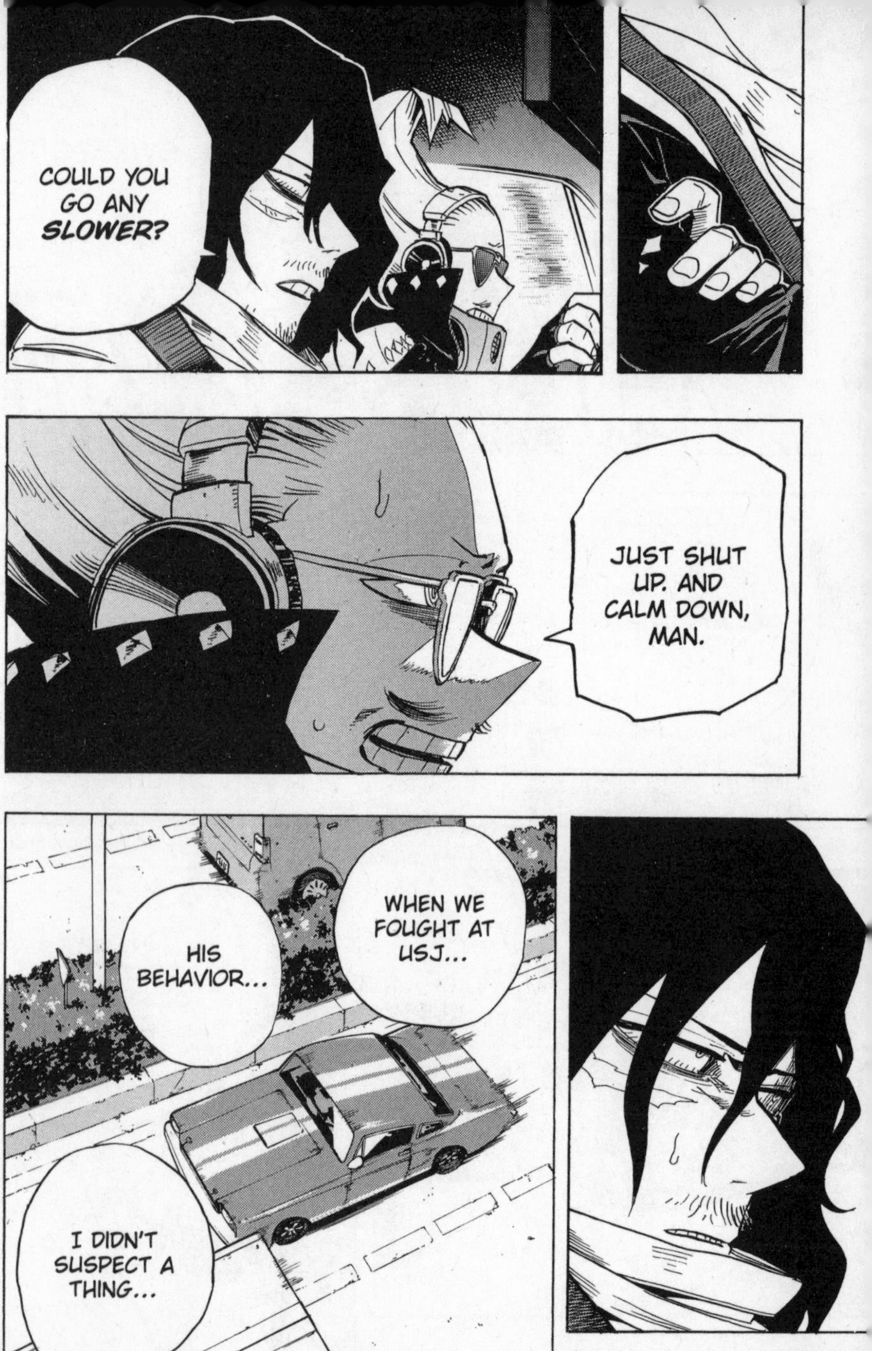
COULD YOU GO ANY SLOWER?
JUST SHUT UP. AND CALM DOWN, MAN.
WHEN WE FOUGHT AT USJ...
HIS BEHAVIOR...
I DIDN'T SUSPECT A THING...

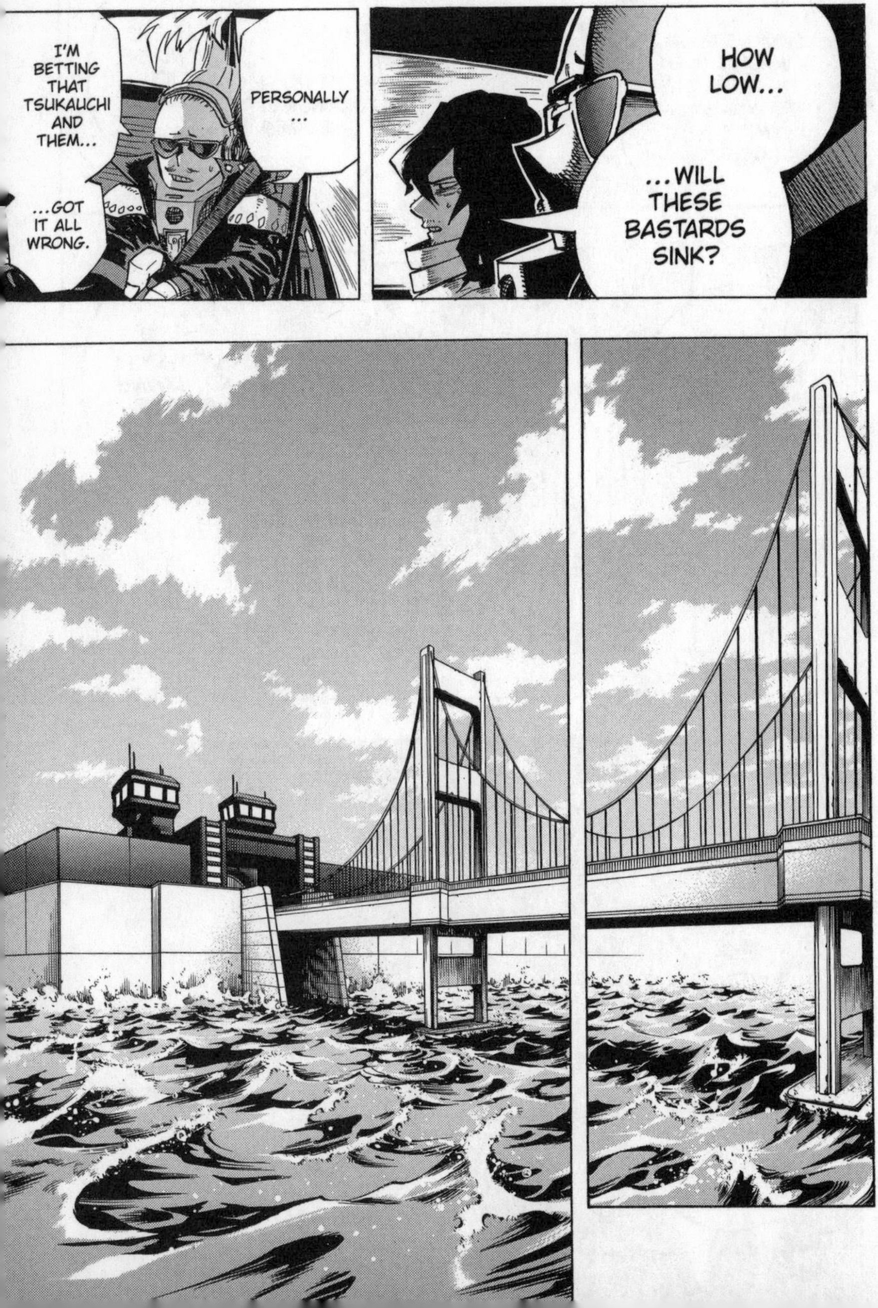
HOW LOW...
...WILL THESE BASTARDS SINK?
PERSONALLY...
I'M BETTING THAT TSUKAUCHI AND THEM...
...GOT IT ALL WRONG.

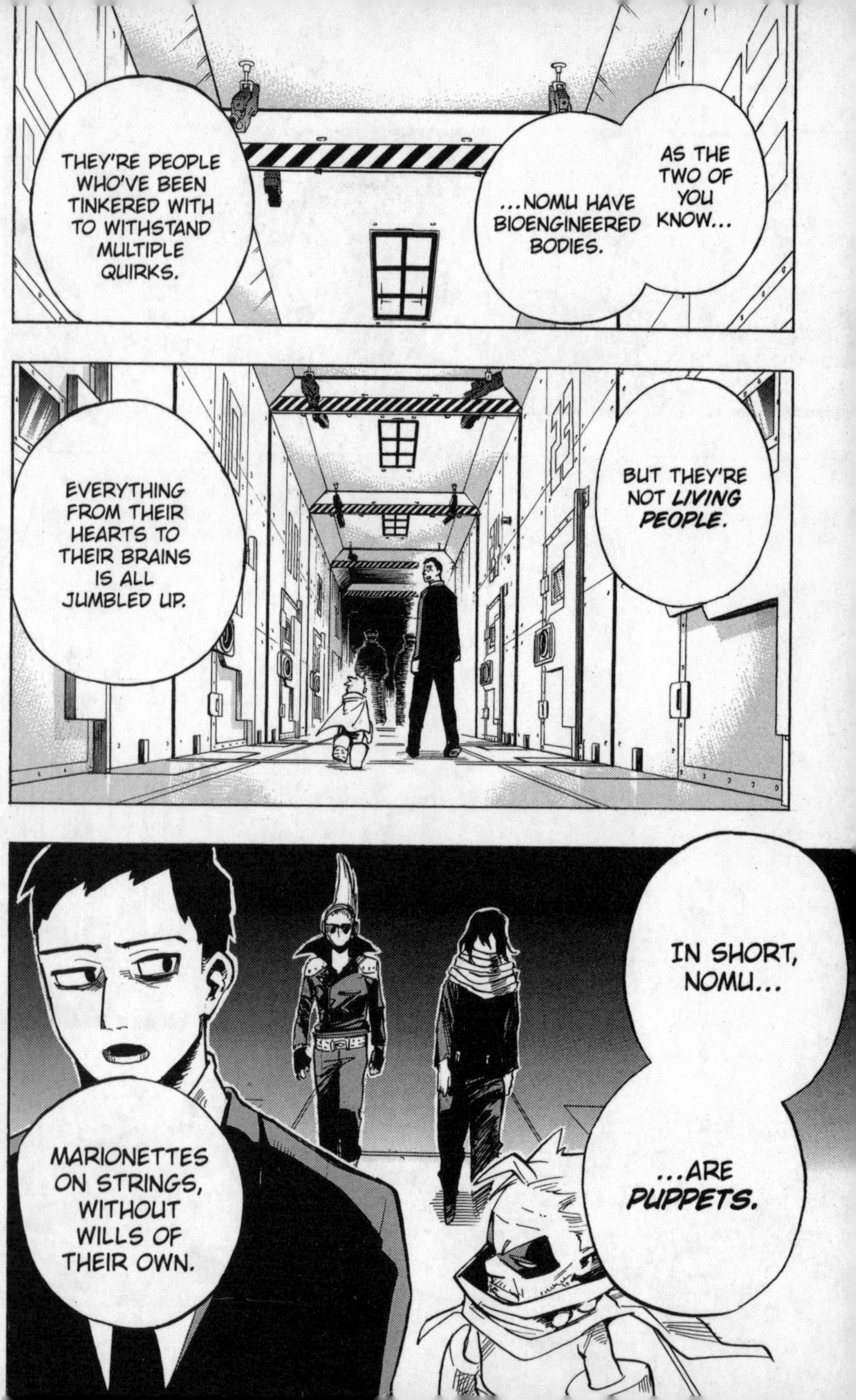
AS THE TWO OF YOU KNOW...
...NOMU HAVE BIOENGINEERED BODIES.
THEY'RE PEOPLE WHO'VE BEEN TINKERED WITH TO WITHSTAND MULTIPLE QUIRKS.
BUT THEY'RE NOT *LIVING PEOPLE*.
EVERYTHING FROM THEIR HEARTS TO THEIR BRAINS IS ALL JUMBLED UP.
IN SHORT, NOMU...
...ARE *PUPPETS*.
MARIONETTES ON STRINGS, WITHOUT WILLS OF THEIR OWN.

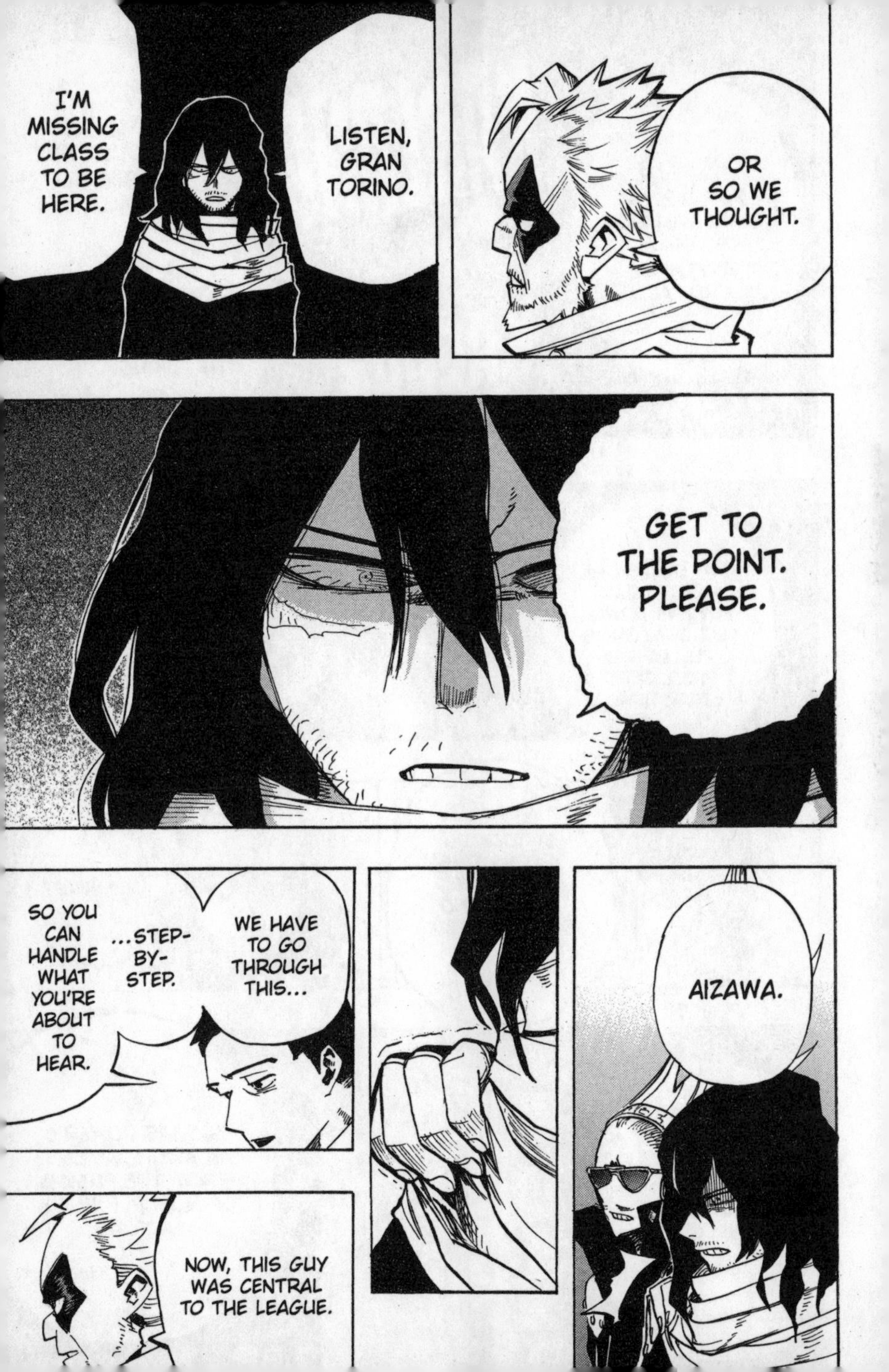
OR SO WE THOUGHT.
LISTEN, GRAN TORINO.
I'M MISSING CLASS TO BE HERE.
GET TO THE POINT. PLEASE.
AIZAWA.
WE HAVE TO GO THROUGH THIS...
...STEP-BY-STEP.
SO YOU CAN HANDLE WHAT YOU'RE ABOUT TO HEAR.
NOW, THIS GUY WAS CENTRAL TO THE LEAGUE.

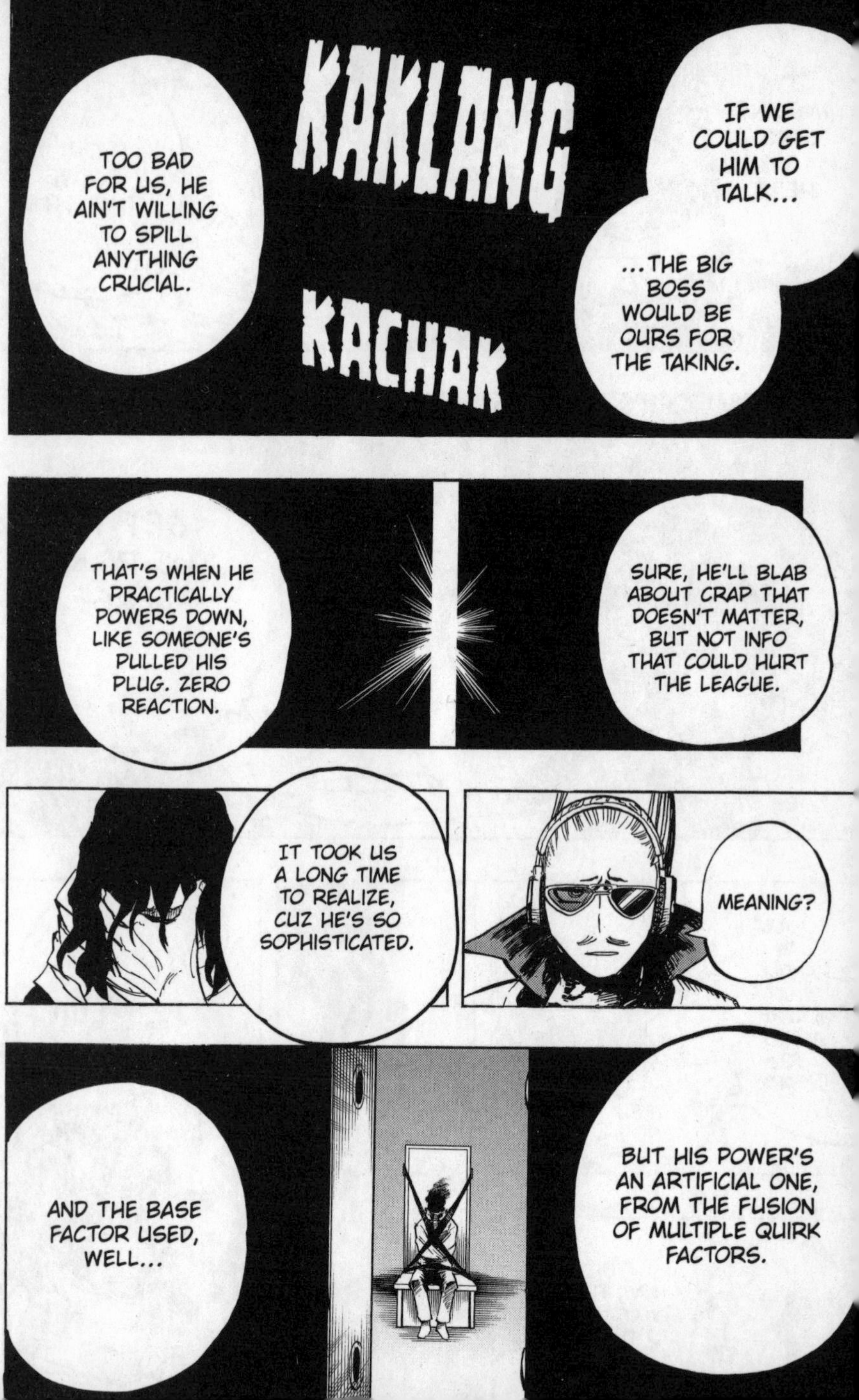
IF WE COULD GET HIM TO TALK...
...THE BIG BOSS WOULD BE OURS FOR THE TAKING.
KAKLANG
KACHAK
TOO BAD FOR US, HE AIN'T WILLING TO SPILL ANYTHING CRUCIAL.
SURE, HE'LL BLAB ABOUT CRAP THAT DOESN'T MATTER, BUT NOT INFO THAT COULD HURT THE LEAGUE.
THAT'S WHEN HE PRACTICALLY POWERS DOWN, LIKE SOMEONE'S PULLED HIS PLUG. ZERO REACTION.
MEANING?
IT TOOK US A LONG TIME TO REALIZE, CUZ HE'S SO SOPHISTICATED.
BUT HIS POWER'S AN ARTIFICIAL ONE, FROM THE FUSION OF MULTIPLE QUIRK FACTORS.
AND THE BASE FACTOR USED, WELL...

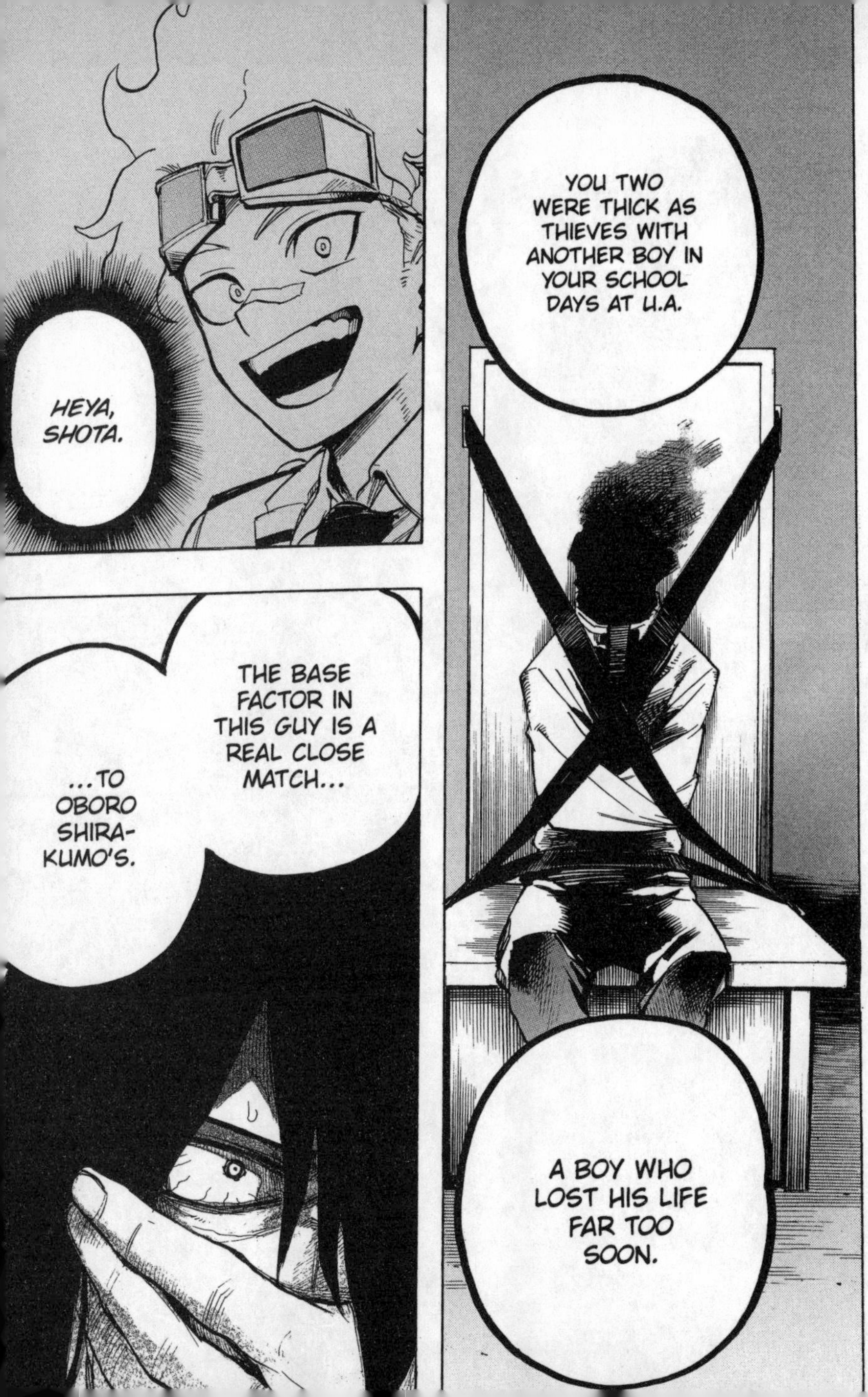
YOU TWO WERE THICK AS THIEVES WITH ANOTHER BOY IN YOUR SCHOOL DAYS AT U.A.
A BOY WHO LOST HIS LIFE FAR TOO SOON.
HEYA, SHOTA.
THE BASE FACTOR IN THIS GUY IS A REAL CLOSE MATCH...
...TO OBORO SHIRA-KUMO'S.

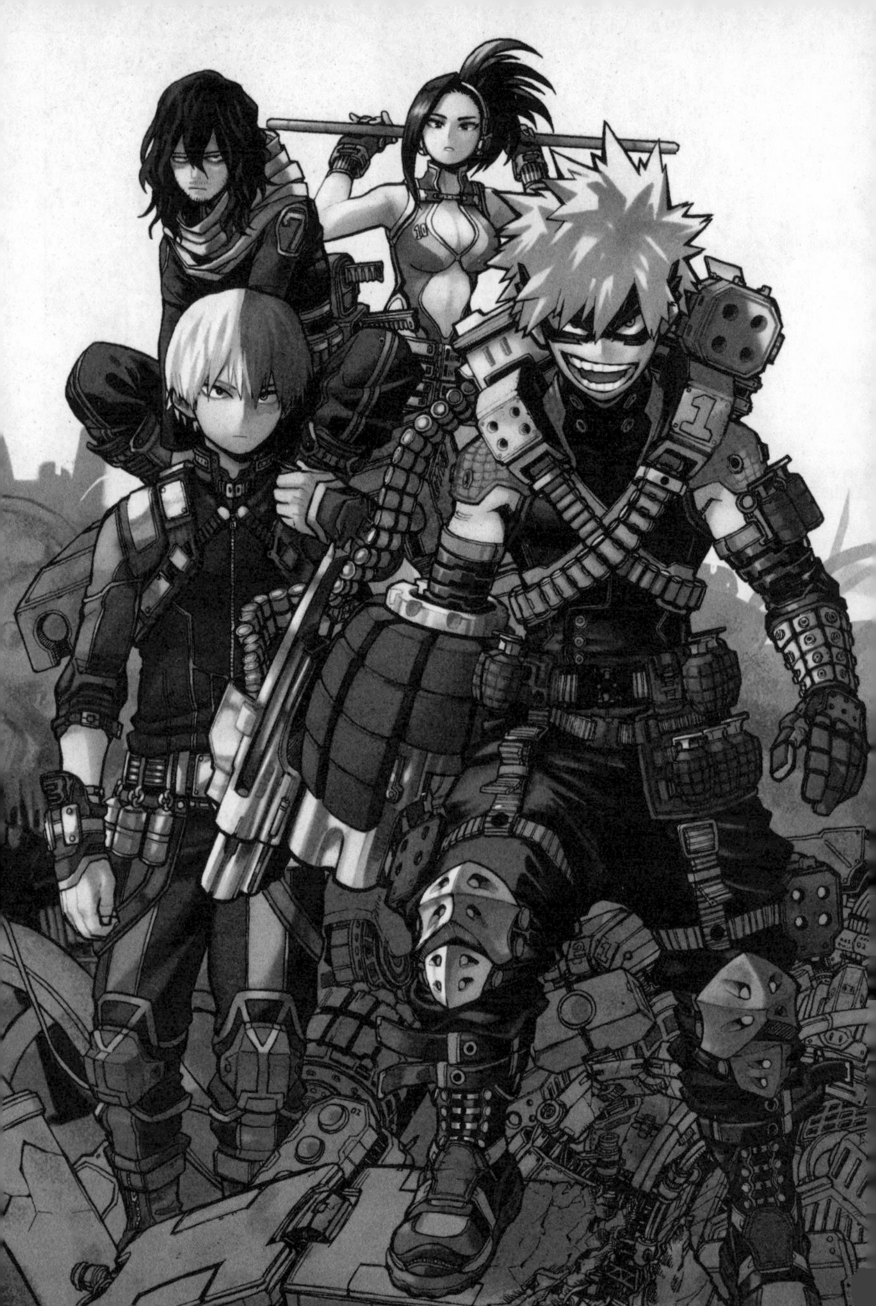

No. 254 - More of a Hero Than Anyone

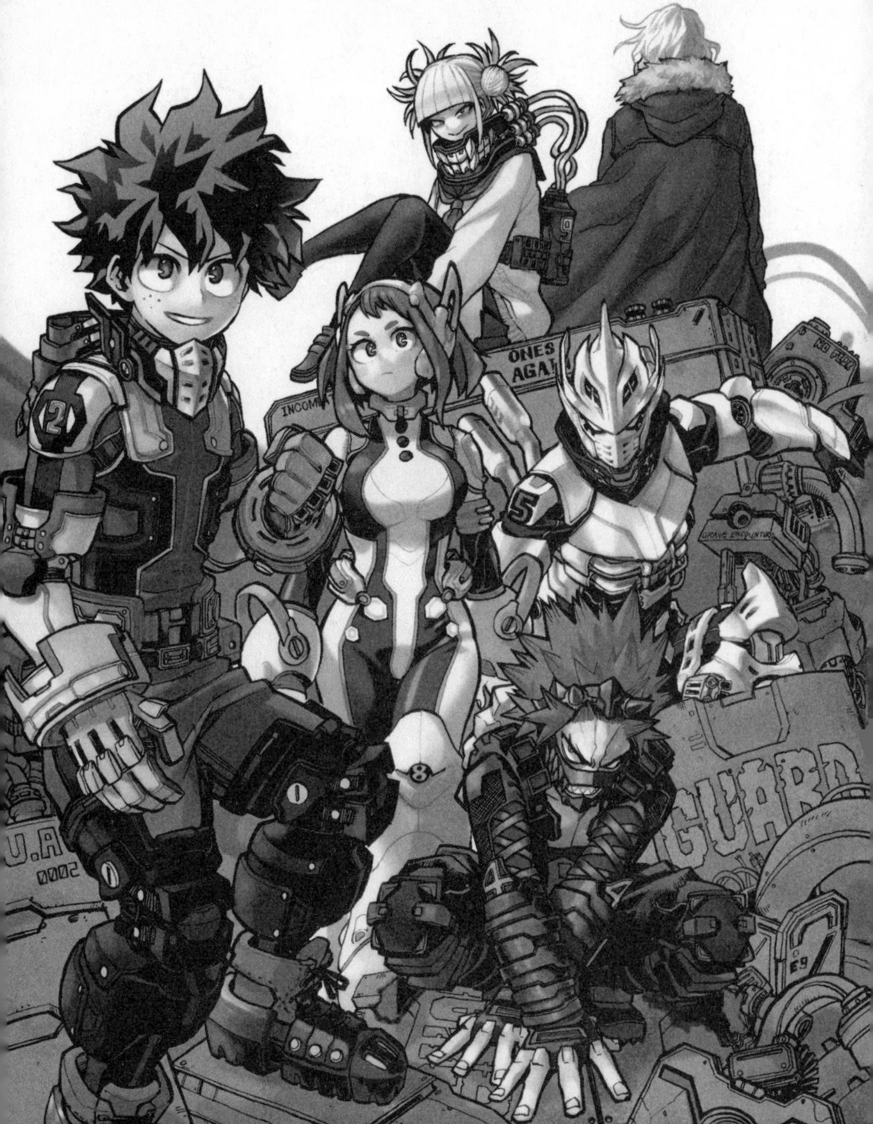
GUARD
U.A
0002
NO FEAR
CAUTION

MY HERO
ACADEMIA

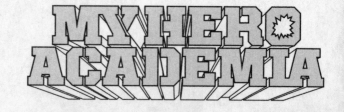

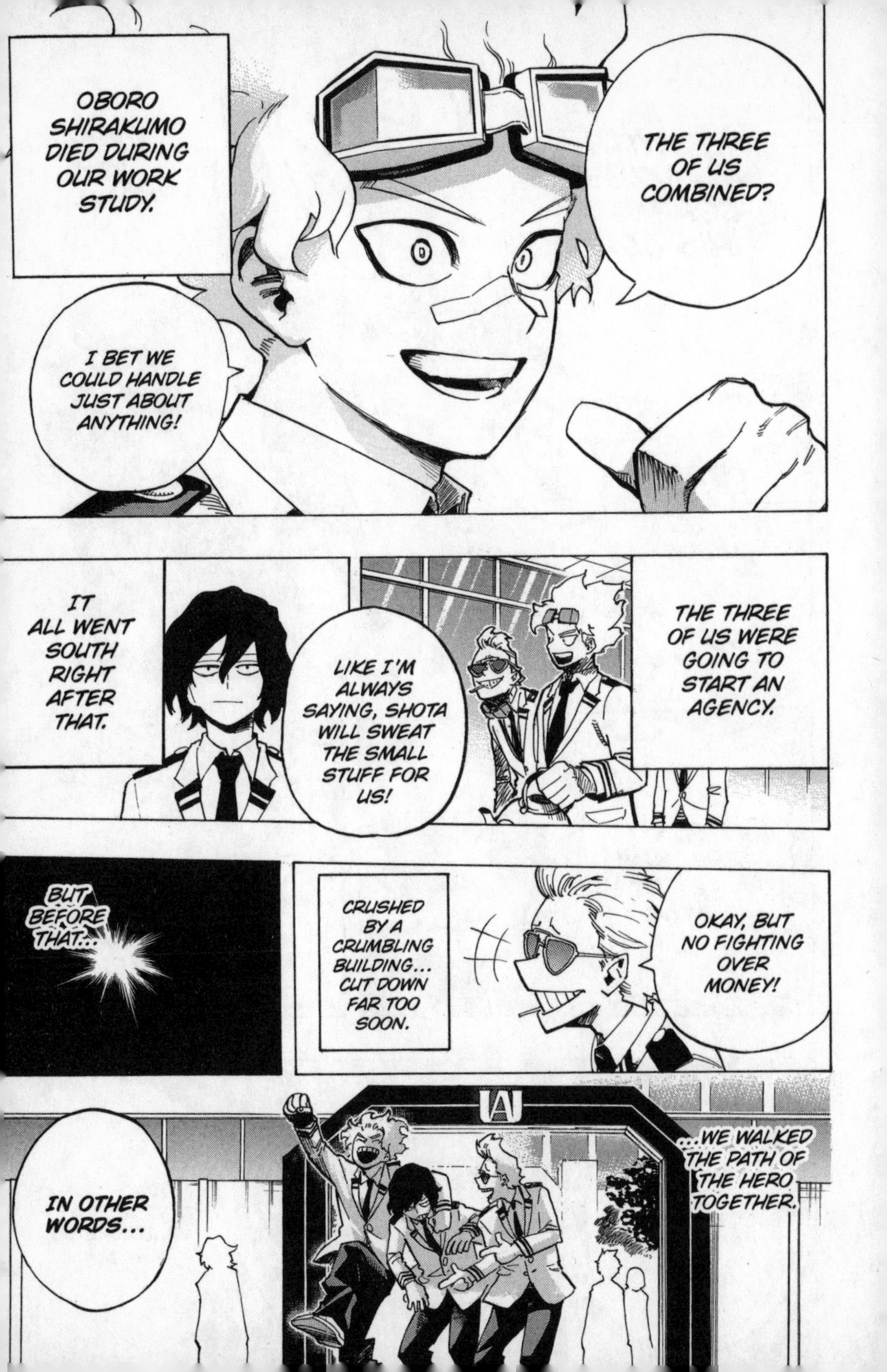
THE THREE OF US COMBINED?
OBORO SHIRAKUMO DIED DURING OUR WORK STUDY.
I BET WE COULD HANDLE JUST ABOUT ANYTHING!
THE THREE OF US WERE GOING TO START AN AGENCY.
LIKE I'M ALWAYS SAYING, SHOTA WILL SWEAT THE SMALL STUFF FOR US!
IT ALL WENT SOUTH RIGHT AFTER THAT.
OKAY, BUT NO FIGHTING OVER MONEY!
CRUSHED BY A CRUMBLING BUILDING... CUT DOWN FAR TOO SOON.
BUT BEFORE THAT...
...WE WALKED THE PATH OF THE HERO TOGETHER.
IN OTHER WORDS...

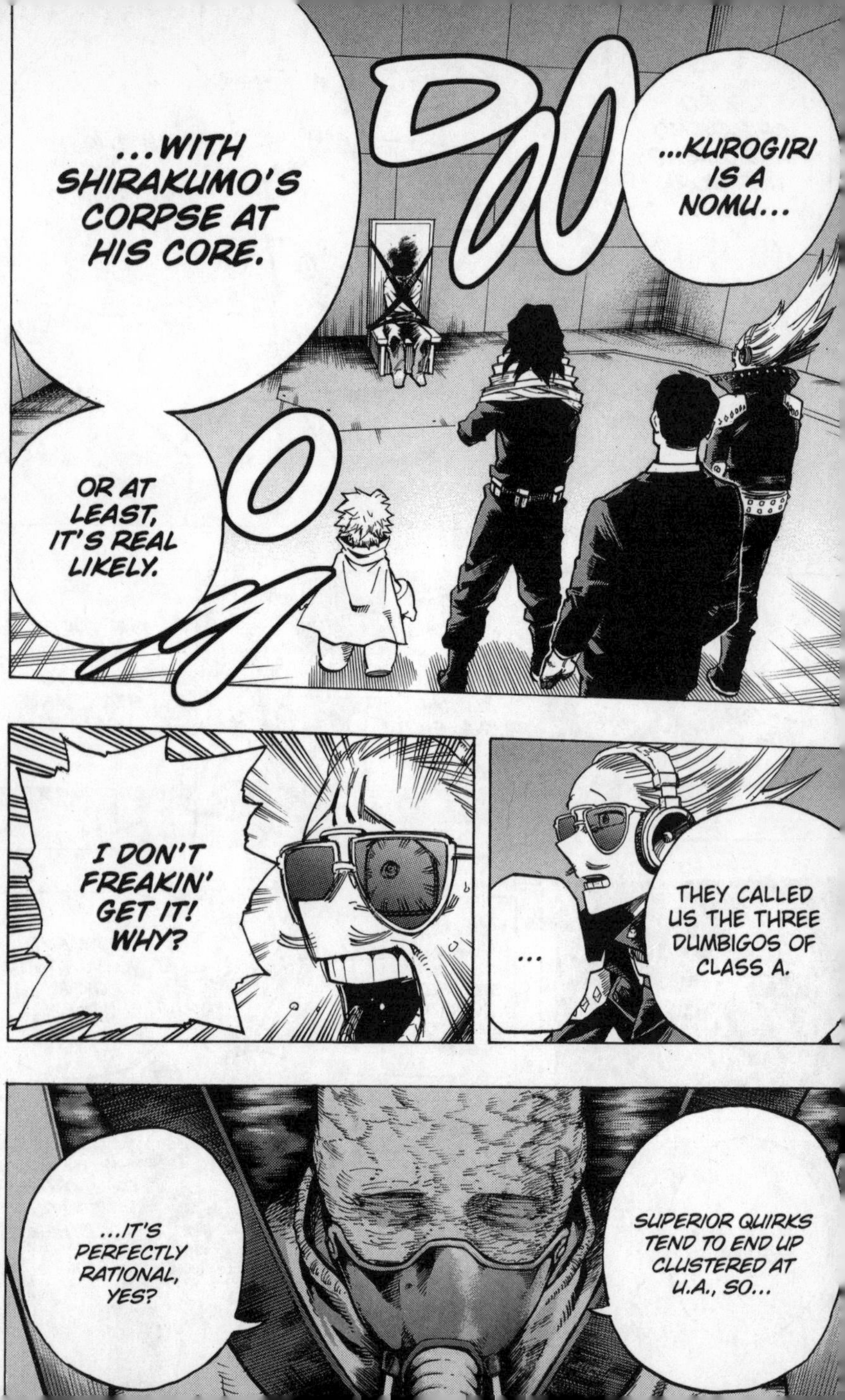
...KUROGIRI IS A NOMU...
...WITH SHIRAKUMO'S CORPSE AT HIS CORE.
OR AT LEAST, IT'S REAL LIKELY.
THEY CALLED US THE THREE DUMBIGOS OF CLASS A.
...
I DON'T FREAKIN' GET IT! WHY?
SUPERIOR QUIRKS TEND TO END UP CLUSTERED AT U.A., SO...
...IT'S PERFECTLY RATIONAL, YES?

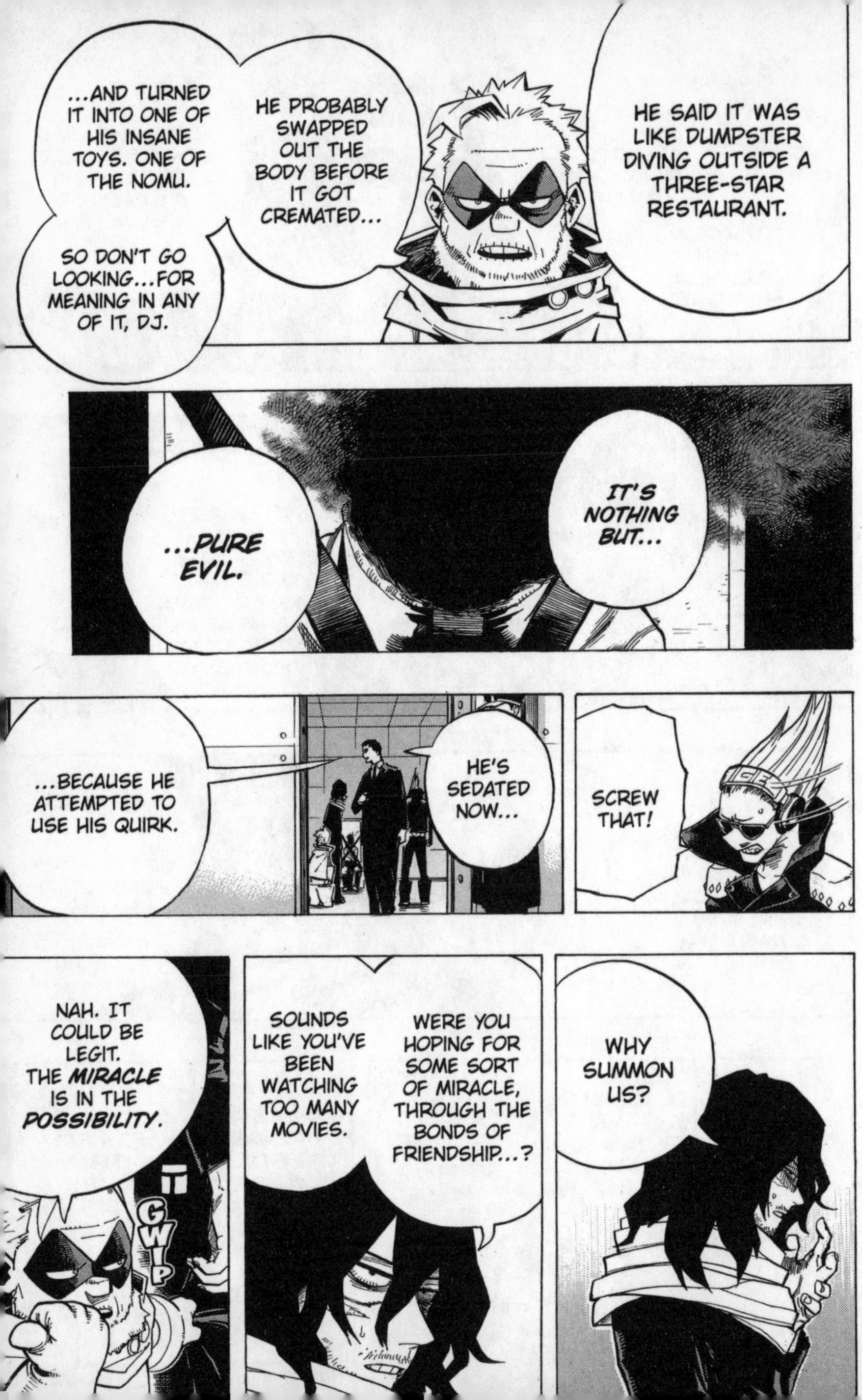
HE SAID IT WAS LIKE DUMPSTER DIVING OUTSIDE A THREE-STAR RESTAURANT.
HE PROBABLY SWAPPED OUT THE BODY BEFORE IT GOT CREMATED...
...AND TURNED IT INTO ONE OF HIS INSANE TOYS. ONE OF THE NOMU.
SO DON'T GO LOOKING...FOR MEANING IN ANY OF IT, DJ.
IT'S NOTHING BUT...
...PURE EVIL.
SCREW THAT!
HE'S SEDATED NOW...
...BECAUSE HE ATTEMPTED TO USE HIS QUIRK.
WHY SUMMON US?
WERE YOU HOPING FOR SOME SORT OF MIRACLE, THROUGH THE BONDS OF FRIENDSHIP...?
SOUNDS LIKE YOU'VE BEEN WATCHING TOO MANY MOVIES.
NAH. IT COULD BE LEGIT. THE ***MIRACLE*** IS IN THE ***POSSIBILITY***.
GWIP

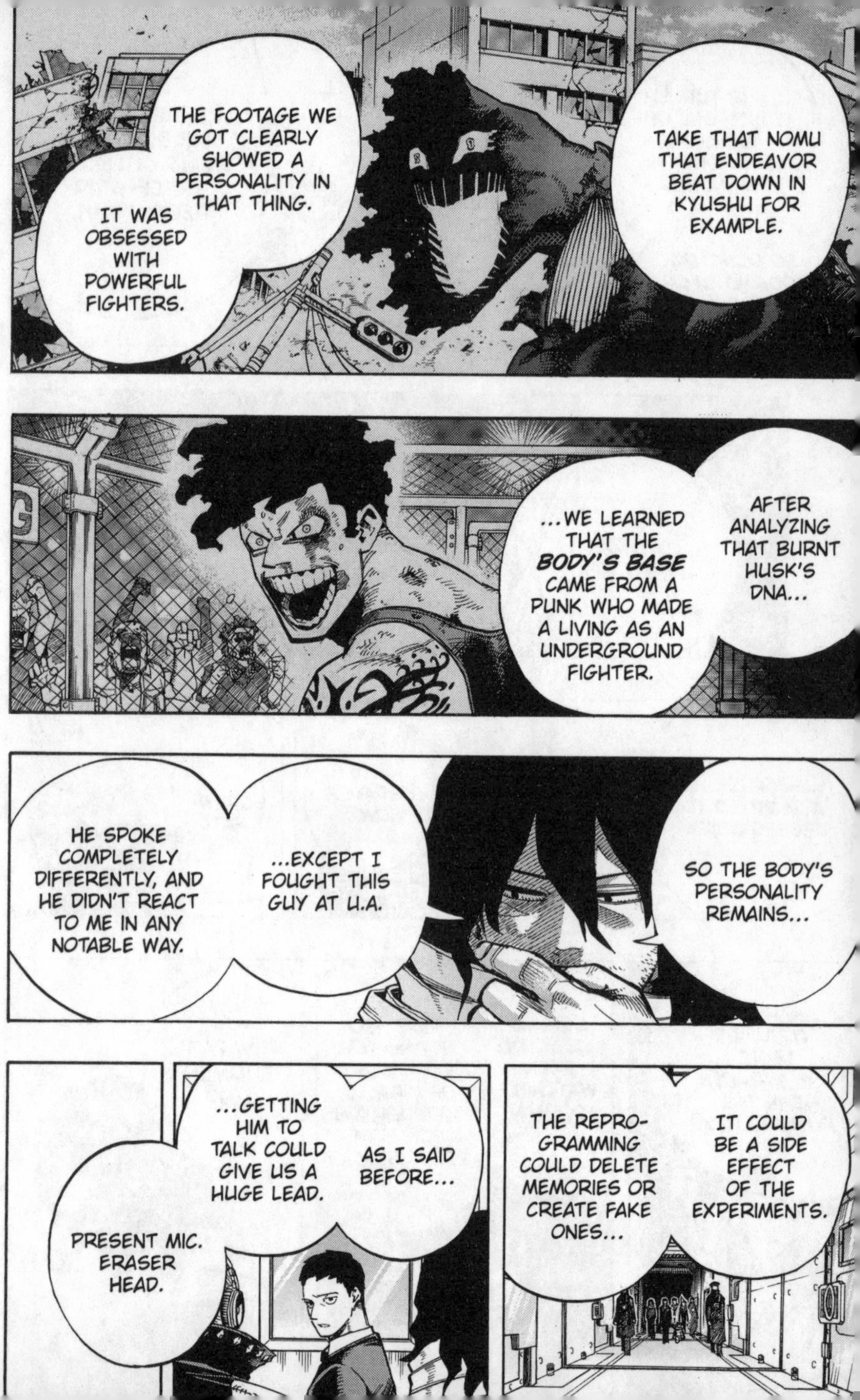
TAKE THAT NOMU THAT ENDEAVOR BEAT DOWN IN KYUSHU FOR EXAMPLE.
THE FOOTAGE WE GOT CLEARLY SHOWED A PERSONALITY IN THAT THING.
IT WAS OBSESSED WITH POWERFUL FIGHTERS.
AFTER ANALYZING THAT BURNT HUSK'S DNA...
...WE LEARNED THAT THE *BODY'S BASE* CAME FROM A PUNK WHO MADE A LIVING AS AN UNDERGROUND FIGHTER.
SO THE BODY'S PERSONALITY REMAINS...
...EXCEPT I FOUGHT THIS GUY AT U.A.
HE SPOKE COMPLETELY DIFFERENTLY, AND HE DIDN'T REACT TO ME IN ANY NOTABLE WAY.
IT COULD BE A SIDE EFFECT OF THE EXPERIMENTS.
THE REPRO-GRAMMING COULD DELETE MEMORIES OR CREATE FAKE ONES...
AS I SAID BEFORE...
...GETTING HIM TO TALK COULD GIVE US A HUGE LEAD.
PRESENT MIC. ERASER HEAD.

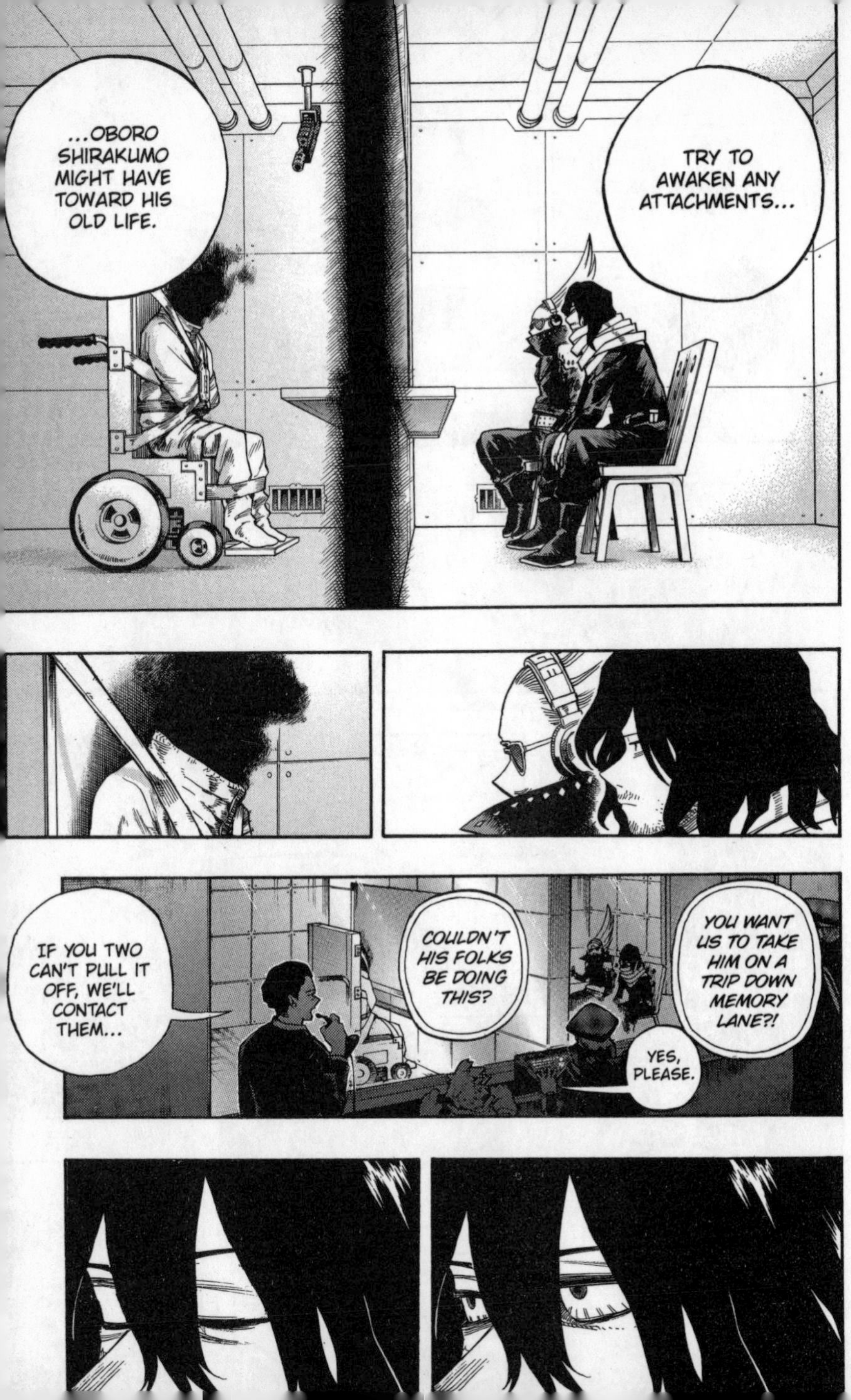
TRY TO AWAKEN ANY ATTACHMENTS...
...OBORO SHIRAKUMO MIGHT HAVE TOWARD HIS OLD LIFE.
YOU WANT US TO TAKE HIM ON A TRIP DOWN MEMORY LANE?!
YES, PLEASE.
COULDN'T HIS FOLKS BE DOING THIS?
IF YOU TWO CAN'T PULL IT OFF, WE'LL CONTACT THEM...

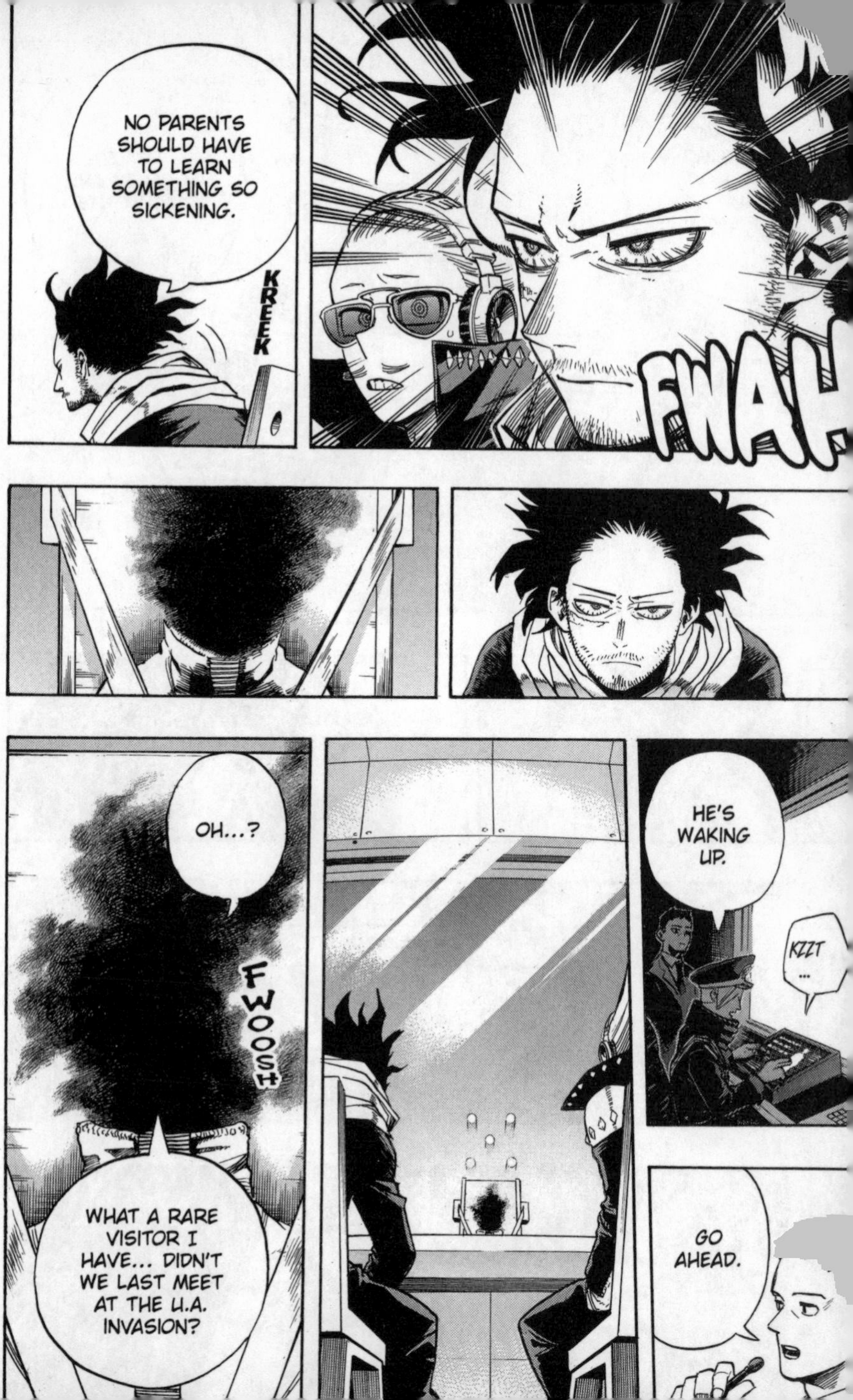
FWAH
NO PARENTS SHOULD HAVE TO LEARN SOMETHING SO SICKENING.
KREEK
HE'S WAKING UP.
KZZT ...
GO AHEAD.
OH...?
FWOOSH
WHAT A RARE VISITOR I HAVE... DIDN'T WE LAST MEET AT THE U.A. INVASION?

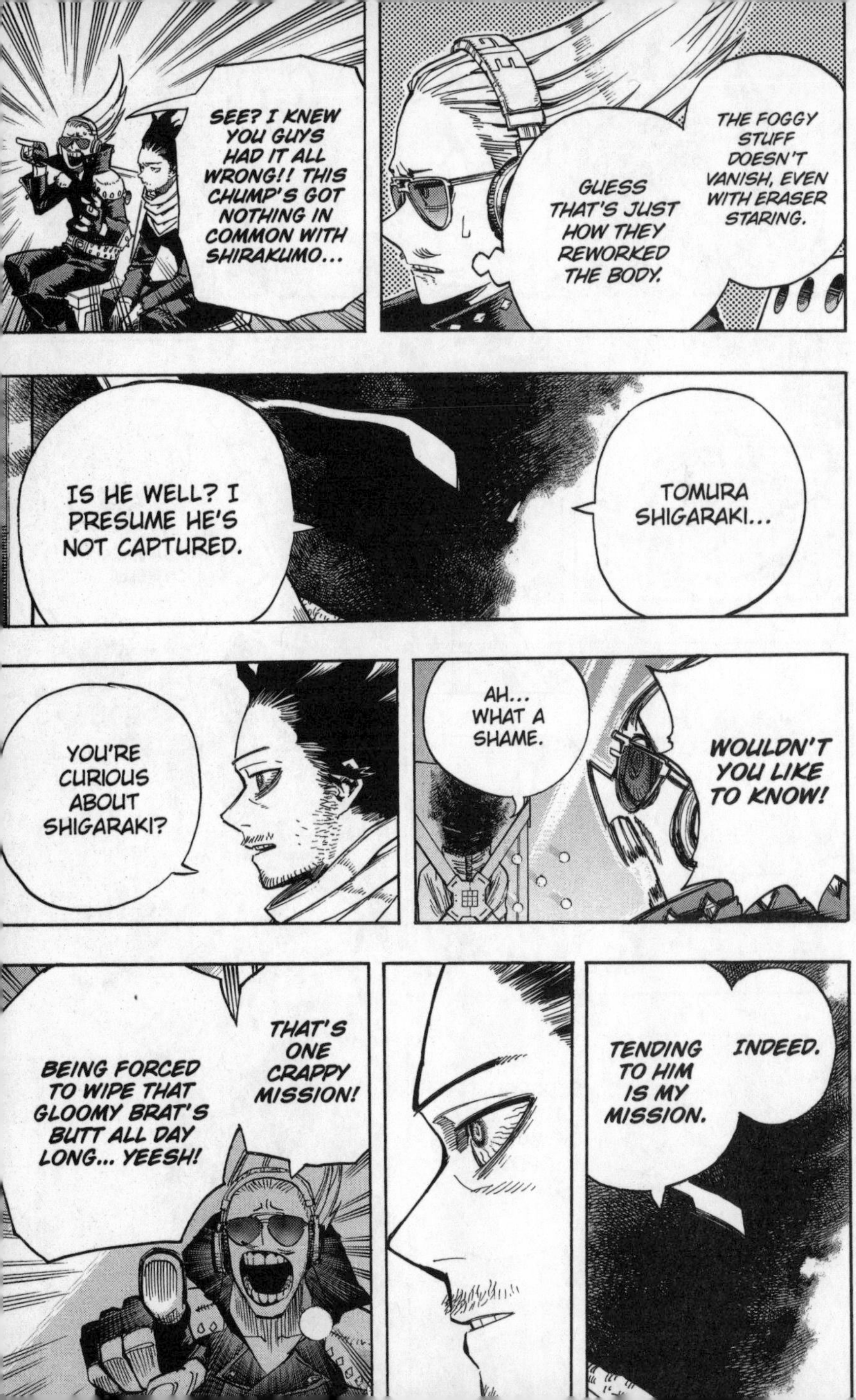
THE FOGGY STUFF DOESN'T VANISH, EVEN WITH ERASER STARING.
GUESS THAT'S JUST HOW THEY REWORKED THE BODY.
SEE? I KNEW YOU GUYS HAD IT ALL WRONG!! THIS CHUMP'S GOT NOTHING IN COMMON WITH SHIRAKUMO...
TOMURA SHIGARAKI...
IS HE WELL? I PRESUME HE'S NOT CAPTURED.
WOULDN'T YOU LIKE TO KNOW!
AH... WHAT A SHAME.
YOU'RE CURIOUS ABOUT SHIGARAKI?
INDEED.
TENDING TO HIM IS MY MISSION.
THAT'S ONE CRAPPY MISSION!
BEING FORCED TO WIPE THAT GLOOMY BRAT'S BUTT ALL DAY LONG... YEESH!

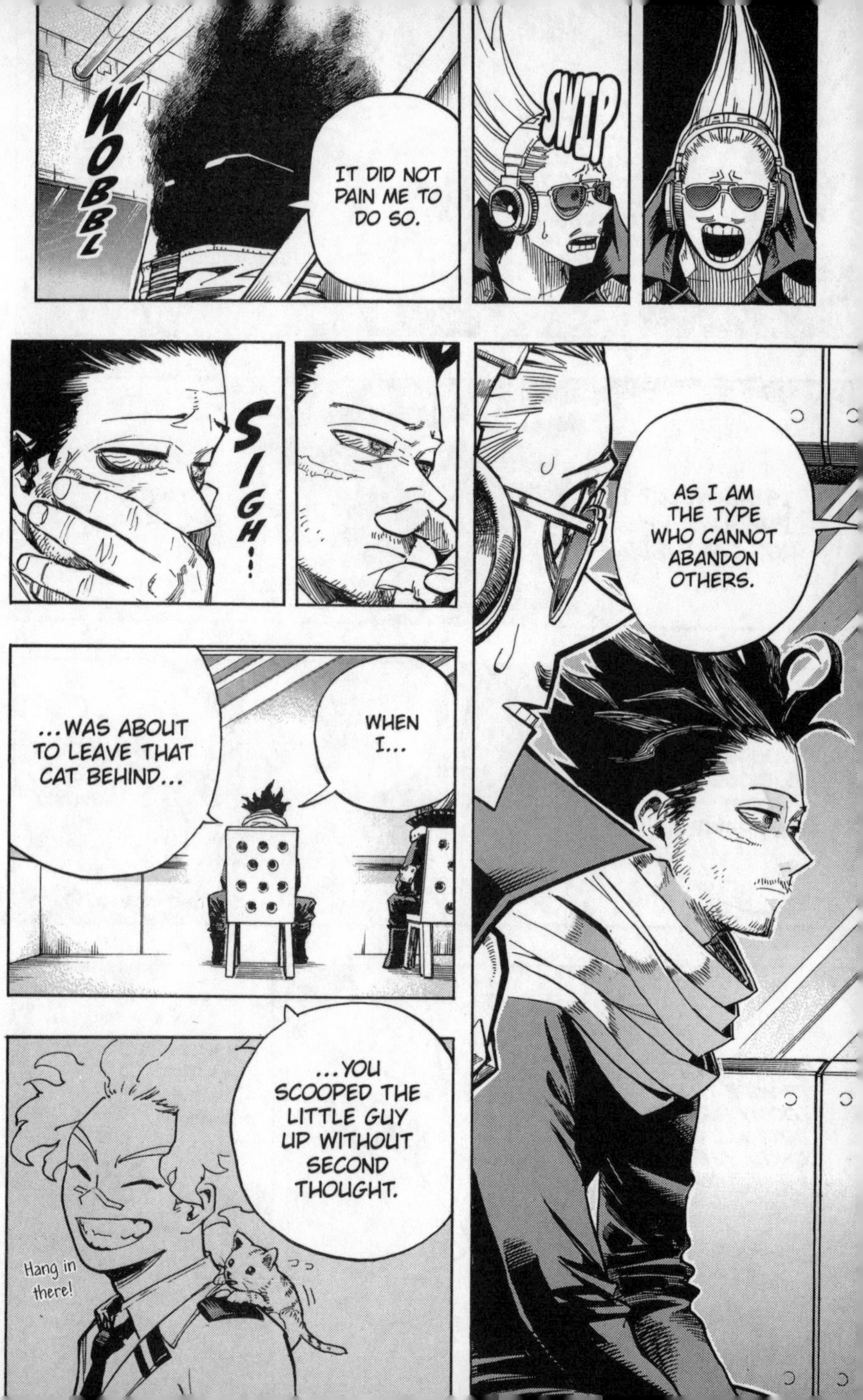
SWIP
WOBBL
IT DID NOT PAIN ME TO DO SO.
AS I AM THE TYPE WHO CANNOT ABANDON OTHERS.
SIGH
WHEN I...
...WAS ABOUT TO LEAVE THAT CAT BEHIND...
...YOU SCOOPED THE LITTLE GUY UP WITHOUT SECOND THOUGHT.
Hang in there!

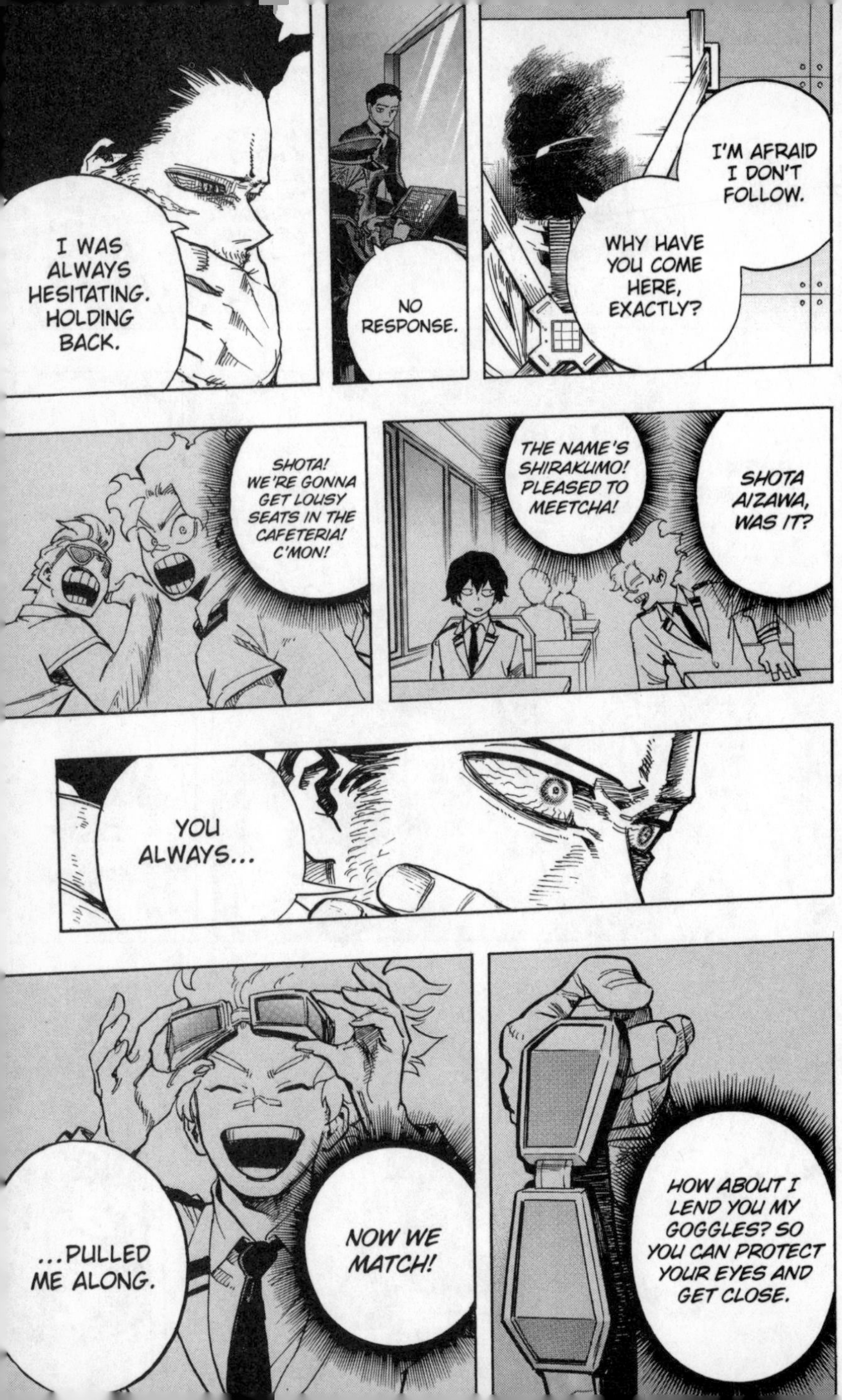
I'M AFRAID I DON'T FOLLOW.
WHY HAVE YOU COME HERE, EXACTLY?
NO RESPONSE.
I WAS ALWAYS HESITATING. HOLDING BACK.
SHOTA AIZAWA, WAS IT?
THE NAME'S SHIRAKUMO! PLEASED TO MEETCHA!
SHOTA! WE'RE GONNA GET LOUSY SEATS IN THE CAFETERIA! C'MON!
YOU ALWAYS...
HOW ABOUT I LEND YOU MY GOGGLES? SO YOU CAN PROTECT YOUR EYES AND GET CLOSE.
NOW WE MATCH!
...PULLED ME ALONG.

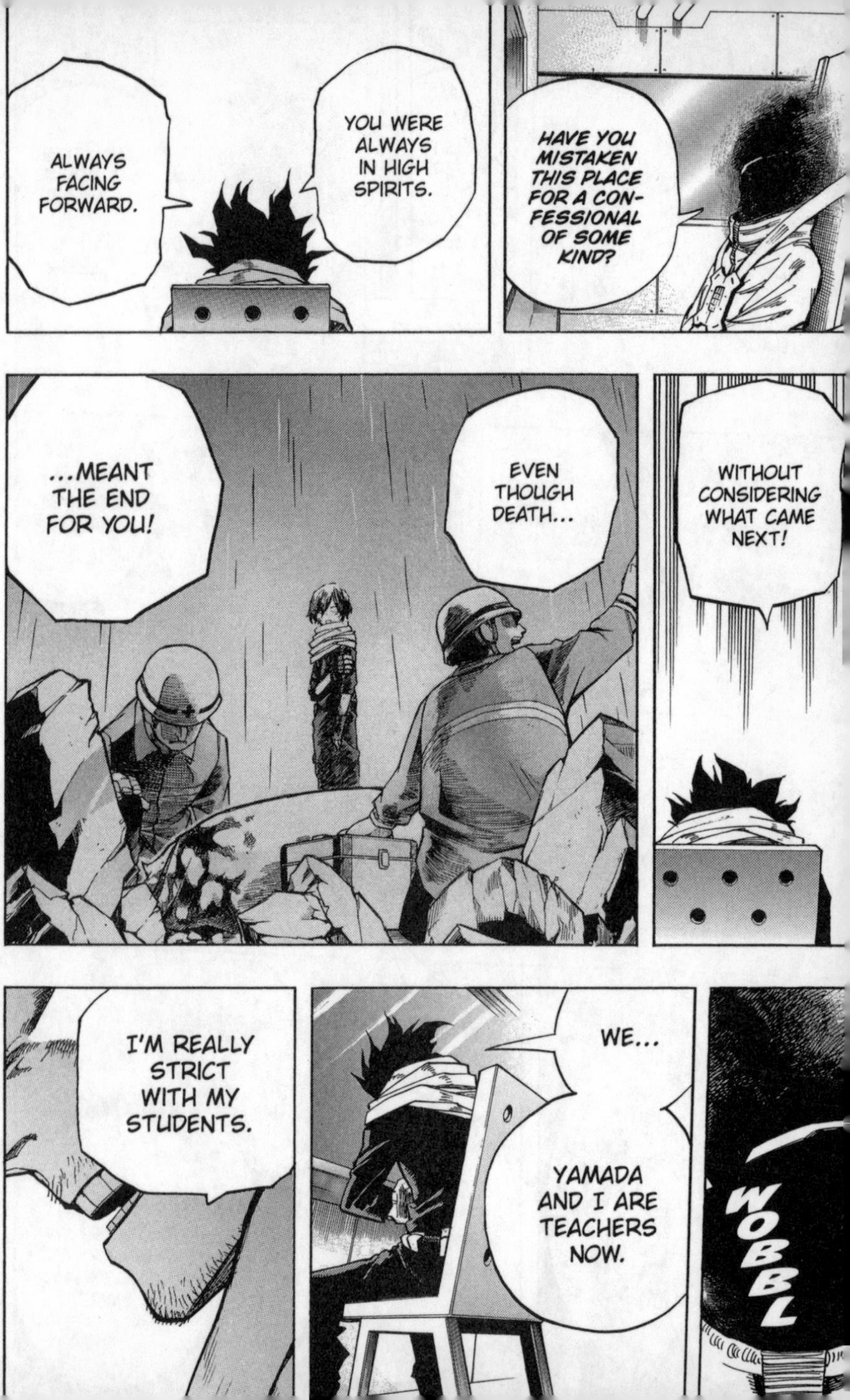
HAVE YOU MISTAKEN THIS PLACE FOR A CONFESSIONAL OF SOME KIND?
YOU WERE ALWAYS IN HIGH SPIRITS.
ALWAYS FACING FORWARD.
WITHOUT CONSIDERING WHAT CAME NEXT!
EVEN THOUGH DEATH...
...MEANT THE END FOR YOU!
WOBBL
WE...
YAMADA AND I ARE TEACHERS NOW.
I'M REALLY STRICT WITH MY STUDENTS.

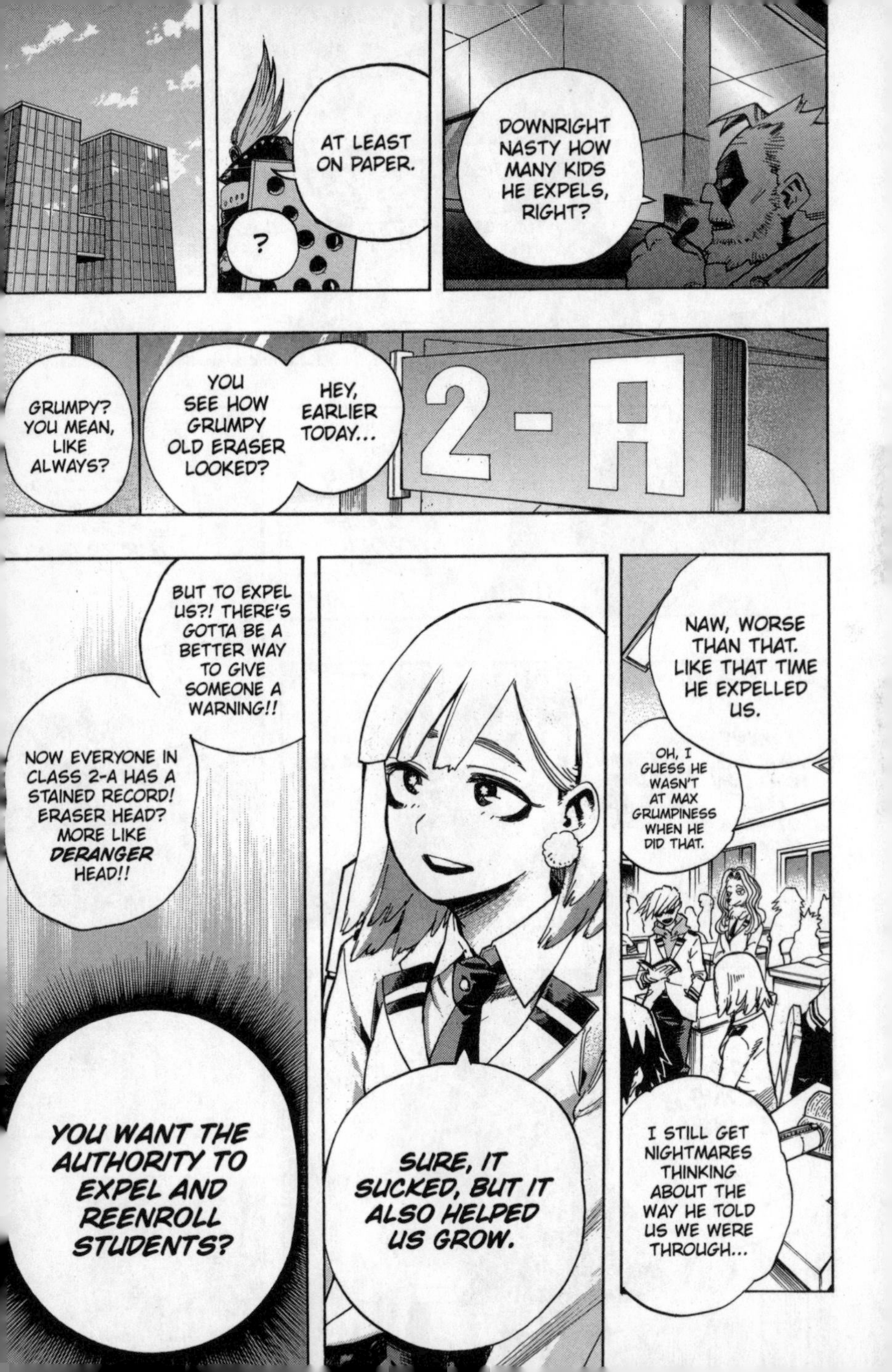
DOWNRIGHT NASTY HOW MANY KIDS HE EXPELS, RIGHT?
AT LEAST ON PAPER.
?
HEY, EARLIER TODAY...
YOU SEE HOW GRUMPY OLD ERASER LOOKED?
GRUMPY? YOU MEAN, LIKE ALWAYS?
2-A
NAW, WORSE THAN THAT. LIKE THAT TIME HE EXPELLED US.
OH, I GUESS HE WASN'T AT MAX GRUMPINESS WHEN HE DID THAT.
I STILL GET NIGHTMARES THINKING ABOUT THE WAY HE TOLD US WE WERE THROUGH...
SURE, IT SUCKED, BUT IT ALSO HELPED US GROW.
BUT TO EXPEL US?! THERE'S GOTTA BE A BETTER WAY TO GIVE SOMEONE A WARNING!!
NOW EVERYONE IN CLASS 2-A HAS A STAINED RECORD! ERASER HEAD? MORE LIKE *DERANGER* HEAD!!
YOU WANT THE AUTHORITY TO EXPEL AND REENROLL STUDENTS?

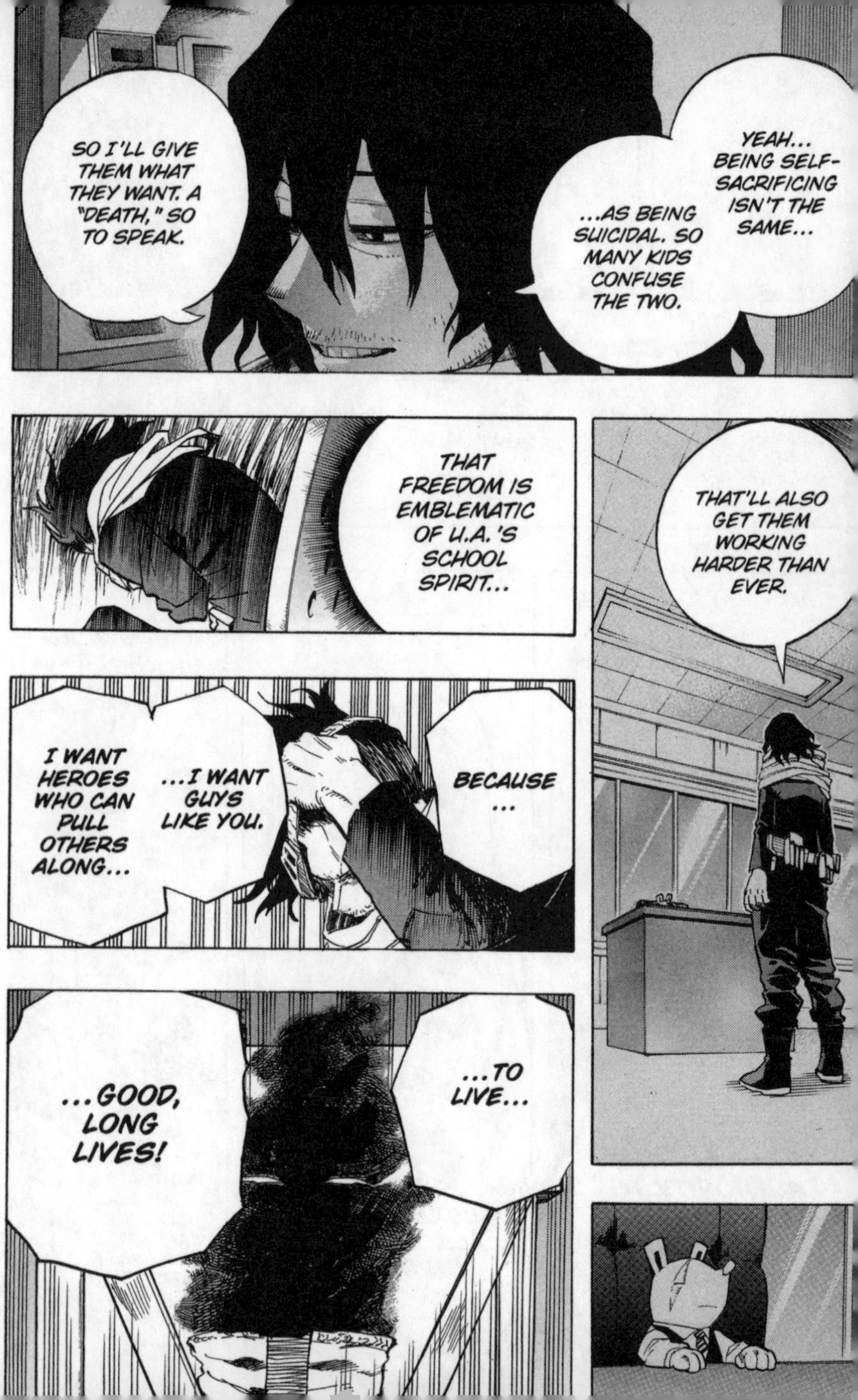
YEAH... BEING SELF-SACRIFICING ISN'T THE SAME...
...AS BEING SUICIDAL. SO MANY KIDS CONFUSE THE TWO.
SO I'LL GIVE THEM WHAT THEY WANT. A "DEATH," SO TO SPEAK.
THAT'LL ALSO GET THEM WORKING HARDER THAN EVER.
THAT FREEDOM IS EMBLEMATIC OF U.A.'S SCHOOL SPIRIT...
BECAUSE ...
...I WANT GUYS LIKE YOU.
I WANT HEROES WHO CAN PULL OTHERS ALONG...
...TO LIVE...
...GOOD, LONG LIVES!

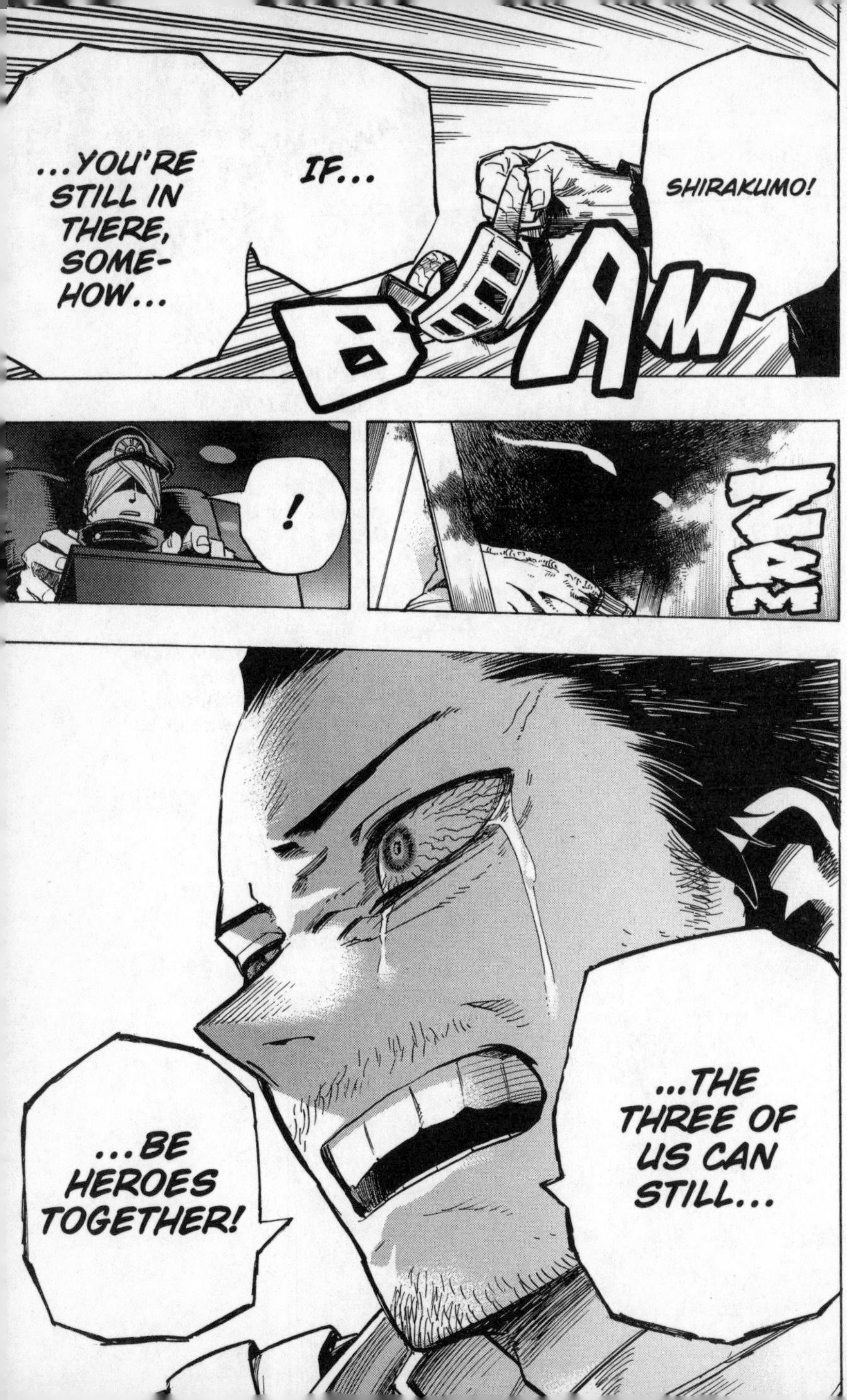
SHIRAKUMO!
IF...
...YOU'RE STILL IN THERE, SOME-HOW...
BAM
!
...THE THREE OF US CAN STILL...
...BE HEROES TOGETHER!

Birthday: 5/10
Height: 155 cm
Favorite Thing: Fluffy sponge cake

THE SUPPLEMENT
In class 2-A of U.A.'s Hero Course.

The debut of the second-years!

Their introduction was always going to coincide with a conversation about Aizawa, but can you believe it took 26 volumes to happen?

Will they ever appear again?!

You bet they will!!

No. 255 - Hero Hopeful

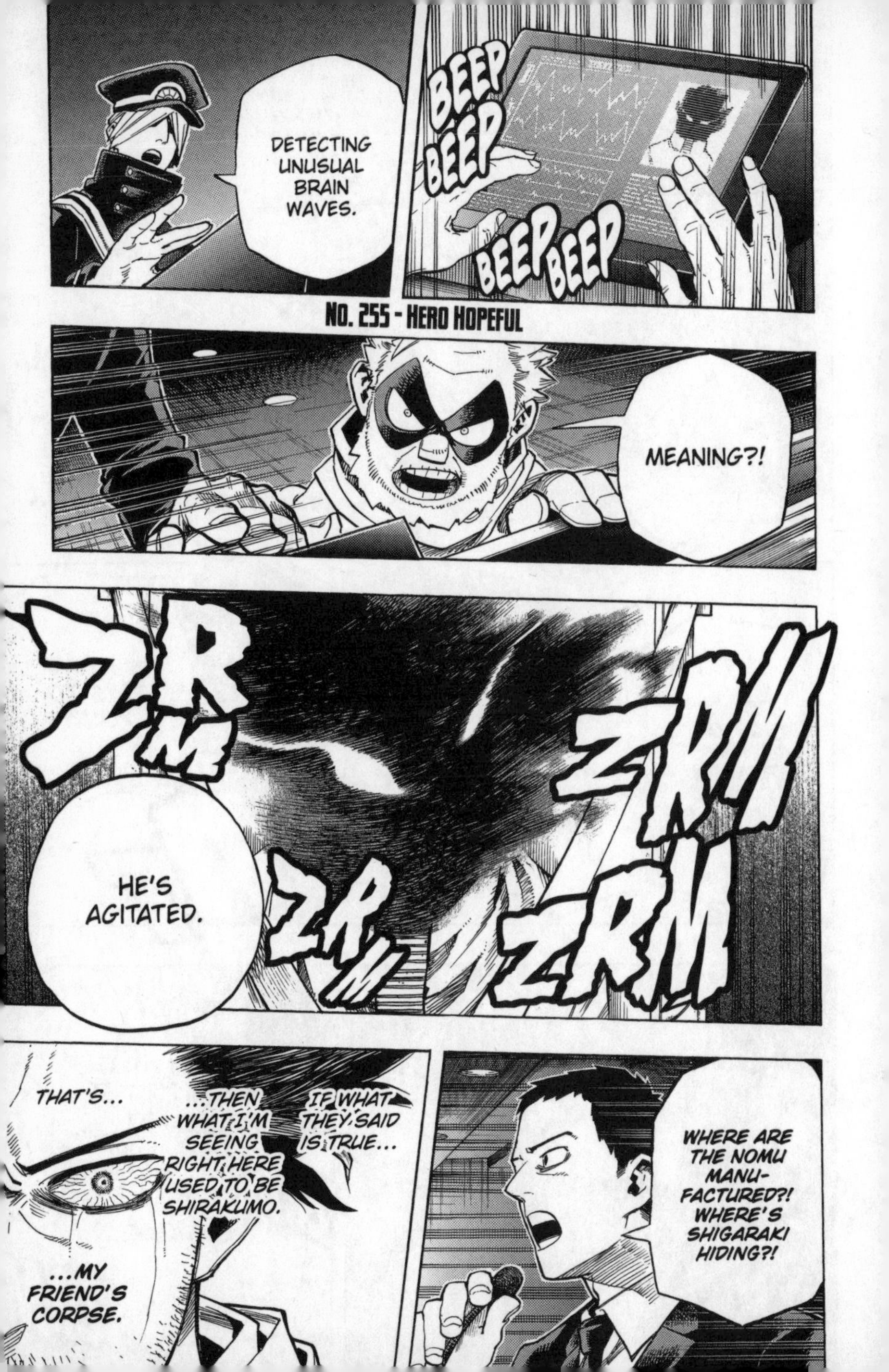
BEEP BEEP
BEEP BEEP
DETECTING UNUSUAL BRAIN WAVES.
MEANING?!
ZRM
ZRM
ZRM
ZRM
HE'S AGITATED.
WHERE ARE THE NOMU MANU-FACTURED?! WHERE'S SHIGARAKI HIDING?!
IF WHAT THEY SAID IS TRUE...
...THEN WHAT I'M SEEING RIGHT HERE USED TO BE SHIRAKUMO.
THAT'S...
...MY FRIEND'S CORPSE.

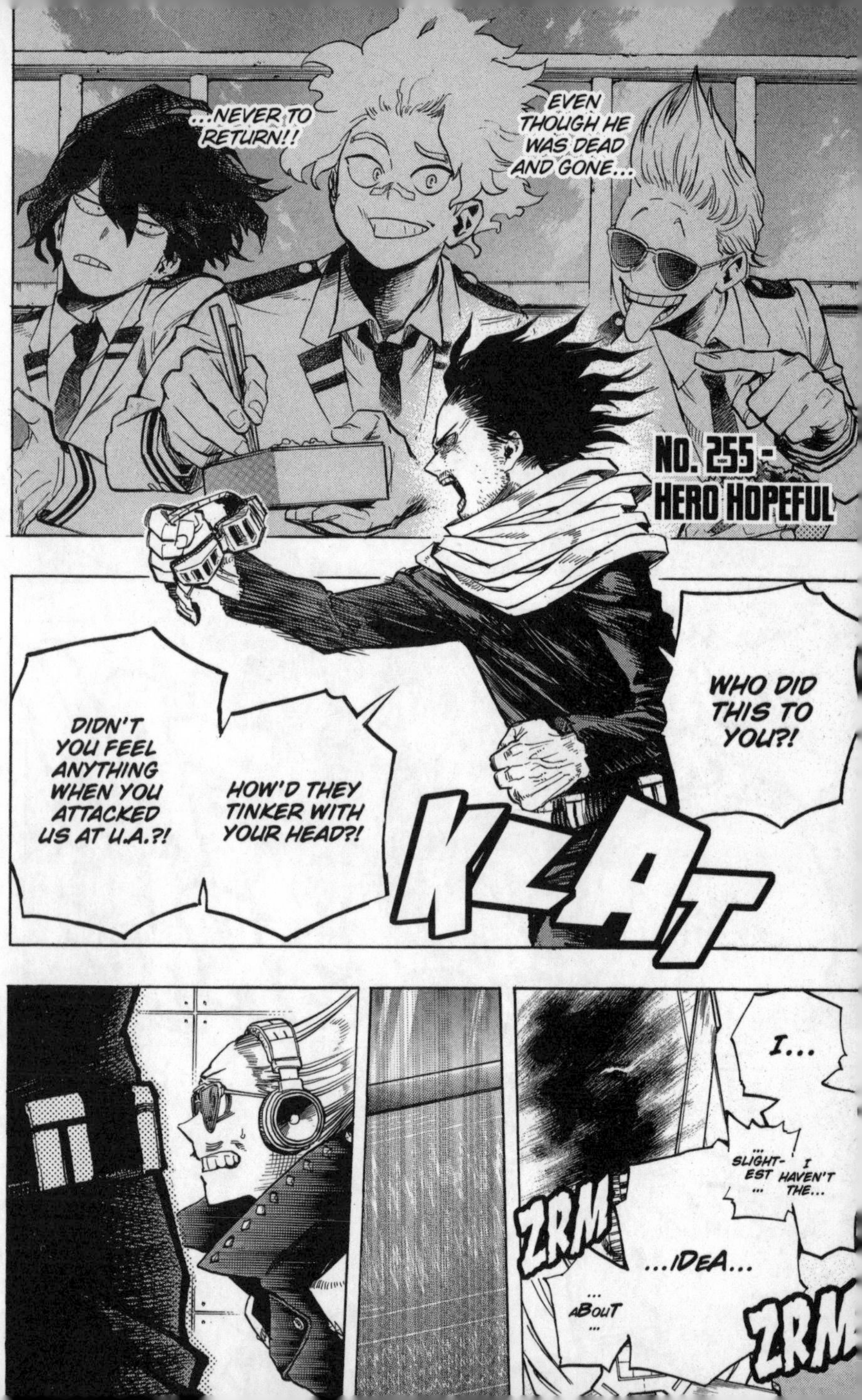
EVEN THOUGH HE WAS DEAD AND GONE...
...NEVER TO RETURN!!
NO. 255 - HERO HOPEFUL
WHO DID THIS TO YOU?!
KZAT
HOW'D THEY TINKER WITH YOUR HEAD?!
DIDN'T YOU FEEL ANYTHING WHEN YOU ATTACKED US AT U.A.?!
I...
I HAVEN'T THE...
...SLIGHT-EST...
ZRM
...IDEA...
...ABOUT...
ZRM

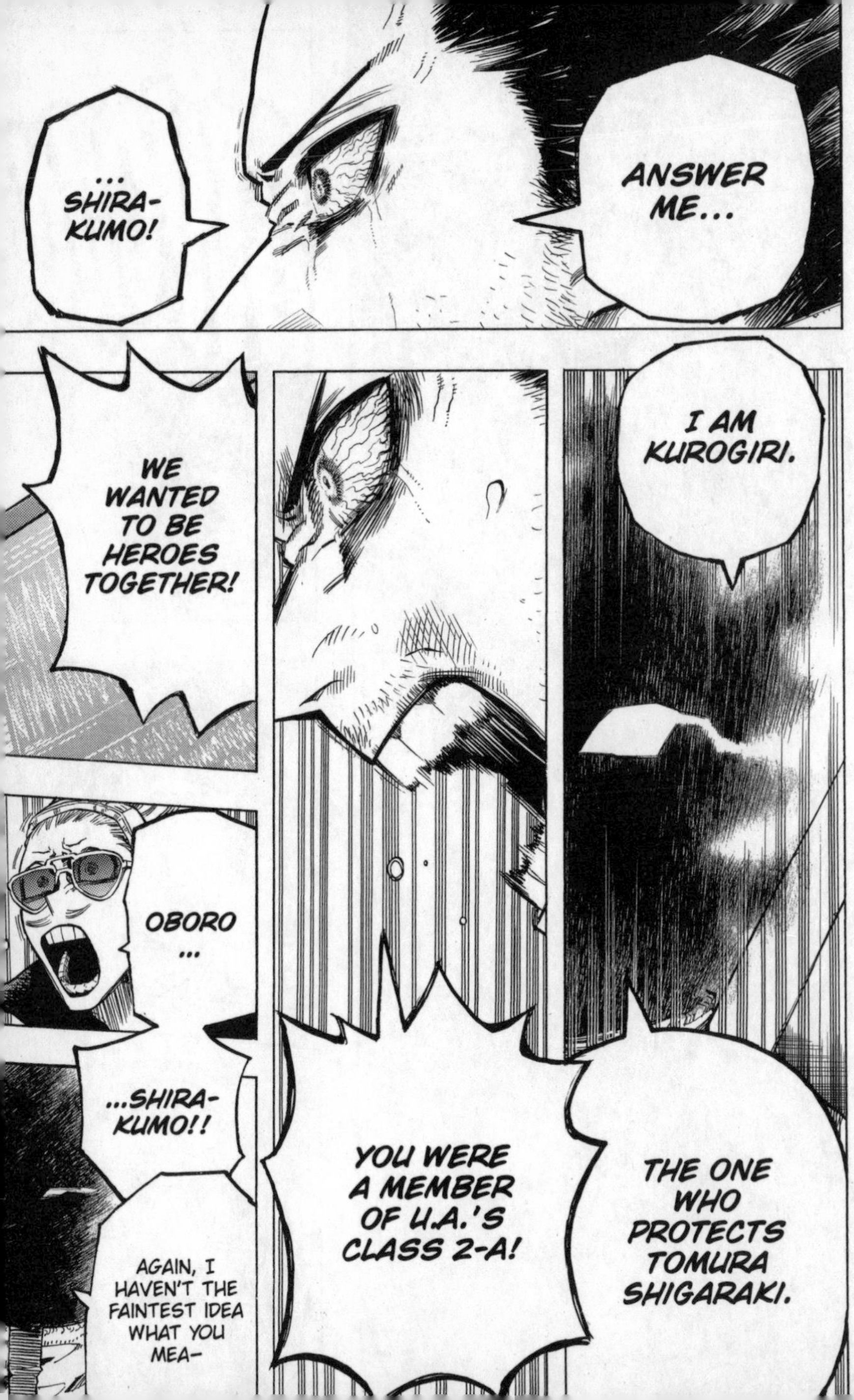
ANSWER ME...
... SHIRA-KUMO!
I AM KUROGIRI.
THE ONE WHO PROTECTS TOMURA SHIGARAKI.
YOU WERE A MEMBER OF U.A.'S CLASS 2-A!
WE WANTED TO BE HEROES TOGETHER!
OBORO ...
...SHIRA-KUMO!!
AGAIN, I HAVEN'T THE FAINTEST IDEA WHAT YOU MEA-

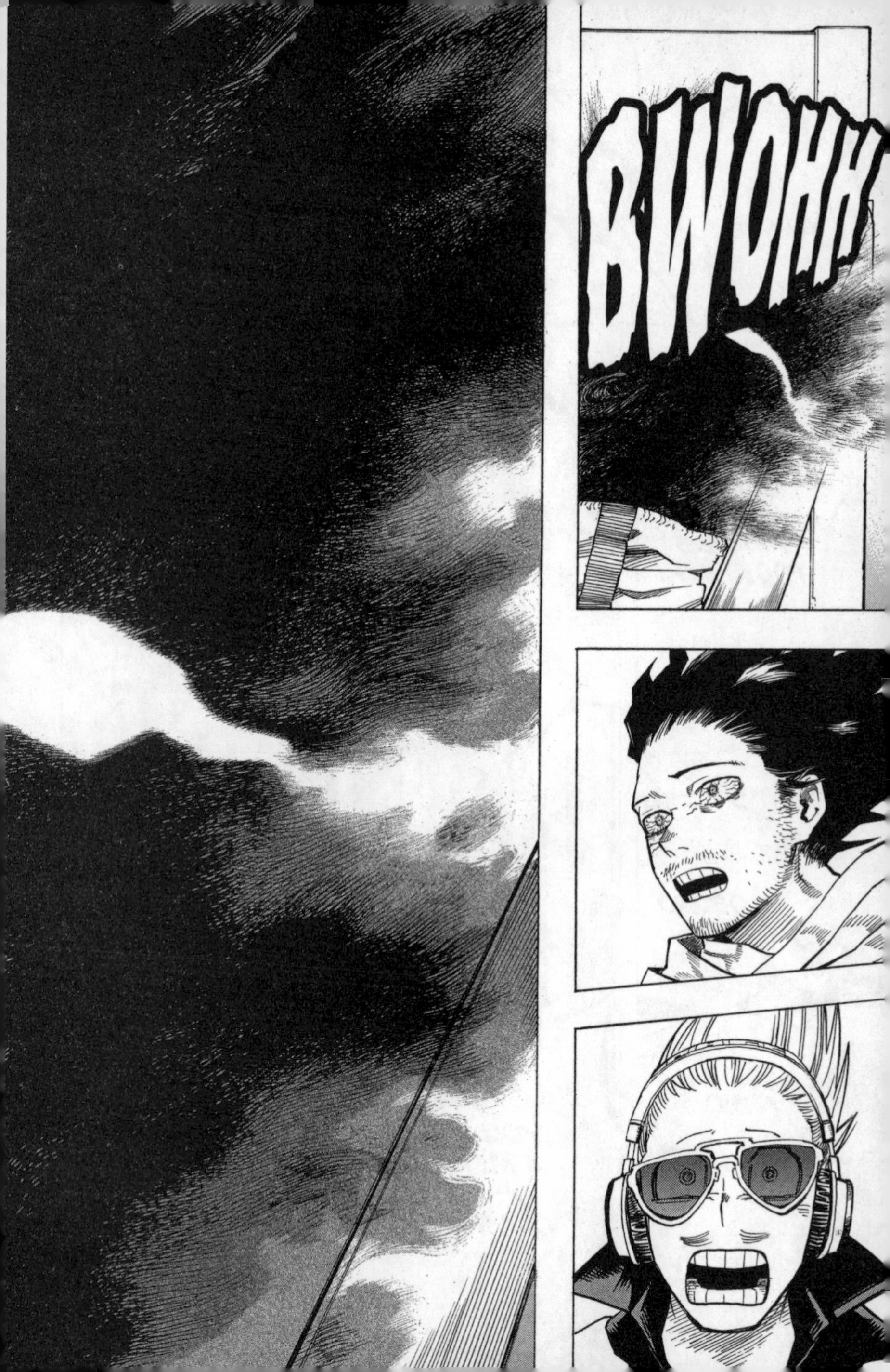
BWOHH

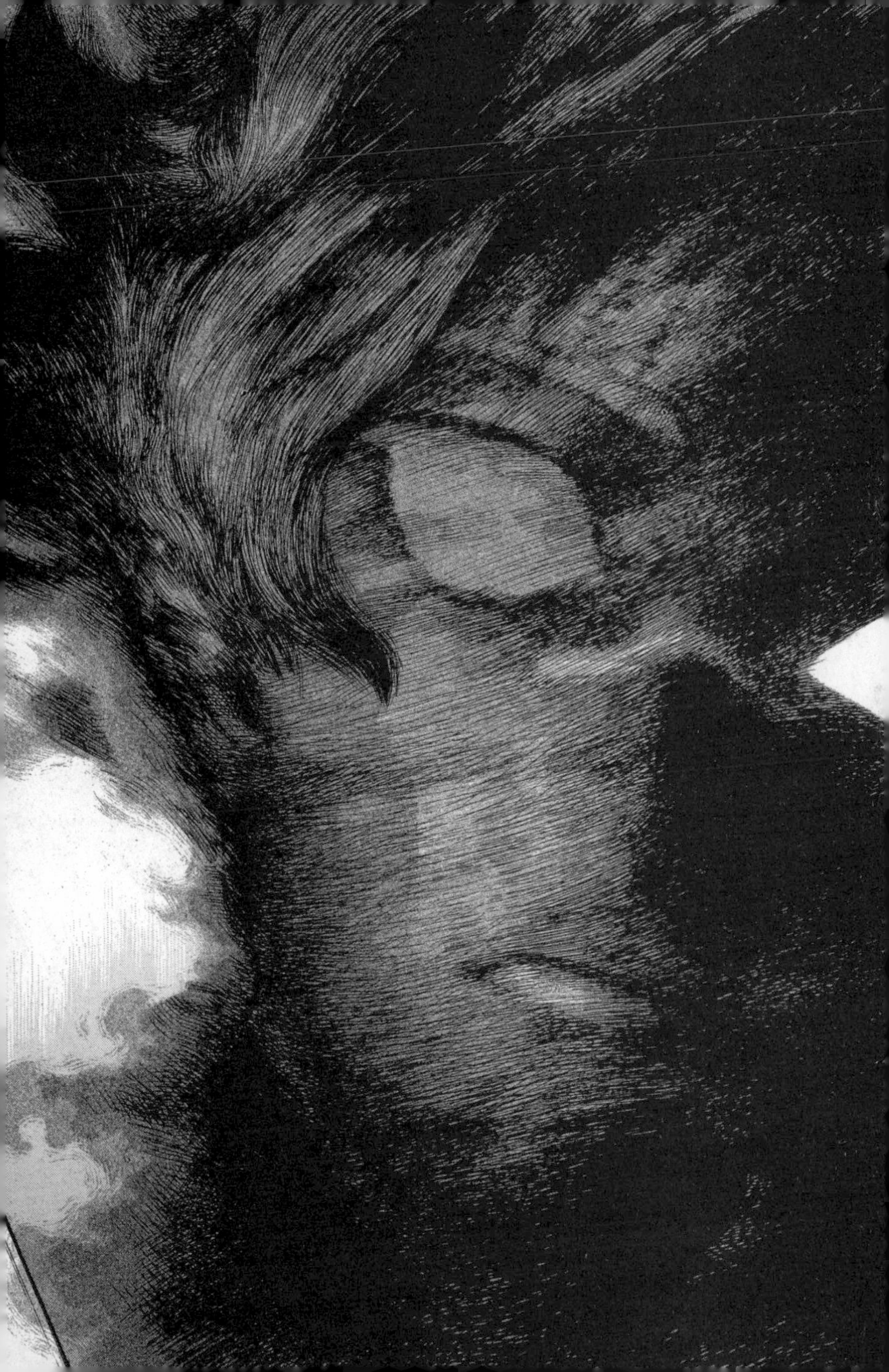

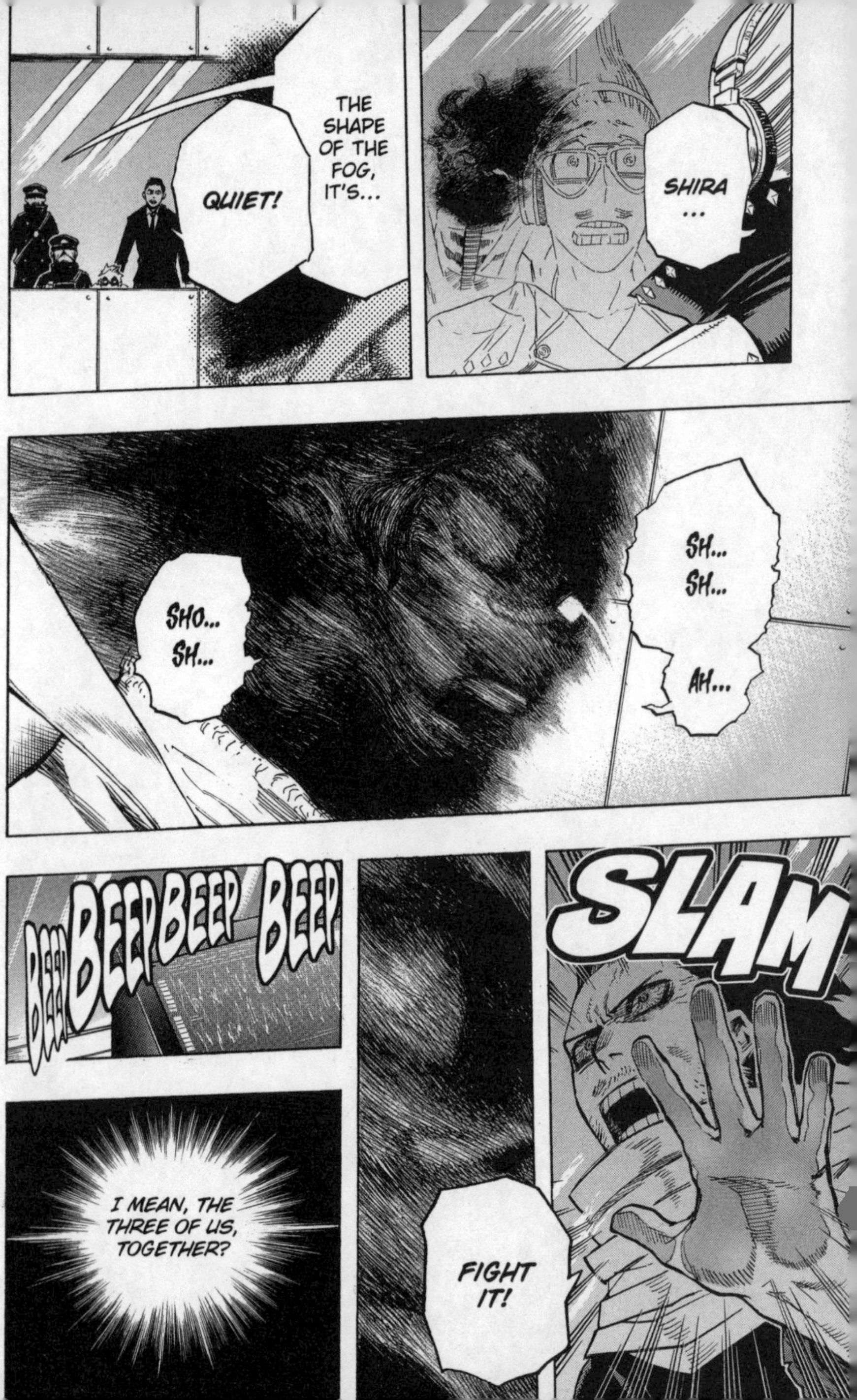
SHIRA...
THE SHAPE OF THE FOG, IT'S...
QUIET!
SH... SH... AH...
SHO... SH...
SLAM
FIGHT IT!
BEEP BEEP BEEP BEEP
I MEAN, THE THREE OF US, TOGETHER?

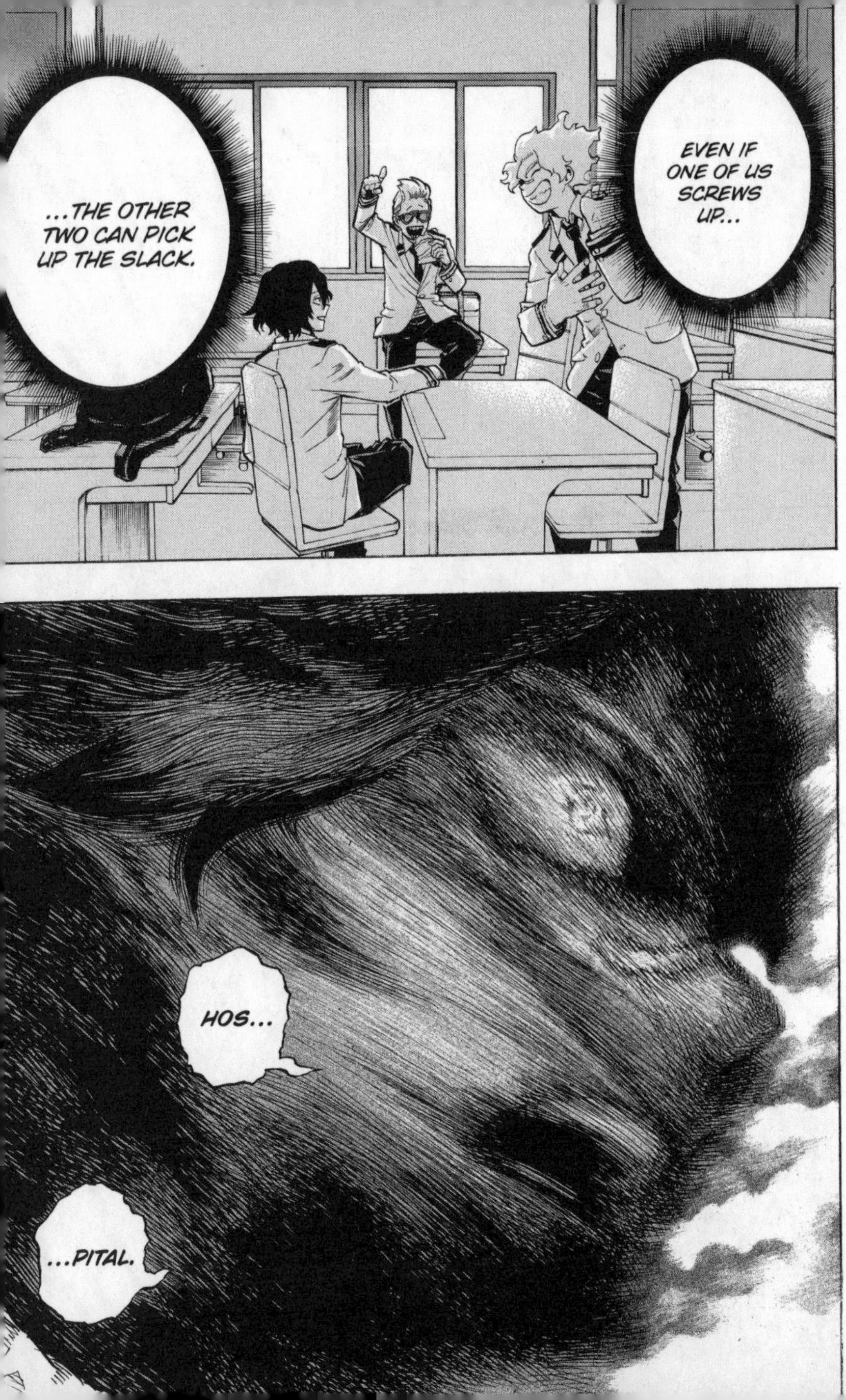
EVEN IF ONE OF US SCREWS UP...
...THE OTHER TWO CAN PICK UP THE SLACK.
HOS...
...PITAL.

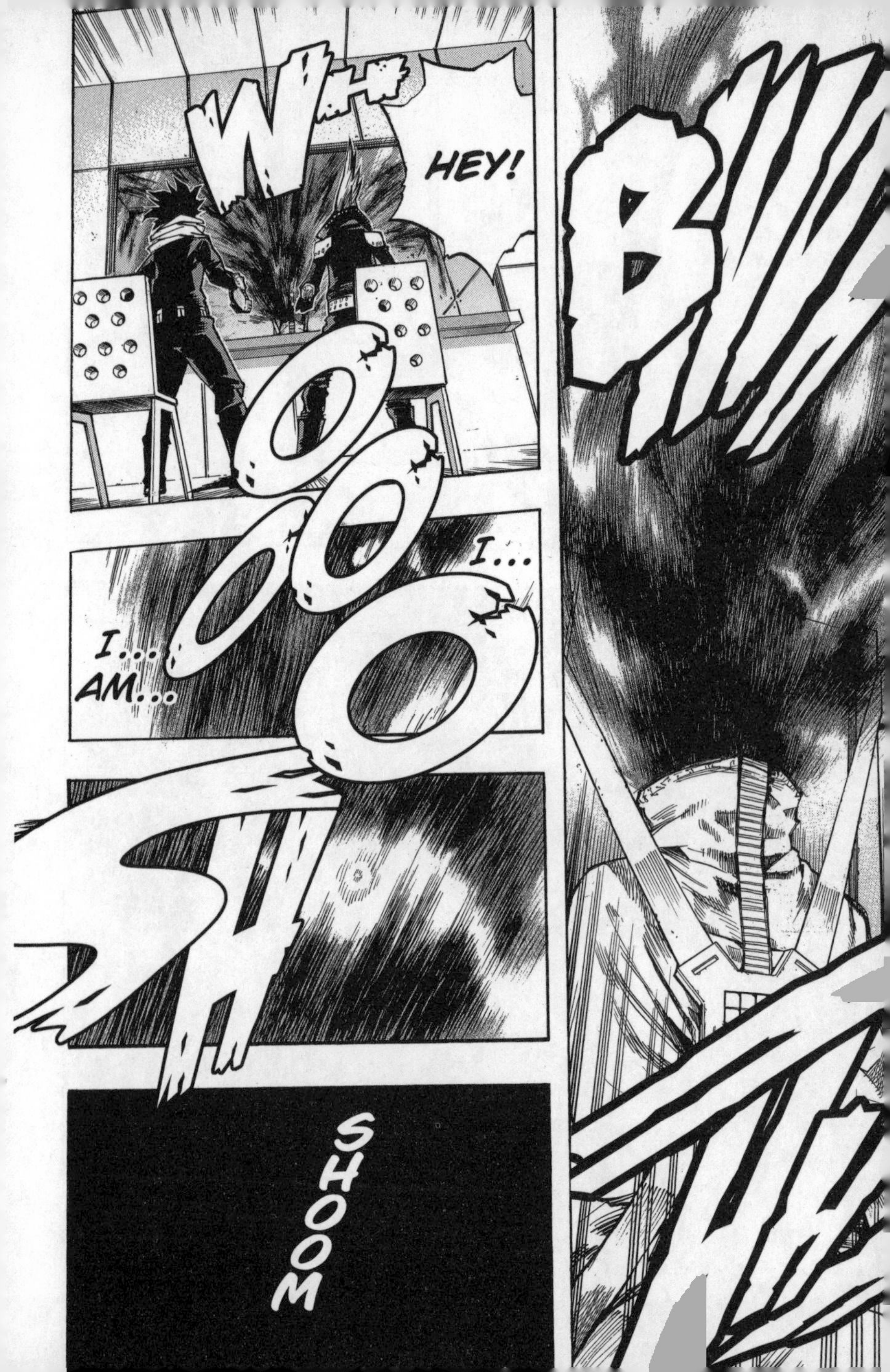
HEY!
I...
I... AM...
SHOOM

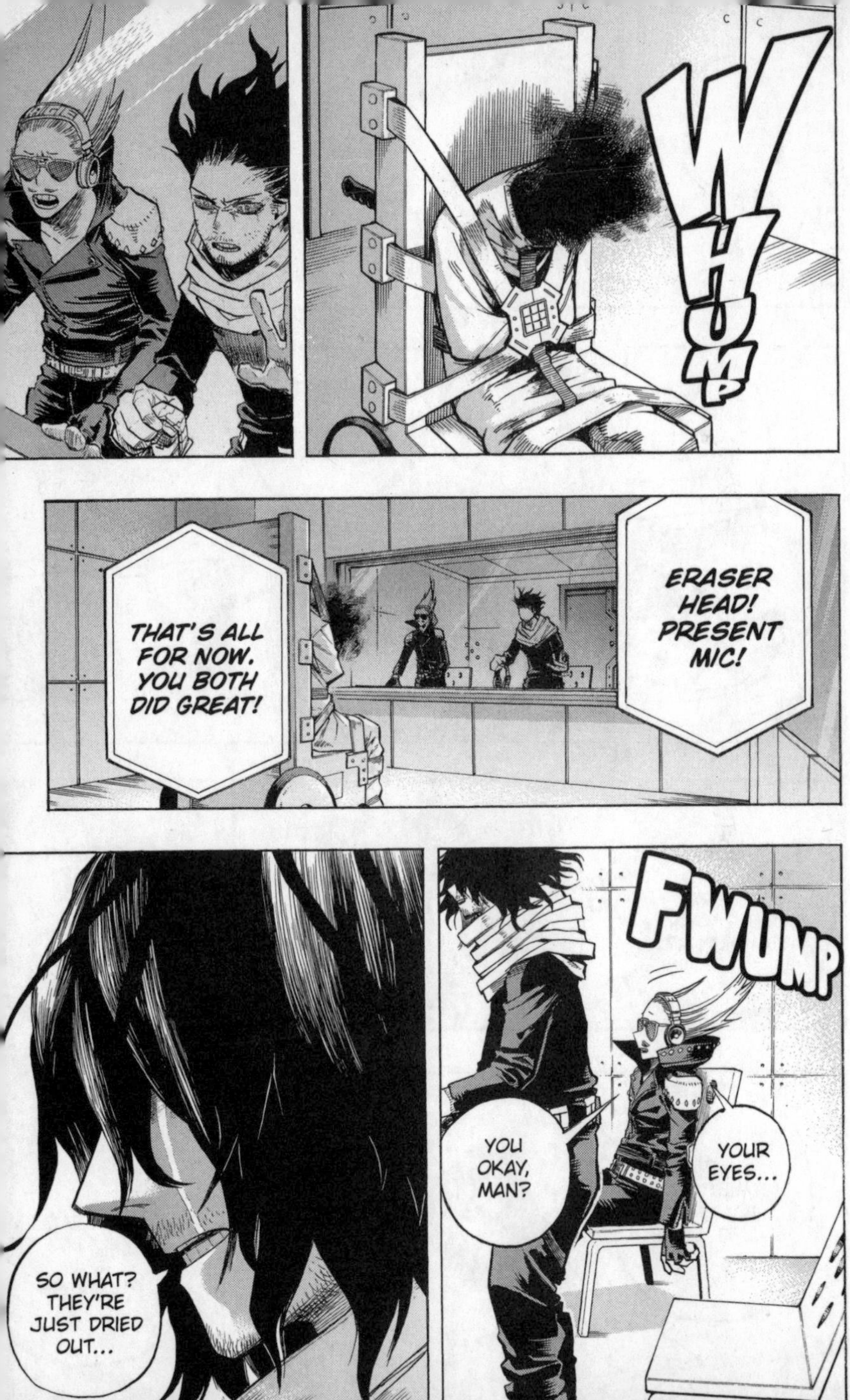
WHUMP
ERASER HEAD! PRESENT MIC!
THAT'S ALL FOR NOW. YOU BOTH DID GREAT!
FWUMP
YOUR EYES...
YOU OKAY, MAN?
SO WHAT? THEY'RE JUST DRIED OUT...

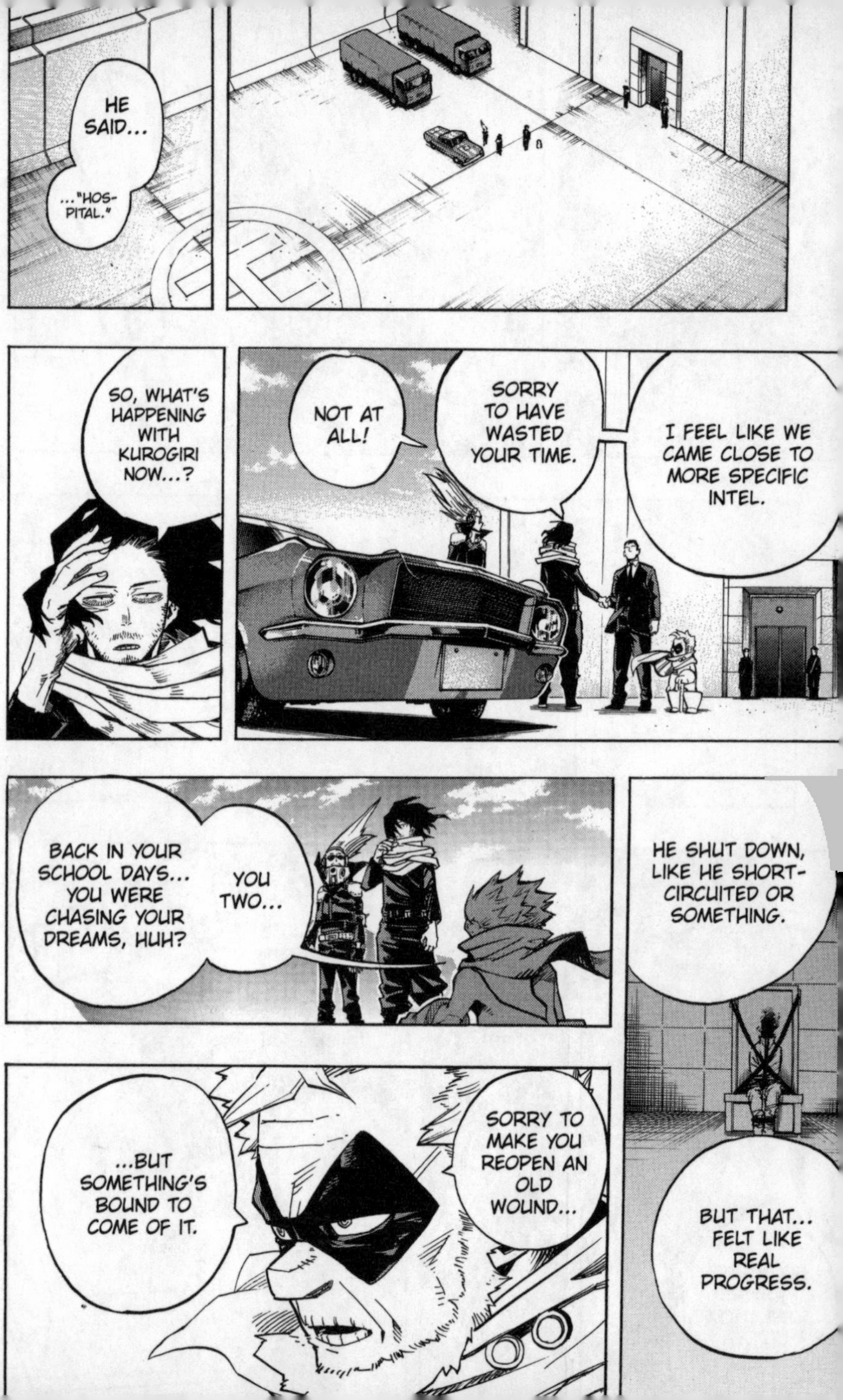
HE SAID...
..."HOS-PITAL."
I FEEL LIKE WE CAME CLOSE TO MORE SPECIFIC INTEL.
SORRY TO HAVE WASTED YOUR TIME.
NOT AT ALL!
SO, WHAT'S HAPPENING WITH KUROGIRI NOW...?
HE SHUT DOWN, LIKE HE SHORT-CIRCUITED OR SOMETHING.
BUT THAT... FELT LIKE REAL PROGRESS.
YOU TWO...
BACK IN YOUR SCHOOL DAYS... YOU WERE CHASING YOUR DREAMS, HUH?
SORRY TO MAKE YOU REOPEN AN OLD WOUND...
...BUT SOMETHING'S BOUND TO COME OF IT.

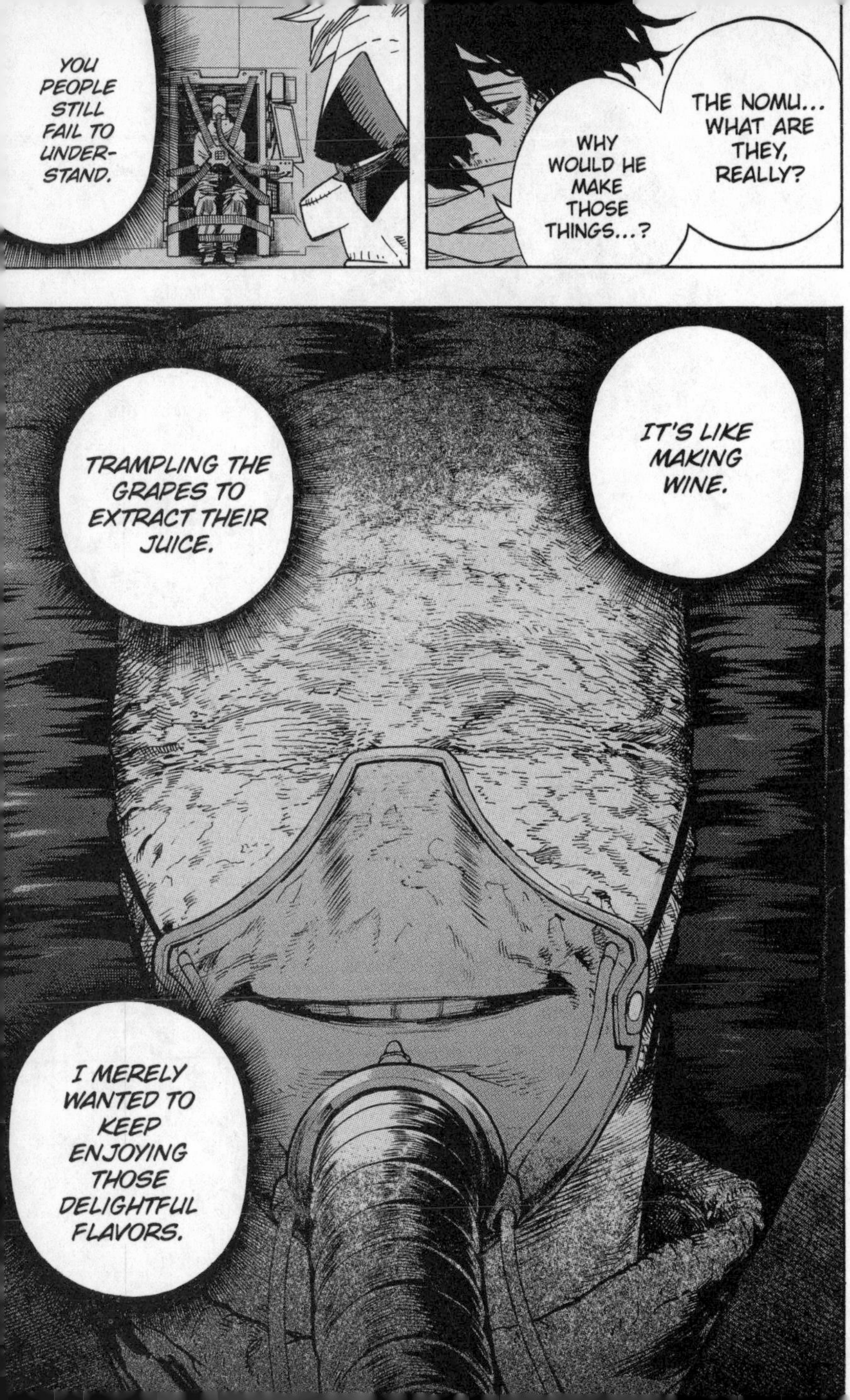
THE NOMU... WHAT ARE THEY, REALLY?
WHY WOULD HE MAKE THOSE THINGS...?
YOU PEOPLE STILL FAIL TO UNDER-STAND.
IT'S LIKE MAKING WINE.
TRAMPLING THE GRAPES TO EXTRACT THEIR JUICE.
I MERELY WANTED TO KEEP ENJOYING THOSE DELIGHTFUL FLAVORS.

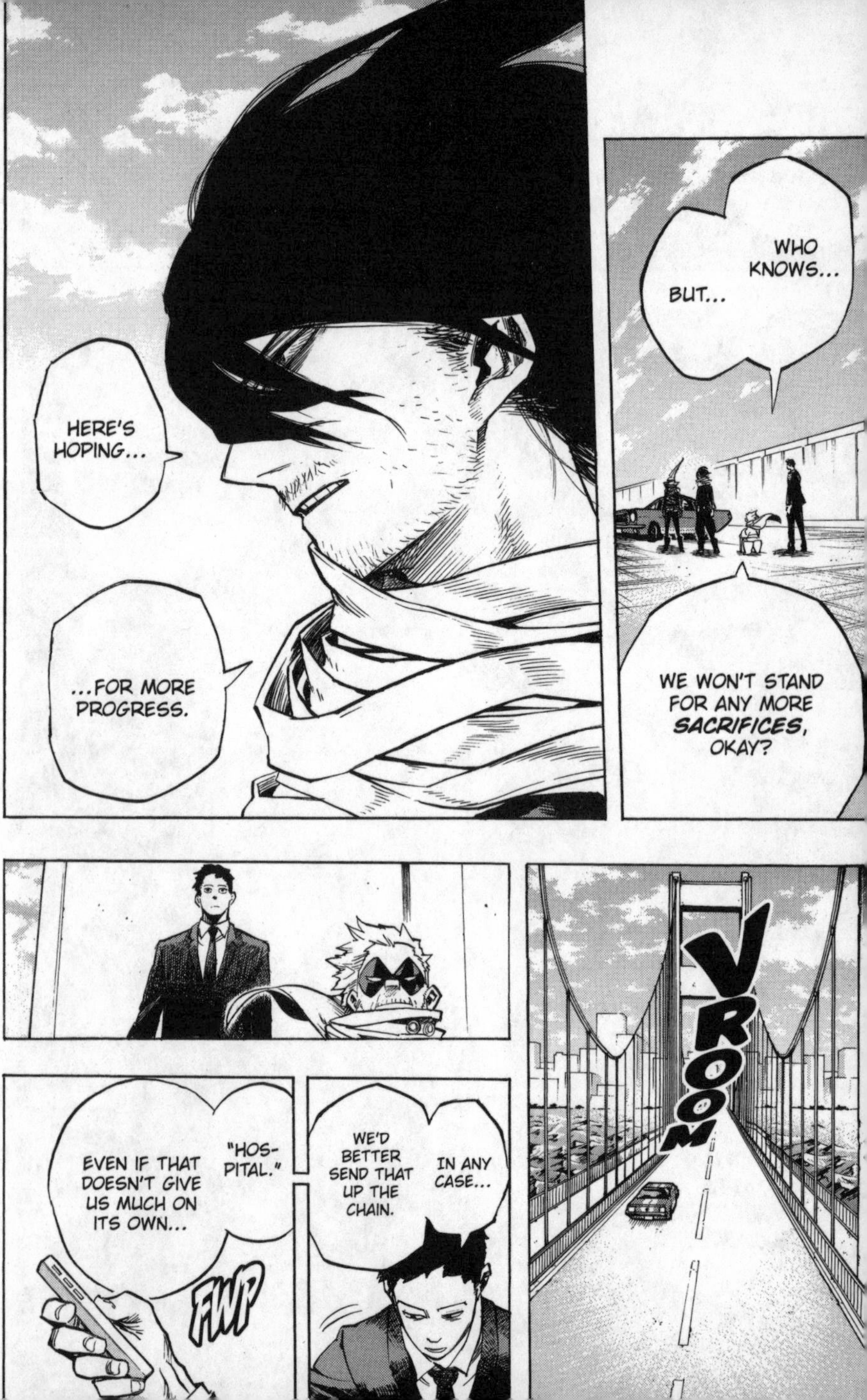

WHO KNOWS...
BUT...
WE WON'T STAND FOR ANY MORE *SACRIFICES*, OKAY?
HERE'S HOPING...
...FOR MORE PROGRESS.
VROOM
IN ANY CASE...
WE'D BETTER SEND THAT UP THE CHAIN.
"HOS-PITAL."
EVEN IF THAT DOESN'T GIVE US MUCH ON ITS OWN...
FWP

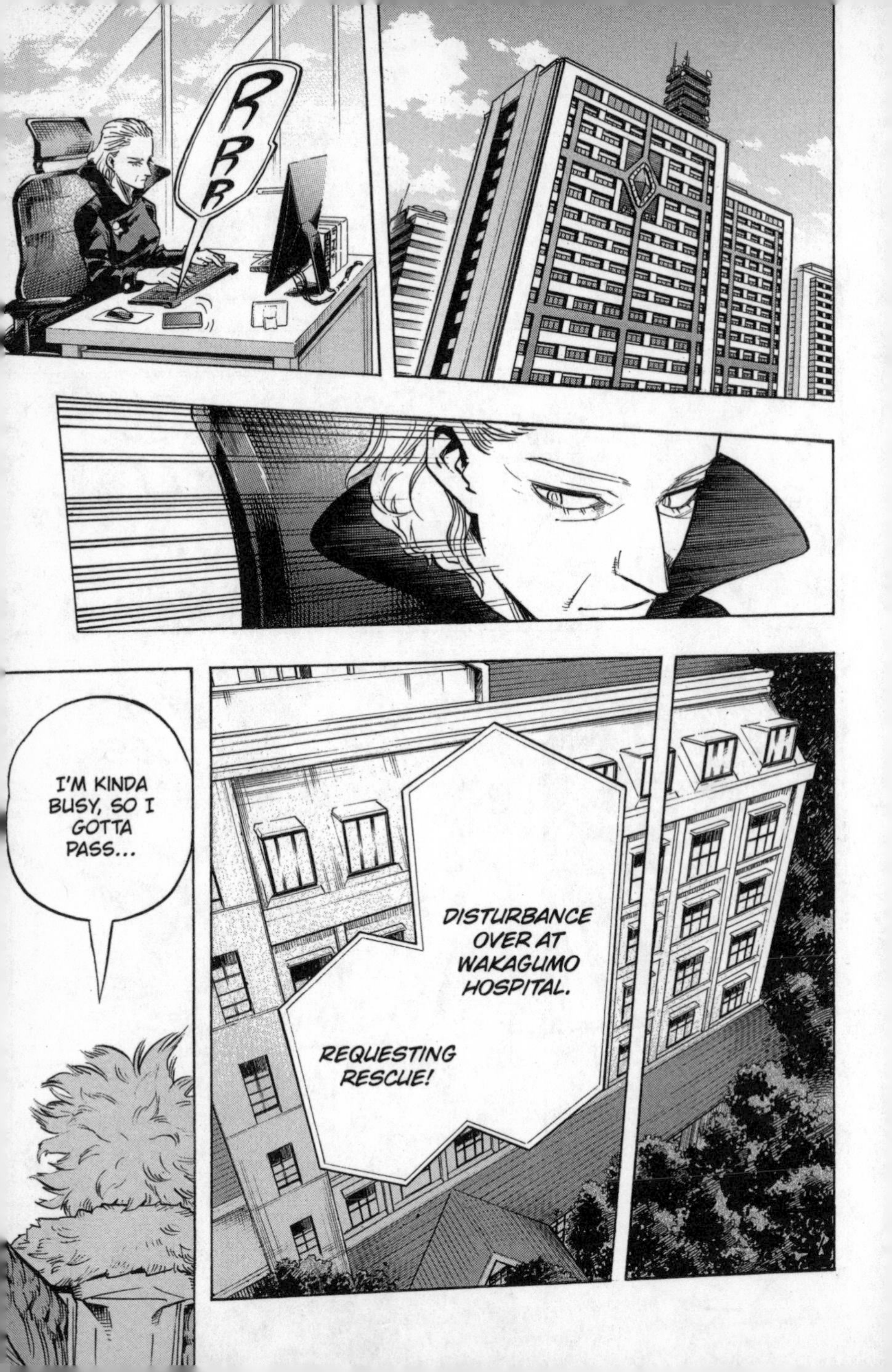
RRR
DISTURBANCE OVER AT WAKAGUMO HOSPITAL.
REQUESTING RESCUE!
I'M KINDA BUSY, SO I GOTTA PASS...

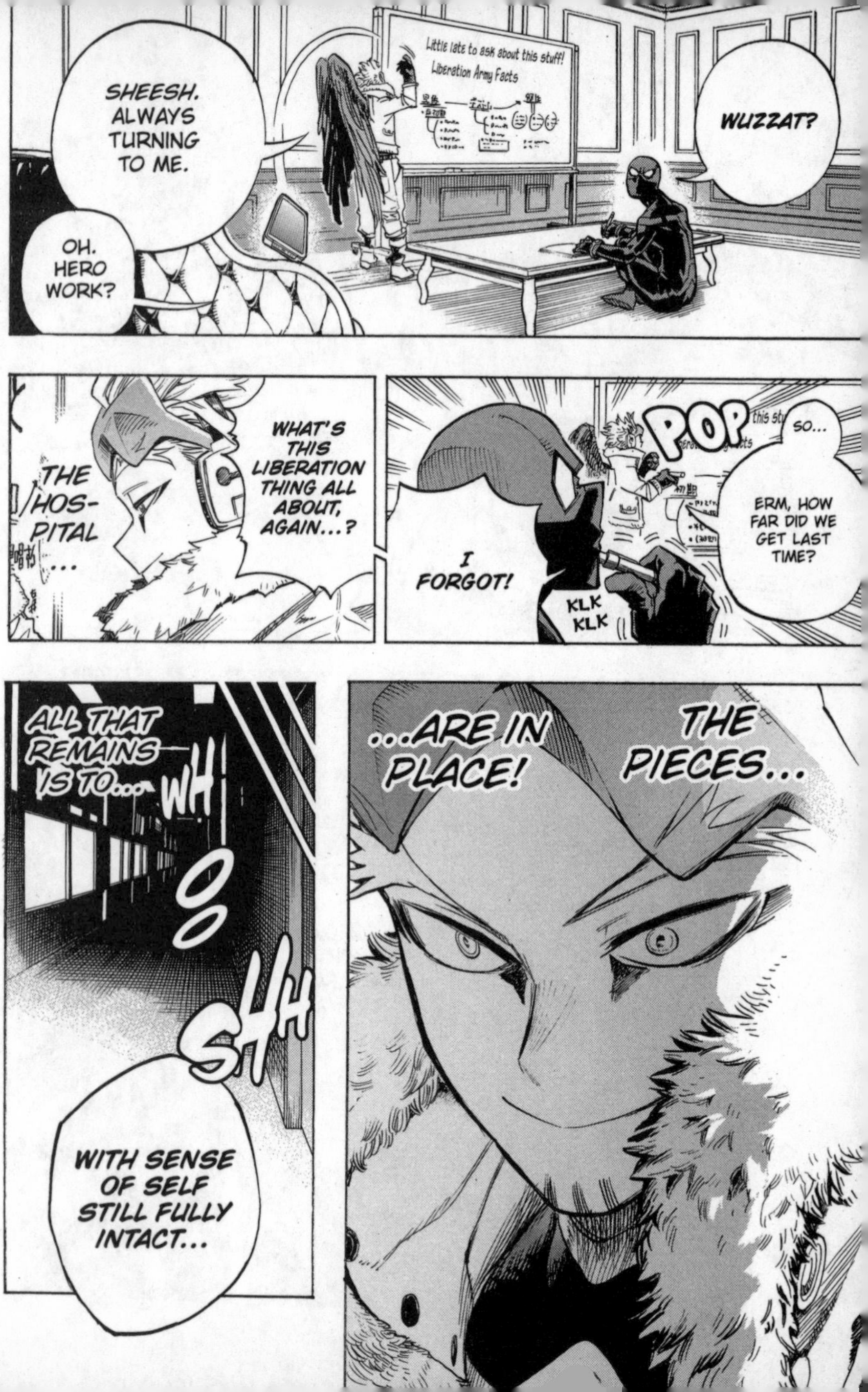
WUZZAT?
Little late to ask about this stuff!
Liberation Army Facts
SHEESH. ALWAYS TURNING TO ME.
OH. HERO WORK?
SO...
ERM, HOW FAR DID WE GET LAST TIME?
POP
I FORGOT!
KLK KLK
WHAT'S THIS LIBERATION THING ALL ABOUT, AGAIN...?
THE HOS-PITAL...
THE PIECES...
...ARE IN PLACE!
ALL THAT REMAINS IS TO...
WHOOSHH
WITH SENSE OF SELF STILL FULLY INTACT...

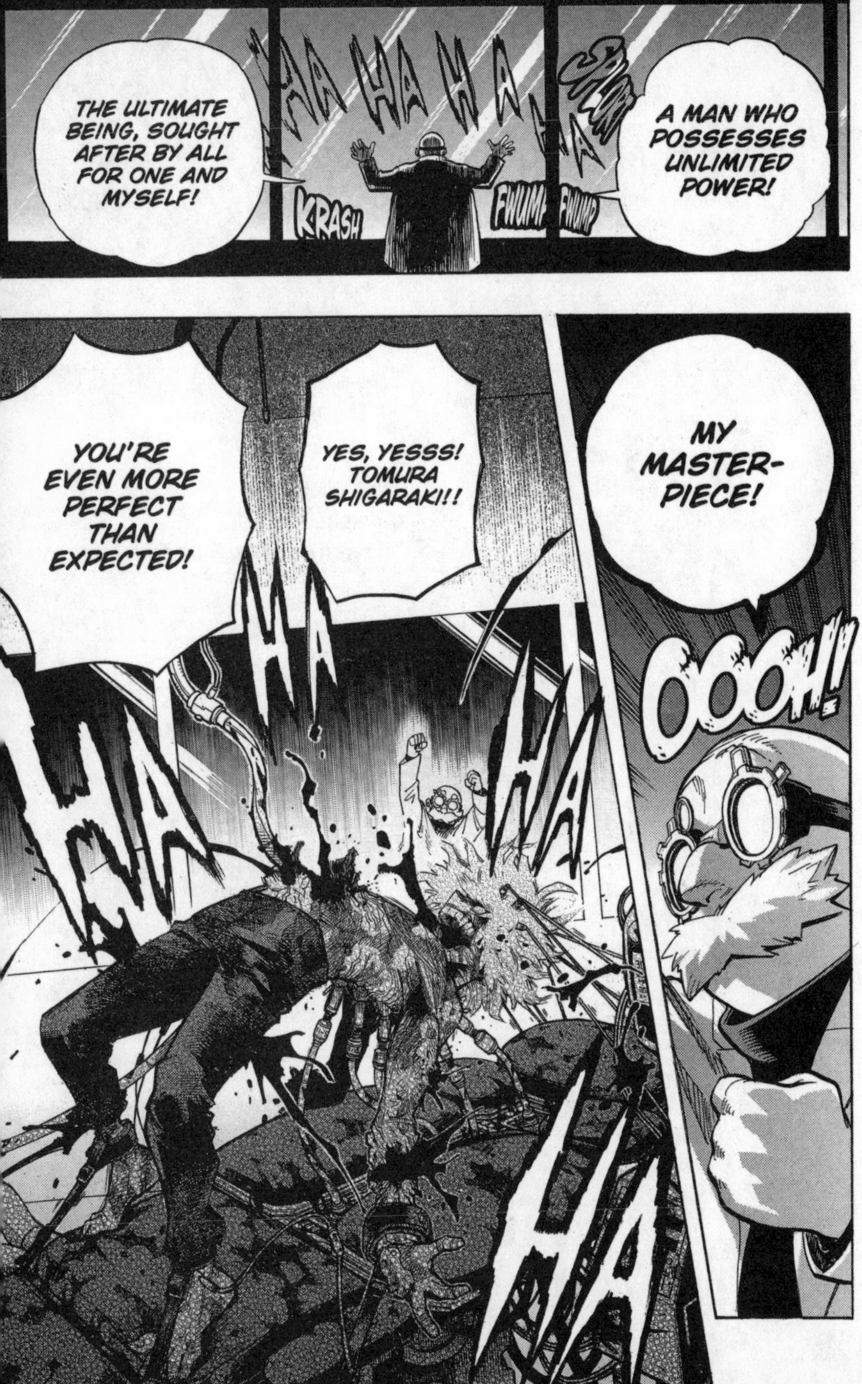
A MAN WHO POSSESSES UNLIMITED POWER!
FWUMP FWUMP
HA HA HA HA
KRASH
THE ULTIMATE BEING, SOUGHT AFTER BY ALL FOR ONE AND MYSELF!
MY MASTER-PIECE!
OOOH!
YES, YESSS! TOMURA SHIGARAKI!!
YOU'RE EVEN MORE PERFECT THAN EXPECTED!
HA HA HA HA HA

OBORO SHIRAKUMO [AGE AT DEATH: 17]

STREET CLOTHES

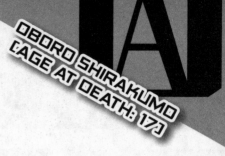

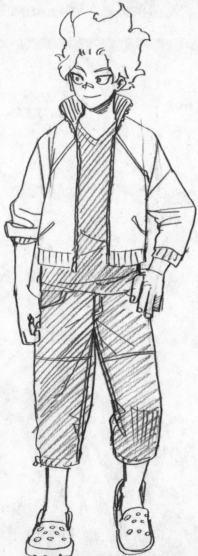

Birthday: 5/5
Height: 187 cm
Favorite Things: Blue skies, the sun

THE *VIGILANTES* SUPPLEMENT

This is Eraser Head and Present Mic's friend from their school days. His name popped up in *MHA* (and he was shown from behind), but you get his full story in the *Vigilantes* spin-off series. Balancing that content between the main series and the spin-off was tricky!!

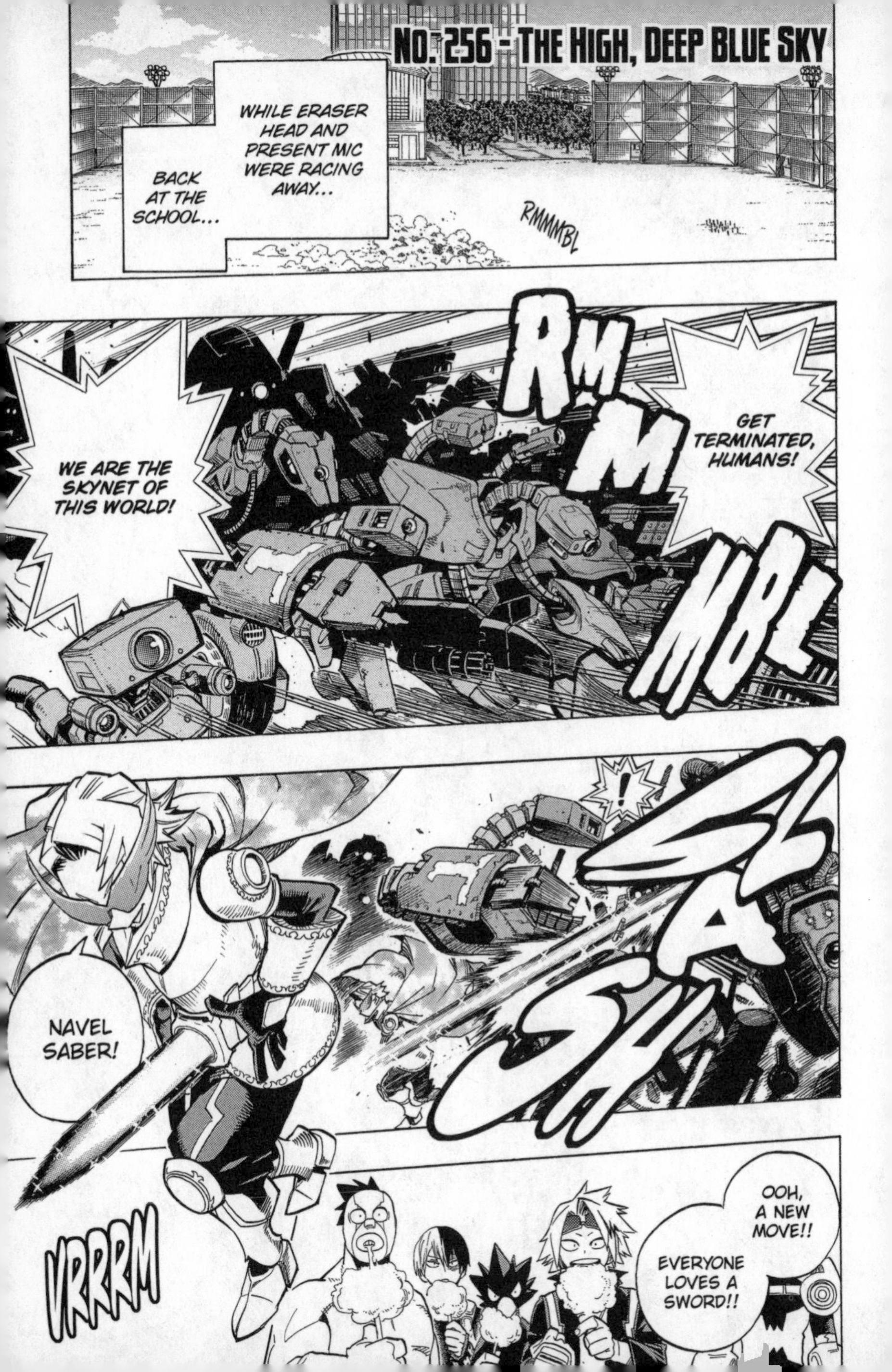
No. 256 - The High, Deep Blue Sky
While Eraser Head and Present Mic were racing away...
Back at the school...
RMMMBL
Get terminated, humans!
RMMMBL
We are the Skynet of this world!
!
SHASH
Navel Saber!
VRRRM
Ooh, a new move!!
Everyone loves a sword!!

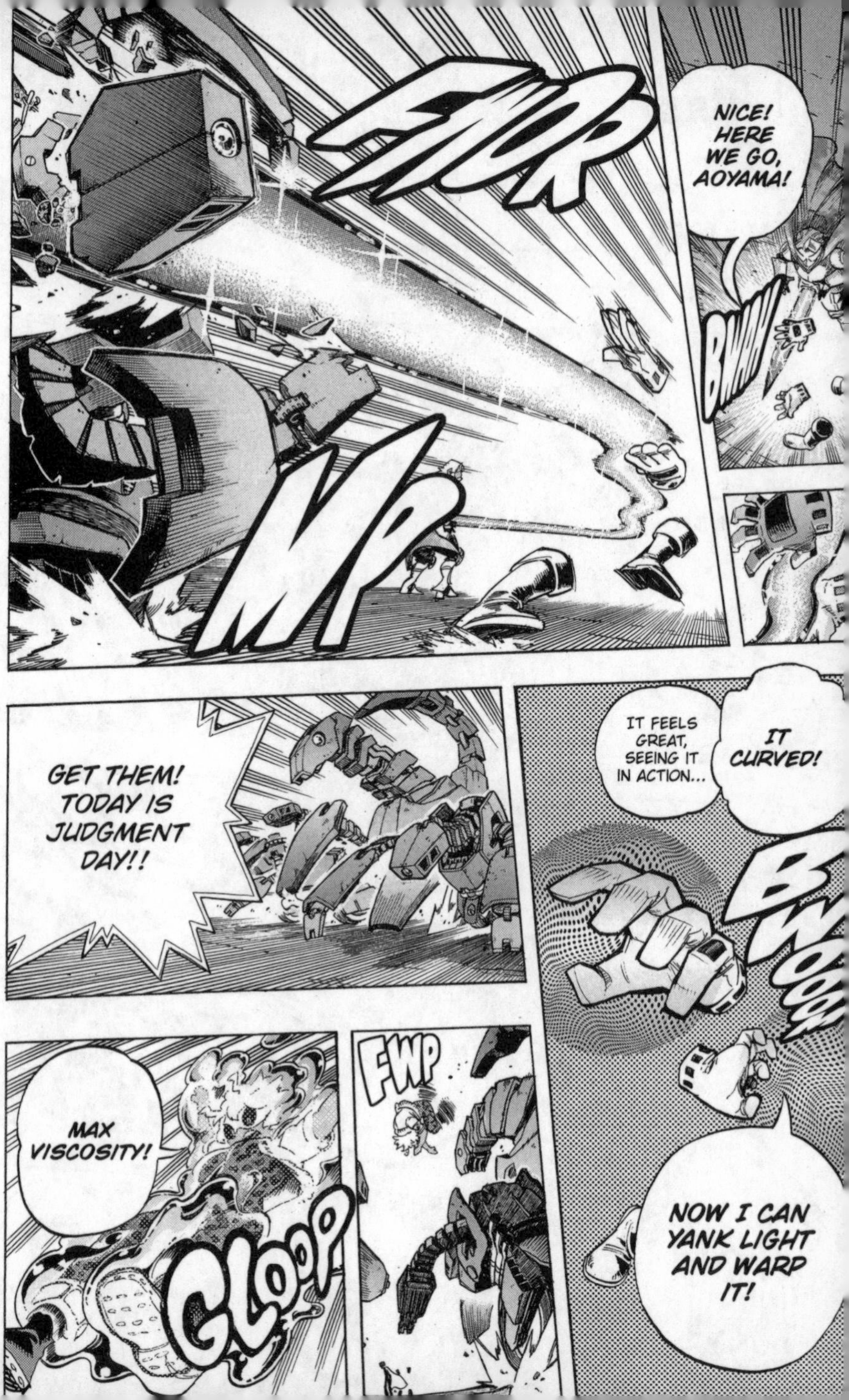
NICE! HERE WE GO, AOYAMA!
IT CURVED!
IT FEELS GREAT, SEEING IT IN ACTION...
NOW I CAN YANK LIGHT AND WARP IT!
GET THEM! TODAY IS JUDGMENT DAY!!
FWP
MAX VISCOSITY!
GLOOP

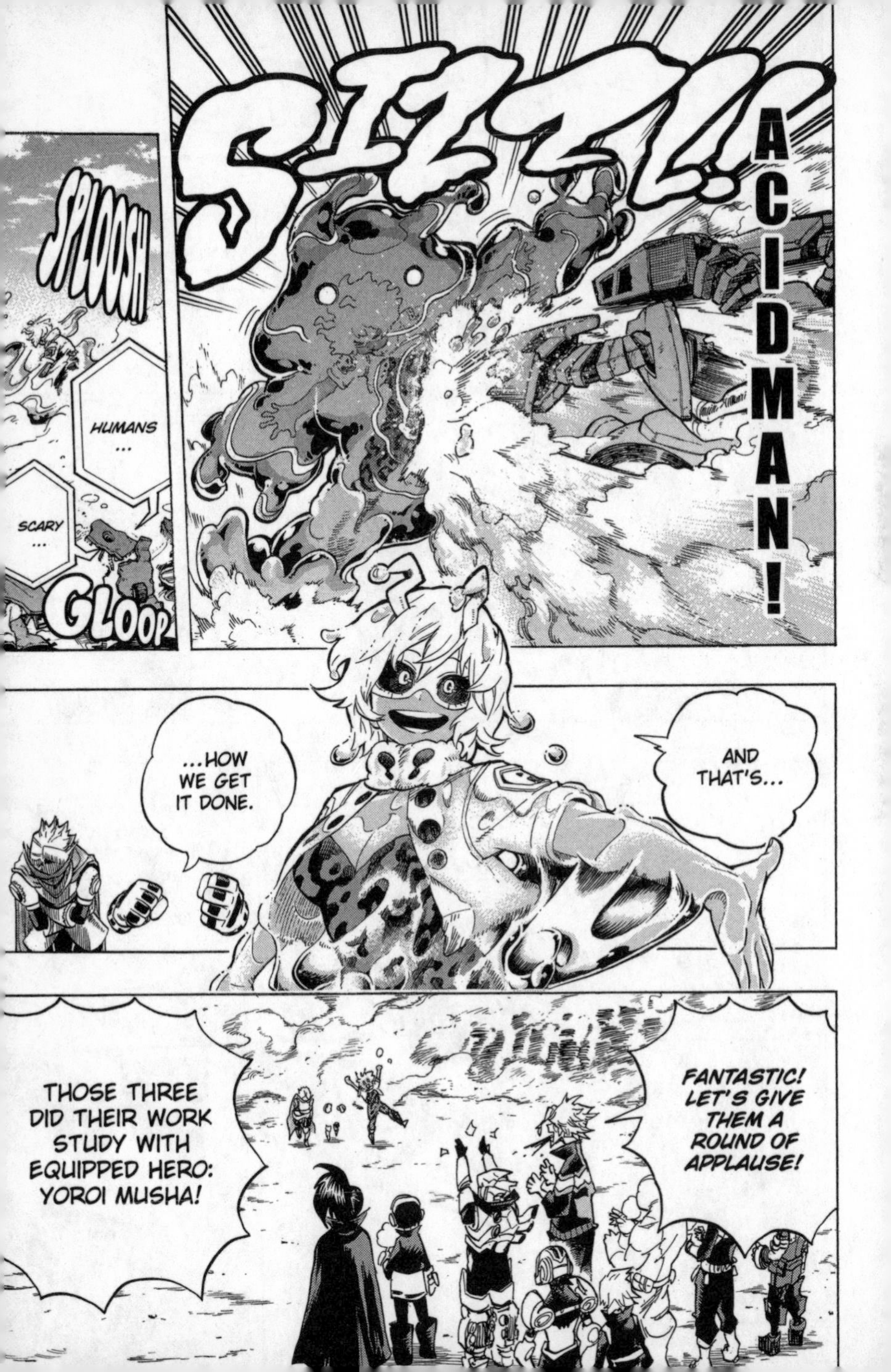

SIZZL!
ACIDMAN!
SPLOOSH
HUMANS ...
SCARY ...
GLOOP
AND THAT'S...
...HOW WE GET IT DONE.
FANTASTIC! LET'S GIVE THEM A ROUND OF APPLAUSE!
THOSE THREE DID THEIR WORK STUDY WITH EQUIPPED HERO: YOROI MUSHA!

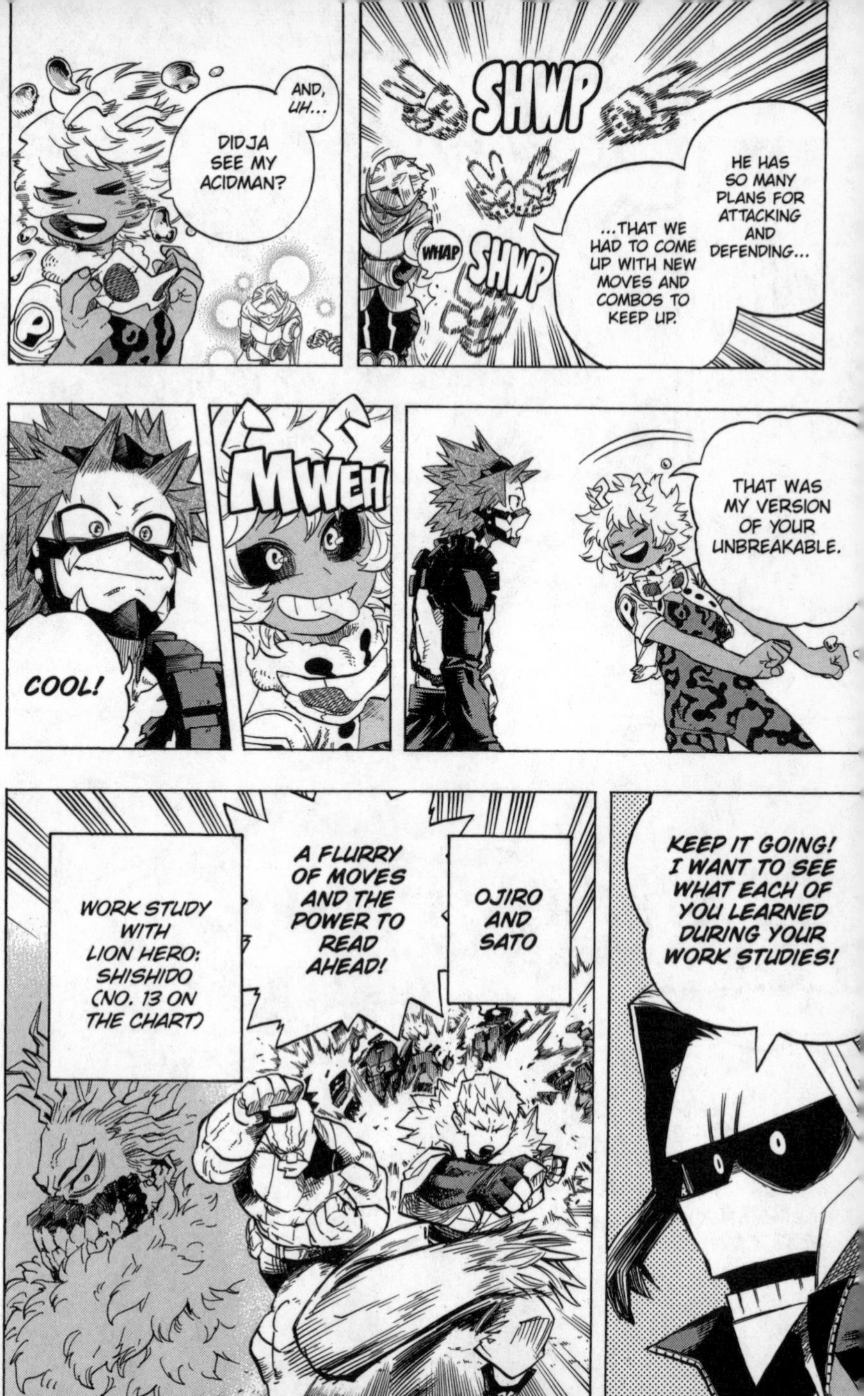
SHWP
HE HAS SO MANY PLANS FOR ATTACKING AND DEFENDING...
...THAT WE HAD TO COME UP WITH NEW MOVES AND COMBOS TO KEEP UP.
WHAP
SHWP
AND, UH...
DIDJA SEE MY ACIDMAN?
THAT WAS MY VERSION OF YOUR UNBREAKABLE.
MWEH
COOL!
KEEP IT GOING! I WANT TO SEE WHAT EACH OF YOU LEARNED DURING YOUR WORK STUDIES!
OJIRO AND SATO
A FLURRY OF MOVES AND THE POWER TO READ AHEAD!
WORK STUDY WITH LION HERO: SHISHIDO (NO. 13 ON THE CHART)

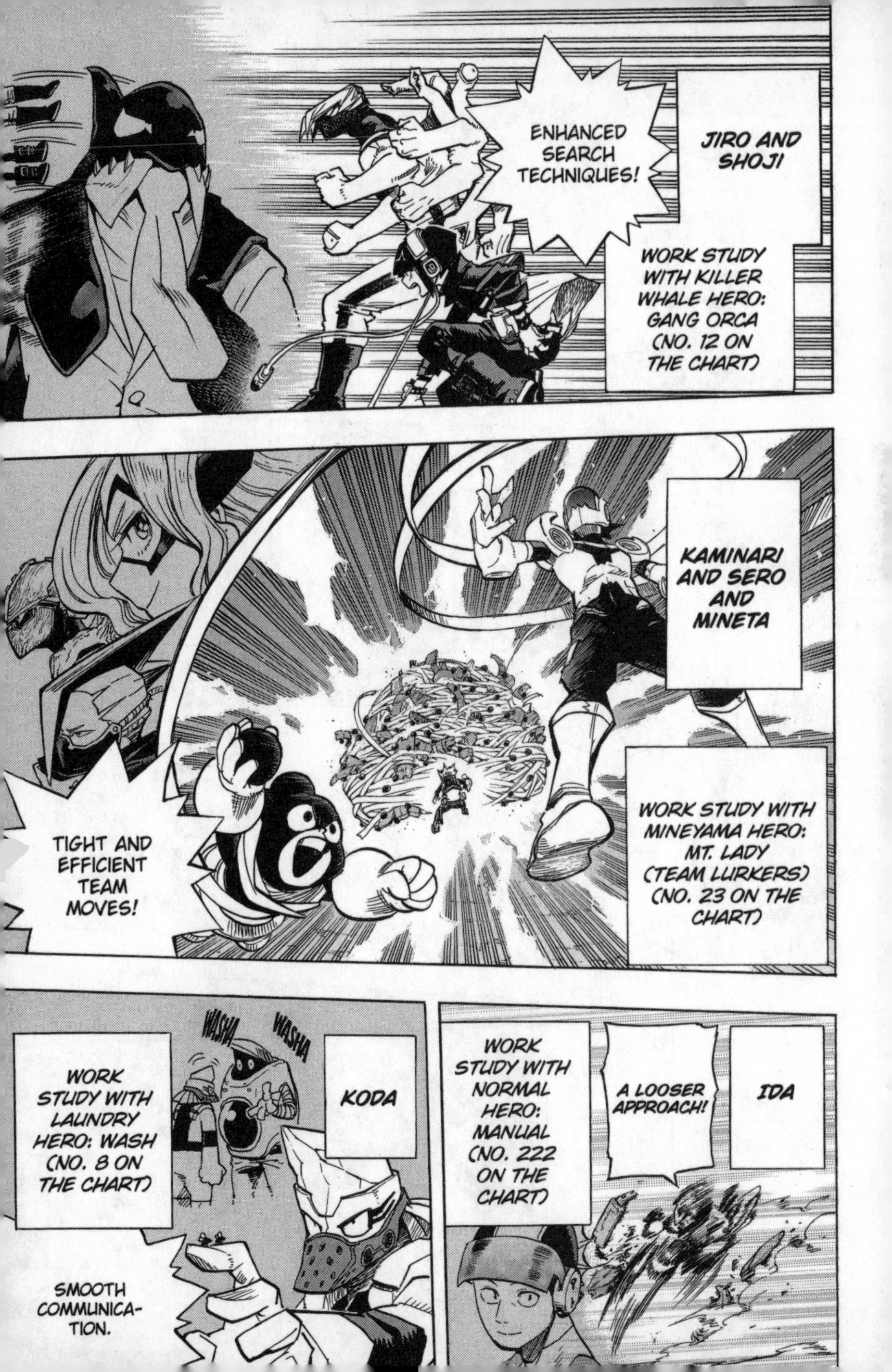
JIRO AND SHOJI
ENHANCED SEARCH TECHNIQUES!
WORK STUDY WITH KILLER WHALE HERO: GANG ORCA (NO. 12 ON THE CHART)
KAMINARI AND SERO AND MINETA
WORK STUDY WITH MINEYAMA HERO: MT. LADY (TEAM LURKERS) (NO. 23 ON THE CHART)
TIGHT AND EFFICIENT TEAM MOVES!
IDA
A LOOSER APPROACH!
WORK STUDY WITH NORMAL HERO: MANUAL (NO. 222 ON THE CHART)
KODA
WASHA
WASHA
WORK STUDY WITH LAUNDRY HERO: WASH (NO. 8 ON THE CHART)
SMOOTH COMMUNICA-TION.

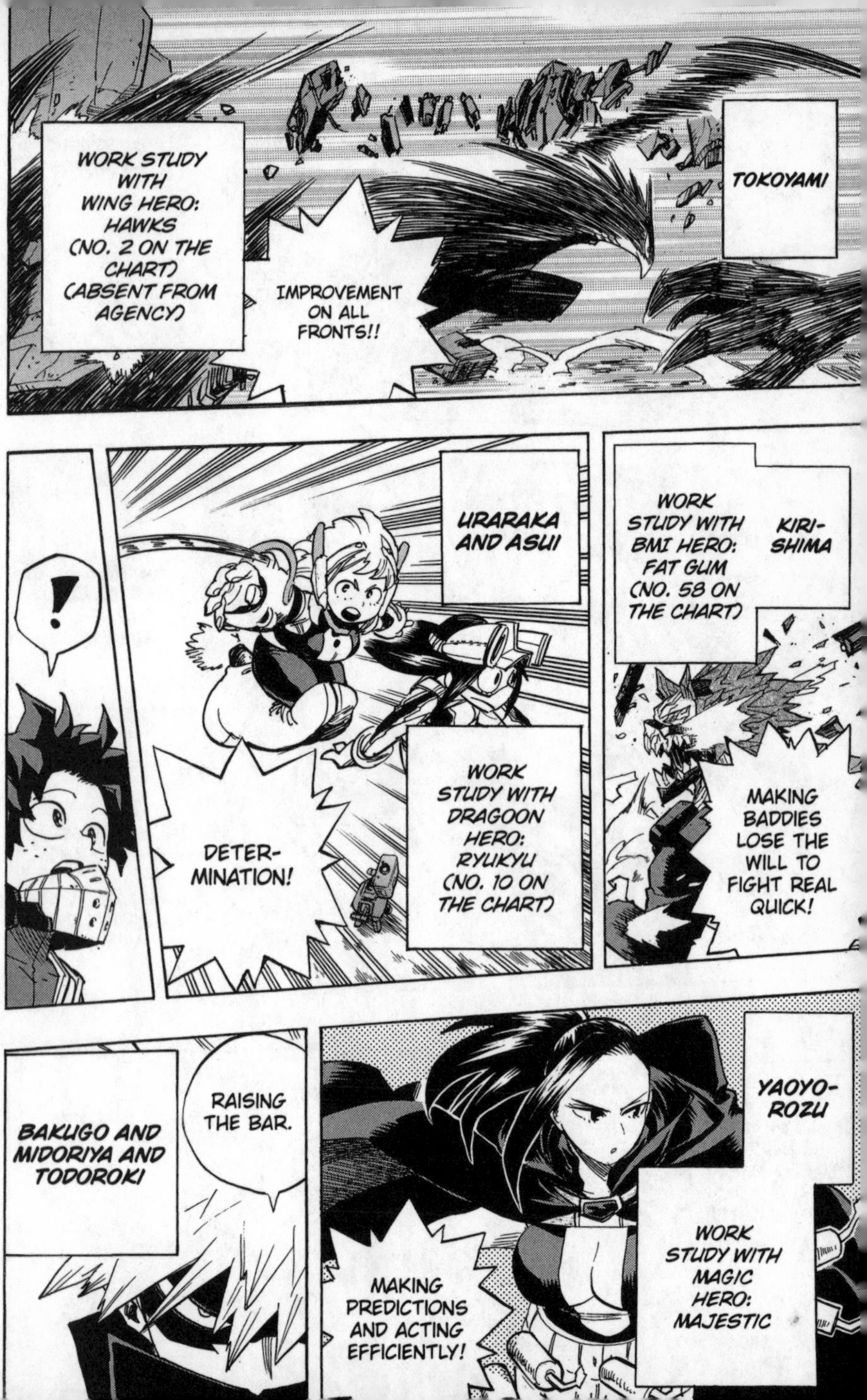
TOKOYAMI
WORK STUDY WITH WING HERO: HAWKS (NO. 2 ON THE CHART) (ABSENT FROM AGENCY)
IMPROVEMENT ON ALL FRONTS!!
KIRI-SHIMA
WORK STUDY WITH BMI HERO: FAT GUM (NO. 58 ON THE CHART)
MAKING BADDIES LOSE THE WILL TO FIGHT REAL QUICK!
URARAKA AND ASUI
WORK STUDY WITH DRAGOON HERO: RYUKYU (NO. 10 ON THE CHART)
DETER-MINATION!
!
YAOYO-ROZU
WORK STUDY WITH MAGIC HERO: MAJESTIC
MAKING PREDICTIONS AND ACTING EFFICIENTLY!
RAISING THE BAR.
BAKUGO AND MIDORIYA AND TODOROKI

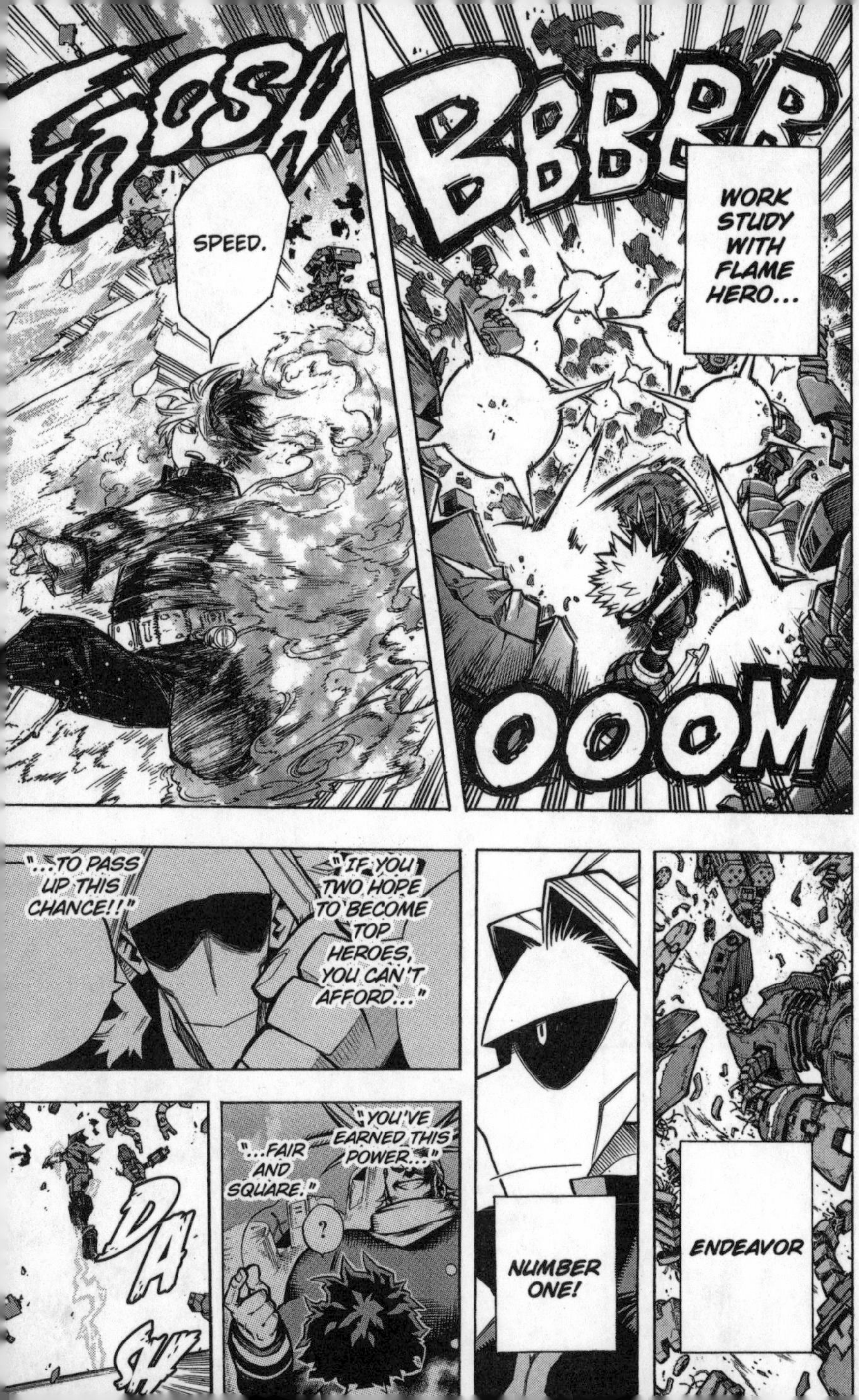
BBBRR
WORK STUDY WITH FLAME HERO...
OOOM
OOSH
SPEED.
ENDEAVOR
NUMBER ONE!
"IF YOU TWO HOPE TO BECOME TOP HEROES, YOU CAN'T AFFORD..."
"...TO PASS UP THIS CHANCE!!"
"YOU'VE EARNED THIS POWER..."
"...FAIR AND SQUARE."
?
DA
SH

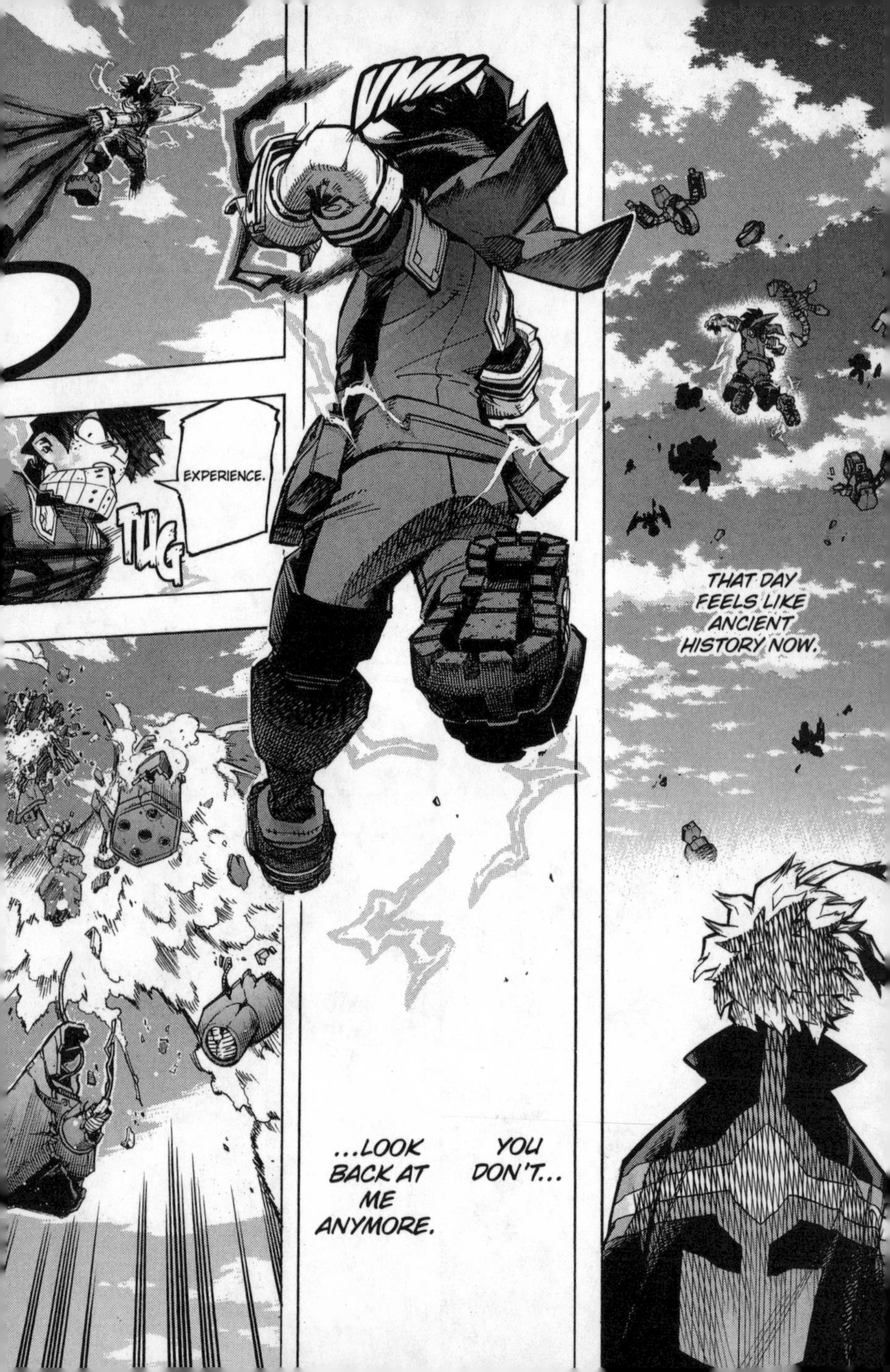
THAT DAY FEELS LIKE ANCIENT HISTORY NOW.
YOU DON'T...
...LOOK BACK AT ME ANYMORE.
EXPERIENCE.
TUG

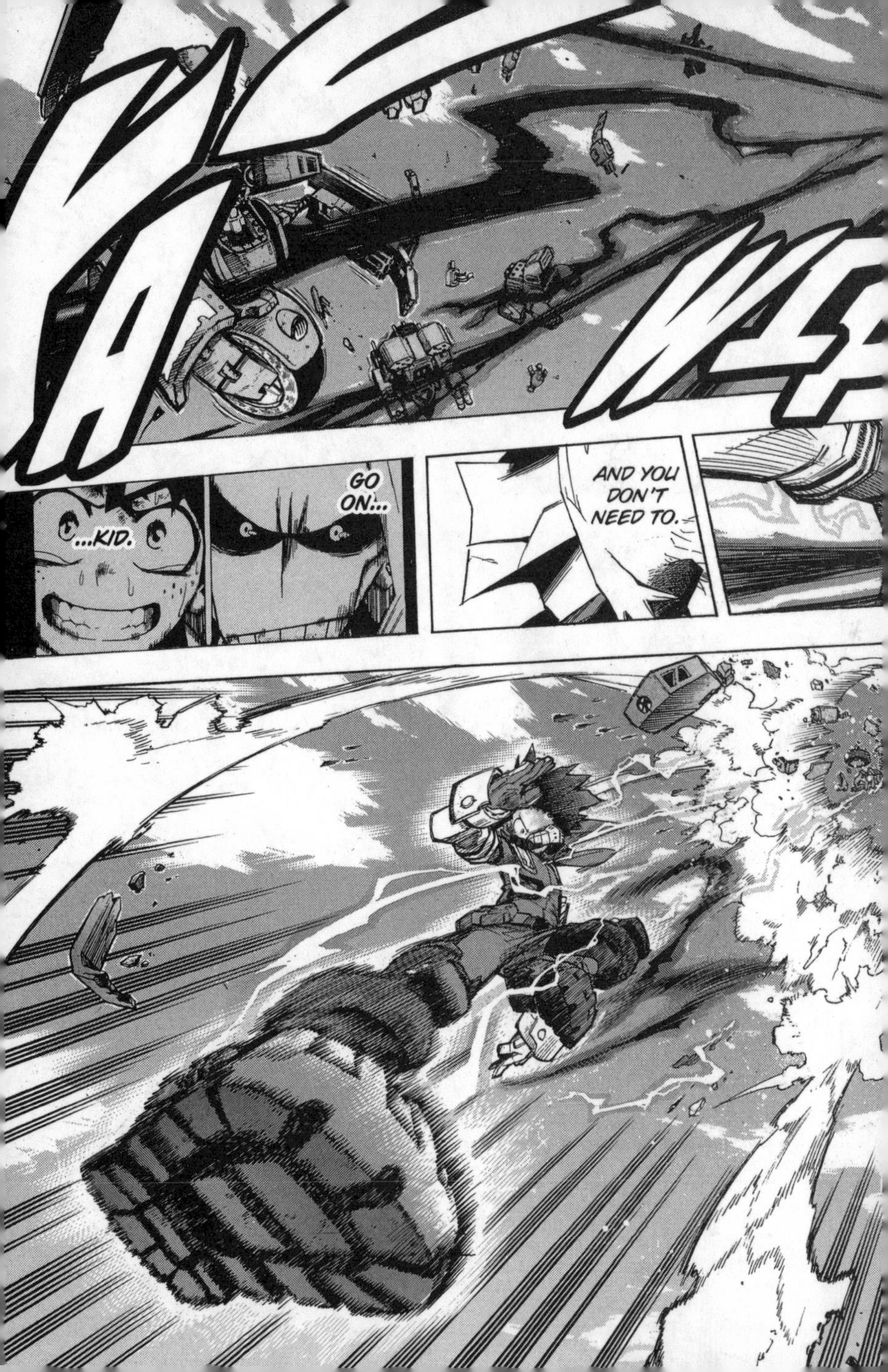
AND YOU DON'T NEED TO.
GO ON...
...KID.

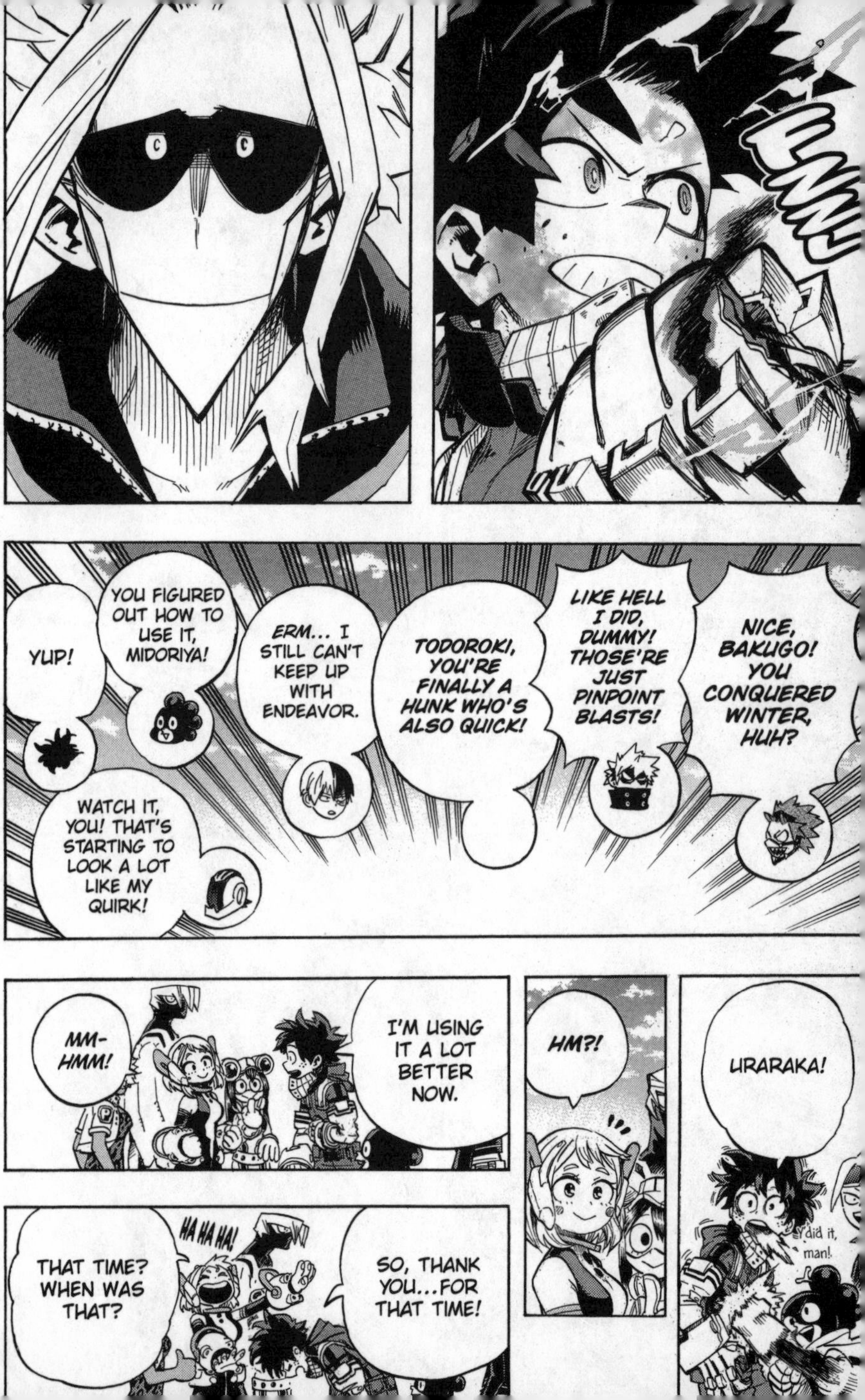
NICE, BAKUGO! YOU CONQUERED WINTER, HUH?
LIKE HELL I DID, DUMMY! THOSE'RE JUST PINPOINT BLASTS!
TODOROKI, YOU'RE FINALLY A HUNK WHO'S ALSO QUICK!
ERM... I STILL CAN'T KEEP UP WITH ENDEAVOR.
YOU FIGURED OUT HOW TO USE IT, MIDORIYA!
YUP!
WATCH IT, YOU! THAT'S STARTING TO LOOK A LOT LIKE MY QUIRK!
URARAKA!
Y'did it, man!
HM?!
I'M USING IT A LOT BETTER NOW.
MM-HMM!
SO, THANK YOU...FOR THAT TIME!
HA HA HA!
THAT TIME? WHEN WAS THAT?

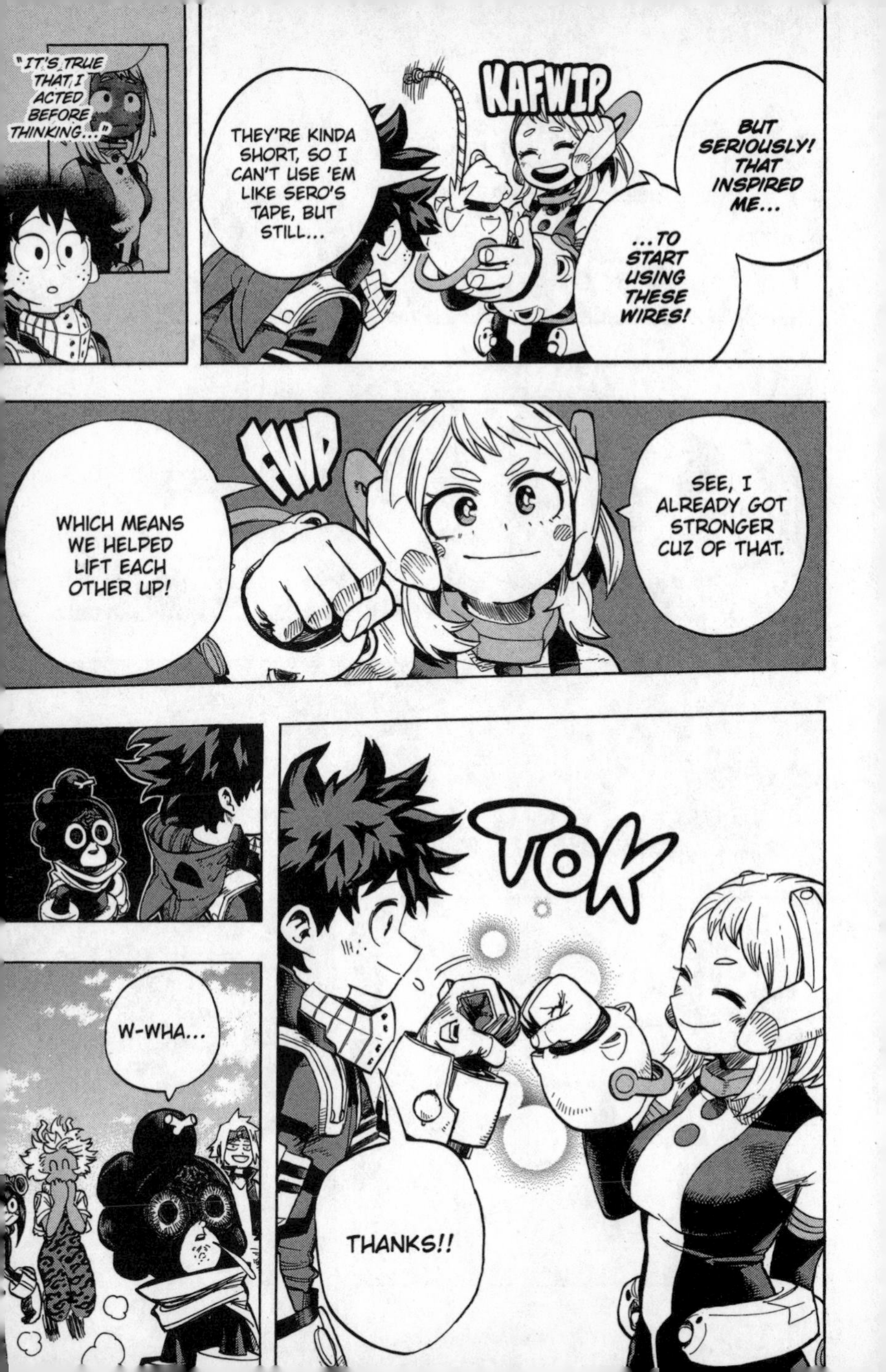
BUT SERIOUSLY! THAT INSPIRED ME...
...TO START USING THESE WIRES!
KAFWIP
THEY'RE KINDA SHORT, SO I CAN'T USE 'EM LIKE SERO'S TAPE, BUT STILL...
"IT'S TRUE THAT I ACTED BEFORE THINKING..."
SEE, I ALREADY GOT STRONGER CUZ OF THAT.
FWD
WHICH MEANS WE HELPED LIFT EACH OTHER UP!
TOK
THANKS!!
W-WHA...

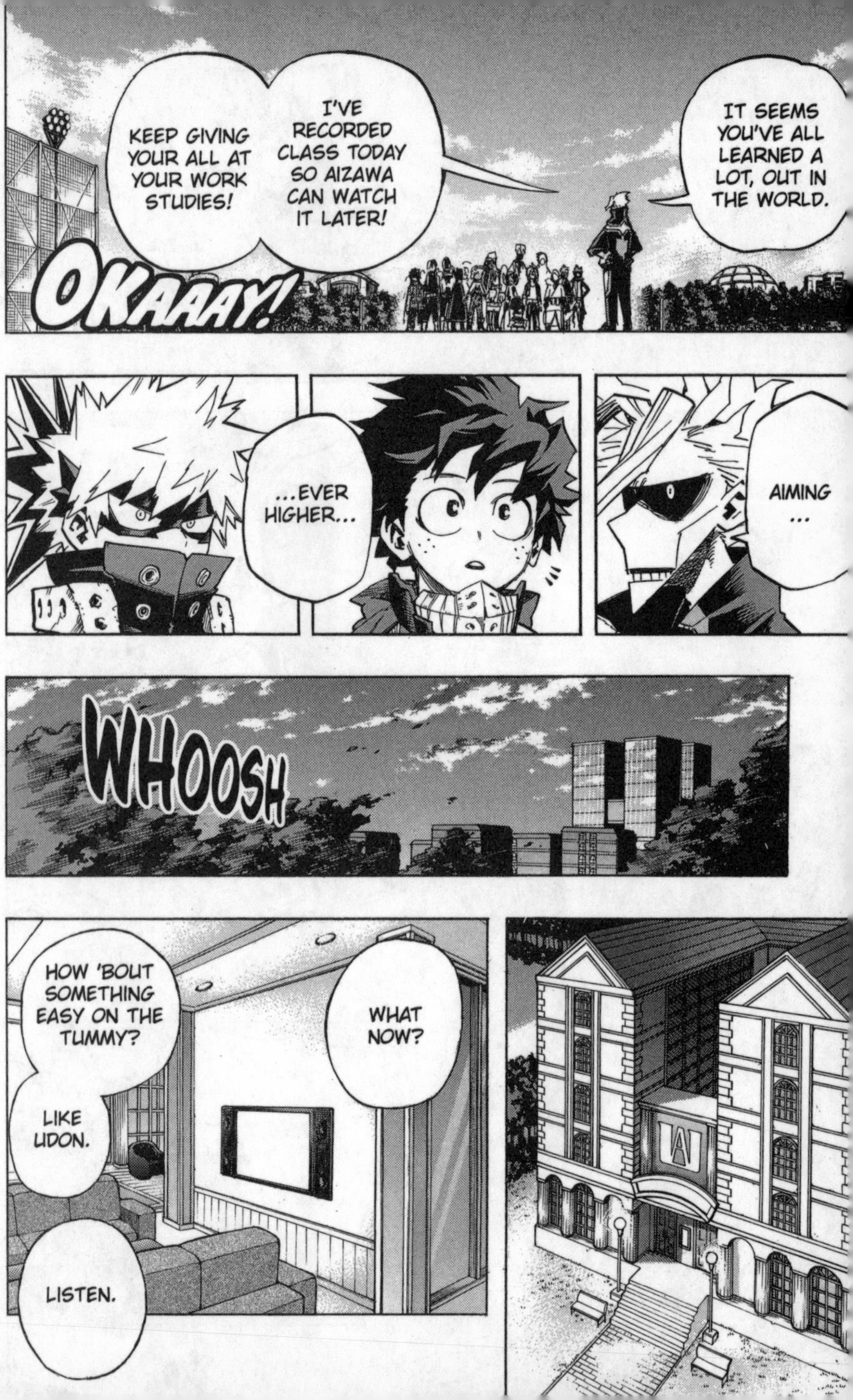
IT SEEMS YOU'VE ALL LEARNED A LOT, OUT IN THE WORLD.
I'VE RECORDED CLASS TODAY SO AIZAWA CAN WATCH IT LATER!
KEEP GIVING YOUR ALL AT YOUR WORK STUDIES!
OKAAAY!
AIMING ...
...EVER HIGHER...
WHOOSH
WHAT NOW?
HOW 'BOUT SOMETHING EASY ON THE TUMMY?
LIKE UDON.
LISTEN.

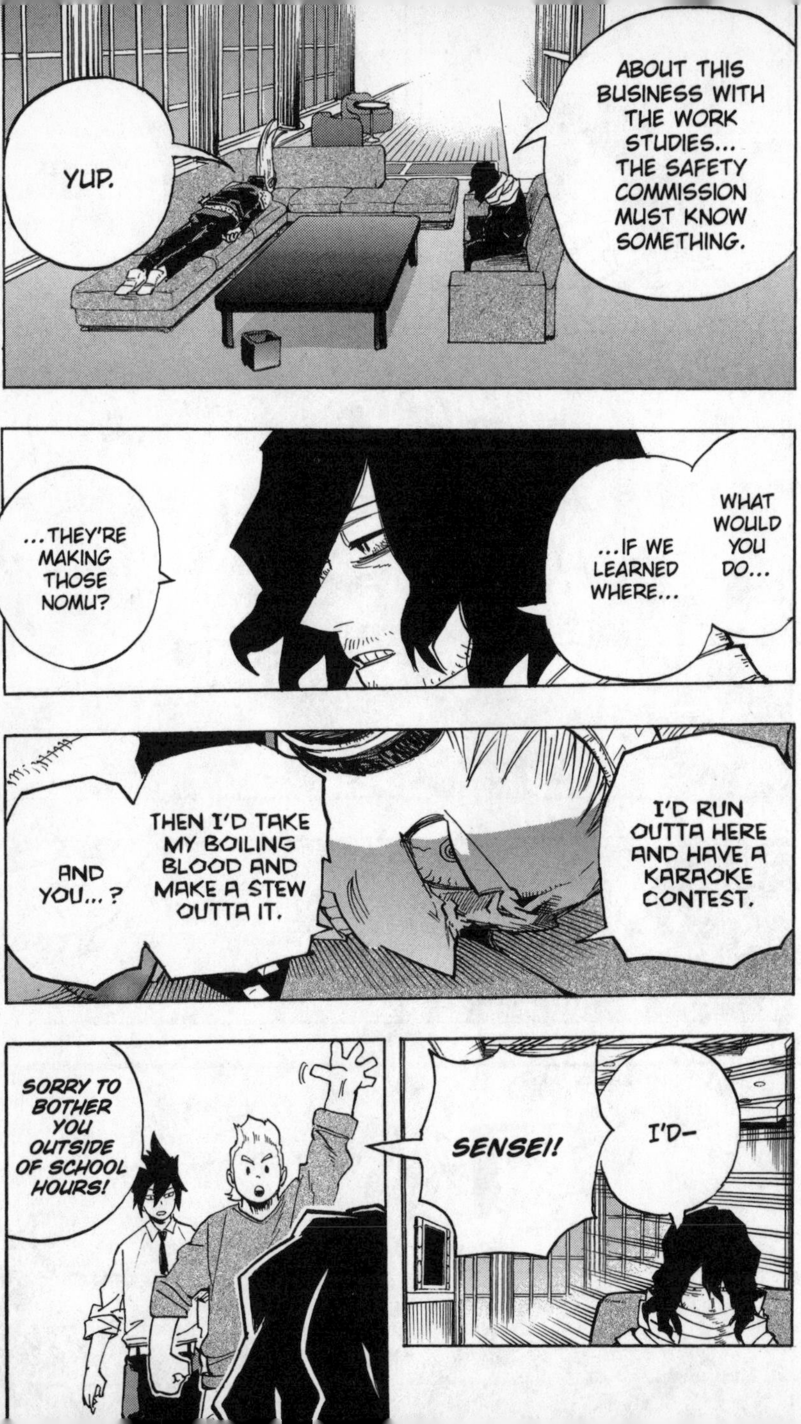
ABOUT THIS BUSINESS WITH THE WORK STUDIES... THE SAFETY COMMISSION MUST KNOW SOMETHING.
YUP.
WHAT WOULD YOU DO...
...IF WE LEARNED WHERE...
...THEY'RE MAKING THOSE NOMU?
I'D RUN OUTTA HERE AND HAVE A KARAOKE CONTEST.
THEN I'D TAKE MY BOILING BLOOD AND MAKE A STEW OUTTA IT.
AND YOU...?
I'D–
SENSEI!
SORRY TO BOTHER YOU OUTSIDE OF SCHOOL HOURS!

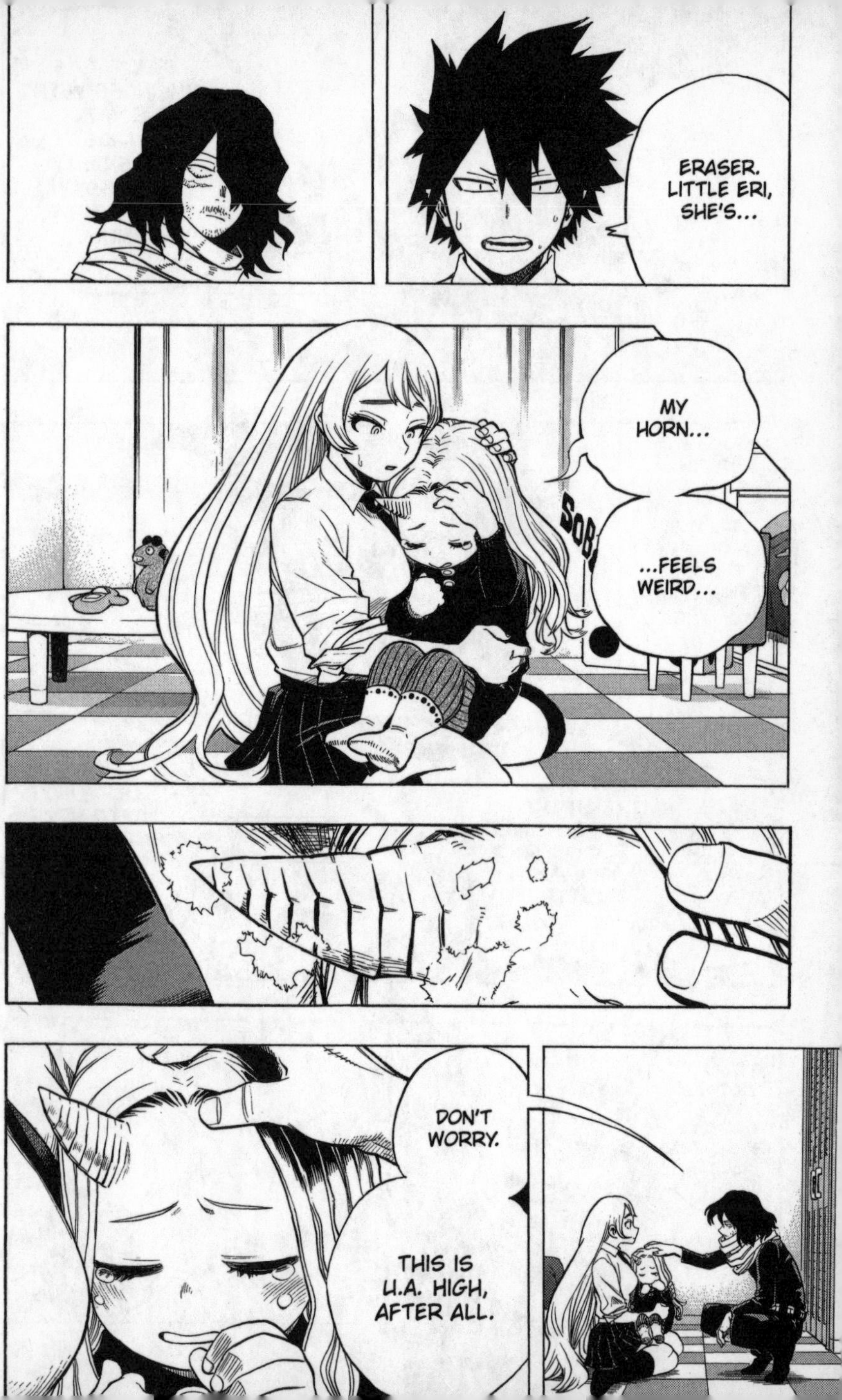
ERASER. LITTLE ERI, SHE'S...
MY HORN...
SOB
...FEELS WEIRD...
DON'T WORRY.
THIS IS U.A. HIGH, AFTER ALL.

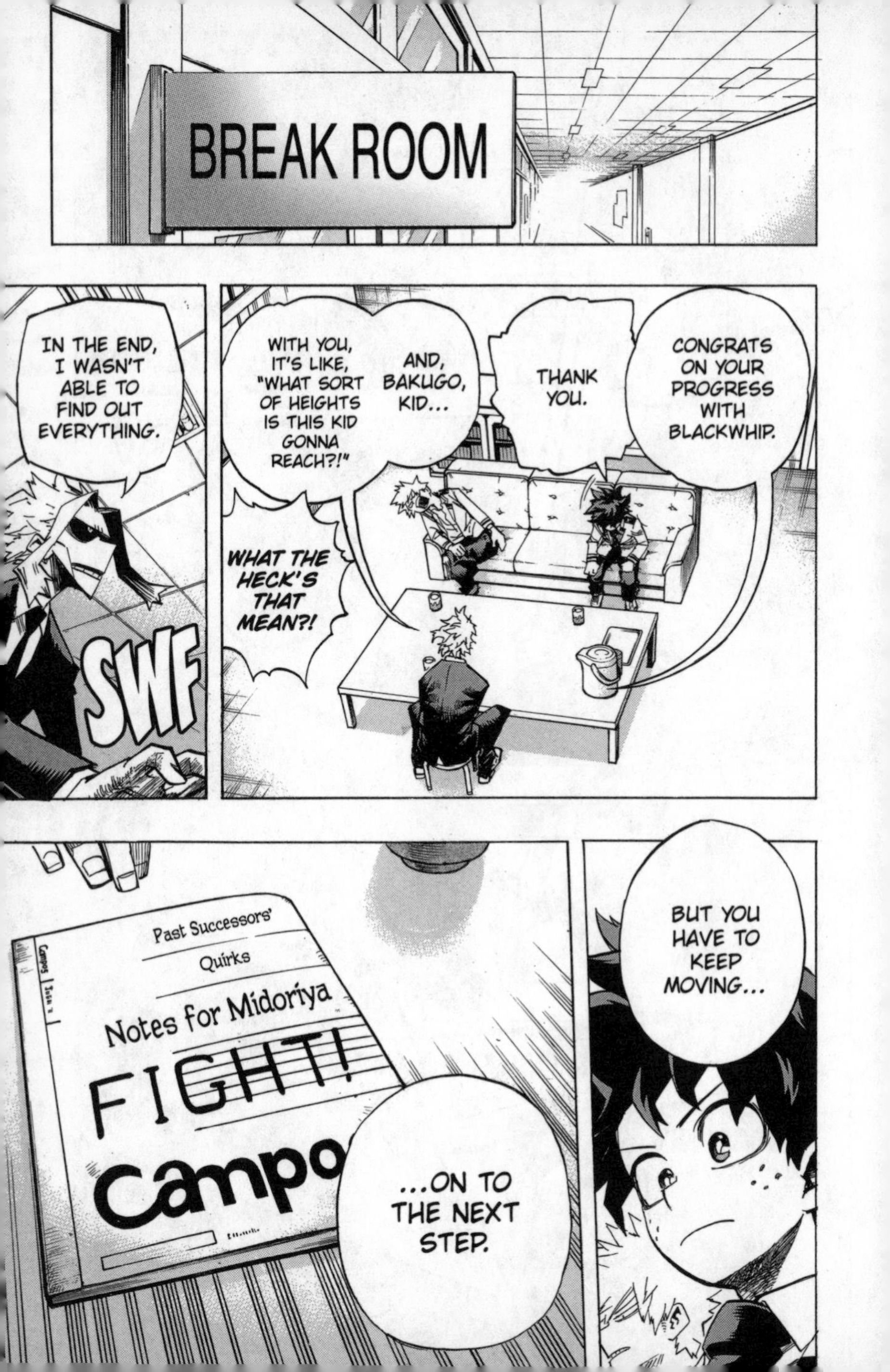
BREAK ROOM
CONGRATS ON YOUR PROGRESS WITH BLACKWHIP.
THANK YOU.
AND, BAKUGO, KID...
WITH YOU, IT'S LIKE, "WHAT SORT OF HEIGHTS IS THIS KID GONNA REACH?!"
WHAT THE HECK'S THAT MEAN?!
IN THE END, I WASN'T ABLE TO FIND OUT EVERYTHING.
SWF
BUT YOU HAVE TO KEEP MOVING...
Past Successors' Quirks
Notes for Midoriya
FIGHT!
Campo
...ON TO THE NEXT STEP.

ASSISTANTS

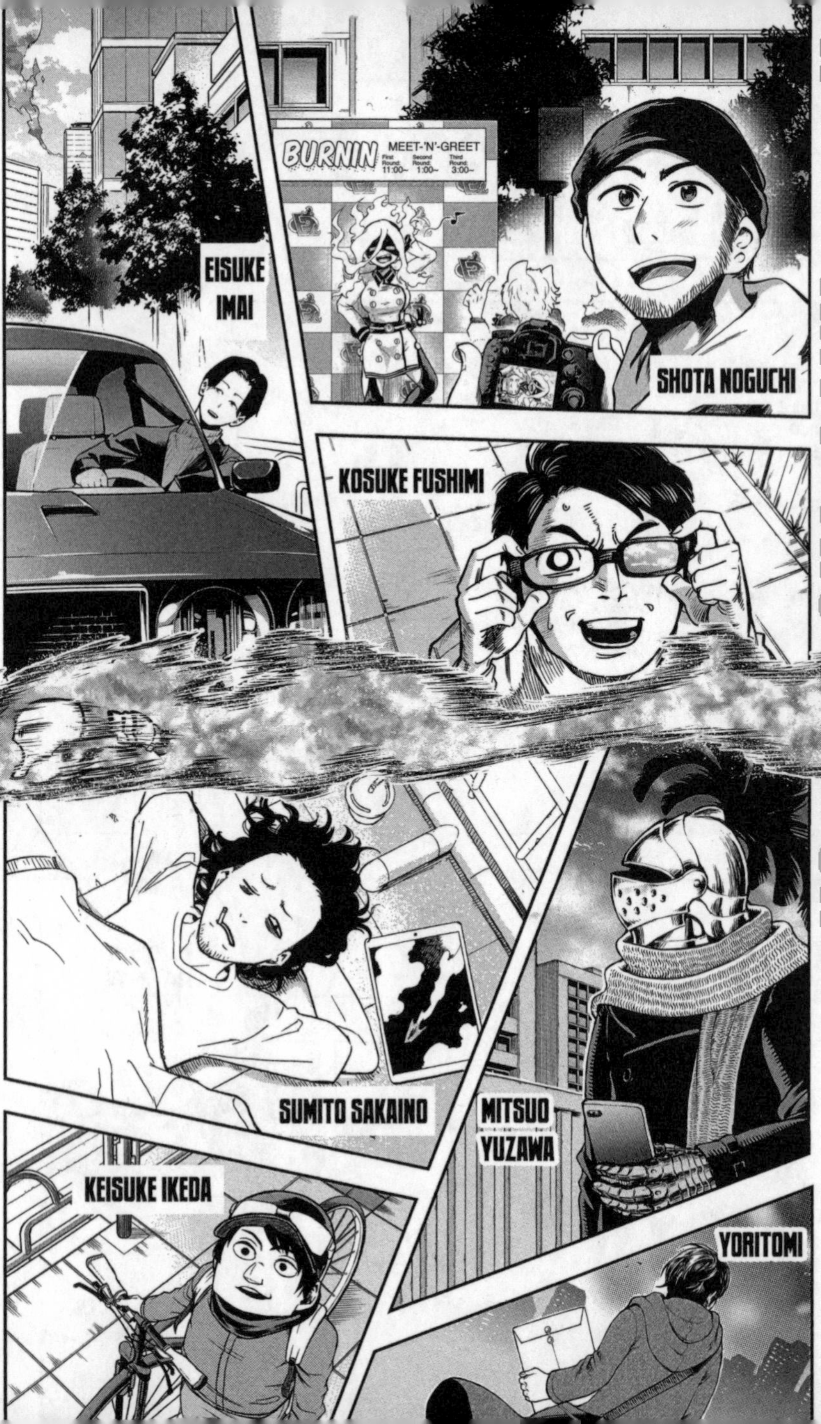
SHOTA NOGUCHI
BURNIN
MEET-'N'-GREET
First Round: 11:00~
Second Round: 1:00~
Third Round: 3:00~
EISUKE IMAI
KOSUKE FUSHIMI
MITSUO YUZAWA
SUMITO SAKAINO
YORITOMI
KEISUKE IKEDA

No. 257 - Pass It Forward, to Whomever

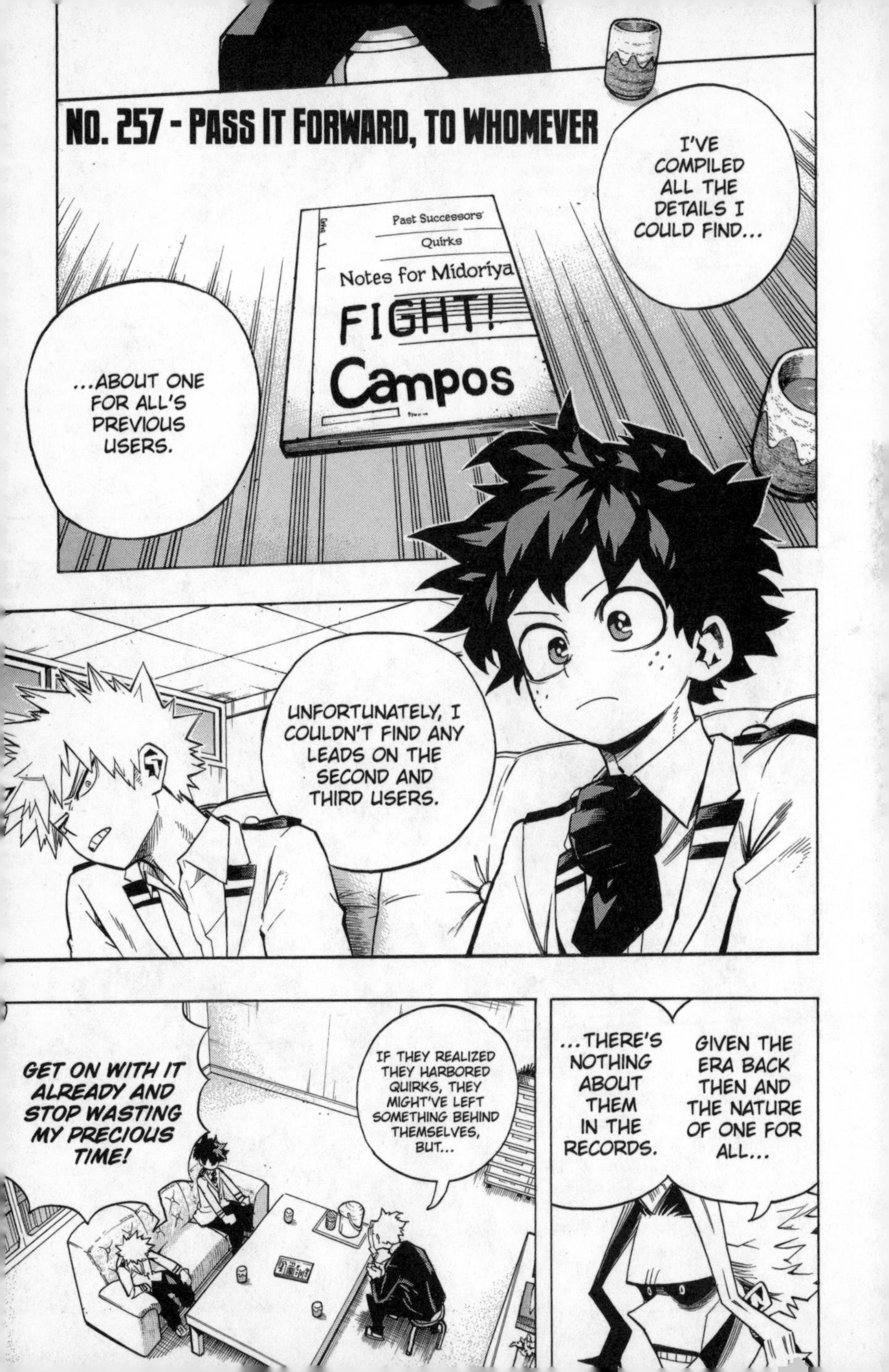

I'VE COMPILED ALL THE DETAILS I COULD FIND...
...ABOUT ONE FOR ALL'S PREVIOUS USERS.
Past Successors' Quirks
Notes for Midoriya
FIGHT!
Campos
UNFORTUNATELY, I COULDN'T FIND ANY LEADS ON THE SECOND AND THIRD USERS.
GIVEN THE ERA BACK THEN AND THE NATURE OF ONE FOR ALL...
...THERE'S NOTHING ABOUT THEM IN THE RECORDS.
IF THEY REALIZED THEY HARBORED QUIRKS, THEY MIGHT'VE LEFT SOMETHING BEHIND THEMSELVES, BUT...
GET ON WITH IT ALREADY AND STOP WASTING MY PRECIOUS TIME!

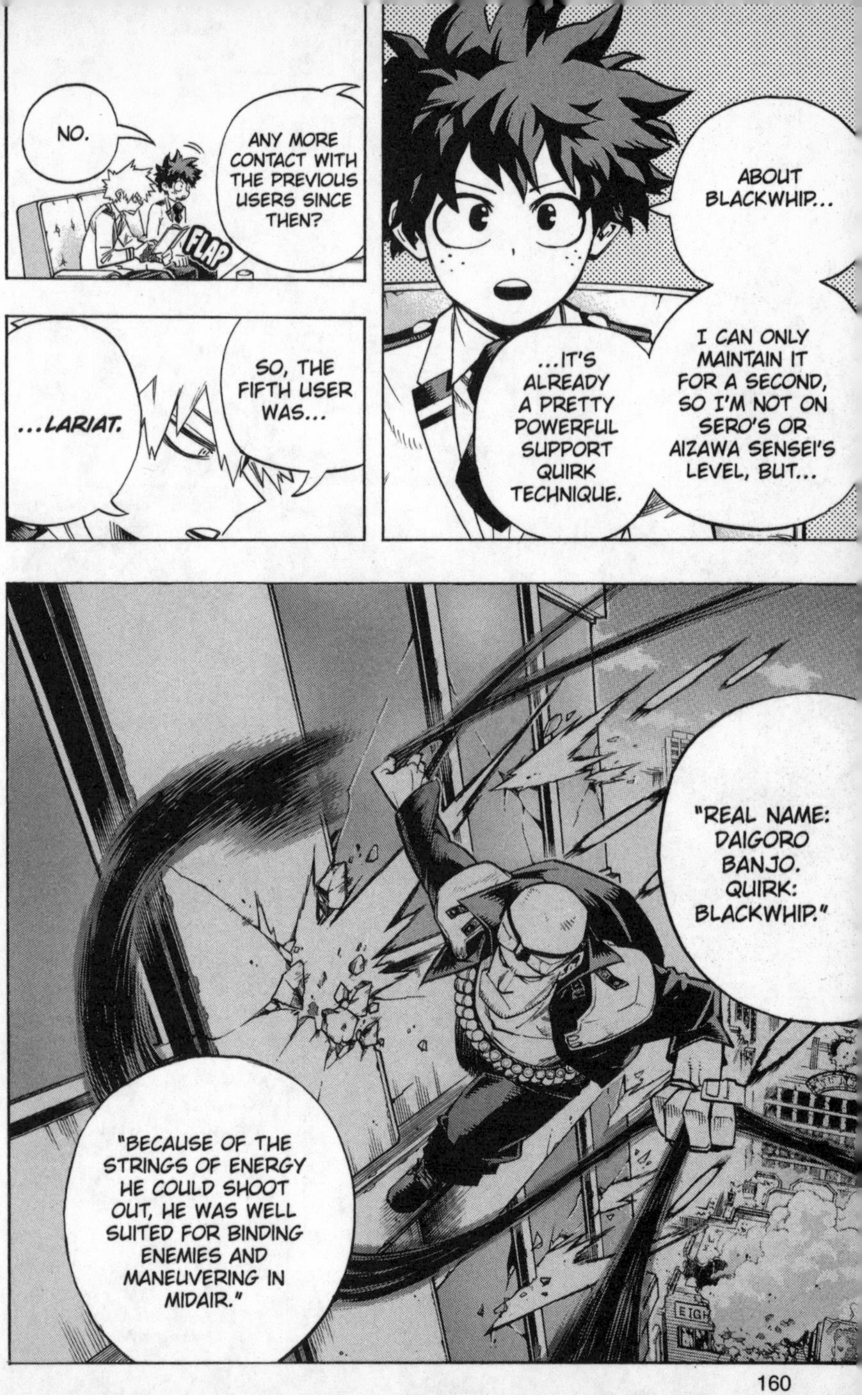
ABOUT BLACKWHIP...
I CAN ONLY MAINTAIN IT FOR A SECOND, SO I'M NOT ON SERO'S OR AIZAWA SENSEI'S LEVEL, BUT...
...IT'S ALREADY A PRETTY POWERFUL SUPPORT QUIRK TECHNIQUE.
ANY MORE CONTACT WITH THE PREVIOUS USERS SINCE THEN?
FLAP
NO.
SO, THE FIFTH USER WAS...
...LARIAT.
"REAL NAME: DAIGORO BANJO. QUIRK: BLACKWHIP."
"BECAUSE OF THE STRINGS OF ENERGY HE COULD SHOOT OUT, HE WAS WELL SUITED FOR BINDING ENEMIES AND MANEUVERING IN MIDAIR."

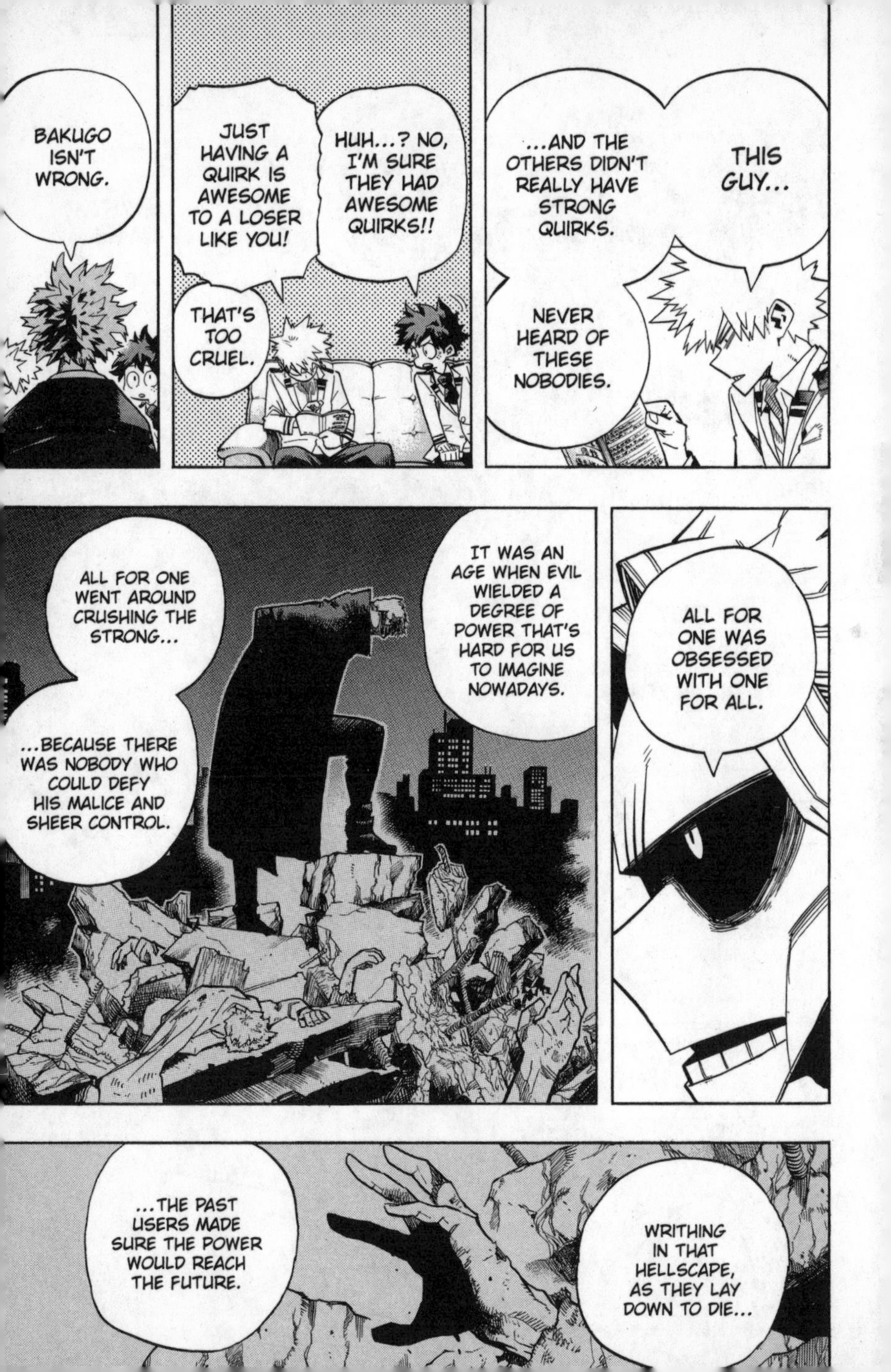
THIS GUY...
...AND THE OTHERS DIDN'T REALLY HAVE STRONG QUIRKS.
NEVER HEARD OF THESE NOBODIES.
HUH...? NO, I'M SURE THEY HAD AWESOME QUIRKS!!
JUST HAVING A QUIRK IS AWESOME TO A LOSER LIKE YOU!
THAT'S TOO CRUEL.
BAKUGO ISN'T WRONG.
ALL FOR ONE WAS OBSESSED WITH ONE FOR ALL.
IT WAS AN AGE WHEN EVIL WIELDED A DEGREE OF POWER THAT'S HARD FOR US TO IMAGINE NOWADAYS.
ALL FOR ONE WENT AROUND CRUSHING THE STRONG...
...BECAUSE THERE WAS NOBODY WHO COULD DEFY HIS MALICE AND SHEER CONTROL.
WRITHING IN THAT HELLSCAPE, AS THEY LAY DOWN TO DIE...
...THE PAST USERS MADE SURE THE POWER WOULD REACH THE FUTURE.

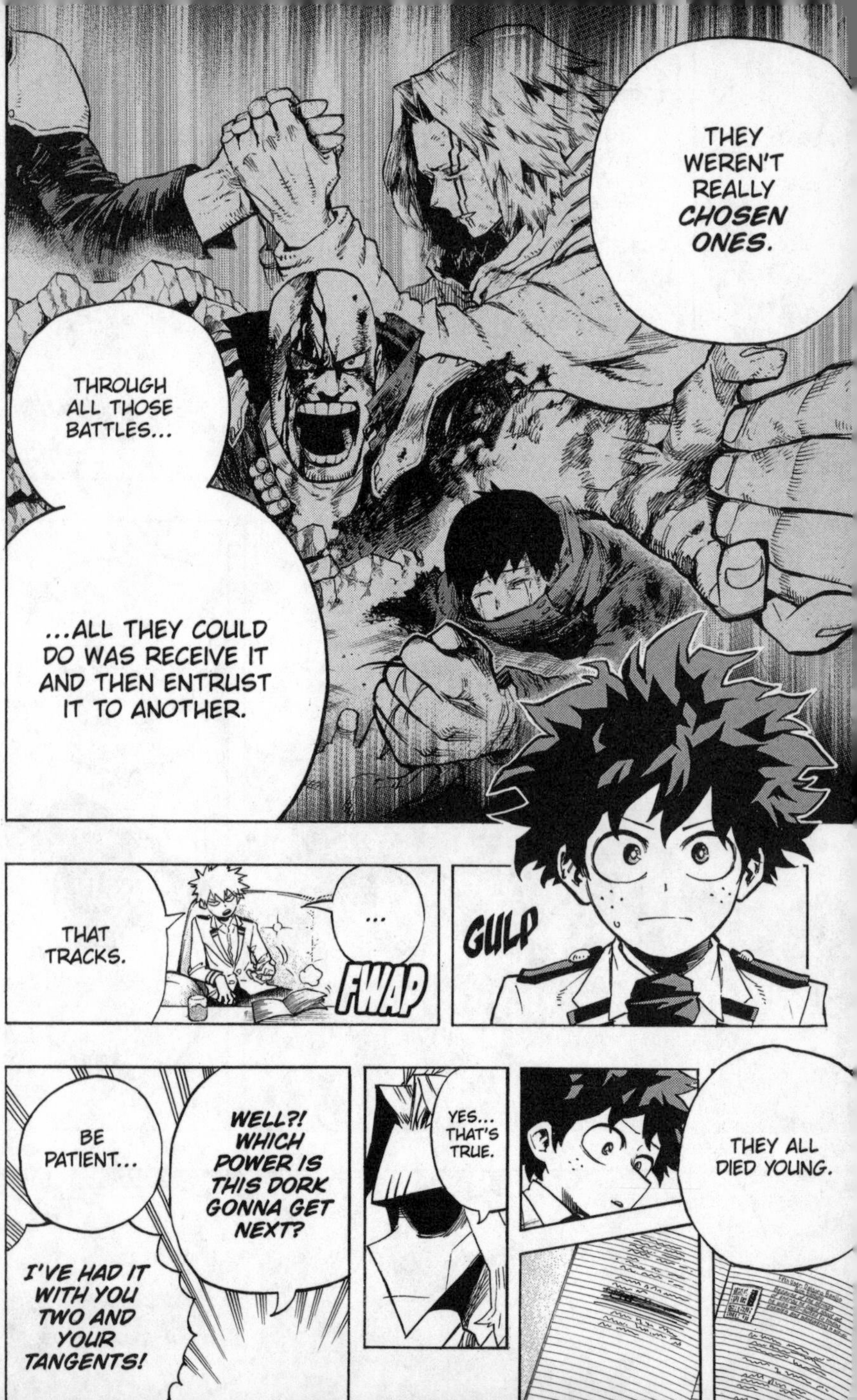
THEY WEREN'T REALLY CHOSEN ONES.
THROUGH ALL THOSE BATTLES...
...ALL THEY COULD DO WAS RECEIVE IT AND THEN ENTRUST IT TO ANOTHER.
GULP
...
FWAP
THAT TRACKS.
THEY ALL DIED YOUNG.
YES... THAT'S TRUE.
WELL?! WHICH POWER IS THIS DORK GONNA GET NEXT?
BE PATIENT...
I'VE HAD IT WITH YOU TWO AND YOUR TANGENTS!

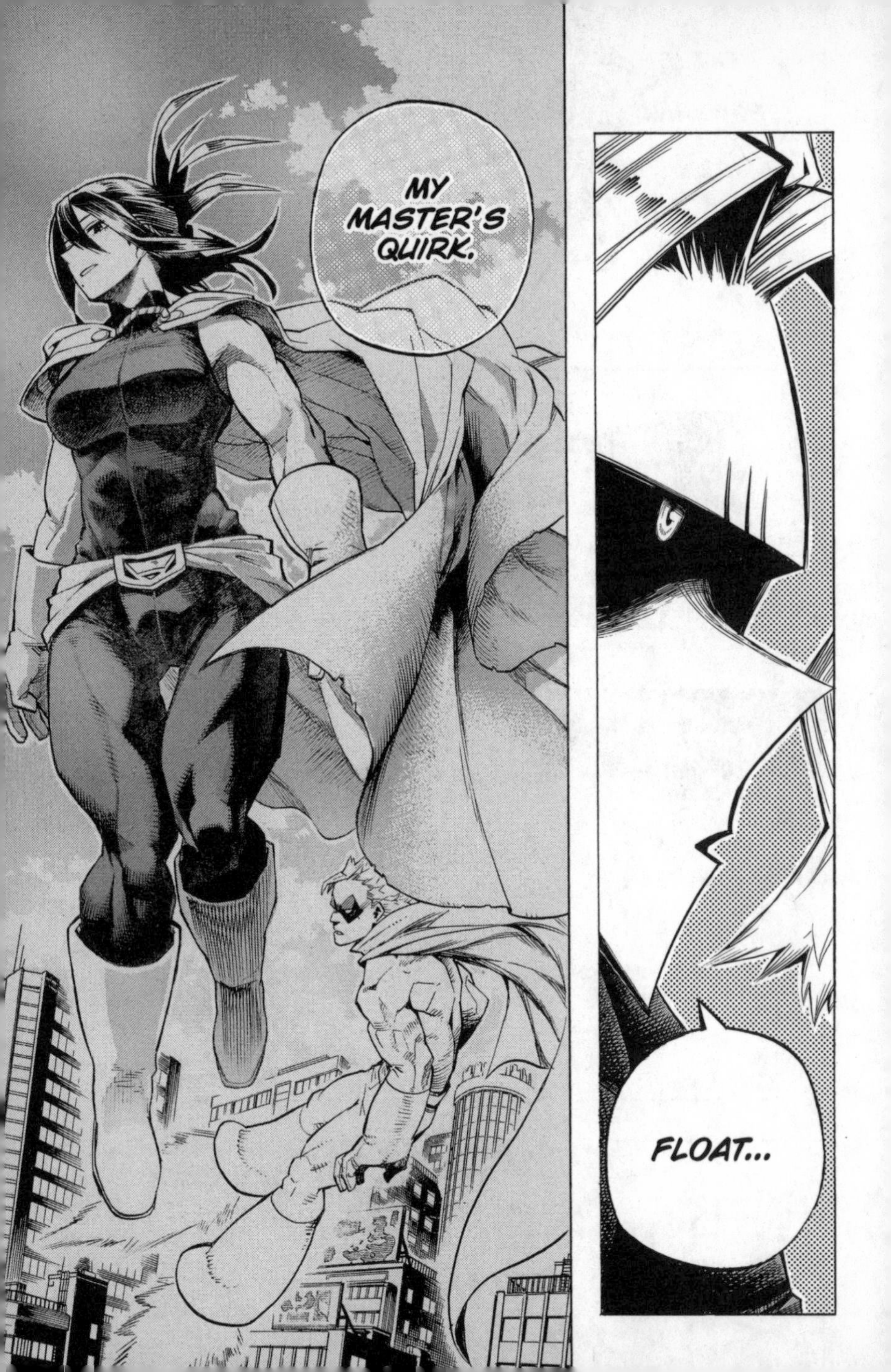
FLOAT...
MY MASTER'S QUIRK.

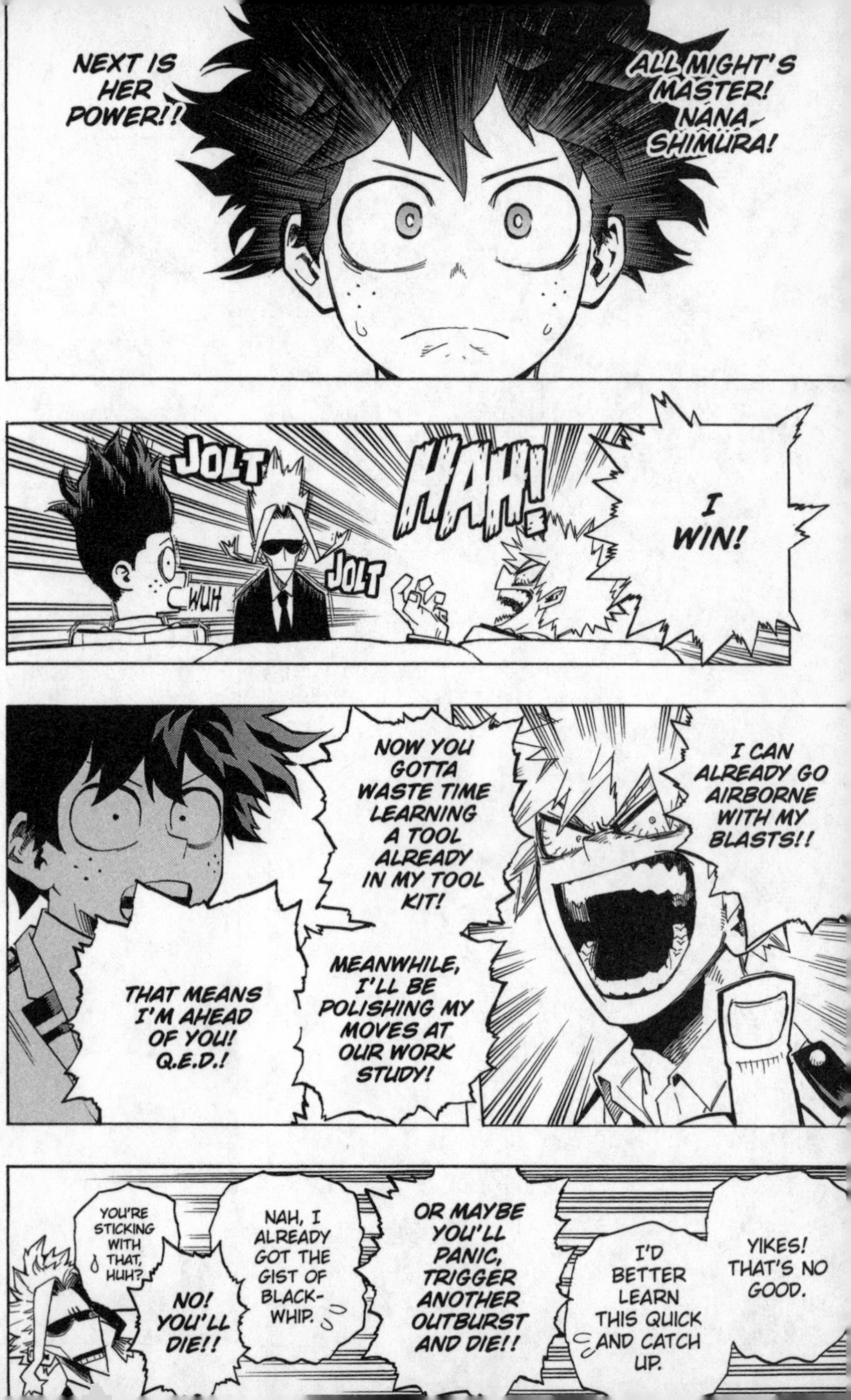
ALL MIGHT'S MASTER! NANA SHIMŪRA!
NEXT IS HER POWER!!
I WIN!
HAH!
JOLT
JOLT
WUH
I CAN ALREADY GO AIRBORNE WITH MY BLASTS!!
NOW YOU GOTTA WASTE TIME LEARNING A TOOL ALREADY IN MY TOOL KIT!
MEANWHILE, I'LL BE POLISHING MY MOVES AT OUR WORK STUDY!
THAT MEANS I'M AHEAD OF YOU! Q.E.D.!
YIKES! THAT'S NO GOOD.
I'D BETTER LEARN THIS QUICK AND CATCH UP.
OR MAYBE YOU'LL PANIC, TRIGGER ANOTHER OUTBURST AND DIE!!
NAH, I ALREADY GOT THE GIST OF BLACK-WHIP.
NO! YOU'LL DIE!!
YOU'RE STICKING WITH THAT, HUH?

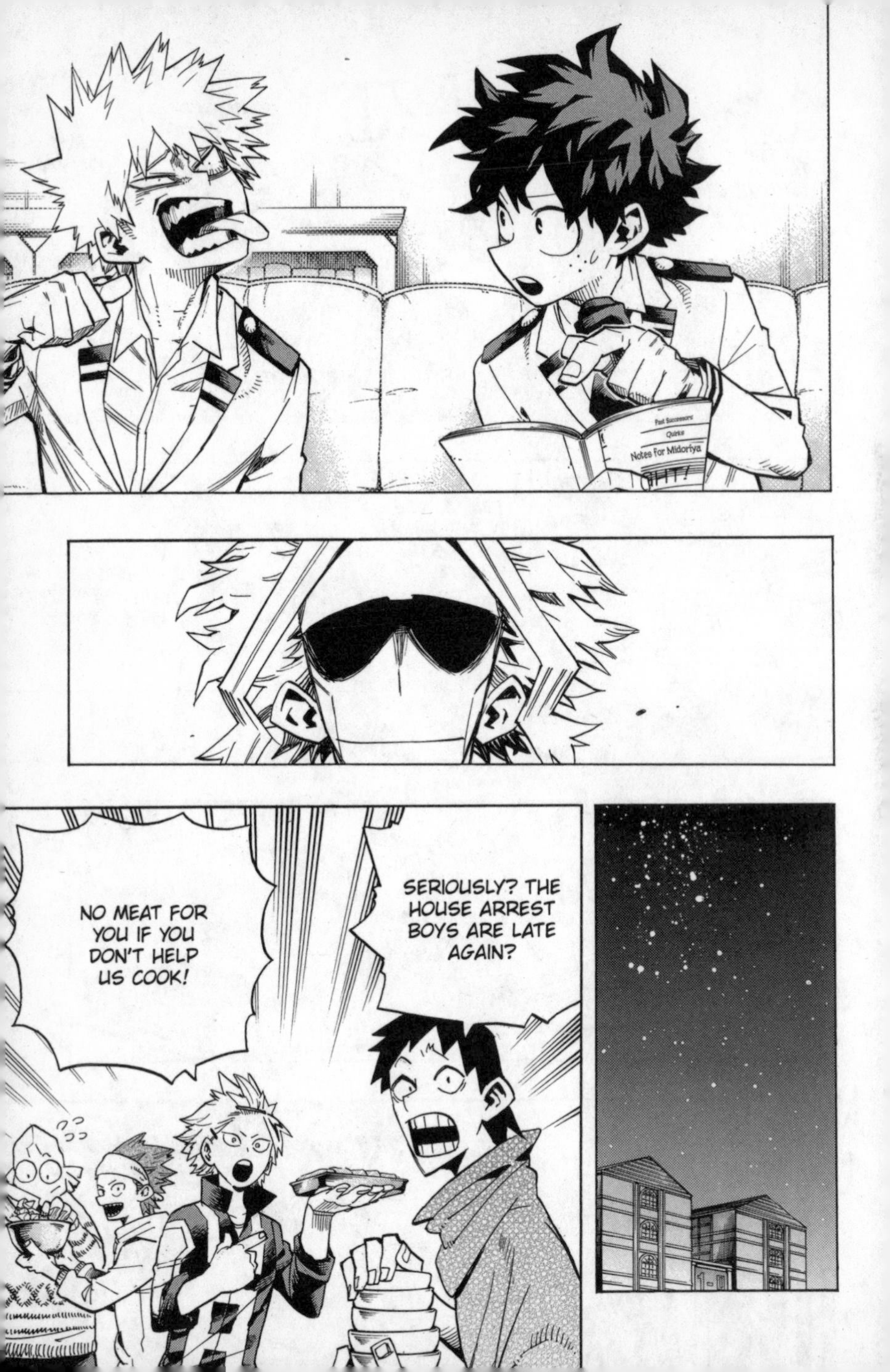
Past Successors
Quirks
Notes for Midoriya
SERIOUSLY? THE HOUSE ARREST BOYS ARE LATE AGAIN?
NO MEAT FOR YOU IF YOU DON'T HELP US COOK!

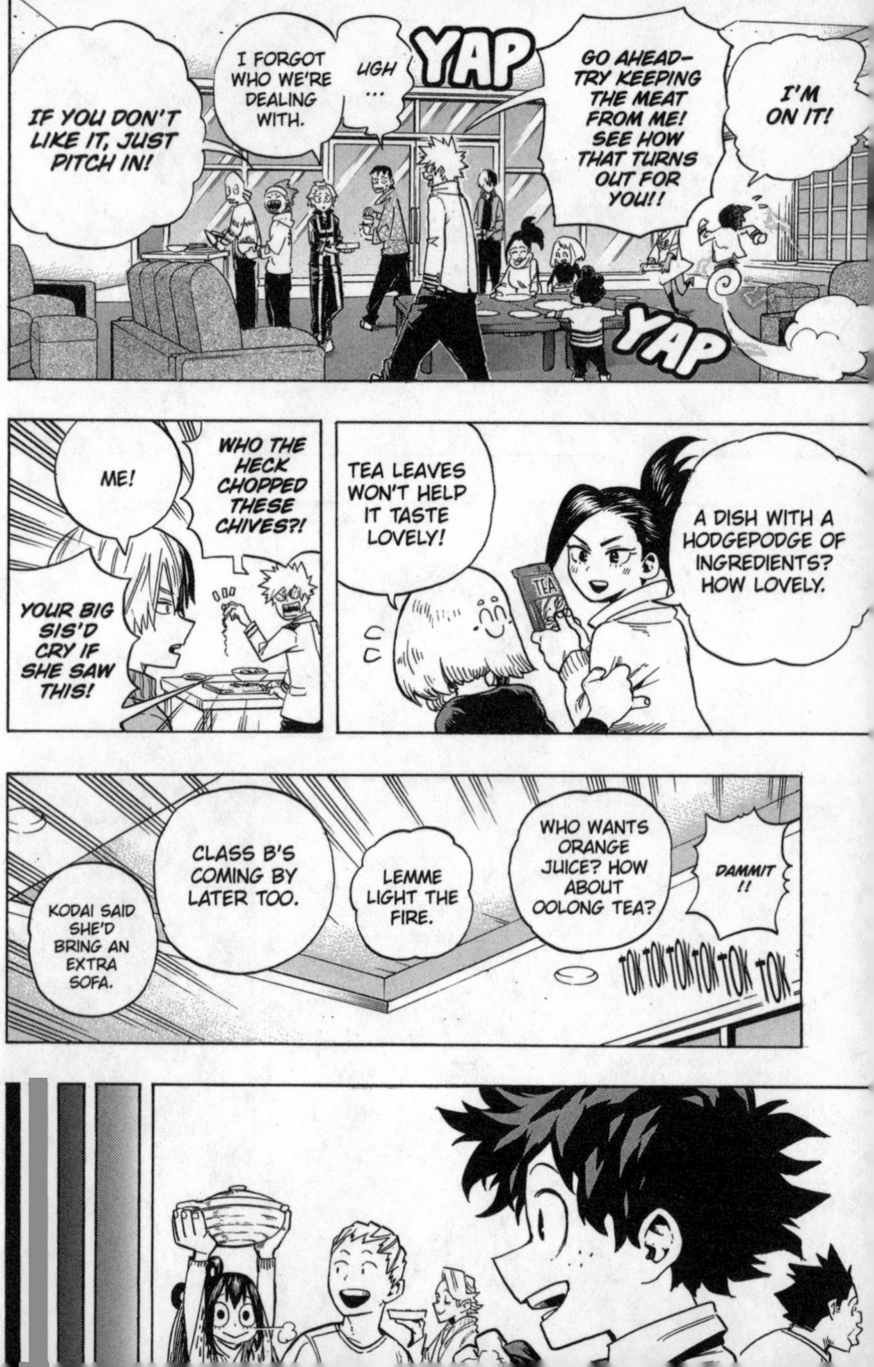
I'M ON IT!
GO AHEAD—TRY KEEPING THE MEAT FROM ME! SEE HOW THAT TURNS OUT FOR YOU!!
YAP
UGH ...
I FORGOT WHO WE'RE DEALING WITH.
IF YOU DON'T LIKE IT, JUST PITCH IN!
YAP
A DISH WITH A HODGEPODGE OF INGREDIENTS? HOW LOVELY.
TEA
TEA LEAVES WON'T HELP IT TASTE LOVELY!
WHO THE HECK CHOPPED THESE CHIVES?!
ME!
YOUR BIG SIS'D CRY IF SHE SAW THIS!
DAMMIT !!
TOK TOK TOK TOK TOK TOK
WHO WANTS ORANGE JUICE? HOW ABOUT OOLONG TEA?
LEMME LIGHT THE FIRE.
CLASS B'S COMING BY LATER TOO.
KODAI SAID SHE'D BRING AN EXTRA SOFA.

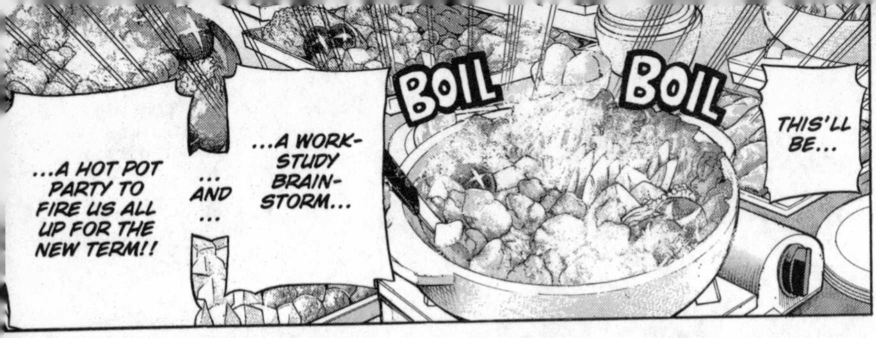
BOIL
BOIL
THIS'LL BE...
...A WORK-STUDY BRAIN-STORM...
...AND...
...A HOT POT PARTY TO FIRE US ALL UP FOR THE NEW TERM!!

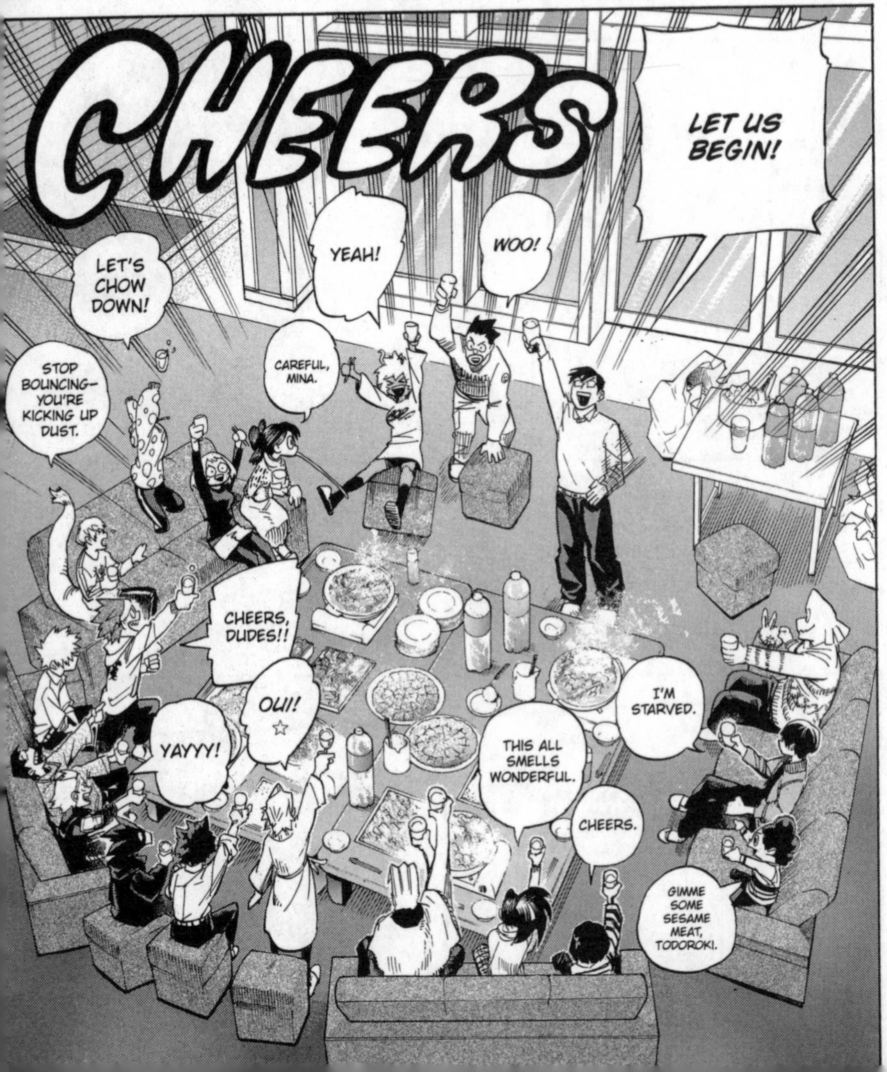
LET US BEGIN!
CHEERS
WOO!
YEAH!
LET'S CHOW DOWN!
CAREFUL, MINA.
STOP BOUNCING-YOU'RE KICKING UP DUST.
I'M STARVED.
CHEERS, DUDES!!
THIS ALL SMELLS WONDERFUL.
OUI! ☆
YAYYY!
CHEERS.
GIMME SOME SESAME MEAT, TODOROKI.

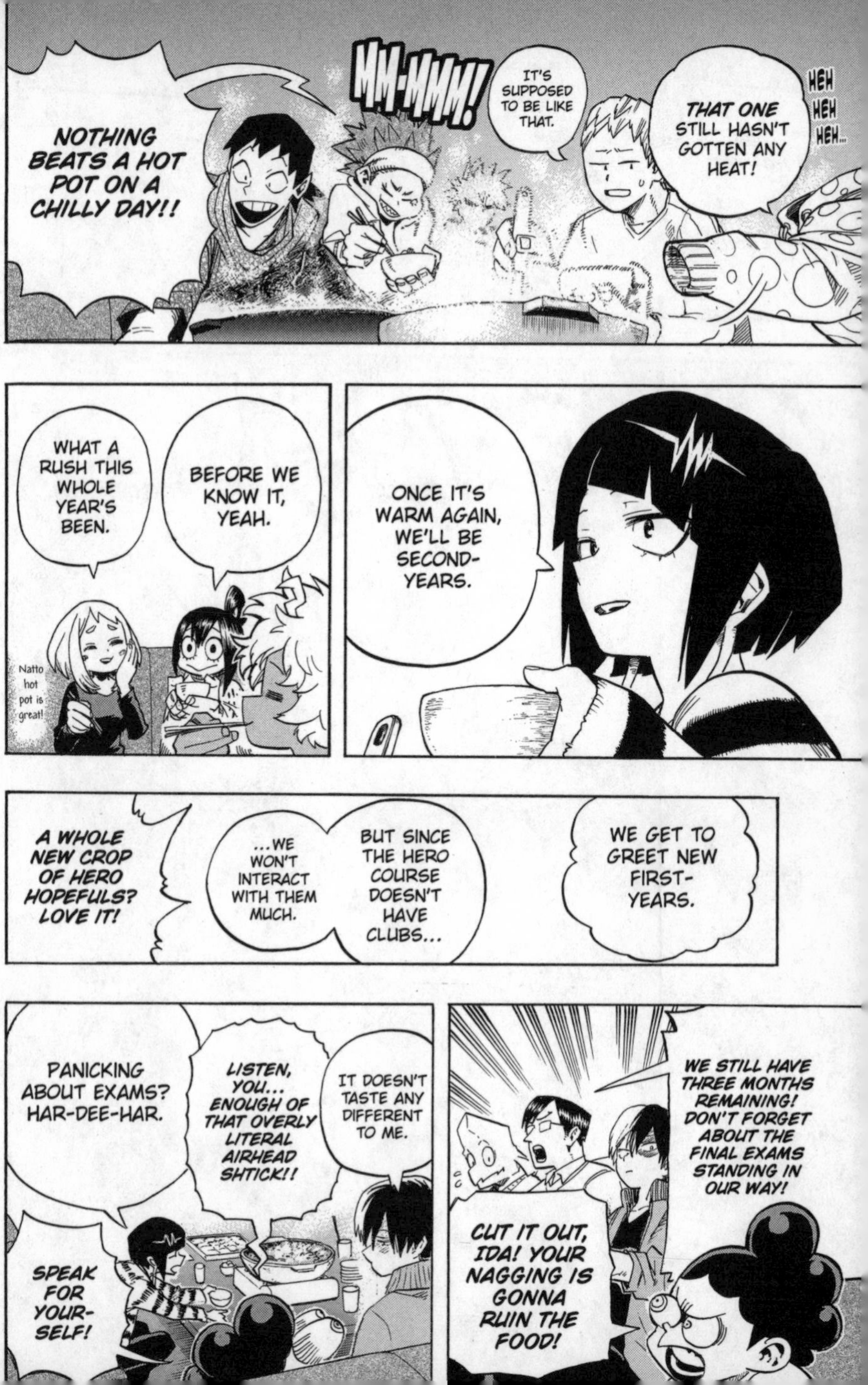
HEH HEH HEH...
THAT ONE STILL HASN'T GOTTEN ANY HEAT!
IT'S SUPPOSED TO BE LIKE THAT.
MM-MMM!
NOTHING BEATS A HOT POT ON A CHILLY DAY!!
ONCE IT'S WARM AGAIN, WE'LL BE SECOND-YEARS.
BEFORE WE KNOW IT, YEAH.
WHAT A RUSH THIS WHOLE YEAR'S BEEN.
Natto hot pot is great!
WE GET TO GREET NEW FIRST-YEARS.
BUT SINCE THE HERO COURSE DOESN'T HAVE CLUBS...
...WE WON'T INTERACT WITH THEM MUCH.
A WHOLE NEW CROP OF HERO HOPEFULS? LOVE IT!
WE STILL HAVE THREE MONTHS REMAINING! DON'T FORGET ABOUT THE FINAL EXAMS STANDING IN OUR WAY!
CUT IT OUT, IDA! YOUR NAGGING IS GONNA RUIN THE FOOD!
IT DOESN'T TASTE ANY DIFFERENT TO ME.
LISTEN, YOU... ENOUGH OF THAT OVERLY LITERAL AIRHEAD SHTICK!!
PANICKING ABOUT EXAMS? HAR-DEE-HAR.
SPEAK FOR YOURSELF!

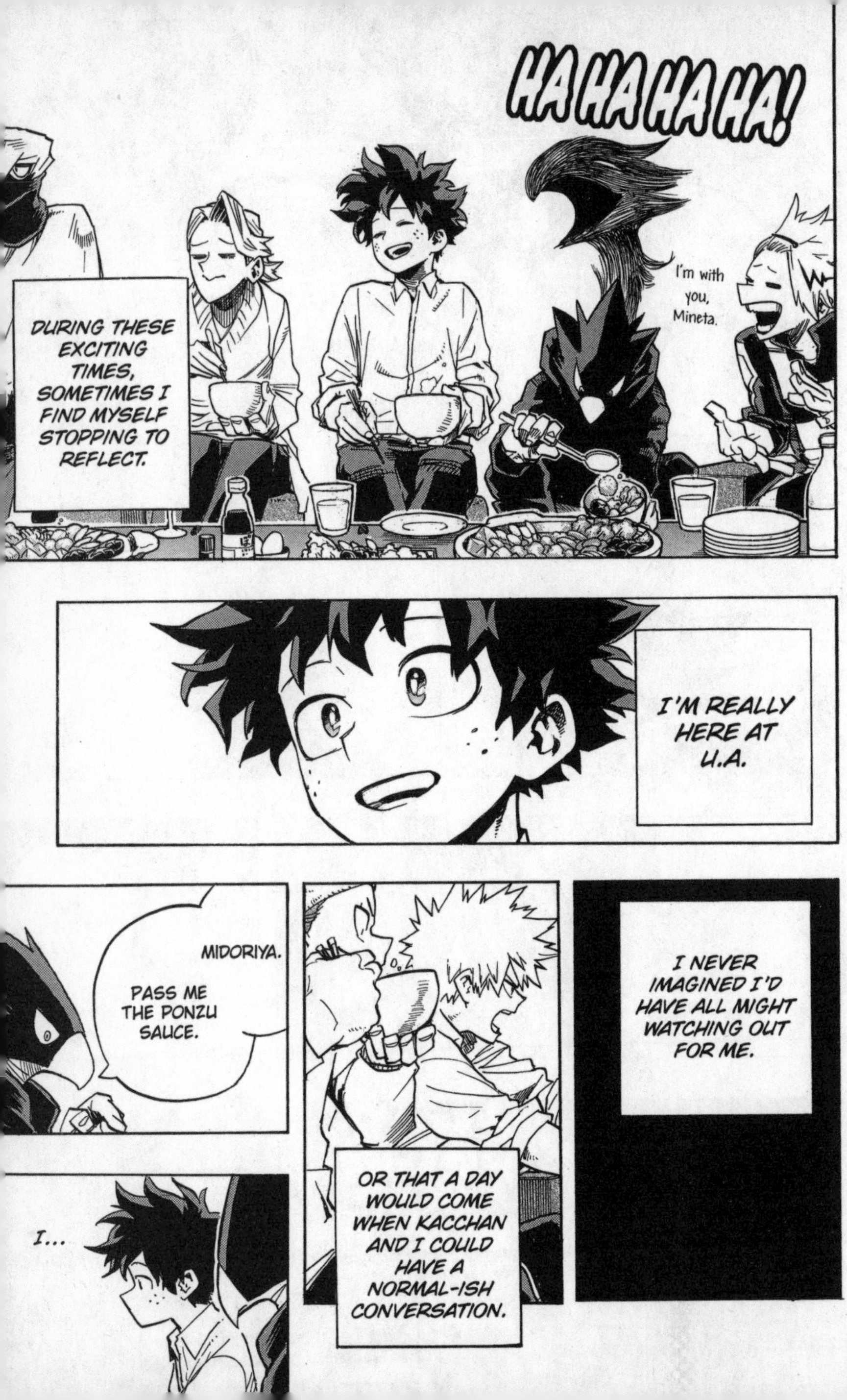
HA HA HA HA HA!
I'm with you, Mineta.
DURING THESE EXCITING TIMES, SOMETIMES I FIND MYSELF STOPPING TO REFLECT.
I'M REALLY HERE AT U.A.
I NEVER IMAGINED I'D HAVE ALL MIGHT WATCHING OUT FOR ME.
OR THAT A DAY WOULD COME WHEN KACCHAN AND I COULD HAVE A NORMAL-ISH CONVERSATION.
MIDORIYA.
PASS ME THE PONZU SAUCE.
I...

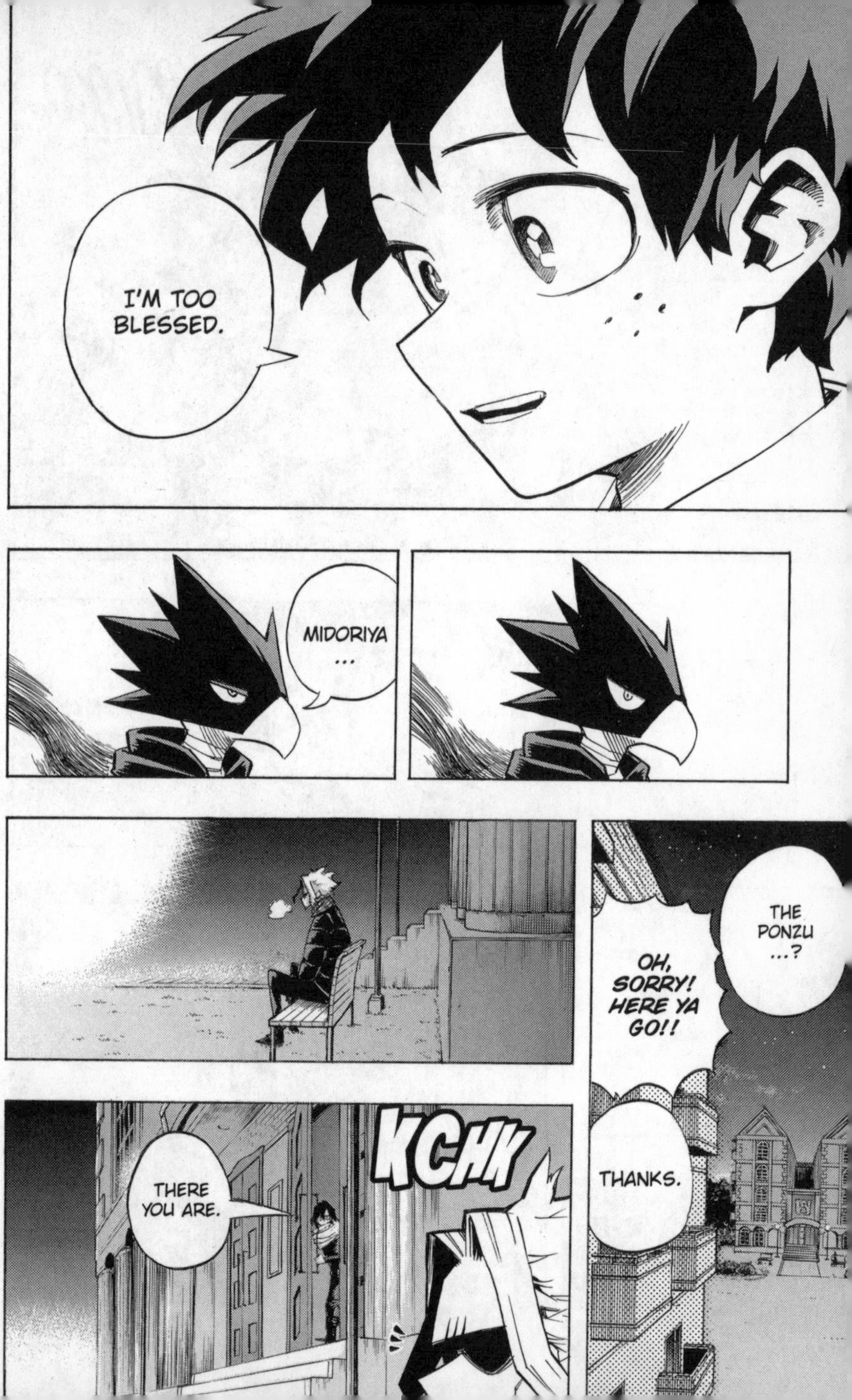
I'M TOO BLESSED.
MIDORIYA ...
THE PONZU ...?
OH, SORRY! HERE YA GO!!
THANKS.
KCHK
THERE YOU ARE.

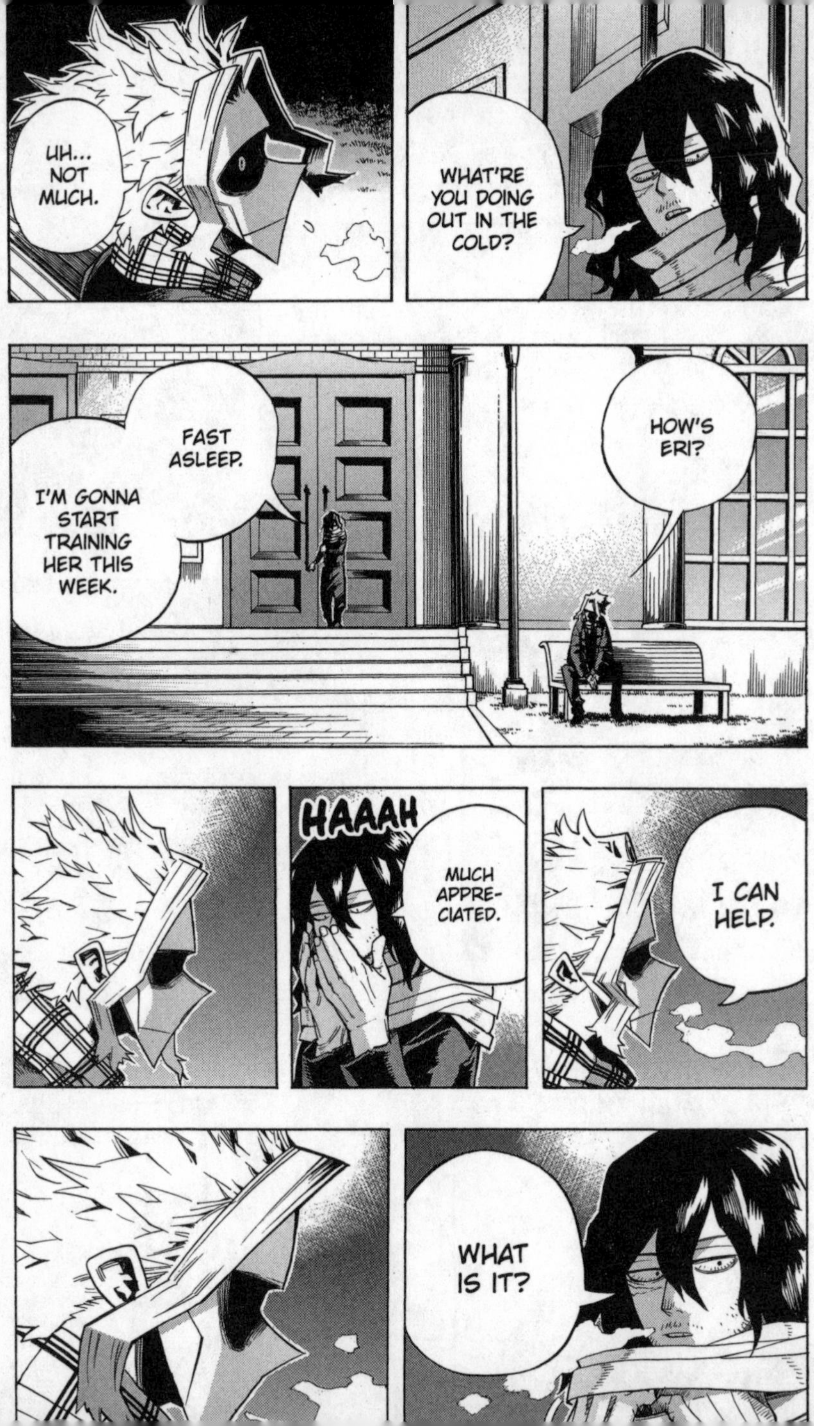
WHAT'RE YOU DOING OUT IN THE COLD?
UH... NOT MUCH.
HOW'S ERI?
FAST ASLEEP.
I'M GONNA START TRAINING HER THIS WEEK.
I CAN HELP.
HAAAH
MUCH APPRE-CIATED.
WHAT IS IT?

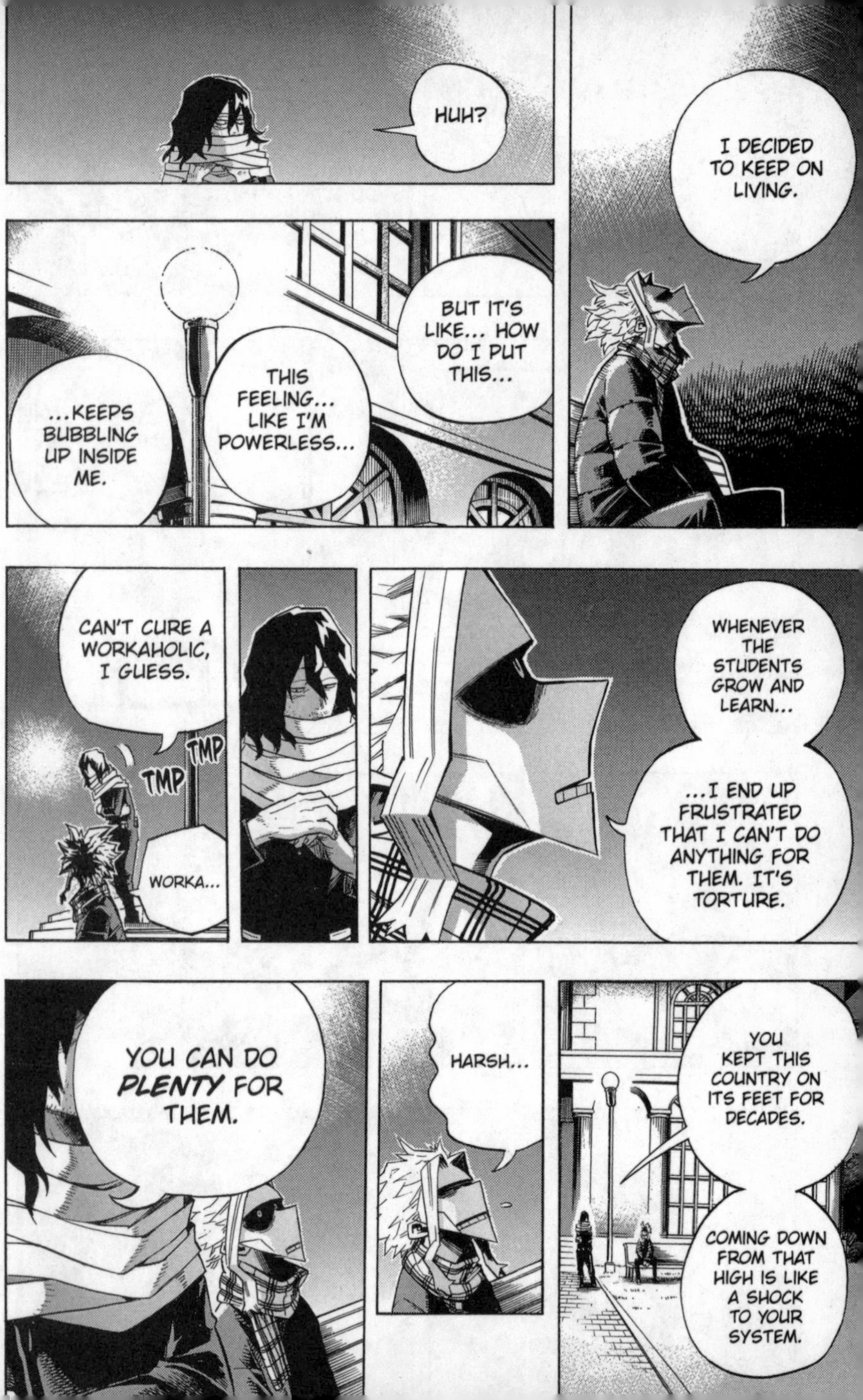
I DECIDED TO KEEP ON LIVING.
HUH?
BUT IT'S LIKE... HOW DO I PUT THIS...
THIS FEELING... LIKE I'M POWERLESS...
...KEEPS BUBBLING UP INSIDE ME.
WHENEVER THE STUDENTS GROW AND LEARN...
...I END UP FRUSTRATED THAT I CAN'T DO ANYTHING FOR THEM. IT'S TORTURE.
CAN'T CURE A WORKAHOLIC, I GUESS.
TMP
TMP
WORKA...
YOU KEPT THIS COUNTRY ON ITS FEET FOR DECADES.
COMING DOWN FROM THAT HIGH IS LIKE A SHOCK TO YOUR SYSTEM.
HARSH...
YOU CAN DO *PLENTY* FOR THEM.

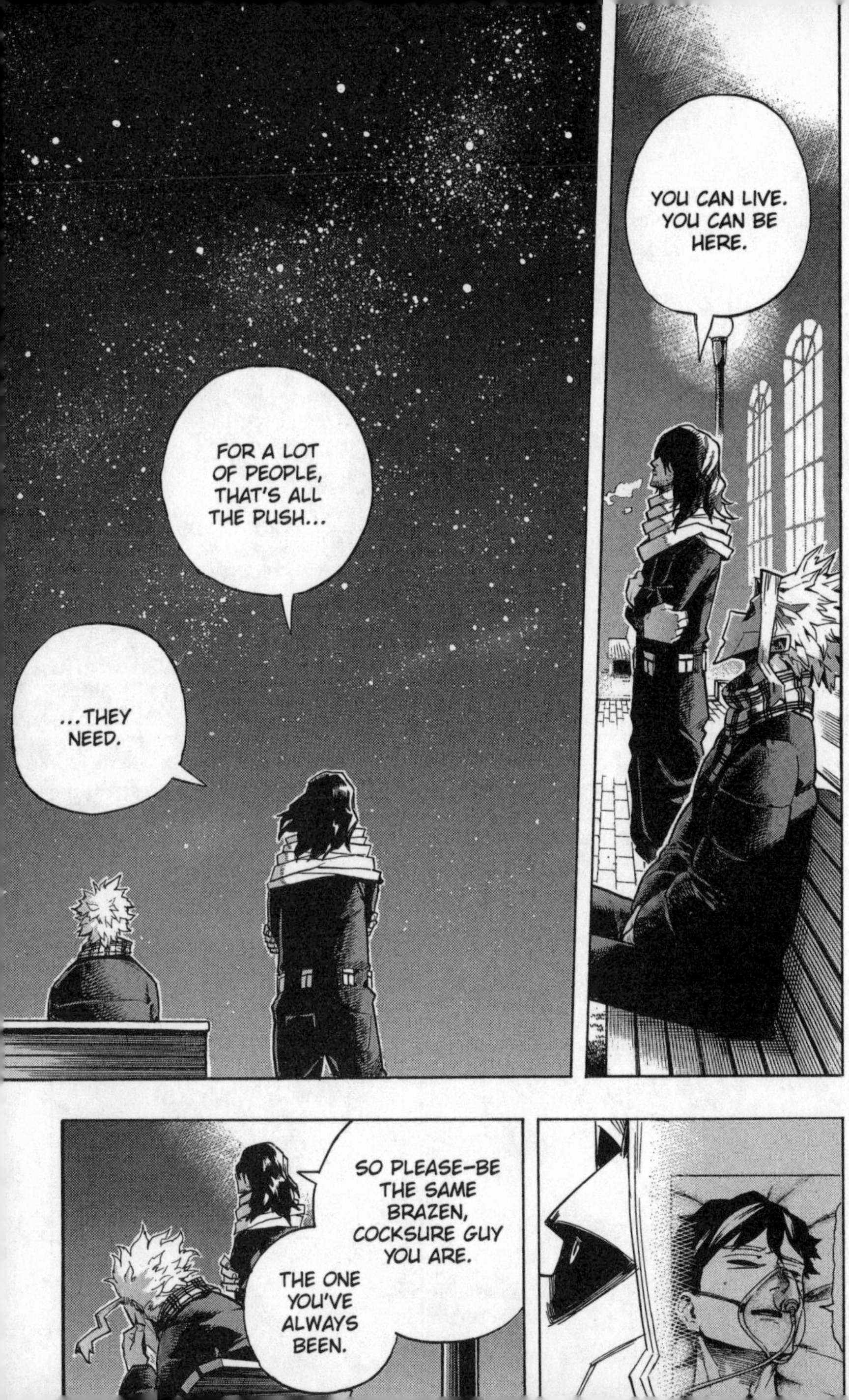
YOU CAN LIVE. YOU CAN BE HERE.
FOR A LOT OF PEOPLE, THAT'S ALL THE PUSH...
...THEY NEED.
SO PLEASE—BE THE SAME BRAZEN, COCKSURE GUY YOU ARE.
THE ONE YOU'VE ALWAYS BEEN.

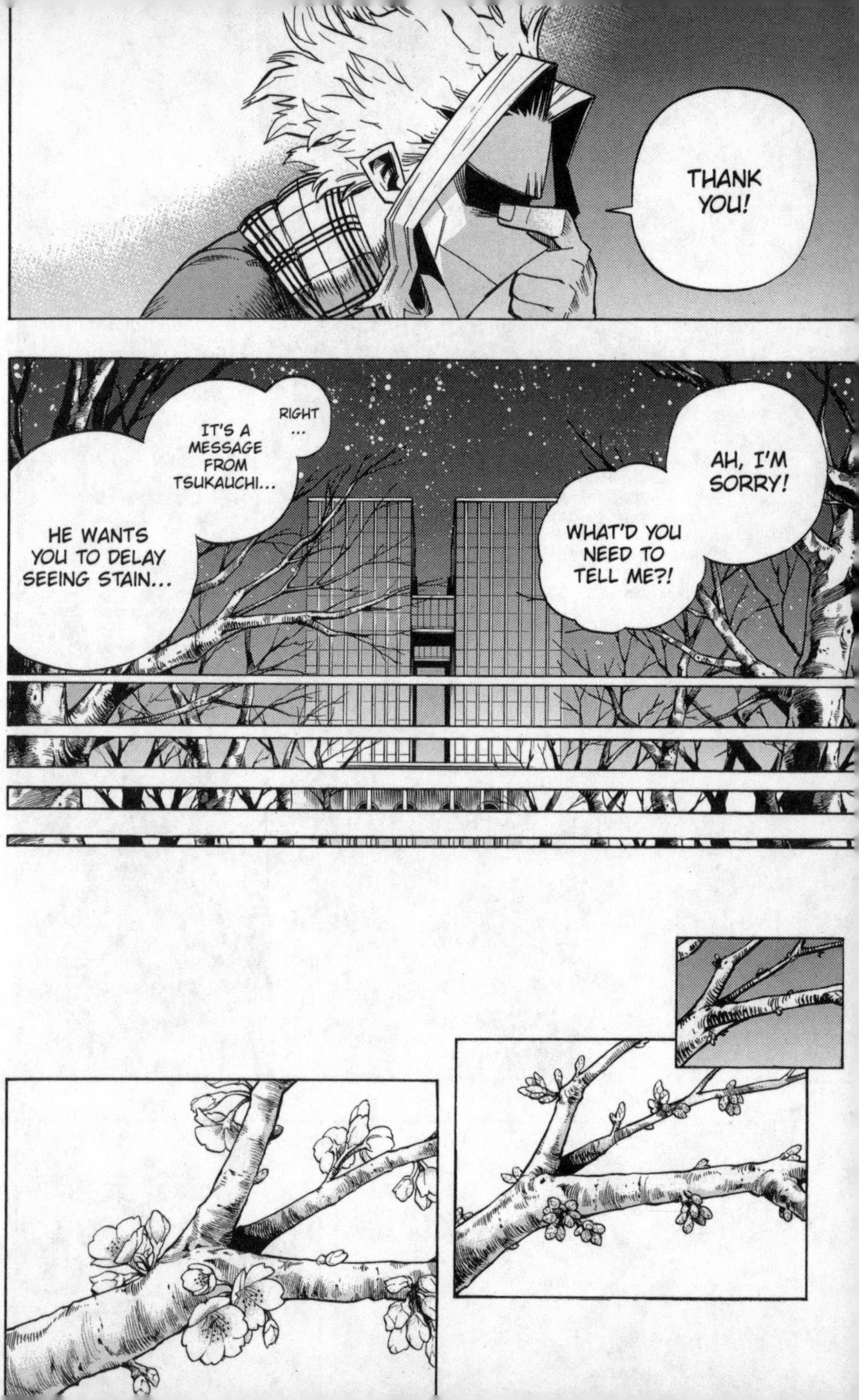
THANK YOU!
AH, I'M SORRY!
WHAT'D YOU NEED TO TELL ME?!
RIGHT...
IT'S A MESSAGE FROM TSUKAUCHI...
HE WANTS YOU TO DELAY SEEING STAIN...

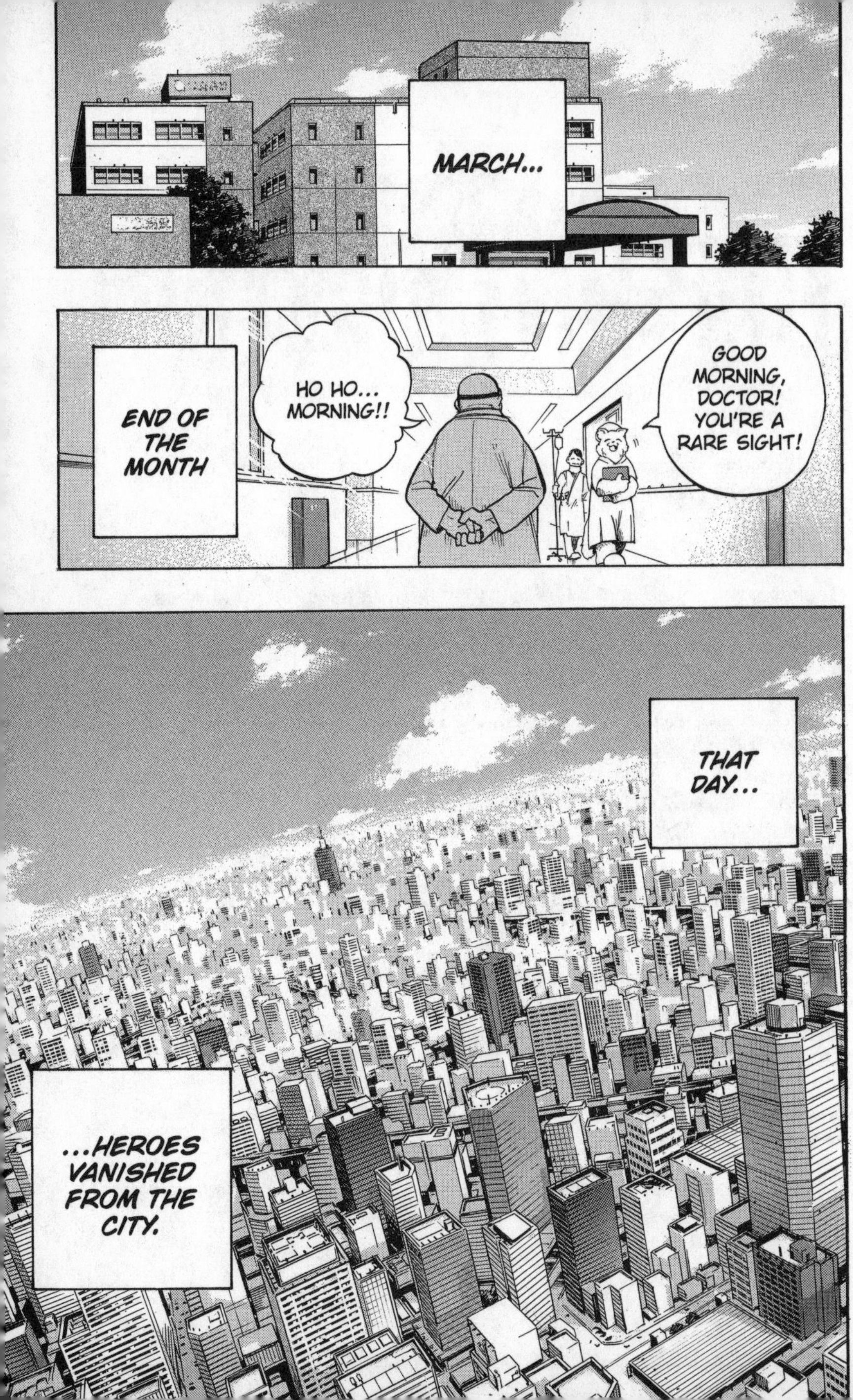
MARCH...
GOOD MORNING, DOCTOR! YOU'RE A RARE SIGHT!
HO HO... MORNING!!
END OF THE MONTH
THAT DAY...
...HEROES VANISHED FROM THE CITY.

THE CONTRIBUTION

This is becoming a tradition! I received art from the artists behind two of the spin-off series!

As I probably mentioned before, my heart and head stopped maturing in preschool, so I absolutely love doing art trades like these.

Having other people draw my characters is thrilling.

Getting to draw their characters is also a blast. Nothing but good vibes.

First, we have a piece from Betten Sensei, the artist for *My Hero Academia: Vigilantes*, which runs in *Jump Plus*.

Volumes 8 and 9 of *Vigilantes* tell the tale of Eraser Head's past.

I make an effort to write *MHA* so that you don't necessarily have to read *Vigilantes* to get what's going on, but the spin-off does provide extra insight about how Eraser Head is feeling. It's heart-wrenching.

Next, we have some art from Akiyama Sensei, the one doing *My Hero Academia: Team-Up Missions*!

Akiyama Sensei has already provided so much help with *MHA*, and now she has her own full-fledged spin-off series!

I love getting to see interactions and team-ups between characters that you don't get in the main series. Volume 1 of that is out now in Japan!

She does such a bafflingly amazing job with her drawings that they could be mistaken for my own.

Ahh, so happy. The corresponding volumes of *Vigilantes* and *Team-Up Missions* also have drawings from me in them, so if you're interested, check them out!

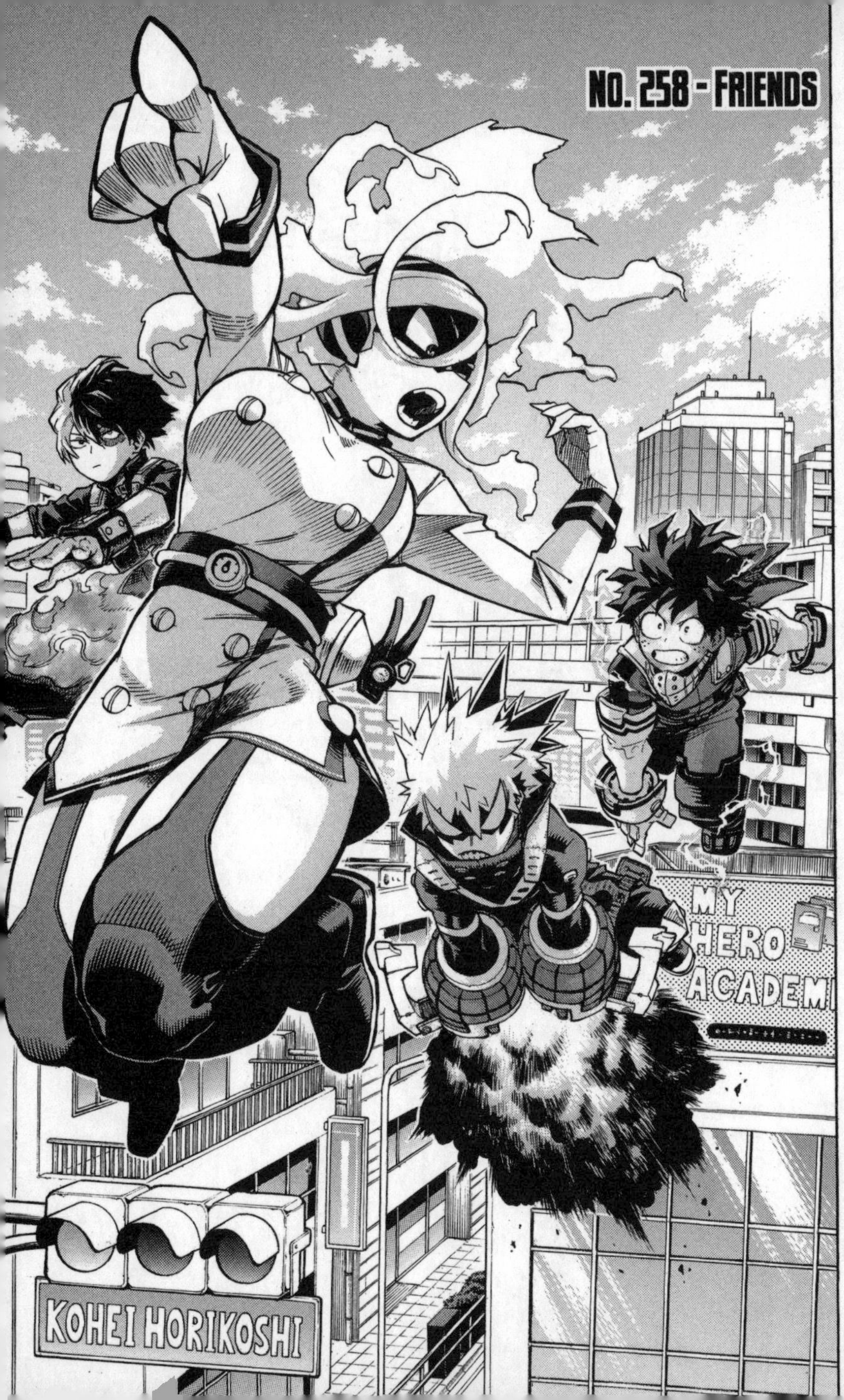
NO. 258 - FRIENDS
MY HERO ACADEMI
KOHEI HORIKOSHI

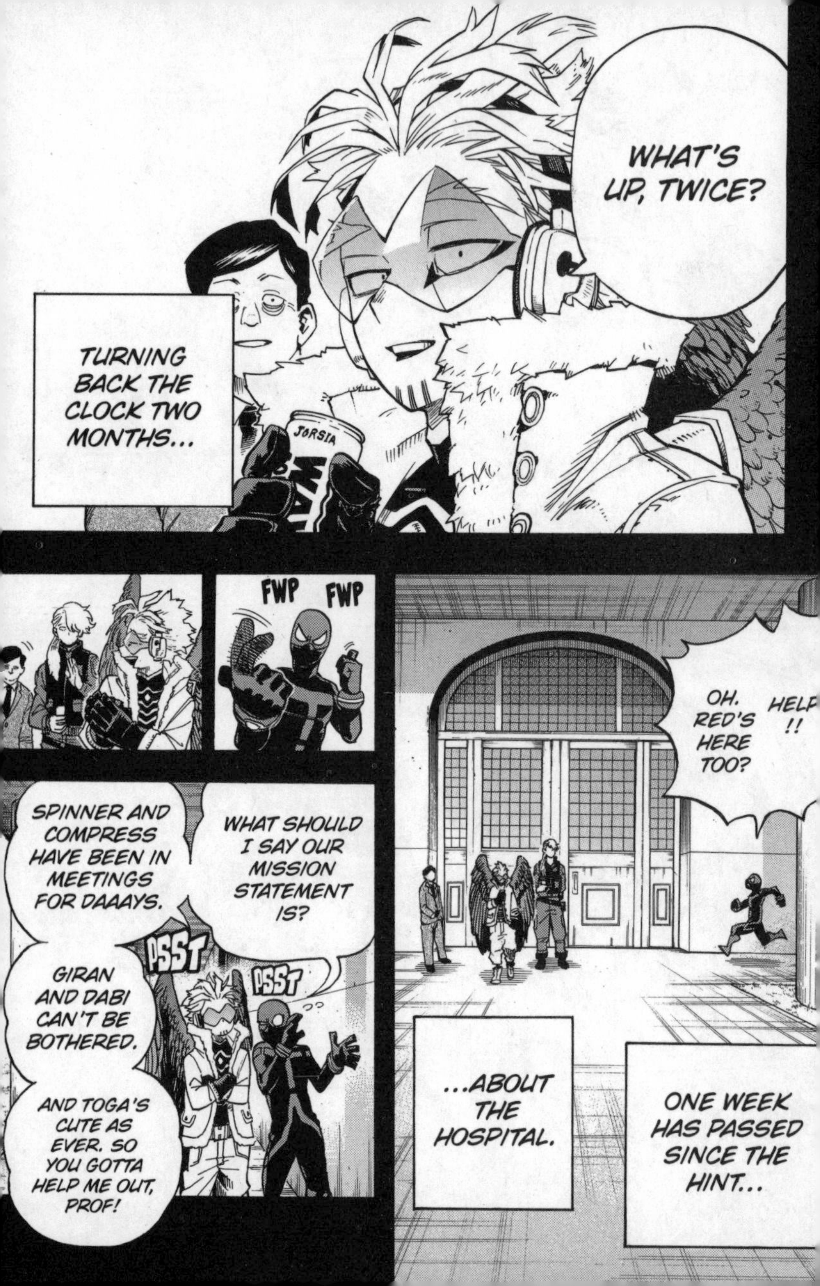
WHAT'S UP, TWICE?
TURNING BACK THE CLOCK TWO MONTHS...
HELP !!
OH. RED'S HERE TOO?
ONE WEEK HAS PASSED SINCE THE HINT...
...ABOUT THE HOSPITAL.
FWP
FWP
PSST
PSST
SPINNER AND COMPRESS HAVE BEEN IN MEETINGS FOR DAAAYS.
GIRAN AND DABI CAN'T BE BOTHERED.
AND TOGA'S CUTE AS EVER. SO YOU GOTTA HELP ME OUT, PROF!
WHAT SHOULD I SAY OUR MISSION STATEMENT IS?

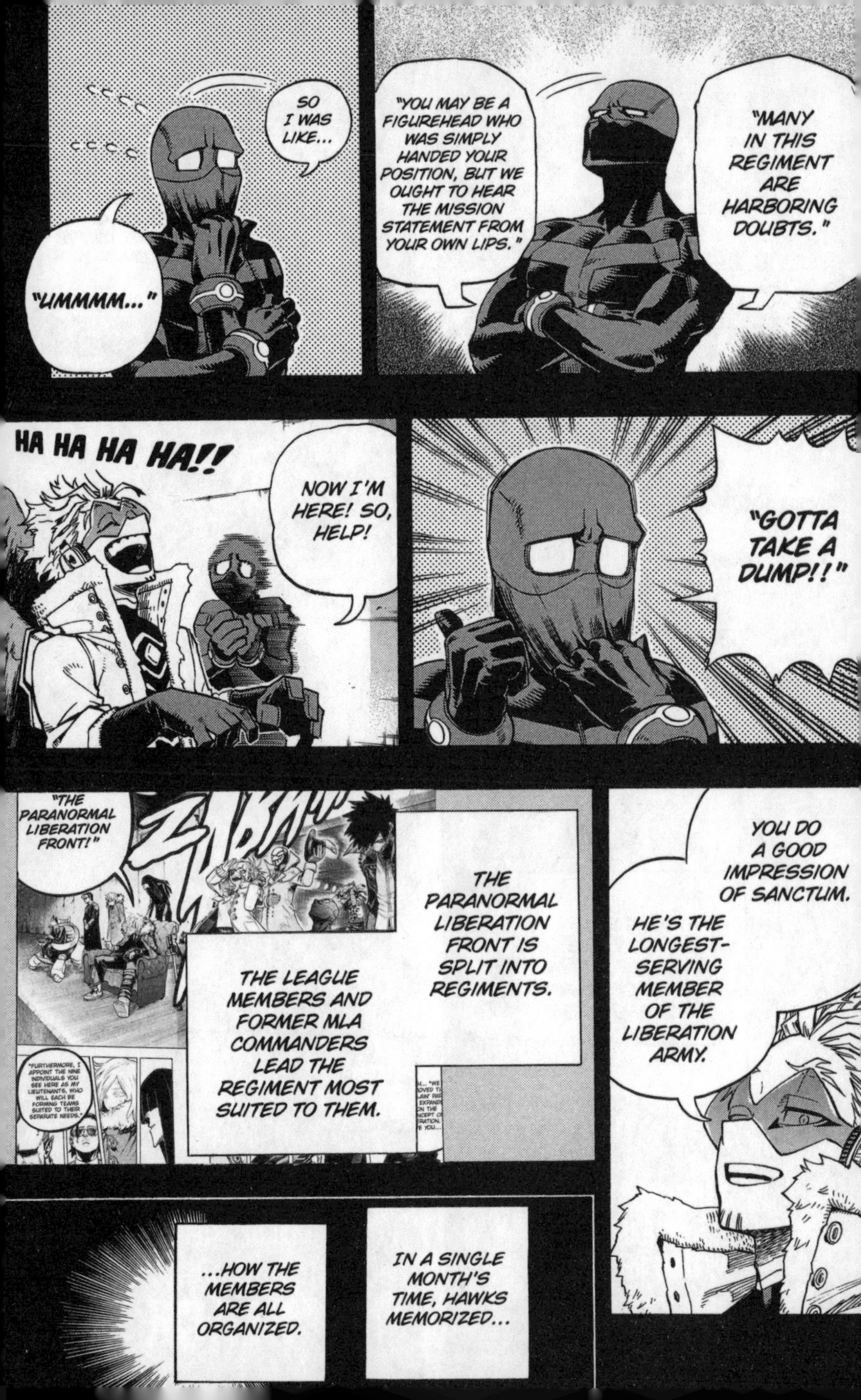
"MANY IN THIS REGIMENT ARE HARBORING DOUBTS."
"YOU MAY BE A FIGUREHEAD WHO WAS SIMPLY HANDED YOUR POSITION, BUT WE OUGHT TO HEAR THE MISSION STATEMENT FROM YOUR OWN LIPS."
SO I WAS LIKE...
"UMMMM..."
"GOTTA TAKE A DUMP!!"
NOW I'M HERE! SO, HELP!
HA HA HA HA!!
YOU DO A GOOD IMPRESSION OF SANCTUM.
HE'S THE LONGEST-SERVING MEMBER OF THE LIBERATION ARMY.
THE PARANORMAL LIBERATION FRONT IS SPLIT INTO REGIMENTS.
"THE PARANORMAL LIBERATION FRONT!"
THE LEAGUE MEMBERS AND FORMER MLA COMMANDERS LEAD THE REGIMENT MOST SUITED TO THEM.
"FURTHERMORE, I APPOINT THE NINE INDIVIDUALS YOU SEE HERE AS MY LIEUTENANTS, WHO WILL EACH BE FORMING TEAMS SUITED TO THEIR SEPARATE NEEDS."
IN A SINGLE MONTH'S TIME, HAWKS MEMORIZED...
...HOW THE MEMBERS ARE ALL ORGANIZED.

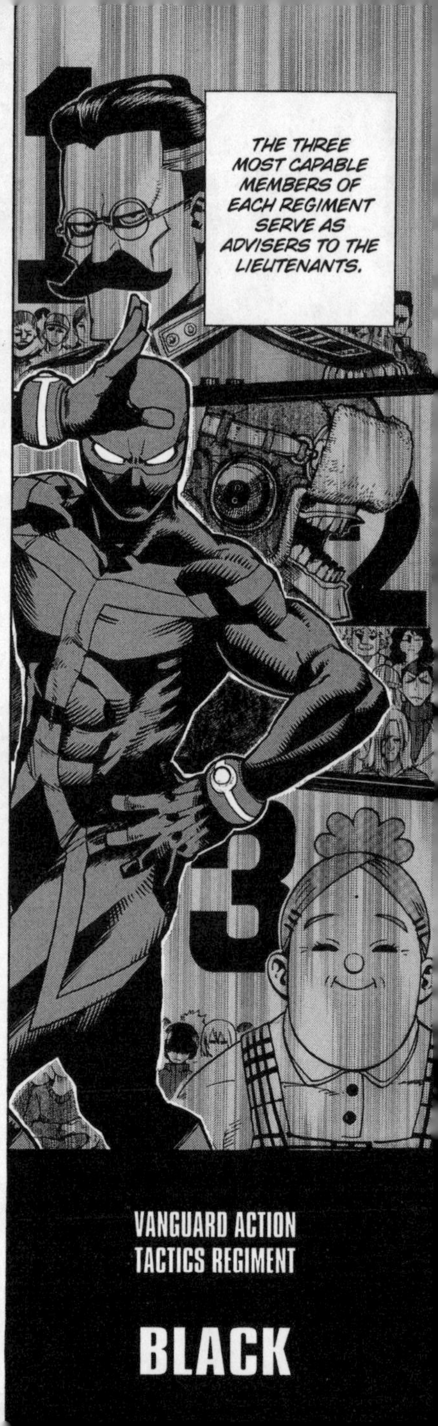
THE THREE MOST CAPABLE MEMBERS OF EACH REGIMENT SERVE AS ADVISERS TO THE LIEUTENANTS.
1
2
3
VANGUARD ACTION TACTICS REGIMENT
BLACK

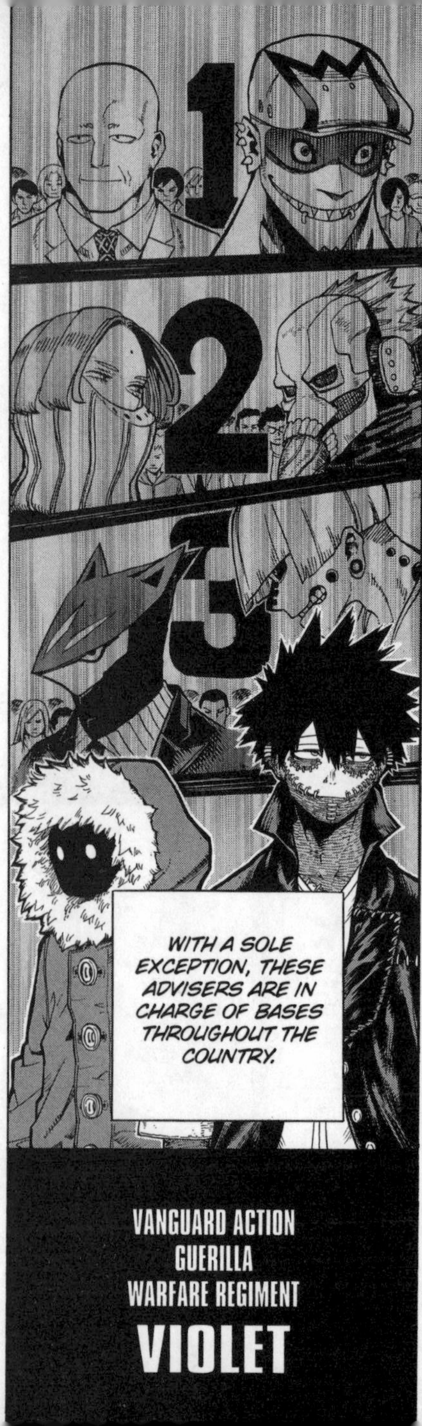
1
2
3
WITH A SOLE EXCEPTION, THESE ADVISERS ARE IN CHARGE OF BASES THROUGHOUT THE COUNTRY.
VANGUARD ACTION GUERILLA WARFARE REGIMENT
VIOLET

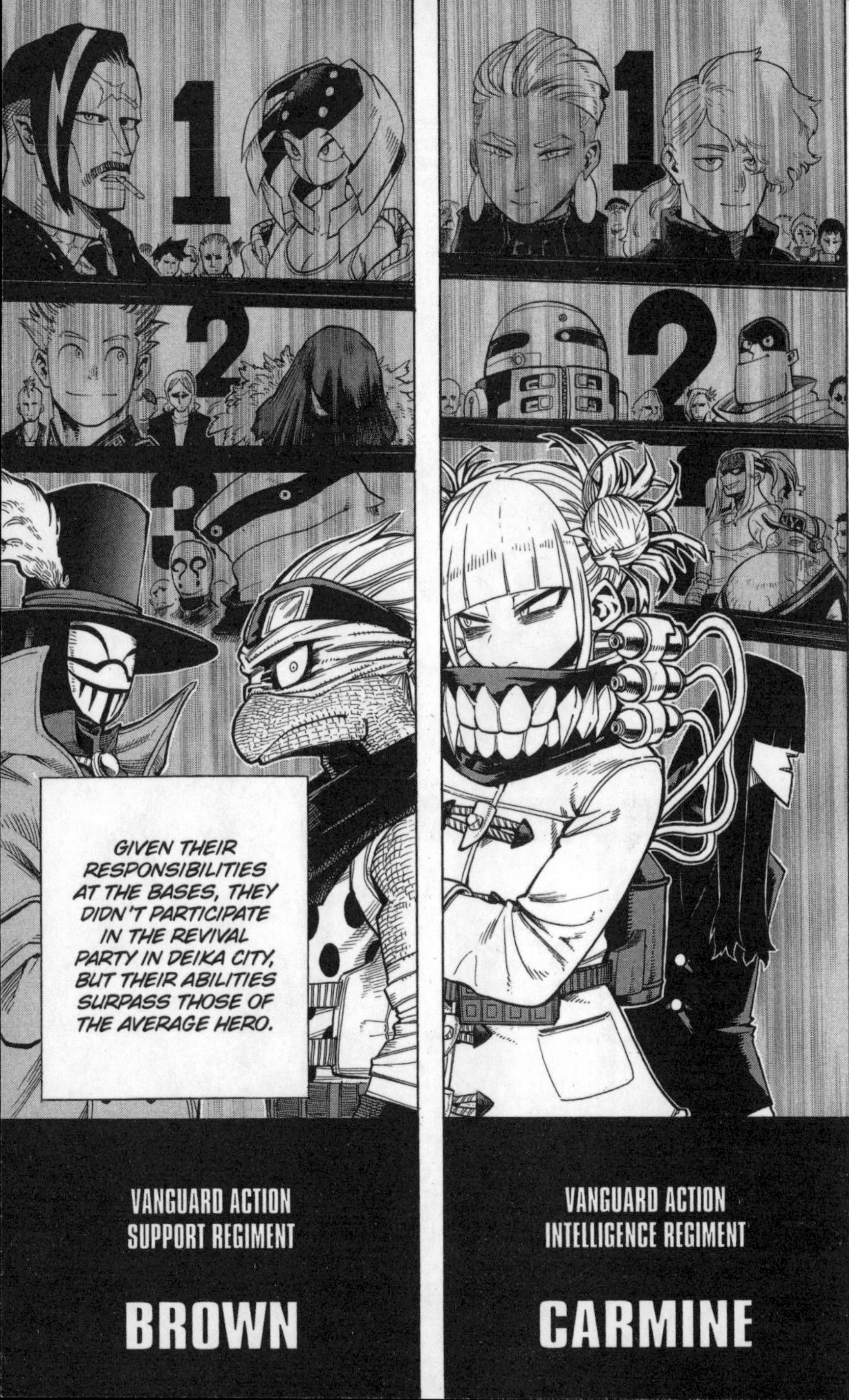
VANGUARD ACTION
INTELLIGENCE REGIMENT
CARMINE
GIVEN THEIR RESPONSIBILITIES AT THE BASES, THEY DIDN'T PARTICIPATE IN THE REVIVAL PARTY IN DEIKA CITY, BUT THEIR ABILITIES SURPASS THOSE OF THE AVERAGE HERO.
VANGUARD ACTION
SUPPORT REGIMENT
BROWN

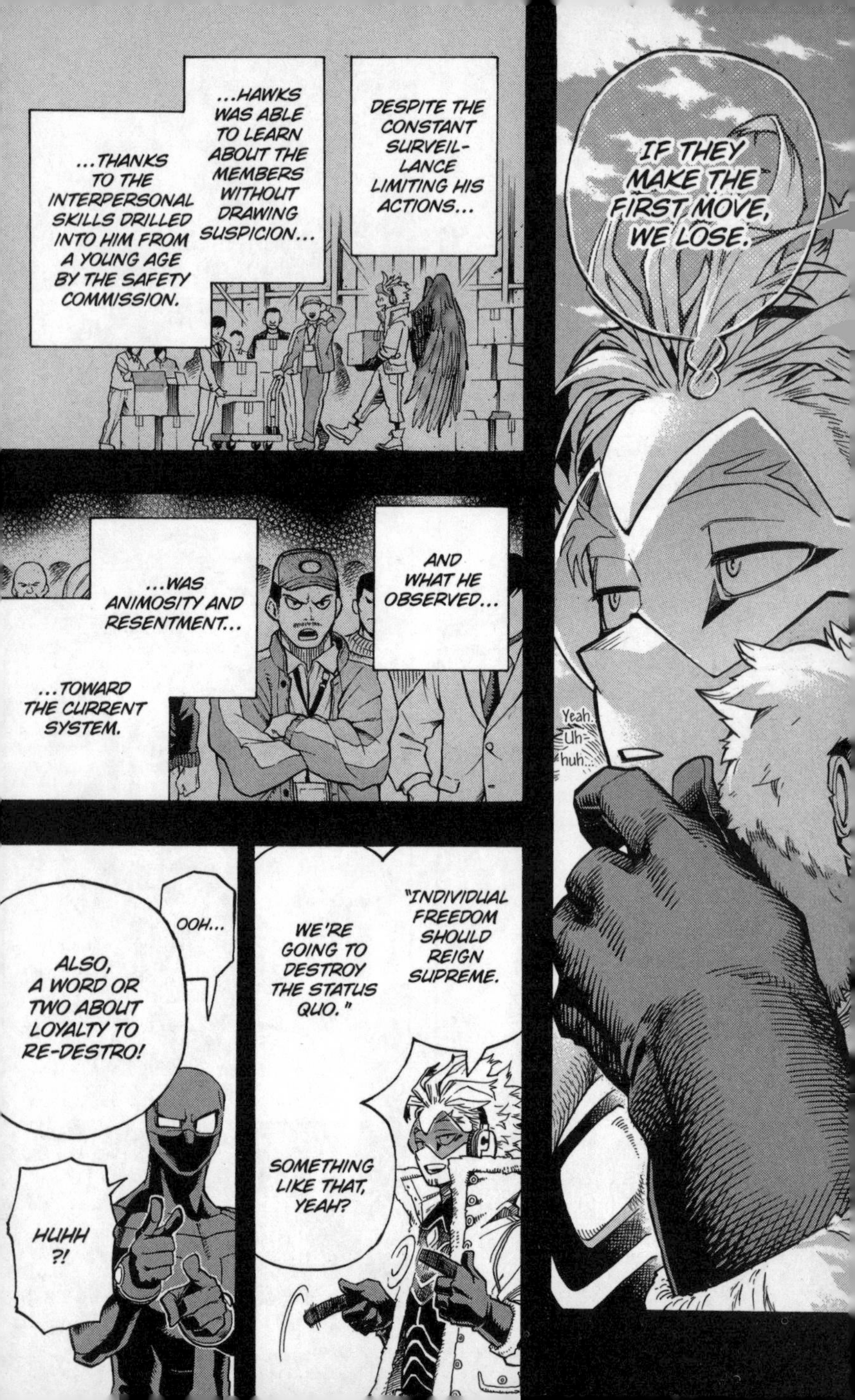
IF THEY MAKE THE FIRST MOVE, WE LOSE.
Yeah. Uh-huh...
DESPITE THE CONSTANT SURVEIL-LANCE LIMITING HIS ACTIONS...
...HAWKS WAS ABLE TO LEARN ABOUT THE MEMBERS WITHOUT DRAWING SUSPICION...
...THANKS TO THE INTERPERSONAL SKILLS DRILLED INTO HIM FROM A YOUNG AGE BY THE SAFETY COMMISSION.
AND WHAT HE OBSERVED...
...WAS ANIMOSITY AND RESENTMENT...
...TOWARD THE CURRENT SYSTEM.
"INDIVIDUAL FREEDOM SHOULD REIGN SUPREME.
WE'RE GOING TO DESTROY THE STATUS QUO."
SOMETHING LIKE THAT, YEAH?
OOH...
ALSO, A WORD OR TWO ABOUT LOYALTY TO RE-DESTRO!
HUHH ?!

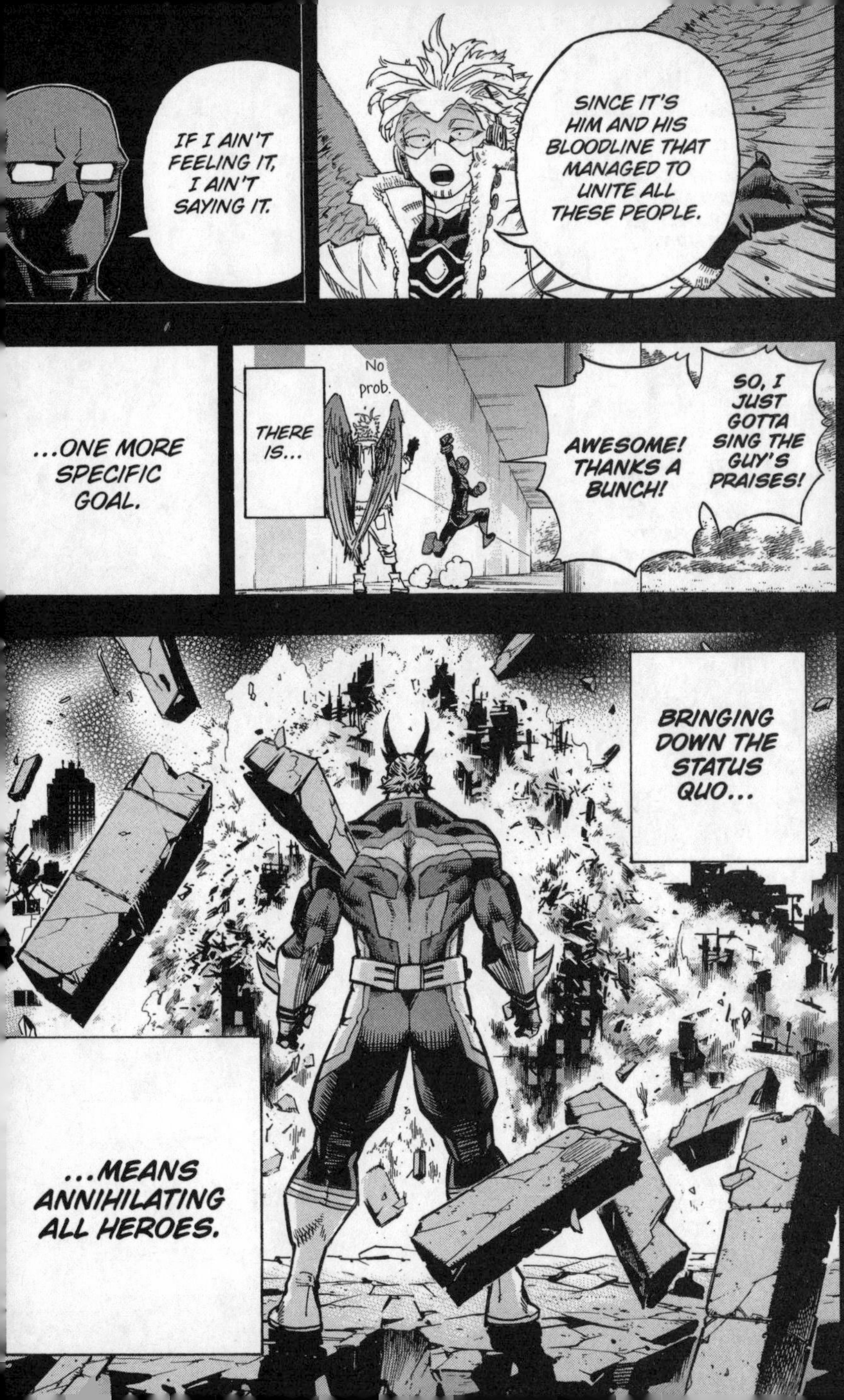
SINCE IT'S HIM AND HIS BLOODLINE THAT MANAGED TO UNITE ALL THESE PEOPLE.
IF I AIN'T FEELING IT, I AIN'T SAYING IT.
SO, I JUST GOTTA SING THE GUY'S PRAISES!
AWESOME! THANKS A BUNCH!
No prob.
THERE IS...
...ONE MORE SPECIFIC GOAL.
BRINGING DOWN THE STATUS QUO...
...MEANS ANNIHILATING ALL HEROES.

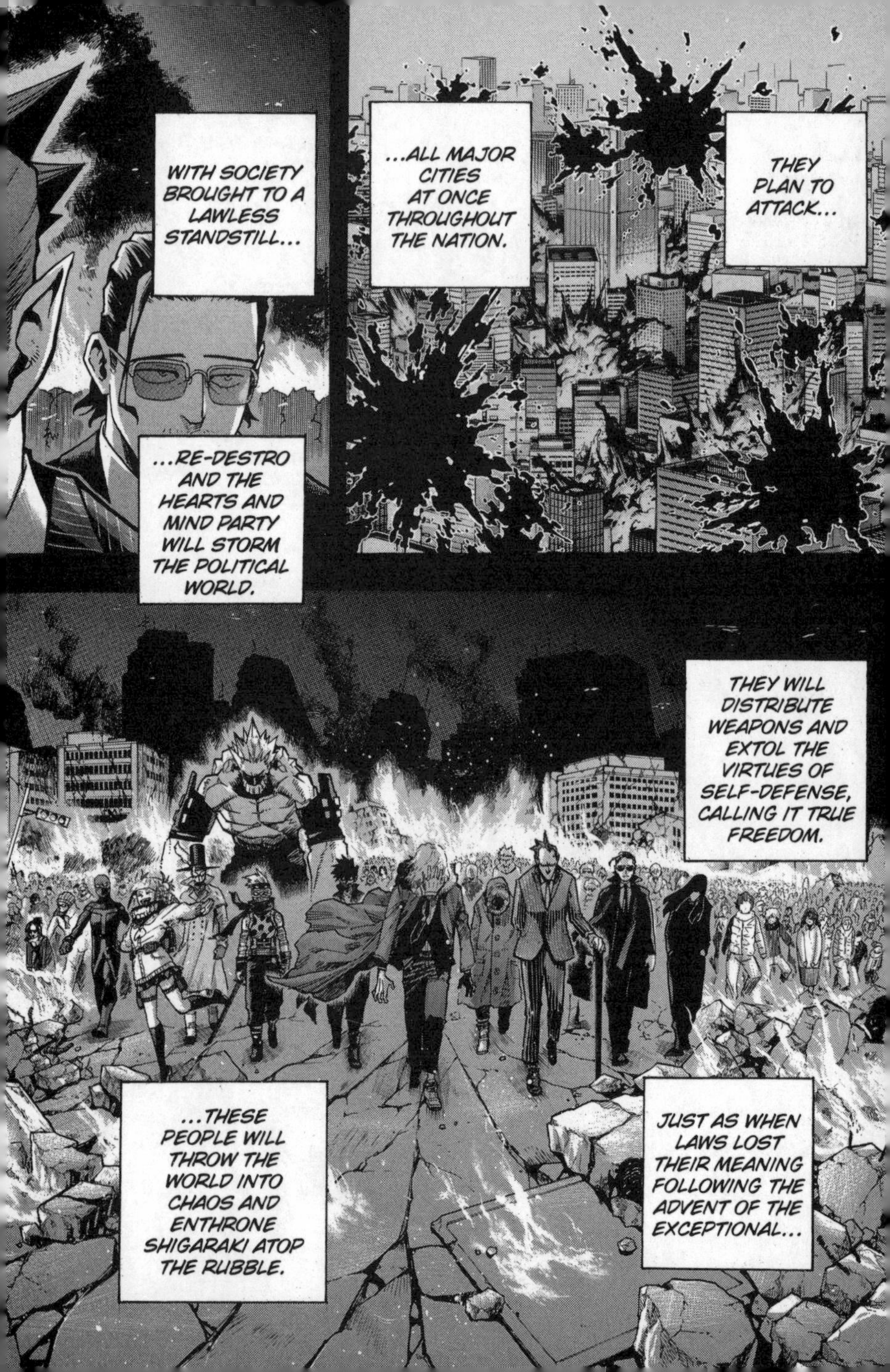
THEY PLAN TO ATTACK...
...ALL MAJOR CITIES AT ONCE THROUGHOUT THE NATION.
WITH SOCIETY BROUGHT TO A LAWLESS STANDSTILL...
...RE-DESTRO AND THE HEARTS AND MIND PARTY WILL STORM THE POLITICAL WORLD.
THEY WILL DISTRIBUTE WEAPONS AND EXTOL THE VIRTUES OF SELF-DEFENSE, CALLING IT TRUE FREEDOM.
JUST AS WHEN LAWS LOST THEIR MEANING FOLLOWING THE ADVENT OF THE EXCEPTIONAL...
...THESE PEOPLE WILL THROW THE WORLD INTO CHAOS AND ENTHRONE SHIGARAKI ATOP THE RUBBLE.

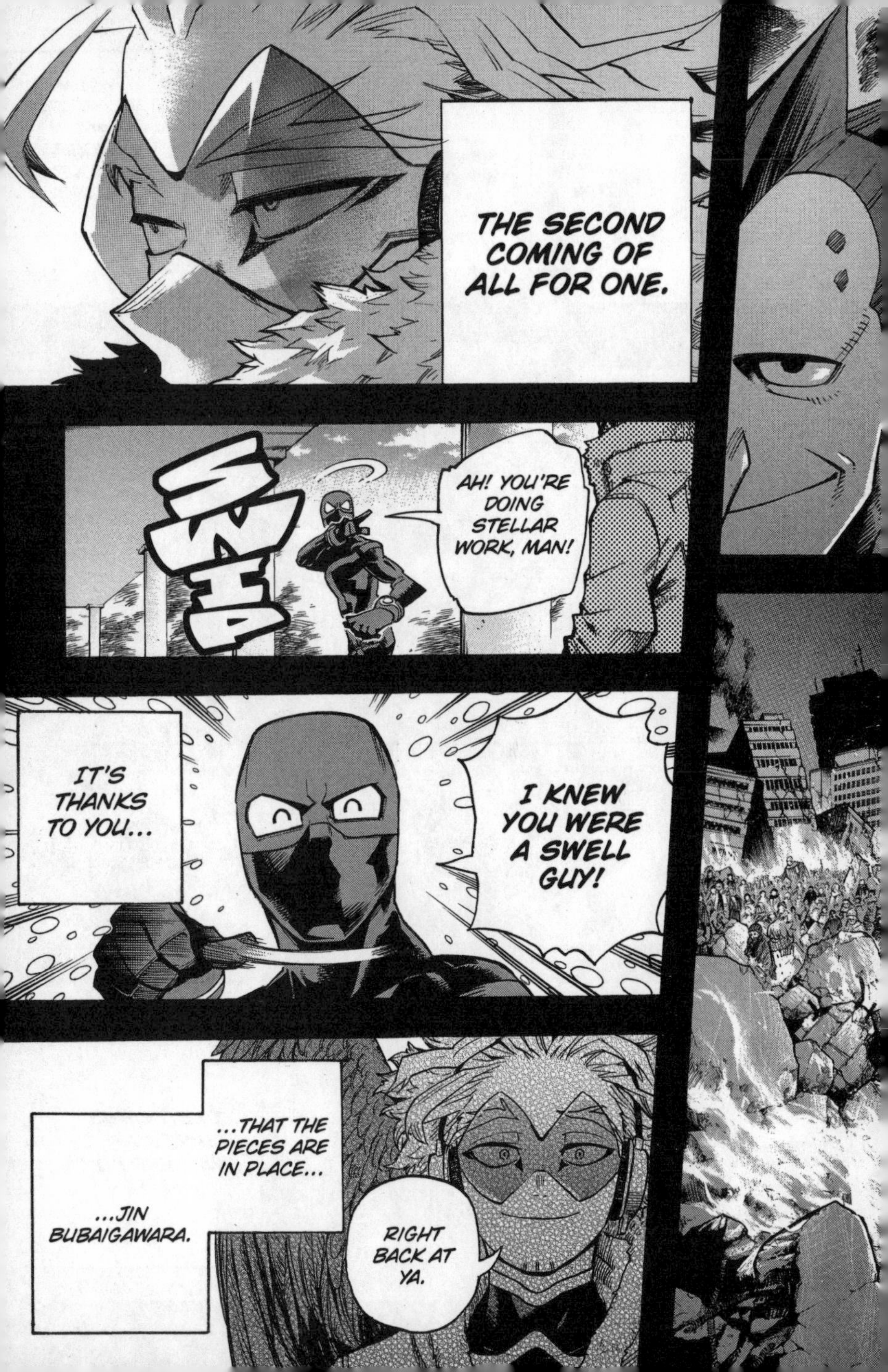
THE SECOND COMING OF ALL FOR ONE.
AH! YOU'RE DOING STELLAR WORK, MAN!
SWIP
I KNEW YOU WERE A SWELL GUY!
IT'S THANKS TO YOU...
...THAT THE PIECES ARE IN PLACE...
...JIN BUBAIGAWARA.
RIGHT BACK AT YA.

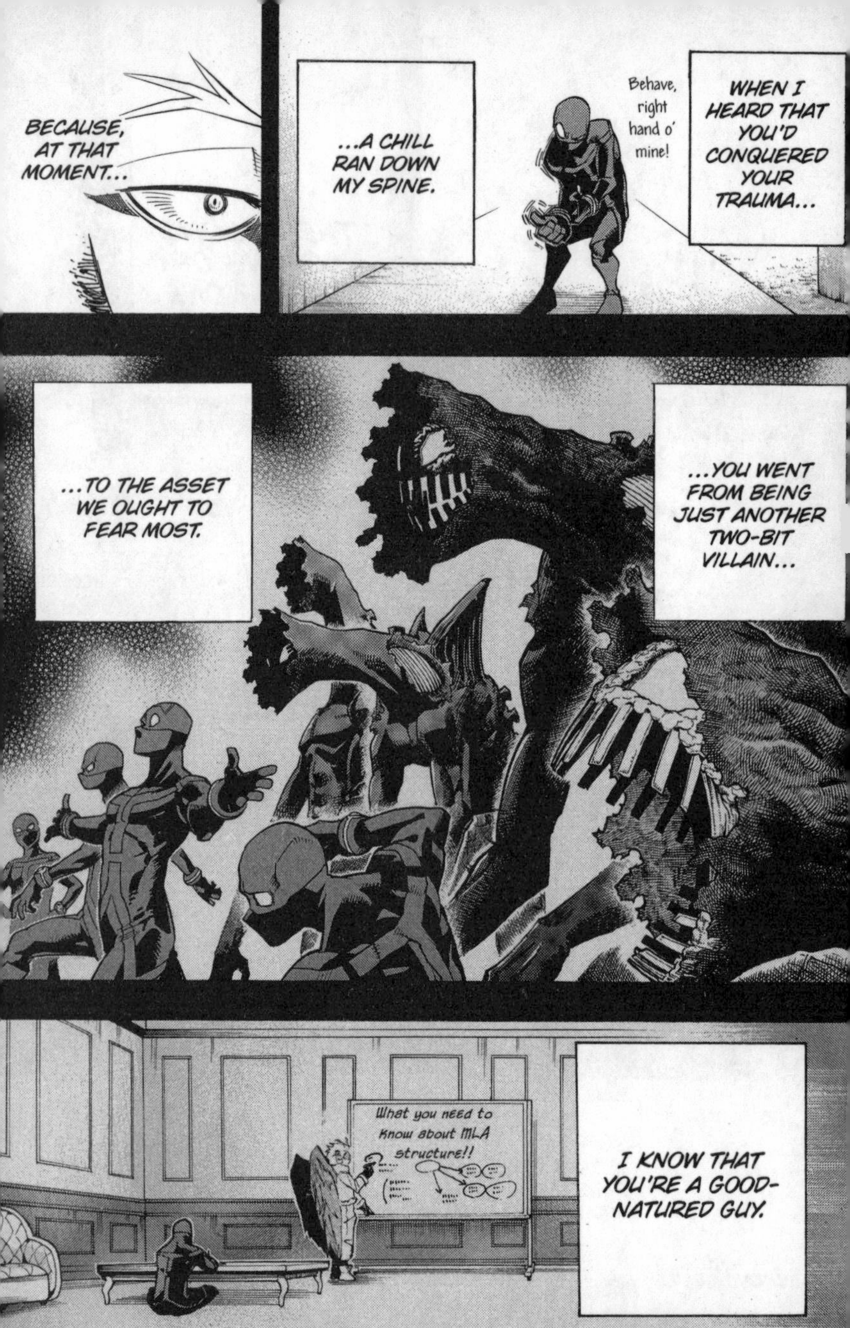
WHEN I HEARD THAT YOU'D CONQUERED YOUR TRAUMA...
Behave, right hand o' mine!
...A CHILL RAN DOWN MY SPINE.
BECAUSE, AT THAT MOMENT...
...YOU WENT FROM BEING JUST ANOTHER TWO-BIT VILLAIN...
...TO THE ASSET WE OUGHT TO FEAR MOST.
I KNOW THAT YOU'RE A GOOD-NATURED GUY.
What you need to know about MLA structure!!

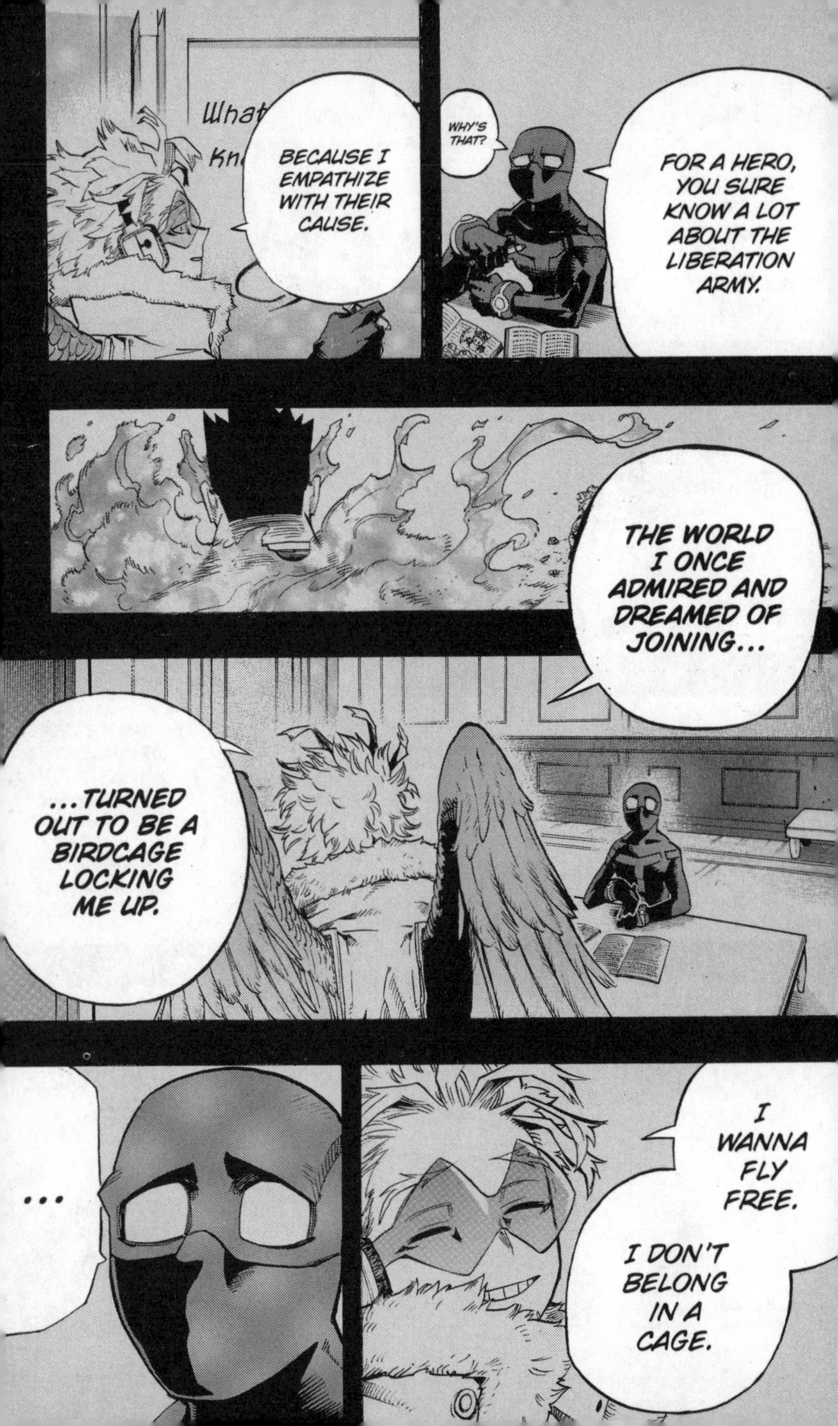

FOR A HERO, YOU SURE KNOW A LOT ABOUT THE LIBERATION ARMY.
WHY'S THAT?
BECAUSE I EMPATHIZE WITH THEIR CAUSE.
THE WORLD I ONCE ADMIRED AND DREAMED OF JOINING...
...TURNED OUT TO BE A BIRDCAGE LOCKING ME UP.
I WANNA FLY FREE.
I DON'T BELONG IN A CAGE.
...

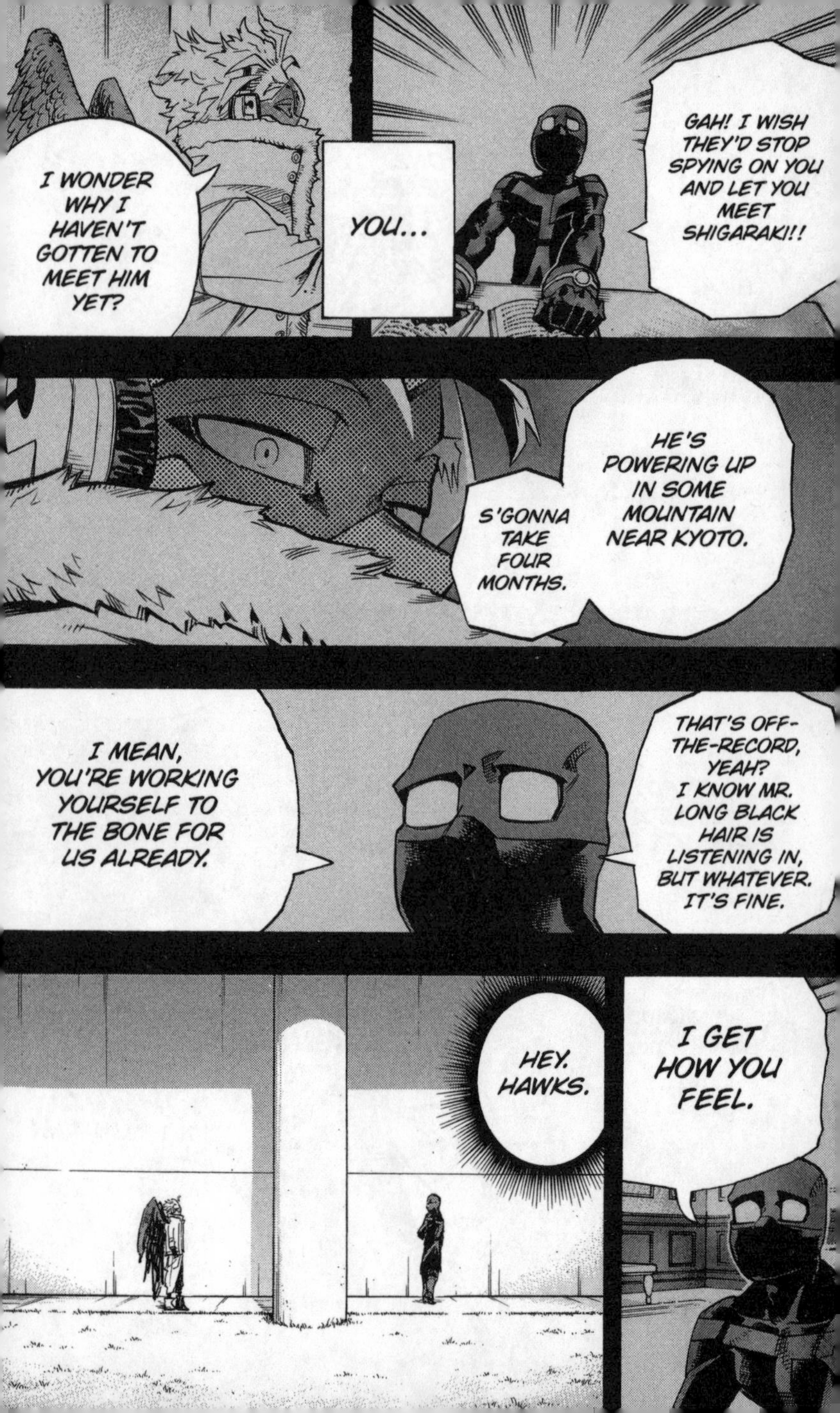
GAH! I WISH THEY'D STOP SPYING ON YOU AND LET YOU MEET SHIGARAKI!!
YOU...
I WONDER WHY I HAVEN'T GOTTEN TO MEET HIM YET?
HE'S POWERING UP IN SOME MOUNTAIN NEAR KYOTO.
S'GONNA TAKE FOUR MONTHS.
THAT'S OFF-THE-RECORD, YEAH? I KNOW MR. LONG BLACK HAIR IS LISTENING IN, BUT WHATEVER. IT'S FINE.
I MEAN, YOU'RE WORKING YOURSELF TO THE BONE FOR US ALREADY.
I GET HOW YOU FEEL.
HEY. HAWKS.

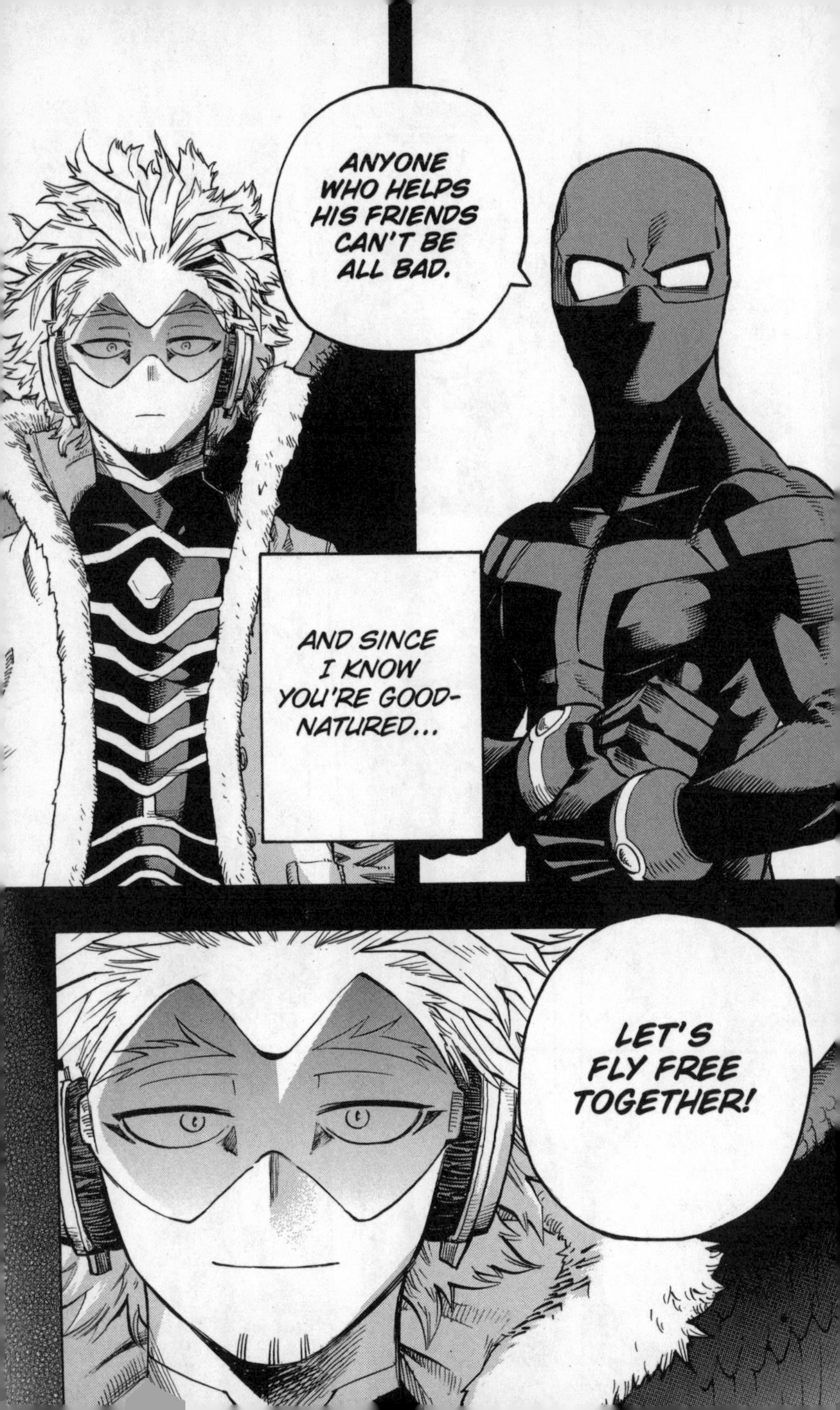
ANYONE WHO HELPS HIS FRIENDS CAN'T BE ALL BAD.
AND SINCE I KNOW YOU'RE GOOD-NATURED...
LET'S FLY FREE TOGETHER!

READY TO TRY YOUR BEST AS A FIRST-YEAR, DAI?

WHOOOSH

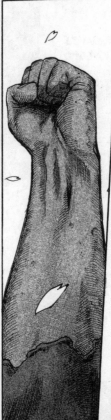

UH-HUH!

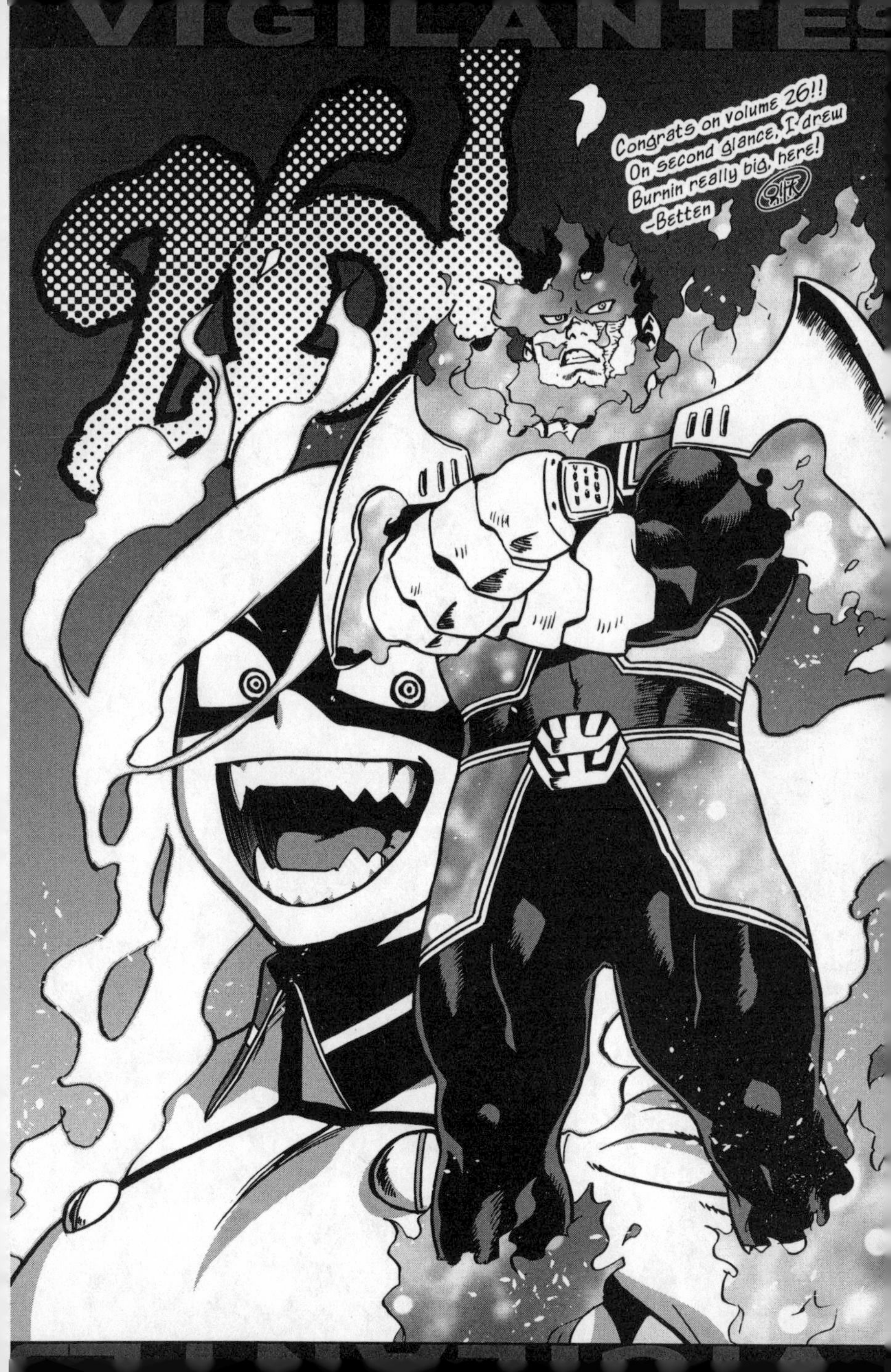

VIGILANTES
Congrats on volume 26!! On second glance, I drew Burnin really big, here! -Betten

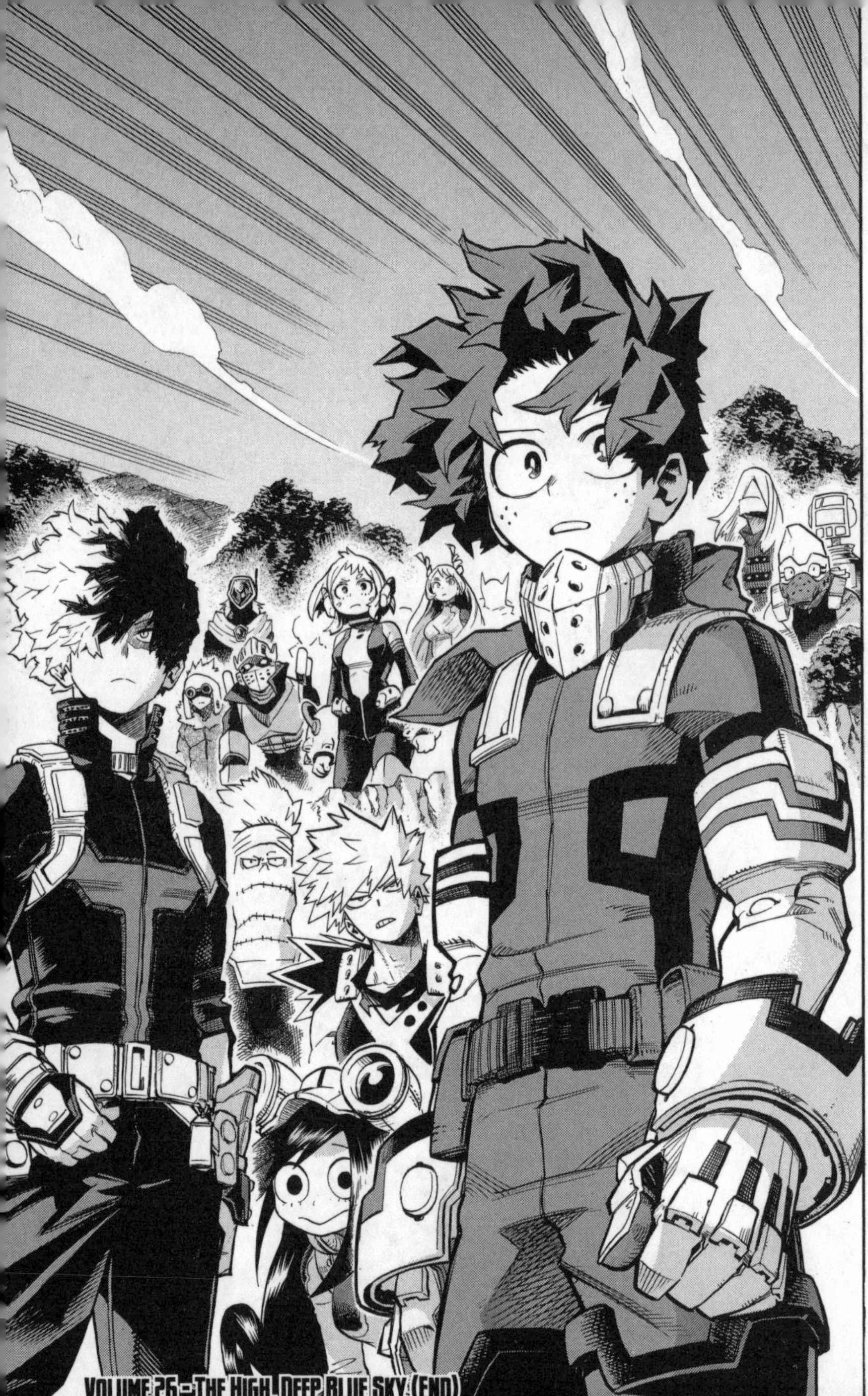

VOLUME 26 - THE HIGH, DEEP BLUE SKY (END)

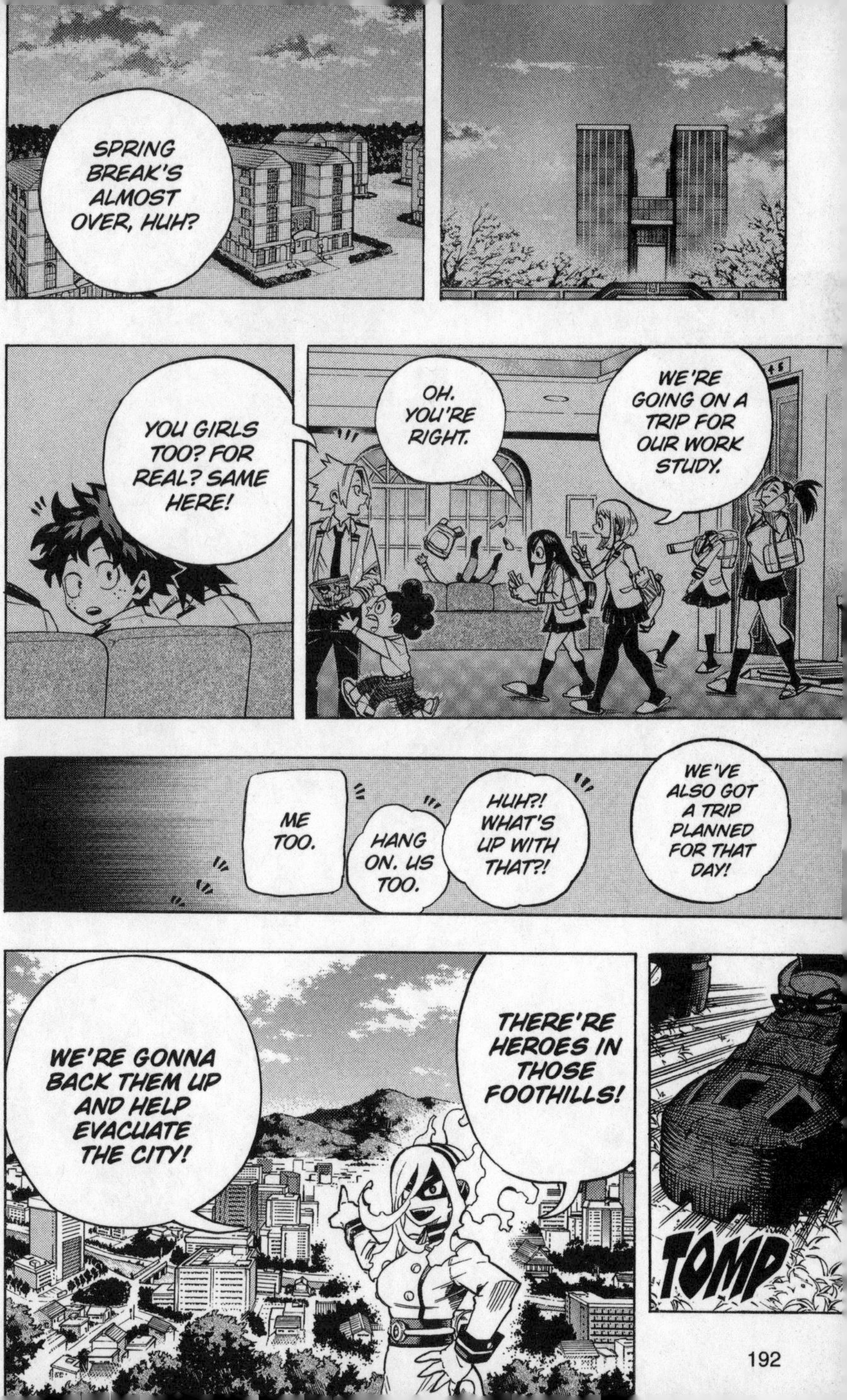
SPRING BREAK'S ALMOST OVER, HUH?
WE'RE GOING ON A TRIP FOR OUR WORK STUDY.
OH. YOU'RE RIGHT.
YOU GIRLS TOO? FOR REAL? SAME HERE!
WE'VE ALSO GOT A TRIP PLANNED FOR THAT DAY!
HUH?! WHAT'S UP WITH THAT?!
HANG ON. US TOO.
ME TOO.
TOMP
THERE'RE HEROES IN THOSE FOOTHILLS!
WE'RE GONNA BACK THEM UP AND HELP EVACUATE THE CITY!

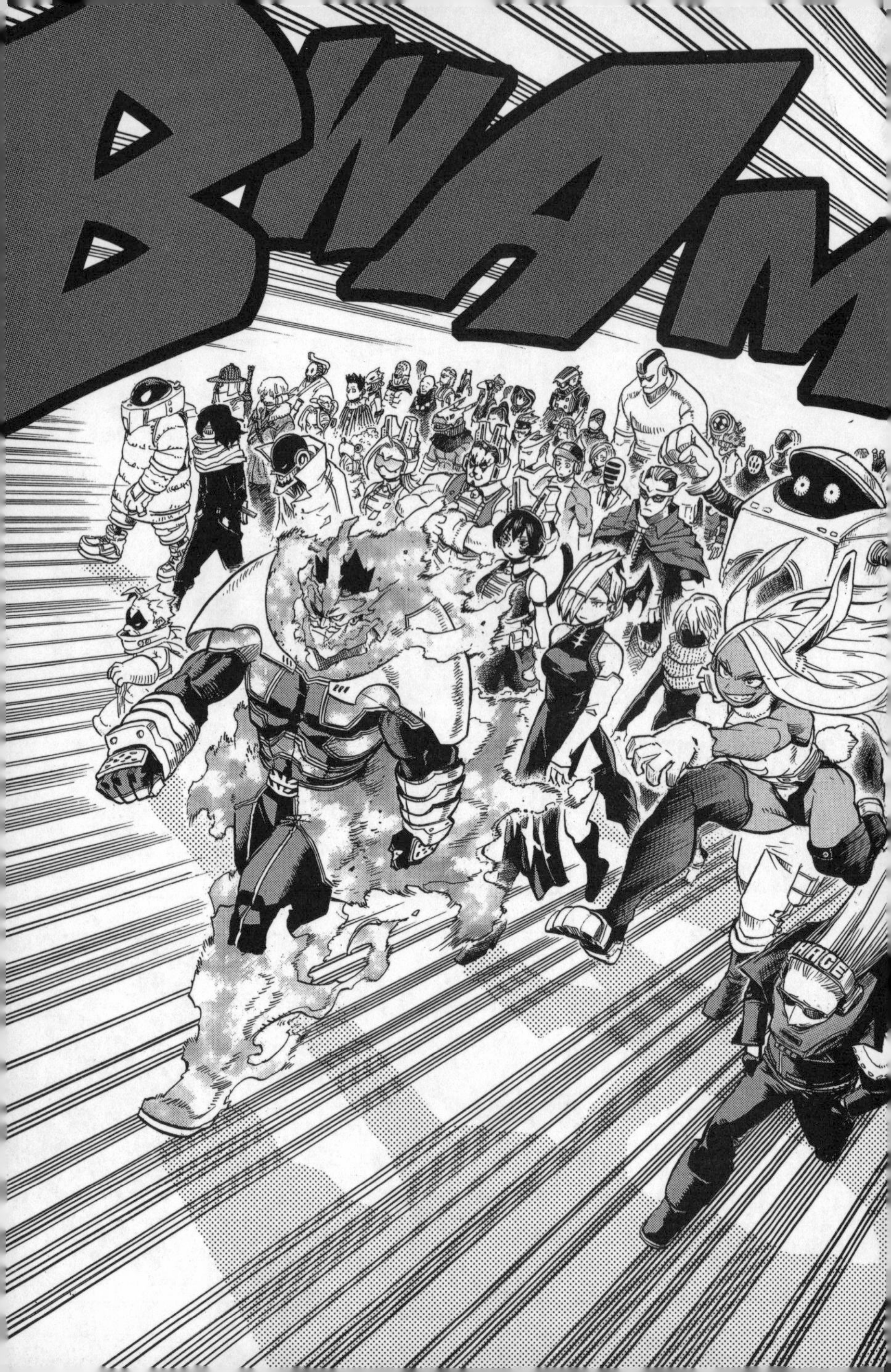
BLAM
RAGE

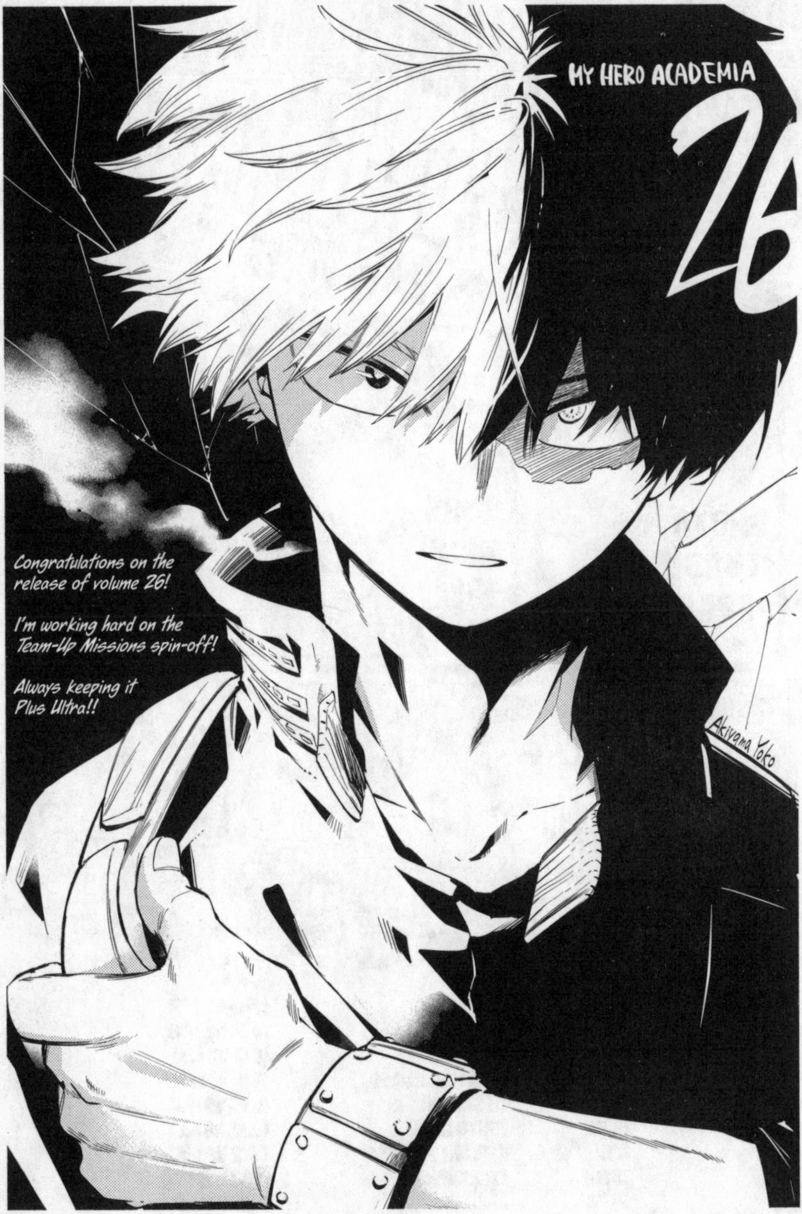
MY HERO ACADEMIA
26
Congratulations on the release of volume 26!
I'm working hard on the Team-Up Missions spin-off!
Always keeping it Plus Ultra!!
Akiyama Yoko

RESULTS OF THE FIFTH ANNUAL CHARACTER POPULARITY POLL!!

HERE ARE THE RESULTS OF THE POLL CONDUCTED (IN JAPAN) IN 2019'S *SHONEN JUMP* ISSUE 33 AND VOLUME 24! EVEN HORIKOSHI SENSEI IS PUMPED ABOUT THIS LIST!!

70,410 VOTES WERE RECEIVED!!

[TOP 20 RESULTS SHOWN]

1ST
KATSUKI BAKUGO
22,876 VOTES
2ND
IZUKU MIDO-RIYA
12,373 VOTES
3RD
SHOTO TODO-ROKI
11,805 VOTES
4TH
EIJIRO KIRI-SHIMA
3,374 VOTES
5TH
TENYA IDA
2,201 VOTES
6TH
TOMURA SHIGA-RAKI
1,880 VOTES
7TH
SHOTA AIZAWA
1,543 VOTES
8TH
OCHACO URA-RAKA
1,143 VOTES
9TH
HIMIKO TOGA
1,104 VOTES
10TH
MOMO YAOYO-ROZU
1,083 VOTES

11TH:	HAWKS	(969 VOTES)
12TH:	KYOKA JIRO	(884 VOTES)
13TH:	ALL MIGHT	(813 VOTES)
14TH:	DENKI KAMINARI	(749 VOTES)
15TH:	YO SHINDO	(644 VOTES)
16TH:	TSUYU ASUI	(602 VOTES)
17TH:	HITOSHI SHINSO	(522 VOTES)
18TH:	ENDEAVOR	(408 VOTES)
19TH:	DABI	(367 VOTES)
20TH:	OVERHAUL	(325 VOTES)

SOMETIMES THOSE WITHOUT A LEGAL WAY TO APPLY THEIR QUIRKS...

...FIND A WAY AROUND THE RULES.

MY HERO ACADEMIA VIGILANTES

In a superpowered society, there is nothing ordinary about evil anymore. Heroes, trained and licensed to protect and defend the public against supervillains, stand above all the rest. Not everyone can be a hero, however, and there are those who would use their powers to serve the people without legal sanction. But do they fight for justice in the shadows, or for reasons known only to themselves? Whatever they fight for, they are called... Vigilantes.

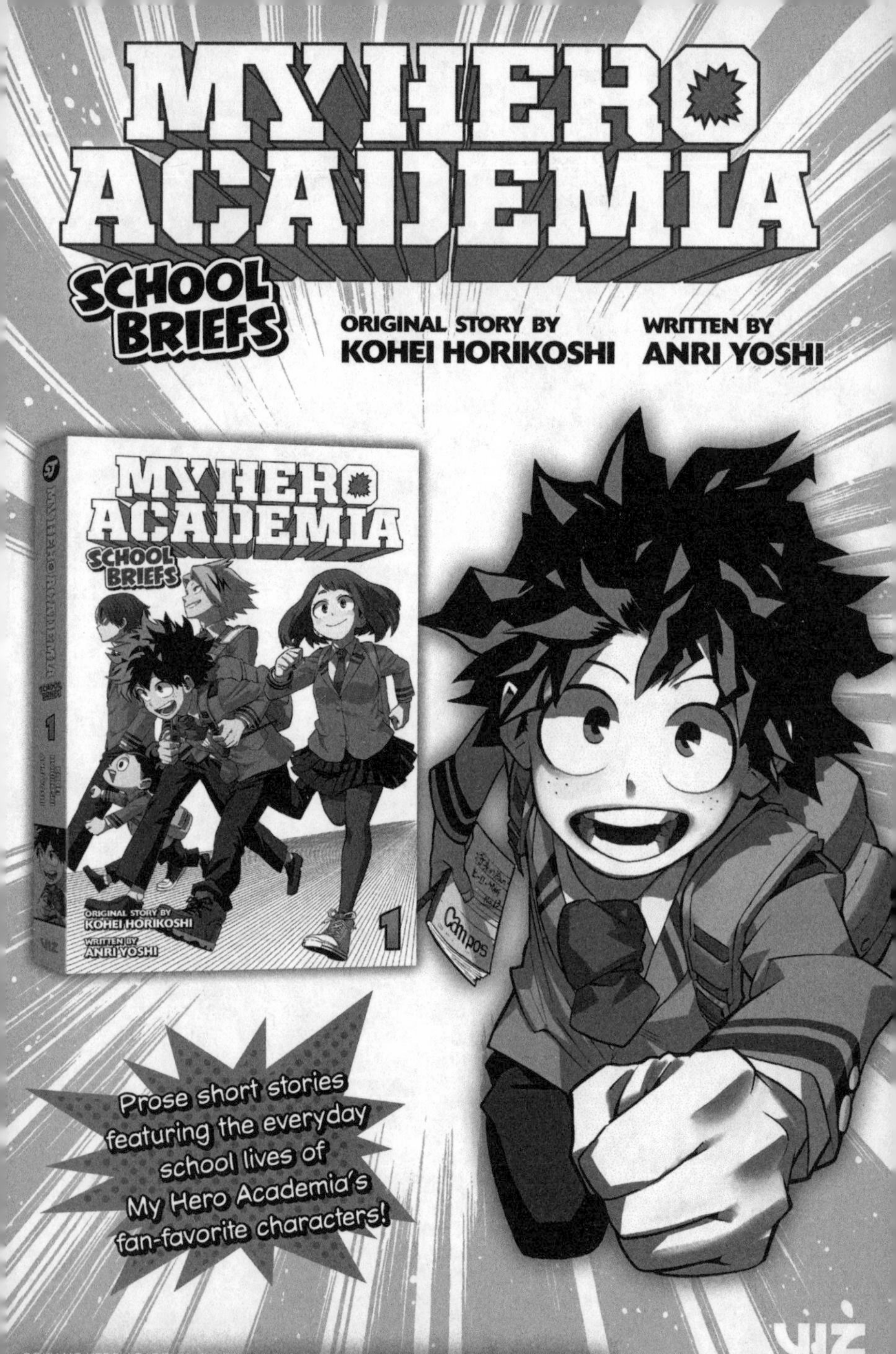
MY HERO ACADEMIA
SCHOOL BRIEFS
ORIGINAL STORY BY
KOHEI HORIKOSHI
WRITTEN BY
ANRI YOSHI
Prose short stories featuring the everyday school lives of My Hero Academia's fan-favorite characters!
VIZ

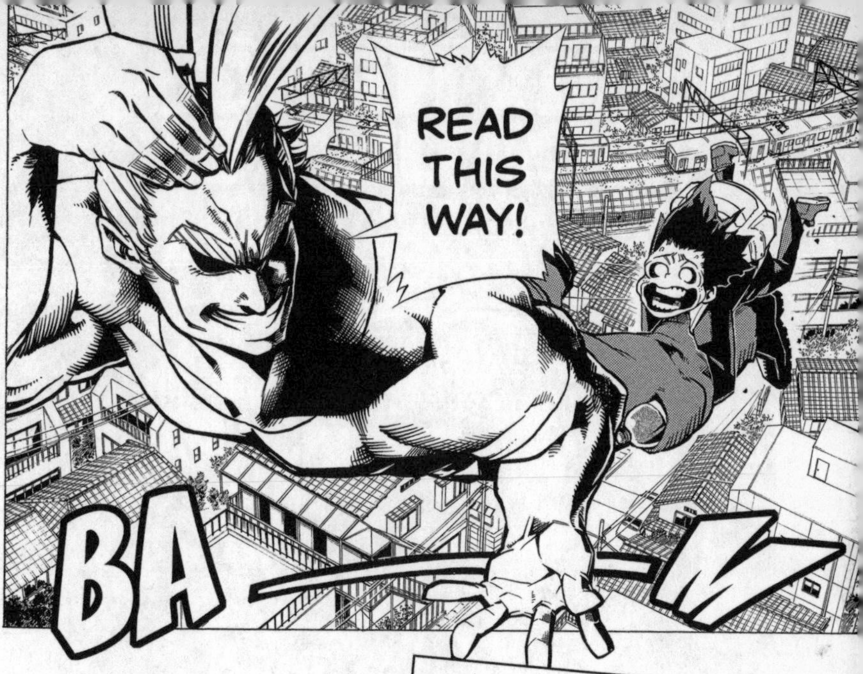
READ THIS WAY!
BA-M

MY HERO ACADEMIA

reads from right to left, starting in the upper-right corner. Japanese is read from right to left, meaning that action, sound effects and word-balloon order are completely reversed from English order.

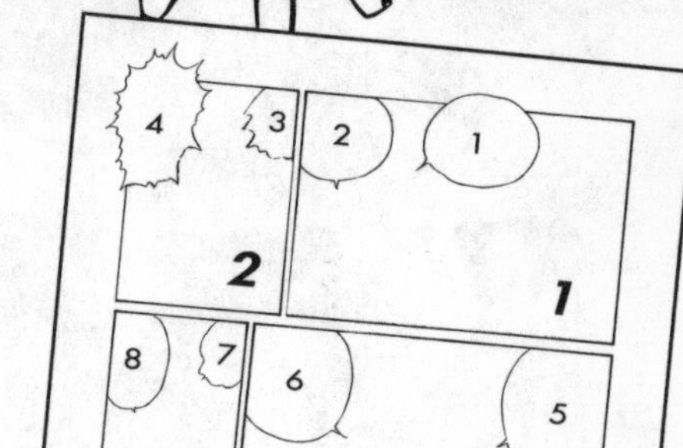
1
2
3
4
5
1
2
3
4
5
6
7
8
9
142

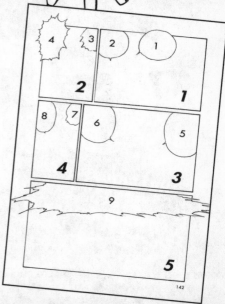

MY HERO ACADEMIA
SMASH!!

Story and Art by Hirofumi Neda
Original Concept by Kohei Horikoshi

HILARIOUS HIJINKS
featuring the characters
and story lines of
MY HERO ACADEMIA!

The superpowered society of *My Hero Academia* takes a hilarious turn in this reimagining of the best-selling series! Join Midoriya, All Might and all the aspiring heroes of U.A. High, plus memorable villains, in an irreverent take on the main events of the series, complete with funny gags, ridiculous jokes and superpowered humor!